The Social and Environmental Effects of Large Dams

The
Social and
Environmental
Effects of
LARGE DAMS

Edward
Goldsmith
and
Nicholas
Hildyard

Sierra Club Books
San Francisco

The Sierra Club, founded in 1892 by John Muir, has devoted itself to the study and protection of the earth's scenic and ecological resources— mountains, wetlands, woodlands, wild shores and rivers, deserts and plains. The publishing program of the Sierra Club offers books to the public as a nonprofit educational service in the hope that they may enlarge the public's understanding of the Club's basic concerns. The point of view expressed in each book, however, does not necessarily represent that of the Club. The Sierra Club has some sixty chapters coast to coast, in Canada, Hawaii, and Alaska. For information about how you may participate in its programs to preserve wilderness and the quality of life, please address inquiries to Sierra Club, 730 Polk Street, San Francisco, California 94109.

LIBRARY OF CONGRESS CATALOGING IN PUBLICATION DATA

Goldsmith, Edward, 1928–
The social and environmental effects of large dams.
Includes index.
1. Dams—Environmental aspects.
2. Dams—Social aspects.
3. Irrigation—History.
I. Hildyard, Nicholas.   II. Title.
TC540.G63   1985   333.73'1   85–2235
ISBN 0–87156–848–9

Jacket design by Mark Shepard
Book design by Wilsted & Taylor
Composition by Wilsted & Taylor
Printed in the United States of America

10 9 8 7 6 5 4 3 2 1

Contents

Tables and Figures

A Ballad of Ecological Awareness

The cost of building dams is always underestimated—
There's erosion of the delta that the river has created,
There's fertile soil below the dam that's likely to be looted,
And the tangled mat of forest that has got to be uprooted.

There's the breaking up of cultures with old haunts' and habits' loss,
There's the education program that just doesn't come across,
And the wasted fruits of progress that are seldom much enjoyed
By expelled subsistence farmers who are urban unemployed.

There's disappointing yield of fish, beyond the first explosion;
There's silting up, and drawing down, and watershed erosion.
Above the dam the water's lost by sheer evaporation;
Below, the river scours, and suffers dangerous alteration.

For engineers, however good, are likely to be guilty
Of quietly forgetting that a river can be silty,
While the irrigation people too are frequently forgetting
That water poured upon the land is likely to be wetting.

Then the water in the lake, and what the lake releases,
Is crawling with infected snails and water-borne diseases.
There's a hideous locust breeding ground when water level's low,
And a million ecologic facts we really do not know.

There are benefits, of course, which may be countable, but which
Have a tendency to fall into the pockets of the rich,
While the costs are apt to fall upon the shoulders of the poor.
So cost-benefit analysis is nearly always sure
To justify the building of a solid concrete fact,
While the Ecologic Truth is left behind in the Abstract.

KENNETH E. BOULDING

(From T. Farvar and J. Milton,
The Careless Technology,
Tom Stacey, London, 1973.)

Preface

THIS BOOK is an attempt to provide an overview of the social and environmental effects of building large dams. Subsequent volumes will provide a collection of case studies and an annotated bibliography. The work has been financed by the Ecological Foundation, to which we are very grateful.

We would also like to thank Peter Freeman, Robert Goodland, and Robert Mann for their encouragement and for all the information they have provided us; Victor Kovda, Jean Pierre Rothé, and John Waterbury for kindly reading and correcting chapters dealing with their particular fields of expertise; and Brent Blackwelder and Philip Williams for correcting the proofs of the book as a whole.

We would also like to thank Hilary Datchens for helping us with the book in all sorts of ways—not least by typing its many versions; Rita Marshall of Rita Marshall Editorial Services for producing the final version on her word processor; and also Ruth Lumley Smith, past managing editor of *The Ecologist*, and Maria Parsons, her successor, for undertaking the proofreading.

Finally, we would like to make it absolutely clear that the conclusions we have come to are not necessarily those of the people who have helped us produce this book. We are alone responsible for these conclusions.

Edward Goldsmith & Nicholas Hildyard

Foreword

Brent Blackwelder, Ph.D.
director of water resources,
Environmental Policy Institute

POPULAR THINKING holds big dams to be of great economic and social benefit because they produce clean power, stop damaging floods, and help combat world hunger by providing water for irrigation. Edward Goldsmith and Nicholas Hildyard have pulled together an unparalleled assemblage of data demonstrating that big dams and water projects have not only failed to achieve those basic objectives but are also leaving a legacy of unsurpassed cultural destruction, disease, and environmental damage. This remarkable study of large water development schemes from around the world shows the dramatic difference between the rhetoric of project promoters and the grim reality of the "superdams."

Goldsmith and Hildyard present telling evidence of the extensive range of problems that large dams have caused throughout the world—from engineering mistakes and operational errors to severe social disruption and the spreading of disease; to the elimination of forests and significant wildlife habitats; to the destruction of estuaries and endangered species; to the ruination of the very land designed to be made productive. Because the pace of large-scale dam building is increasing exponentially, it is imperative that industrialized nations take the warnings in this book to heart. The case against irreversible manipulation of river systems on a global scale is so overwhelming that we proceed with funding of these superdams at our own peril.

A significant percentage of water development programs in the United States has been sadly in error, and developing countries seem intent on replicating our mistakes. America's Tennessee Valley Authority is often held up as a model of how to make the economy of a valley flourish. People from all over the world come to see what TVA has done. Unfortunately, the TVA story is really a myth.* The Environmental Policy Institute's analysis of the costs and benefits experienced by TVA's water projects during its first fifty years showed that the flood control and navigation objectives have yet to pay for themselves by any reasonable standard of accounting. Furthermore, areas in the southeastern United States that did not receive financial aid from TVA did as well as or better than the TVA region, even though they were as poor, or poorer, to begin with.

One outstanding feature of Goldsmith and Hildyard's work is the discussion of ancient or traditional irrigation societies, sustained over centuries. This is in stark contrast with the short-lived, poorly designed irrigation projects that industrialized countries have funded throughout the Third World.

The staggering array of problems created by large-scale water development is so alarming and widespread that an international network has been established to halt the destruction and to propose sensible alternatives. Goldsmith and Hildyard's book stands as a landmark in providing the most comprehensive information and analysis to date on the tragic impacts of the superdams.

WASHINGTON, D.C., 1984

---

*See William V. Chandler, "Water: Stewardship and Development," in Volume Two, *Case Studies*, available from The Ecologist, Worthyvale Manor, Camelford, Cornwall, U.K. (Price: £25 for institutions, £15 for individuals.)

1. The Reasons Given for Building Dams

SINCE THE BEGINNING OF THE HISTORICAL ERA, man has been building dams. The ancient civilizations of Sumeria, Babylonia, Egypt, Ceylon, and Cambodia, for example, were all justifiably famed for their irrigation works. Indeed, the embankments and tanks that remain at such ancient capitals as Anuradhapura in Sri Lanka, or Angkor Wat in Cambodia, still survive to bear proud witness to the engineering skills of those who constructed them. Today, however, advances in concrete technology and the development of vast earth-moving machines (the largest weighing 2,000 tons) have enabled us to build dams of a size and complexity that would have staggered the ancients.

The statistics speak for themselves. In Egypt, the Aswan High Dam is seventeen times heavier than the great pyramid of Cheops. In Ghana, the Volta Dam is large enough to impound a reservoir covering 8,500 square kilometers—5 percent of the total area of the country and an area almost the size of Lebanon. In Brazil, plans to harness the power of the Amazon and its tributaries with a complex of dams capable of providing 66,000 megawatts of electricity will entail flooding an area the size of Montana. The Itaipu Dam on the Paraná River will alone generate 12,600 megawatts of electricity—equivalent to the output of thirteen large nuclear power stations.[1]

Still more ambitious is the Sanxia Dam on China's Yangtse River. Once completed, the dam will generate 40 percent of China's total current electricity output—providing 25,000 megawatts, equivalent to the output of twenty-five large nuclear power stations.[2] The dam will cost up to twelve billion dollars; flood thousands of acres, including 300,000 acres of farmland; and displace two to three million people. In Southeast Asia, plans are afoot to build a complex of dams on the Mekong River Basin at a cost of eight billion dollars, at 1970 prices. This would affect 250,000 square miles of land, including most of Laos and Cambodia, two-fifths of South Vietnam, and one-third of Thailand. At present, thirty million people live in the region; by the end of the century that number could double.

With funding now available from such institutions as the World Bank and the various international aid agencies, the pace of dam construction has accelerated dramatically since the Second World War. Significantly, the very first loan ever made by the World Bank to a developing country—to Chile in March 1948—was for an irrigation and hydropower scheme. By June 1982, the Bank had lent $26.7 billion for agricultural projects, of which $10 billion went to financing no fewer than 285 irrigation projects. About 38 percent of the money advanced by the Bank for agricultural development schemes has been for irrigation projects—and 90 percent of that lending has occurred during the last ten years.[3]

The worldwide total of dams more than 150 meters high is expected to reach 113 by 1990; of these, 49 will have been built during the 1980s.[4] In the Philippines alone, an estimated 861 dams are in the offing. Thirty-nine are already in operation, 12 are under construction, and 177 are awaiting construction. A further 31 are being studied, and more than 361 have been identified for study. Feasibility studies have been completed on 12 and tentative planning studies are under way on another 229.[5]

Even more impressive than the dams themselves are the vast reservoirs whose waters they serve to impound. In 1970, there were at least 260 man-made reservoirs with a surface area of 100 to 1,000 square kilometers, and 40 with a surface area of more than 1,000 square kilometers.[6] The volume of water stored in those reservoirs—some 4,000 cubic kilometers—has been estimated to be "approximately equal to one-third of the water of the earth's atmosphere." Small wonder, perhaps, that the reservoirs behind today's "superdams" are said to be the only man-made structures on this planet that are clearly visible from space.

PLANS FOR THE FUTURE: DAM THEM ALL?

For the future, even more ambitious schemes are planned, many of which involve the diversion of whole rivers, the transfer of water from one river basin to another and, even, the reversal of the flow of rivers.

In the Soviet Union, plans are afoot to build the Siberian Diversion Scheme, which involves blocking the flow of the River Ob and pumping its waters via a canal through Kazakhstan in order to irrigate land 1,500 kilometers away. The water will eventually be flushed into the Aral Sea, where the water level is already sinking due to the demands of industry and irrigation, and the salinity is seriously increasing. The initial investment is expected to cost at least $41.6 billion. Closer to the capital, there are plans to dam the Pecara River to the northeast of Moscow in order to transfer water to a southern tributary of the Volga.[7]

In China, a canal is to be built to divert water from the Chang Jiang (Yangtse) River to agricultural areas in the arid north of China. Three possible routes have been proposed: a western route, a middle route, and an eastern route. The western route has never been properly surveyed; the eastern route was surveyed in detail in 1978 and the middle route in 1979. At the time of writing, the middle route appears to be favored. It will require the construction of a 1,265-kilometer canal to Beijing, which will cross the Huang He River just west of Zhengzhou and then pass through the Nanyang Basin in Southern Henan.[8] The scheme is expected to irrigate 3.8 million hectares of farmland and to guarantee regular water supplies to a further 1.3 million hectares. Almost 7.4 cubic kilometers of water will be provided for industrial, mining, municipal, and domestic uses.[9] Giant pumping stations

TABLE I

Proposed Massive Water Diversion Projects in Selected Countries

Country	Volume (million acre-feet)	Distance (kilometers)	Estimated Cost* (Billion $)
UNITED STATES			
Peripheral Canal	16.3	70	5.1–23.0
High Plains Canals	6–7.2	580–1,360	13.4–40.0
CHINA			
Chang Jiang (Yangtze) Canal			
Middle Route	19.2	1,265	6.6
Eastern Route	11.3–24.3	1,150	6.6
SOVIET UNION			
Siberian Diversion	48.6	2,300	41.4
INDIA			
Ganges-Cauvery Canal		3,340	4.0

SOURCE: Bruce Stokes, "Bread and Water: Growing Tomorrow's Food," Worldwatch Institute, Washington, D.C., 1980.

*Cost estimates made in various years and do not include total infrastructure costs.

are also to be built to drain excess water from an area of 18,000 square kilometers at a rate of 5,000 cubic meters a second.[10]

In India, a series of canals is being built to divert water from the Brahmaputra, the Ganges, and the Indus rivers to the drought-prone regions of Madhya Pradesh in Central India, to Rajasthan in the West, and to Tamil Nadu in the South. Those canals will "radiate" out from the 2,000-mile Ganges/Cauvery River Canal, which will run down almost the entire length of the country.[11]

In the United States, similar schemes include the Texas Water System and the NAWAPA Project. The latter (the North American Water and Power Alliance—hence its acronym) would channel water from Alaska and Canada in order to irrigate Mexico and the southwestern United States, at a cost of some two trillion dollars. An area of 1.3 million square miles would have to be drained; 177 lakes and reservoirs would need to be built; and the scheme would require the cooperation of three nations, 36 states, 11 provinces, and thousands of cities.[12]

The Texas Water System, as originally conceived in 1968, involved transferring water from the humid eastern region of Texas to the arid and semiarid western region of the state—in addition to "importing" massive amounts of water from the Mississippi Basin via the state of Louisiana. "The key to the Texas Water System," writes Charles Greer, of Indiana University, "is a series of reservoirs on the major rivers of east and central Texas, which drain into the Gulf of Mexico. Ultimately the system of reservoirs, large and small, would be more than two hundred in number, with a combined reservoir capacity of 125×10^9 cubic metres. The role of these reservoirs in the Texas Water System would be to store water, from the rivers of East Texas as well as from out-of-state imports, prior to conveyance through two major canal systems: the Coastal Canal System and the Trans-Texas Canal System."[13] Together, these two canals make up the Texas Water System. The coastal canal "would extend approximately 600 kilometres south-westward, flowing by gravity from the Sabine River on the eastern edge of Texas to the southern tip of the State." As for the Trans-Texas Canal, it would extend "about 1,200 kilometres westward from the Upper Sulphur River basin in North-east Texas." Although the original plan was turned down by a local referendum in 1969, a revised version (no less ambitious) has been proposed.

GLITTERING PRIZES: THE CLAIMED BENEFITS OF LARGE-SCALE WATER DEVELOPMENT PROJECTS

There is little doubt that at least some of those involved in building the massive "water development" projects described above sincerely believe that they are improving the lot of mankind. In 1975, the former commissioner of the U.S. Bureau of Reclamation, Gilbert G. Stamm, told a congressional committee: "Water resource projects have many positive environment effects. When water management practices regulate and augment low flows of rivers and streams, decrease erosion, prevent floods, eliminate waste of water, and in many instances change deserts into gardens where man can comfortably live and prosper, the result is betterment of environmental conditions."[14]

In a similar vein, the U.S. Army Corps of Engineers assured the American public in a 1977 publication that by building dams, it aimed "to preserve the unique and important ecological, aesthetic and cultural values of our national heritage; to conserve and use wisely the natural resources of our nation for the benefit of present and future generations; to restore, maintain and enhance the natural and man-made environment in terms of productivity, variety, spaciousness, beauty and other measures of quality . . . and to create new opportunities for the American people to enjoy the environment and the use of natural resources."[15]

Indeed, reading the official literature on large-scale dams and other water development projects—that is to say, the literature put out by the dam-building industry—one might be forgiven for thinking that such projects can bring nothing but good for mankind. Little mention is made of their social, let alone their ecological, impact. (A 1982 report by the International Commission on Large Dams, for instance, makes only one reference to the likelihood of irrigation schemes' causing salinization, a problem which, as we shall see, is putting hundreds of thousands of acres out of production every year.)[16] Instead, we are presented with a long and glowing list of the benefits to be accrued from developing the rivers of the world, benefits ranging from ensuring supplies of potable water (a critical consideration for the majority of the Third World countries, where unhygienic water supplies are a major cause of disease) to creating jobs and controlling floods.

But, most important of all, dams and other water projects are seen as having a vital role to play in ensuring future economic development. By supplying hydroelectricity, dams supply "the power to progress." And by providing water for irrigation, they will help boost food production—and thus, it is argued, enable more people to be fed. Let us consider those two goals in a little more detail; in particular, let us examine their implications for the pace of future dam building.

THE LURE OF HYDROPOWER

Recently the less-developed countries have begun to exploit their hydropower potential in earnest. Their new-found enthusiasm for hydroelectricity is understandable: power—in particular, cheap power—is considered a sine qua non of development. And, on the face of it, hydroelectric power is extremely cheap. In 1973, the cost per kilowatt of installed generating capacity of hydroelectricity was $300 to $400. Today it has climbed to $1,000, but even at that price, it is still far cheaper than electricity produced by a thermal power plant, let alone a nuclear reactor. It should be noted, however, that the cost of hydroelectricity varies considerably from one project to another.

Dams with just over 123,000 megawatts of hydroelectric capacity are currently under construction, and facilities that could add another 239,000 megawatts are in the planning stage. Once built, those dams will double world capacity.[17] Even then, however, only one-third of the world's hydroelectric potential will have been tapped. Indeed, if all the energy contained in the rivers of the world were to be harnessed by dams, then an estimated 73,000 terawatt-hours could be produced every year—as against the 1,300 terawatt-hours produced today.

Inevitably, technical difficulties preclude the exploitation of much of that energy. Nonetheless, the World Energy Conference (WEC) still considers it possible to tap 19,000 terawatt-hours a year. That would require the construction of 2,214,700 megawatts of hydroelectric capacity. Others less optimistic than WEC project massive increases in the amount of energy produced by hydropower schemes. Dr. Daniel Deudney of the Washington-based Worldwatch Institute estimates that "even taking all constraints into account, world hydro-power production could reach between four and six times its present level."[18] Table 2 presents estimates of the hydroelectricity potential of individual continents.

Lured on by the carrot of cheap energy, Third World governments have embarked on massive hydroelectricity schemes to exploit to the very full the energy of their rivers. In Brazil, for example, a complex of dams is now being built to power the "Grande Carajas" project, a massive development scheme designed to transform one-sixth of Brazilian Amazonia into a vast industrial area. If the project goes ahead as planned, a total of $39 billion will be spent on an assortment of mineral and metallurgical schemes, on agriculture, and on ranching and forestry in the area. Twenty-two billion dollars alone will be invested in building the infrastructure—the roads, motorways, cities, and ports—necessary to "open up" the Carajas region. Among the planned projects are the world's largest open-pit iron mine, a bauxite mine capable of producing 8 million tons of bauxite a year, and an aluminum smelter that will produce 800,000 tons of aluminum and 320,000 metric tons of aluminum oxide a year for sale to Japan.[19]

In Central America, the Guatemalan government has made a detailed study of its hydropower potential—although no concrete plans for developing the area have yet been issued. At present, the country uses some 226 megawatts of electricity a year. According to two consultants employed by the Guatemalan government to prepare an "Electricity Masterplan" for the country, the gross energy potential of Guatemala's rivers—at 50 percent discharge—is 7,436 megawatts.[20] The Masterplan identifies 240 dam sites for development and another 431 as "technically feasible" for hydroelectricity production. Of these sites, Gaertner and Morariu deem 121 economically feasible to develop and recommend that they be included in the "optimum development chains for the river basins investigated." Those development chains would provide 4,951 megawatts of electricity, nearly twenty times the amount at present used by Guatemala.

Similar estimates have been made for the hydroelectricity potential of countries throughout Oceania, Asia, and Africa. Indeed, it seems to be assumed by governments throughout the world that it is their duty to exploit every last kilowatt from their rivers. If they do so, then very few rivers will remain free to flow

TABLE 2
Potential and Current Hydropower Development, by Continent
(after UN Water Conference Secretariat, 1978)

Continent	Potential available 95% of time (10³ kw) (1)	Potential output 95% of time (10⁶ kwh/yr) (2)	Present installed capacity (10³ kw) (3)	Current annual production (4)	$\frac{(4)}{(2)} \times 100$ (5)
Africa	145,218	1,161,741	8,154	30,168	2.6
Asia	139,288	1,114,305	47,118	198,433	17.8
Europe (including USSR)	102,961	827,676	135,498	505,317	61.0
North America	72,135	577,086	90,210	453,334	78.5
Latin America	81,221	649,763	18,773	91,415	14.1
Oceania	553,810	4,434,468	307,362	1,307,564	29.5

SOURCE: A. K. Biswas et al., eds., *Water Management for Arid Lands in Developing Countries*, Pergamon, Oxford, 1980.

unimpeded to the sea. Kassas makes the same point. According to him, it is likely that "in the near future, practically all the world's major rivers will be brought under control." He goes on to write: "Some rivers will even be sealed off by estuary barrages (e.g., barrages across Morecombe Bay and the Solway Firth in the UK). But rivers represent an important agency in the hydrologic cycle: collecting surface drainage and discharging it into seas and oceans. Estimates of world total run-off of water from land to sea (mostly river flow) are in the order of 24,000 × 10⁹ gal. (103 × 10⁹m³) per day. This is equivalent to about 7 per cent of the total evaporation from land and sea . . . Rivers discharge into the Northeastern and Pacific ocean between California and the Aleutian Islands about 21,000 m³/sec. Freshwater discharges into the Bering Sea by Alaskan and Siberian rivers average 10,000 m³/sec. The Columbia River discharges about 3,200 m³/sec. and its surface water of the ocean is perceptible several hundreds of kilometres out to sea. The water masses emerging from the Bering Strait northward to the Chikchi Sea bring fresh waters and sediments together with warmth. What would be the effects of sealing off these rivers on climate, biota and hydrological cycle?" (Mohammed Kassas, "Environmental Aspects of Water Resources Development" in Asit K. Biswas et al. (eds.) *Water Management for Arid Lands in Developing Countries*, Pergamon Press, Oxford, 1980, p. 75).

THE LURE OF IRRIGATION

Irrigated agriculture is one of the most productive farming systems known to man. In the United States, a Nebraska corn farmer can produce 40 bushels of corn a year on one acre of unirrigated land. By introducing sprinkler irrigation, that yield can be increased to an average of 115 bushels an acre.[21] Irrigation can similarly increase the yields of sugar beet and legumes by five to eight times; and fodder by nine to ten times. Under irrigation, new varieties of rice, wheat, and maize can produce yields of up to twelve metric tonnes per hectare (a metric tonne equals 1.1 U.S. "short" tons; a hectare is approximately 2.47 acres).

Elsewhere—most notably in Southern Asia, where 63 percent of the world's irrigated land is to be found—the successes of irrigated agriculture are even more dramatic. "Yields of rice and wheat," writes Robert P. Ambroggi in *Scientific American*, "have almost doubled, and the cropping intensity has almost doubled too, reaching an average value of 1.3. As a result, total production has increased almost fourfold."[22] He goes on to comment: "The most efficient agricultural system in the world is an Asian one and is almost entirely under irrigation. It is the system of Japanese rice culture, where 0.045 hectare of land suffices to provide 2,500 calories per day for one person. In the US, twice as much land is needed to provide the same diet, and under the Indian system of agriculture, almost seven times as much land is needed."

It is not at all clear just how much land is at present under irrigation. Professor Gilbert White, one of the world's leading authorities on the subject, himself admits that "Accurate data on existing and potential irrigated lands do not exist for most of the world."[23]

Nonetheless, estimates abound. In 1971, Milós Holy, president of the Czechoslovak National Committee of the International Commission on Large Dams, calculated that some 13 percent of the world's arable lands were irrigated, and that they required approximately 1,400 billion cubic meters of water a year. He also estimated that the area under irrigation was then increasing at an annual rate of 2.9 percent. By contrast, the amount of nonirrigated land coming into production was increasing at only 0.7 percent a year.[24]

Writing in 1976, Dr. Roger Revelle, of the University of California at San Diego, estimated that some 223 million hectares— 14 percent of the world's total cultivated land—was irrigated.[25] More recently, Professor Victor Kovda, of the University of Moscow, suggested that 250 million hectares are under irrigation, of which 120 million to 130 million have been irrigated only within the last thirty years. Kovda expects the amount of irrigated land at the beginning of the twenty-first century to be about 350 million hectares.[26]

Others use lower figures. Professor M. El Gabaly, of the University of Alexandria, estimates that only 11.8 percent of the world's total agricultural land is now irrigated—a figure equivalent to 10 percent of the earth's total land area. By the end of this century, he predicts, some 250 million hectares will be under irrigation, more than six times the area irrigated at the beginning of the century (40 million hectares) and almost half as much again as was irrigated in the early 1970s (180 million hectares).[27]

Whatever the statistical divergences about the amount of land under irrigation, there is general agreement among conventional agronomists that more land must be irrigated if food production is to be increased. In 1979, the International Food Policy Research Institute (IFPRI) estimated that over the next decade, three-fifths of the food production increases it projected for all developing countries would result from extending the amount of land under irrigation. For the eight countries it studied in Asia, IFPRI asserted that nearly three-quarters of the projected increases would result from improving existing irrigation schemes, from developing new means of increasing yields on irrigated land, and from extending the amount of land under irrigation. A study for the Trilateral Commission came to a similar conclusion: indeed, it argued that extending irrigation would prove "the single most important factor in increasing rice yields in Asia."

Meanwhile, the UN Food and Agriculture Organization (FAO) puts the total amount of land under irrigation in 1982 at 220 million hectares. That figure compares with 148 million hectares in 1962 and 179 million hectares in 1972. FAO predicts that if the present rate of conversion is maintained, another 100 million hectares will be brought under irrigation by the year 2000, thereby permitting a 10 percent increase in per capita food consumption.

In its study *Agriculture: Toward 2000*, FAO assumes that the area under irrigation will expand at a rate of 1.7 percent a year from now until the end of the century. The FAO also recommends that rehabilitation work be carried out on 42 million hectares of degraded land already under irrigation.[28]

Others argue that the expansion of irrigation will have to proceed even faster, if the world's hungry are to be fed. Bruce Stokes, a former researcher at the Worldwatch Institute, for example, argues that 70 million hectares must be brought under irrigation within the next decade to keep pace with food demand.[29] With the world's population predicted to rise by 1.5 billion by the year 2000, another 556 million tons or so of grain will be needed just to maintain present levels of consumption. If affluence also increases, bringing about a rise in the demand for meat, then still more wheat will be required in order to feed livestock.

It is quite clear, however, that with 50 percent of the earth's surface classified as "arid" or "semiarid," we are unlikely to extend the amount of irrigated land without dramatically increasing the supply of water for agriculture.* The question seems to be: how best to increase that supply?

---

*Asit Biswas, one of the world's leading authorities on irrigation schemes and other water development projects, argued that the future rate of expansion for irrigated lands cannot realistically be expected to exceed 1.7 percent a year: "With real investment costs reaching $2,000 to $10,000 per hectare, funds will not be available in the future for massive developments." (Asit Biswas, Foreword *in* A. K. Biswas et al. (eds.), *Long Distance Water Transfers*, Tycooly, Dublin, 1983, p.xii.)

To date, the answer has generally been to tap groundwater resources. Recent years have thus seen a substantial increase in the number of wells sunk for irrigation purposes. The Chinese have sunk nearly a million wells in North China since the mid-fifties.[30] In the 1960s and 1970s, 1.6 million tube wells were sunk in India. As a result, the proportion of agricultural land irrigated by groundwater increased from 29 percent in the early 1950s to 40 percent in the mid-1970s. In the United States, the number of wells in the High Plains has risen from a few hundred in the early 1970s to between 150,000 and 200,000 today. In fact, in 1980, groundwater supplied two-fifths of the water used in the United States for irrigation; practically all the new land brought under irrigation in recent years derived its water from this source.

There is a limit, however, to the number of wells that can be sunk—and that limit appears to have been exceeded in many parts of the world. Indeed, underground water is now being mined on such a massive scale that, in some areas, water levels are falling dramatically. In the Southwest of the United States, the huge Ogallala aquifer will be depleted by 40 percent within the next twenty to forty years. Already, as a result of overexploitation, the cost of water for irrigation is becoming prohibitive; considerable areas of agricultural land have therefore been taken out of irrigation. Unless other water sources are made available, the future of farming in the US Southwest—which produces some 20 percent of America's food—is extremely precarious.

Two other sources of water remain. One, desalinated seawater, is too expensive. The other, rainwater, is too diffuse and unpredictable: of the 100,000 cubic kilometers of rainwater that falls annually on the earth, 30 to 40 percent runs off directly to the oceans, two-thirds of it in flood flow. Frequently, therefore, the water is available neither *where* it is required nor *when* it is required.

The ability of large dams to compensate for the unpredictability of nature is what makes them so attractive; dams can store peak flow during the rainy season for use as irrigation water during the dry season. Moreover, large dams can irrigate land in those very areas that are likely to be the most fertile, namely, the rich alluvial soils of the world's major river basins and river valleys. Such basins and river valleys include those of the Nile, the lower Mekong, the Indus, the Ganges, and the Brahmaputra, the Tigris and the Euphrates, the Grijalva and Papaloapan in Mexico, the São Francisco valley in Brazil, and the Lower Colorado in the United States. Once dammed, those rivers will yield their rich alluvial soils for irrigation throughout the year, with their annual flood waters impounded in a reservoir and released when required. No longer will their waters be wasted on the journey to the sea.

PLAYING WITH WATER: PLAYING WITH FIRE?

Such then are the two *major* benefits claimed for large-scale water development projects. Given that food and energy are the two commodities in shortest supply throughout the Third World, is it any wonder that so many developing countries now see large-scale dams as the touchstone of future prosperity? In a world where millions go to bed hungry and where few have access to even the cheapest material goods that we take for granted in the West, a demand that the further building of large-scale dams should cease forthwith must sound churlish. Would not doing so effectively condemn still more people to death by starvation? And if the experts insist that dams provide the route to material prosperity for impoverished millions, who are we to gainsay them?

But there is another aspect to the dam-building issue, one that the industry is less than keen to display. It includes massive ecological destruction, social misery, and increasing ill-health and impoverishment for those very people who are expected to benefit most. That underside of the issue is the subject of this book. In our examination, we shall see—

1. How little of the extra food grown through irrigation schemes ever reaches those who need it most; how, in the long run, those irrigation schemes are turning vast areas of fertile land into salt-encrusted deserts; and how, too, the industry powered

by dams is further undermining food supplies through pollution and the destruction of agricultural land;

2. How millions of people have been uprooted from their homes to make way for the reservoirs of large dams; how their social lives have been shattered and their cultures destroyed; and how, also, their health has been jeopardized by the water-borne diseases introduced by those reservoirs and their associated irrigation works;

3. How dams are now suspected of triggering earthquakes; how they have failed to control floods and have actually served to increase the severity of flood damage; and how, in many instances, they have reduced the quality of drinking water for hundreds of millions of people;

4. And, finally, how the real beneficiaries of large-scale dams and water development schemes have invariably been large multinational companies, the urban elites of the Third World, and the politicians who commissioned the projects in the first place.

Truly, by playing with water, we are in a very real sense—in terms of the metaphor—playing with fire.

PART II
BEFORE THE FLOOD

2. Dams and Society:
The Problems of Resettlement

ONE OF THE INEVITABLE CONSEQUENCES of flooding an area is that people who had been living there have to be resettled. In some cases, such resettlement has involved the movement of vast numbers. Ghana's Volta Dam, for example, saw the evacuation of some 78,000 people from more than 700 towns and villages. Lake Kainji in Nigeria displaced 42,000; the Aswan High Dam, 120,000; the Kariba Dam, 50,000; Turkey's Keban Dam, 30,000; Thailand's Ubolratana Dam, 30,000. The Pa Mong project in Vietnam uprooted 450,000 people.[1]

Exact figures for the numbers of people who are likely to be resettled as a result of future projects are hard to come by. The following are a few representative estimates.

In China, the vast Three Gorges Dam scheme will displace 1,400,000 people.[2]

In Brazil, eight planned hydroelectric projects are expected to flood between 91,000 and 351,000 hectares of Indian lands, threatening the livelihood of some thirty-four indigenous tribes. "For some Indian groups, the loss will be total," reports Dr. Robin Wright of the U.S. Anthropology Resource Center. "The areas to be affected include the Kaingang, Guarani and Kokleng reservations in southern Brazil; the Truka, Tuxa, Parakana Gavioes, Suriri and others in northeastern Brazil; the Kingu and Iriri river basin tribal lands in central Brazil; and the Waimiri-

17

Atroar reservation of the northwest."[3] One of the dams, the Itai-pu Project (due to be completed in 1988) will displace 50,000 people, including 5,500 Guarini Indians. Another, the Tucuruí Project, will flood six towns; leave 20,000 to 30,000 homeless; submerge two Indian reserves; and "lacerate" a third by "the incursion of a power transmission line, an electrified iron-ore railroad, and by construction and maintenance roads."[4] One of those reserves, Parakanan, is the last refuge of a tribe that has already been reduced to only 200 people as a result of disease and contact with white settlers.

In Panama, the first stage of the multidam Teribe-Changuinola project will flood land now supporting 2,000 Guyami Indians. By the time the project is completed, the land of 60,000 Indians will have been affected.[5]

In the Philippines, forty new large dams are planned over the next twenty years. Those dams, asserts Robin Wright, could affect "the homes of more than 1.5 million people."[6] Among the more controversial projects is the Chico Dam complex, shelved for the moment after massive local opposition. If the project is resurrected (a distinct possibility, according to many observers), then up to 100,000 more people would need to be resettled.

In Canada, the Slave River Dam, a scheme that will divert three major river systems, will require the resettlement of some 10,000 Dene Indians from the Northwest Territories. The dam will provide irrigation and power for farms and industries in Southern Alberta. Among its possible side effects are the likely depletion of groundwater reserves and the drying up of rivers in the North.[7]

A RECORD OF FAILURE

If the past is anything to go by, those resettlement schemes will bring nothing but untold misery. Indeed, there is scarcely a scheme in existence that has avoided the twin problems of cultural disruption and social alienation—a point that was not lost on NEDECO, the Dutch consultants who undertook one of the main feasibility studies for Sri Lanka's Mahaweli scheme. In its

1979 report to the Sri Lanka government, it warned: "On the basis of the scenario adopted by the consultants about 50,000 families, or 250,000 people, have to be settled between 1980 and 1985. *It is hard to find examples elsewhere in the world of successful settlement of such a large number of people in such a short time* [emphasis added]."[8] In fact, 1.5 million people will have to be resettled.

NEDECO is not alone in pointing to the failure of past resettlement schemes. Dr. Robert Goodland, a senior ecologist at the World Bank and a world authority on the environmental effects of large dams, is equally critical. "In the past," he writes, "people were often relocated or resettled without regard to their individual, community or societal needs. Concern was often lacking for their future welfare; how or whether they would find employment, receive education and health care, retain their cultural and societal identity, and ensure their safety and social continuity. It was not uncommon for the displaced peoples to be placed in habitational settings foreign to their cultures or to be located in proximity to other peoples with whom they had no affinity or even longstanding enmity."[9]

In a similar vein, Professor William Ackermann told a 1976 conference on the effects of large-scale dams: "From the human point of view, relocation has been one of the least satisfactory aspects of reservoir projects. . . . Settlement schemes have a high failure rate around the world."[10] Noting that resettlement inevitably imposes "physiological, psychological and sociocultural stress," Ackermann went on to comment: "Even where planning is effective, some (especially the aged) will never come to terms with their new homes. For them, the transition period ends only with death."

GOVERNMENT INSENSITIVITY

To politicians, the concern that flooding a plot of land might destroy a people's culture is often incomprehensible. Whatever anthropologists might say, the politicians prefer to dismiss the talk of ancestral shrines, cultural patterns, and the like as mere "sentimentalism." For some, even the motives of the anthropologists are suspect. At the height of the Jonglei Canal controversy, for example, Sudan's southern regional president, Abel Alier, told the local regional assembly:

> The people of the South cannot even have one full meal a day, and children of school age cannot go to school because of our under-development, backwardness, and poverty. Yet we are asked to accept all this . . . and remain in a sort of human zoo for anthropologists, tourists, environmentalists and adventurers from developed countries of Europe to study us, our origin, our plights, the sizes of our skulls and the shape and length of our customary scars. . . . I wish to say that although the Jonglei scheme is a Central Government Project, the Regional Government supports it and stands for it. *If we have to drive our people to paradise with sticks, we will do so for their good and the good of those who come after us* [emphasis added].[11]

That intolerance of criticism—combined with a dogmatic belief in the benefits of technical "progress"—has characterized all too many resettlement schemes. Inevitably, it has often led to a patronizing and frequently dictatorial attitude toward those who are to be resettled. Such an attitude is found by no means only in the Third World—or behind the Iron Curtain, where the KGB is responsible for all water development projects. In drawing up its plans for the James Bay Project, for example, the Quebec provincial government apparently saw no reason to consult the Cree and Inuit Indians who would be uprooted by the scheme. It presented the project as a *fait accompli*, telling the Indians that the scheme would go ahead regardless of their opposition.[12]

The Akawaio Indians of Guyana were treated with similar brusqueness. Their headmen were simply summoned to Georgetown to be told by the minister of energy and natural resources, Hubert Jack, that their villages would be flooded as part of the Upper Mazaruni Hydroelectric Project. It was, he said, too late for the decision to be reconsidered, let alone reversed, and the government expected their cooperation in resettling their four thousand compatriots. The project was presented as an opportunity for the Indians "to contribute to the development of their country."[13] If their help was not forthcoming, they would lose the chance of government aid for resettlement. "There was no discussion of where the Akawaio were to move to," reported Stuart Wavell in the *Guardian*, "nor any mention of compensation. Although, at a meeting with the government authorities, one of the Akawaio captains 'opposed the scheme vigorously,' the other four present were induced to sign a statement agreeing to the drowning of their villages. . . . The meeting was called at such short notice that two village captains were unable to attend, and those that did were not given an opportunity to talk together, let alone consult the communities they represented. The captain who refused to sign was told that he would be barred from any resettlement committee. He was later removed from office."[14] Unlike the majority of Guyana's other Amerindians, the Akawaio had no formal title to their lands, despite a recommendation by the 1966 Amerindian Lands Commission that such title should be granted. In the government's view, therefore, they could be moved without even being compensated. Indeed, in the opinion of Prime Minister Forbes Burnham, the Akawaio were no more than "squatters" on their ancestral lands.[15]

The Upper Mazaruni Dam Project has now been shelved. The experience of the Akawaio is of interest, however, because it is typical of the treatment meted out to other tribal groups that have been earmarked for resettlement. As Robert Goodland notes in a general overview of resettlement schemes:

> Treatment of people arbitrarily forced out of their homes by construction of a reservoir varies tremendously. At one end of the scale, the people receive scarcely a warning that the waters will rise; others may be notified, but neither compensated nor assisted to move. Some communities may be offered the services of a government truck for a day to transport moveable belongings to dry ground; others may be provided with grass for houses while their own are burned. Lengthy police intervention, military coercion, and the bulldozer sanction, which is used in places, is acclaimed as successful if bloodshed can be avoided.[16]

But bloodshed is not always avoided. Indeed, in the case of the Chico Dam, the Philippines government brought in units of both the police and the army in order to quash opposition to the dam. At times, the methods used by those troops were brutal in the extreme, and arbitrary arrests were commonplace. It is even alleged that the army was responsible for the assassination of one of the main opponents of the dam, Apo Pangat Macli-ing Dulag, and the attempted murder of one of his chief lieutenants, Pedro Dungoc.[17]

LACK OF COMPENSATION AND INFERIOR LAND

Had the Chico Dam gone ahead, the local Bontocs and Kalinga tribesmen would have been resettled on land already declared unfit for the type of terraced agriculture they practice. "Years ago," reports the Australian-based Purari Action Group, "the people tried to transform the proposed resettlement areas into rice terraces and found this to be an impossibility."[18] Moreover, the compensation they were promised for the loss of their ancestral lands and villages was minimal.

Those twin problems—lack of adequate compensation and resettlement on inferior lands—are a feature of numerous resettlement schemes. For example, only those living on the actual site of Indonesia's Asahan Dam and its accompanying aluminum smelter were compensated for the loss of their land. As a result, 60 percent of those resettled under the project received nothing at all, even though their land will be used for roads and power lines. The amount paid in compensation is reported to have been "minimal." It had to be: the government was given only six million dollars to cover the cost of resettlement by the Japanese consortium building the dam—and the Indonesian government clearly had no intention of losing out.[19]

In Sri Lanka, those families being resettled in the Mahaweli Scheme received just £90 in compensation (3,000 rupees). Although those who owned a home were given the market value of their house, few of those resettled actually owned homes. Each family was being offered just one hectare of land in the resettlement scheme, land that was generally covered with scrub or forest, which had to be cleared before planting could take place. The Victoria Dam, funded by Britain, will ultimately flood 123 villages; a minimum of 45,000 people will be affected. "Yet," reports John Madeley in *New Scientist*, "those people were not consulted before the project started and there has been no public inquiry of any kind."[20]

For landless squatters, the problem of compensation is aggravated by the absence of legal rights. In Brazil, for example, those claiming compensation are bound by various articles under the Codigo Civil. To obtain compensation, explains Robert Goodland, they must "prove both humility and to be law-abiding and the fact that the land in dispute has been exploited by them uninterruptedly for 40 years on federal, unowned land. On land subsequently found to be owned, 20 years is adequate, or 15 years 'in good faith,' according to the Codigo Civil of 1973."[21] Those squatters who are unable to establish such rights "will be indemnified only for whatever dwelling they have constructed." As a result, many squatters receive little or no compensation. Thus, reports Goodland, between one-third and two-thirds of those squatters affected by the Tucuruí Project will be unable to support their claims. "Even though the squatters may be well-established, they will not be indemnified at the same rate as that for title holders. The treatment of squatters could provoke enormous hardship for the large numbers—possibly 10,000—of already impoverished people to be displaced by the reservoir."

Before building the Pantabangan Dam in Luzon, the Philippines government promised the 9,500 people who were to be resettled that they would be compensated for the loss of both land and housing. "It was to be a simple case of returning value for value," writes the Purari Action Group. "Land for land, house for house. Where such exchange was impractical, such as in the case of trees and plants and other improvements, cash payments would come in. The people could even opt for cash payments for everything lost."[22] The government also promised that new communities would be built and that those displaced would be employed on building the dam. Few of the promises were kept.

No land came to the people, save the homelots on rugged, desolate mountainsides and hilltops: resettlements sprawled in clusters on the rolling arid terrain. Within them, there is hardly a place to farm. There are only houses—some corehouses only, others almost finished; some painted, others not; all of them completely exposed to the elements and looking badly battered by the dusty winds and rains. . . . Homelots and farmlots which were to be leased to the people for a period of 40 years and renewable for the same length of time, are nowhere in sight. In one area, the farmlots could no longer be given to the resettlers since the authorities designated the land as a watershed area. Even worse, the government is presently studying the possibility of transferring the people to other lands more than 300 kilometers from where they are now.

Although it was intended that every farmer resettled under Ghana's Upper Volta Project should receive twelve acres, the land clearing got so behind that only 8,000 acres of an intended 54,000 acres were cleared before flooding. Much of that land was already earmarked for new villages. Describing the initial resettlement scheme as a "disaster," Warren Linney and Susan Harrison of the Nairobi-based Environment Liaison Centre report:

Originally, the people were to be resettled on a self-help basis 3–4 years before the flooding under the government's policy of "No one worse off as a result of the dam." In reality, only 2 years were available because of financing problems. The physical movement of the people and their possessions to 52 resettlement sites was carried out successfully in 1964; 67,000 people elected to move into the official settlement, the rest receiving cash compensation. By 1968, only 25,000 of the original settlers remained in the planned settlements. The failure of the agriculture programme was the major cause of exodus of the 42,000 original settlers. [That] programme failed mainly because of a lack of good land. The siting of the settlement had taken the wishes of the people into account and located the towns on their traditional lands, but there was already a high pressure on the land from other people. Only 6,000 hectares of new land was cleared, and half of this was required for the actual townsites.[23]

Many settlers found that they had no land to farm and were forced to rely on food distributed by U.S. AID and other agencies for the first two years of their resettlement. As a result, they were reduced from "independent subsistence farmers . . . to a landless peasantry, dependent on food handouts and government social spending."[24]

Had Guyana's Upper Mazaruni Dam gone ahead, the Akawaio Indians would have been forced to abandon the forests they had lived in for generations. The area where they were to have been resettled consisted of barren, rocky mountains and an occasional stretch of savannah where little grows except the odd stunted shrub. At the time that the dam was first proposed, the Akawaio expressed fears that they would not be able to adapt to such harsh conditions. "How can we who are not like mountain birds ascend the mountain to make gardens?" asked one village headman.[25] For their part, the Guyanese authorities talked enthusiastically about large, modern farms being created around the dam and in the lowlands beyond—this despite a clear warning in the 1950s from a British soil survey team that the Mazaruni area was unsuited to intensive agriculture.

It is now appreciated by a growing number of ecologists that traditional swidden methods of farming are the only means of cultivating the jungle without causing extensive environmental damage. For despite the lush canopy, the profusion of plants, and the incredible variety of species, the jungle's soils are some of the most fragile in the world. To farm them without causing ecological degradation takes an intimate knowledge of the local environment and the sort of skill that comes from generations of experience. Each garden has to be hewn out of the virgin forest—the smaller trees cut down, the rest burnt. In among the stumps the crops are then planted, and constant weeding is required to protect them. After three years or so, the soil's fertility drops so dramatically that the gardens have to be abandoned and the farmers must move elsewhere. This method takes a particular type of social organization and it cannot be learned overnight.

Those who have attempted to farm the jungle using modern

intensive agriculture have learned quickly and expensively that rain forests cannot support such techniques. Where this has been tried, it has been disastrous. "At Iata, an equatorial wonderland in the heart of the Amazon basin, the Brazilian government set up an agricultural colony," writes Dr. Mary McNeil, then development geologist for Lockheed Aircraft International.

> Earth-moving machinery wrenched a clearing from the forest and crops were planted. From the very beginning there were ominous signs of the presence of laterite. Blocks of ironstone stood out on the surface in some places: in others nodules of the laterite lay just below a thin layer of soil. What had appeared to be rich soil, with a promising cover of humus, disintegrated after the first or second planting. Under the equatorial sun, the iron-rich soil began to bake into brick. In less than five years, the cleared fields became virtually pavements of rock. Today, Iata is a drab despairing colony.[26]

Those Egyptian Nubians uprooted by the Aswan High Dam were moved to a new settlement area known as New Nubia, a crescent-shaped strip of land some 60 kilometers long and 3 kilometers wide. When the dam was closed, much of the new land was not ready to farm; monthly food subsidies were necessary to prevent starvation. Two years later, there were still bitter disputes about how the land was to be allocated. "A temporary distribution then took place in some villages, providing only a one-feddan farm plot to every family," reports Hussein Fahim, author of *Dams, People and Development*. "In 1971, upon completion of the reclamation and cultivation of most of the land allocated to New Nubia, another redistribution gave every beneficiary a good piece of land in addition to another of lesser quality. This caused difficulties for both the settlers and the administration. Disputes over soil quality, irrigation facilities and the distances between allocated land and the home village were some of the problems."[27] Those problems were further aggravated by the government's insistence that settlers with suitable soils should plant 40 percent of the acreage with sugar cane—a crop totally unfamiliar to the Egyptian Nubians and, consequently, hard to cultivate.

Other problems were caused by the poor quality of the soil in New Nubia and by the lack of drainage.

"The problem of land shortage presented by relocation was obvious from the start to all government officials concerned," Professor Thayer Scudder of the California Institute of Technology charges in appraising the Kariba Dam resettlement scheme in Zimbabwe and Zambia. "After resettlement had been completed, it was known that approximately one-third of the population would find themselves in serious straits within ten years. The rest were more fortunate, although there was little room for population increase in some areas and all areas could easily be degraded in the years ahead through erosion, overcultivation and overgrazing."[28]

Even before the dam was built, land shortages and population pressure had led to overcultivation, the reduction of fallow periods, and the exhaustion of many local "gardens." Resettlement greatly exacerbated the problem, in large part because those lands least susceptible to degradation were flooded. Of the land in the area resettled, much was marginal:

> Under the local system of agriculture, less than 40 percent . . . could support semipermanent cultivation (category 1), which involves five to ten years of continuous cropping, followed by a fallow period of approximately equal length. The rest (category 2) ranging in quality from fair to poor, could support at best cultivation for about six years, followed by a twenty-year fallow. With almost all of the arable land in the valley surveyed, this meant that semipermanent cultivators needed an absolute minimum of two acres per capita, whereas bush fallow cultivators needed five or more. The situation in Mwemba was by far the worst; 9,000 people had access to approximately 20,000 acres of category 2 soil, much of it in the less fertile and more easily eroded gardens. To meet their needs, at least 40,000 more acres were necessary.[29]

The result was erosion on a devastating scale. Yet the measures proposed for dealing with the problem were ones which the authorities knew in advance would be unacceptable to the Tonga. Thus attempts to stop the Tonga from cultivating the banks of river tributaries, which was their custom, were singularly unsuccessful—largely because the soil on the river's edge was the most fertile available. "While those Tonga involved were well aware of the dangers of erosion, they saw no option but to continue as in the past."[30] Similarly, efforts to persuade the Tonga to practice regular crop rotation and manuring were stymied because they conflicted with traditional farming practices. As for attempts to introduce "contour ridges" as a protection against erosion, these never even got underway. "Well aware that the valley residents did not really understand the basis for contouring, the Native Authority did not wish to associate itself with a potentially unpopular measure." It therefore did nothing. Where contour ridges were dug (1,230 miles of ridges protecting 14,247 acres were completed) they were poorly maintained and quickly fell into disrepair. In some cases they were actually torn down to make way for new gardens, such was the lack of land.

Nor was the lot of the Tonga made any the easier by the unpredictability of the rise and fall of Lake Kariba's waters. Between October, 1963, and March, 1964, the water level dropped 20 feet, leaving two miles of shoreline exposed. That land was cultivated by evacuees living on the lake's shores, and the first harvest produced "some of the best maize ever reaped in the Valley" before the water rose again.[31] The next season, however, the lake's waters dropped just two feet, and rose considerably earlier than expected, passing the previous high-water mark in January as opposed to March. "Any Tonga who had tried to repeat the successful 1963–64 experiment by again planting maize in November would have had his entire crop flooded out prior to its harvest."[32] Tragically, many farmers were wiped out—at a time when food shortages were often critical.

Even in the industrialized world, those resettled as a result of dam projects often receive scant compensation. Testifying before a U.S. Senate subcommittee in 1979, Geneva Sherman told how the Army Corps of Engineers had assessed compensation for those who were resettled under the Paintsville Lake Project. "Sherman referred to the Corps's method of land acquisition as robbery," reports Fred Powledge, author of *Water: The Nature, Uses and Future of Our Most Precious and Abused Resource*. "In almost every case, she said, the Corps takes its own land survey and claims that a landowner owns less acreage than his or her deed says—from 10 to 50 percent less. In this manner, the Corps can pay less for the land it confiscates. But when the Corps is finding comparable land for those evicted, it does not do its own survey, preferring then to take the deed's word for it."[33]

3. Social and Cultural Destruction

RESISTANCE TO RESETTLEMENT

Not surprisingly, those earmarked for resettlement are frequently unwilling to move. This widespread attitude led the authors of a paper prepared for Papua New Guinea's Office of Environment and Conservation to remark: "Love of birthplace, no matter how inhospitable it may appear to strangers, is quite possibly a universal human characteristic."[1]

When the society that must be resettled is a tribal one, that "love of land" takes on a significance far greater than is the norm in societies where land is viewed as just another commodity to be bought and sold. Land is the very charter on which a tribal culture is based, the resting place of ancestors and the source of spiritual power; it is thus frequently regarded with a reverence rarely understood in the West.

That sense of reverence is remarked upon time and again by anthropologists: it is also expressed in mythopoetic language by the tribal people themselves—often in last-minute pleas to be allowed to remain unmolested by the forces of "progress." For example, at the height of the controversy over the proposed Upper Mazaruni Hydroelectric Scheme, the headmen of Guyana's Akawaio Indians wrote to the prime minister, Mr. Forbes Burnham:

This land is where we belong—it is God's gift to us and has made us as we are. This land is where we are at home, we know its way: and the things that happen here are known and remembered, so that the stories the old people told are still alive here. This land is needed for those who come after us. . . . [It] is the place where we know where to find all that it provides for us—food for hunting and fishing, and farms, building and tool materials, medicines. Also the spirits around us know us and are friendly and helpful. This land keeps us together within its mountains—we come to understand that we are not just a few people or separate villages, but one people belonging to a homeland. If we had to move, we would be lost to those who remain in other villages. This would be a sadness to us all, like the sadness of death. Those who moved would be strangers to the people and spirits and places where they are made to go.[2]

That mythopoetic view of the world, alien as it is to Western minds, is fundamental to Akawaio culture. Flood their lands, and one would be flooding not only earth and rocks but also a *moral* map, for their moral and cultural values are etched into their landscapes as incisively as the Ten Commandments were supposedly etched onto Moses' tablets. As Survival International, the London-based organization set up to protect tribal rights, explained in its report *The Damned*:

The Akawaio have invested the landscape with special significance. It is an environment transformed by their ancestors in conjunction with the mystic forces of the universe. All its features— its rivers, falls, mountains, rocks, savannahs and valleys—were designed by their forebears, whose names and deeds are recorded in myth, song, dance and poetry. The vital forces of each locality are linked to the human community. They protect, guide, feed and even chastise its members. *Thus the landscape is dynamic, every part is living, functional, has meaning and moral value.*[3]

Summing up the feelings of the Cree Indians, who have been resettled as a result of Canada's James Bay Project, Boyd Richardson notes:

From one end of the region to the other, it is the same refrain. If you destroy the land, you destroy the animals, and if you destroy the animals, you destroy the Indians. Money? We do not want money. Jobs? How long will these jobs last? Money and jobs are impermanent. They disappear. They do not last. When they are gone, the land will still be there. If the land is not destroyed, we can return to it—live off it as we have always done. That is the only way we know how to live.[4]

One of the most bitter complaints voiced by the 57,000 Tonga resettled under the Kariba Dam scheme was that they were being forced to leave the land where their ancestors were buried. "Women in particular felt close identification with alluvial gardens (and their associated shelters) which had been cultivated and inherited by members of their matrilineage for longer than they could remember," reports Professor Thayer Scudder. "Tied to other gardens as well as to shrines by ancestral sanctions, neighbourhood ritual leaders feared for their health and that of their kin should they move elsewhere."[5]

Before the Chico Dam was halted in 1982, the Bontoc and Kalinga tribesmen who were to have been resettled made numerous deputations to the Philippine government to argue their case against the dam. Like the Akawaio, they stressed their bond with the land, a bond molded (in the case of the Kalinga) by the belief that the god Kabunian had entrusted the land to them for safekeeping. "To them the land is sacred," wrote Ceres P. Doya in Manila's *Bulletin Today*. "The God Kabunian has gifted them with the land and, therefore, they must be good stewards of the gift. . . . Their dead do not go away forever. They are buried right in their very own yards to form part of the earth which they have worked and caressed. The dead become one with the guardian spirits who make the land yield flowers and fruit abundantly."[6]

Anthropologists who have studied the region take a more "functionalist" view of the Kalinga's bond to the land. It is worth quoting at some length from a paper delivered shortly before the dam project was cancelled, at the 3rd National Annual Conference of the Anthropological Association of the Philippines:

The traditional religion of the people of the Chico Valley is characterised by ancestor worship, belief in and fear of the spirits of forest and field. Even today, where some accept Christianity, the respect for the power and integrity of the traditional ancestors and gods over all areas of day-to-day living prevails. All the many ancestor and spirit gods are associated in the people's minds with the land of the home region. The remains of all who die, even those who may die many miles away, are brought home. . . . Ancestors and spirits are capable of bringing sickness and misfortune to the living if neglected or not given the proper respect. Most sickness, mental ill-health and accidents are believed to be caused by angry spirits. Once the people allow the villages to be submerged, this will mean the greatest displeasure of the spirits who would forever haunt and bring disaster to the lives of the living. . . .

Aside from the local religion, the political institutions for which the people of the Chico Valley are noted are also tied up with the land of the home region. The peace pact (Kalinga *bodong*, Bontoc *pachen*) prevails over certain defined territories which the present villages occupy. Each separate peace pact between two communities defined the specific land area over which it is to prevail. Submersion of these lands and the dislocation of the people from their communities would mean the destruction of the peace pacts prevailing over the areas.

The peace pact and its system of laws (*pagto to bodong*) is today still the most effective mechanism for social interaction and control in the peace pact areas. The barrios to be submerged by the Chico IV alone hold a total of 180 peace pacts with each other and with other Kalinga, Bontoc and Tinggian communities. Submersion of the land and transfer of the inhabitants would nullify all of these. And if the peace pact system presently prevailing were to be rendered inutile by dam incursion into specific territories, the whole supportive system underlying the social structure of local society would be undermined.[7]

ETHNIC DIFFERENCES IGNORED

Once resettled, those who have been moved frequently have to contend with planning authorities who are often insensitive to their cultural traditions. A case in point is the Volta River Project, where 69,000 people from more than 700 villages were resettled in just fifty-two new settlements. Villages were split up and thou-

sands of people from different ethnic backgrounds—speaking
different languages, worshipping different gods, and following
widely different social customs—were resettled together without
any regard for those differences. "The complex emotional relationships between the different tribes and their lands were not
properly understood," argues Dr. Asit Biswas, a well-known authority on water development projects. "The development of a
socially cohesive and integrated community, having a viable in-
stitutional infrastructure, became hard to achieve."[8] To make
matters worse, the new settlers were bitterly resented by the original inhabitants of the area. Land disputes and outbreaks of violence became increasingly common as the resettlement scheme
got under way.

Those same mistakes were repeated at Khashm el-Girba
(New Halfa), the resettlement project built to rehouse the 30,000
Sudanese Nubians uprooted by the Aswan High Dam. Although,
to their credit, the authorities tried to avoid splitting up villages
after they were resettled, this was not always possible. In some
cases, the population of the old villages was too large to be resettled together. As a result, the social structure of many villages was
severely disrupted. This exacerbated the psychological stress of
resettlement, fomenting considerable social tension.

That tension was further compounded by the decision to settle
three disparate ethnic groups at Khashm el-Girba. Two of those
groups, the Shukyra and the Beja, were pastoralists, settled under a government scheme to "sedentarize" half of the area's nomadic population. The third group consisted of Halfans, a
people with a long tradition of agriculture and with a proud cultural past. "After being the dominant group in their former area,
the Halfans became just one of several ethnic groups living in the
Khashm el-Girba region," reports Dr. Hussein Fahim, in his
study of the resettlement program. "The resettled Halfans still
fear that their contact with the nomads and other groups in the
scheme will eventually erode the distinctive qualities of their traditional Sudanese Nubian culture."[9]

The Halfans' wariness of other tribes in the area is fully recip-
rocated. The Halfans consider the nomads aggressive and dis-

honest, and the nomads consider the Halfans to be intruders on their lands. The nomads see no reason why they should cease grazing their sheep on the land now farmed by the Halfans, even though it has been bought by the Sudanese government. To them the land is theirs, simply because it has always been theirs. For the same reason, they refuse to pay for bus tickets when the bus is traveling in their traditional homelands.

The obvious consequence has been numerous and bitter disputes over land rights, disputes that became so heated in 1974 that the army had to be called in to keep the peace by preventing the nomads from grazing on cultivated land. Small wonder that one settler likened the Khashm el-Girba project to "a cage where the government put a lamb and a wolf and asked them to figure out one way or another to live peacefully." Naturally, he told Fahim, the experiment had not worked.[10]

INAPPROPRIATE HOUSING

The nomads at Khashm el-Girba also resented the fact that the Halfans had been rehoused in modern buildings, whereas the nomads had been given traditional mud-and-wattle housing. Paradoxically, but not surprisingly, the Halfans themselves were also dissatisfied with their new houses. It was not that the houses lacked modern facilities—indeed, by Sudanese standards they were luxurious—but rather that the designers had paid little heed to the social needs of the uprooted settlers. As Hussein Fahim notes:

> Part of the dissatisfaction was due to the assignment of the new buildings according to the estimated cost of the old ones, instead of according to the size of the families who were to live in them. Large families, whose old homes were valued at less than 100 Sudanese pounds, received two-room houses and thus were unable to accommodate their members, whose numbers ranged between seven and nine persons on average. The addition of extra rooms was practically impossible because of the sloping tin roof and the cost of construction in the area. Furthermore, many of the houses were poorly built: their design ignored the basic social aspects of

Nubian architecture, such as the need for high walls to provide security and privacy. The seclusion of women, a traditional notion supported by their Islamic religion, was always emphasised in old Nubian house designs.[11]

Across the border, the Egyptian Nubians were experiencing similar problems:

The old Nubian houses were large and spacious. Built on one floor with walls as high as 6 to 8 metres, each house had several wide rooms roofed with either brick vault domes or palm trunks and reed, which in either case suited the hot dry weather. These rooms, which had several holes near the roof for ventilation, usually opened into a large open-air courtyard, an essential feature of Nubian architecture. The lack of these elements has been given, among others, as an important reason for the Nubians' displeasure with their new living quarters. . . . The basic design did, and still does, constitute a major source of stress among the relocatees. The transfer from spacious homes to compact, contiguous dwellings with relatively low walls has also caused problems. In addition, the distribution of the new houses on the basis of the family size resulted in the fragmentation and dispersion of the already established social and economic units of the family-based neighbourhoods. Widowed, divorced and elderly people, who previously lived with their immediate relatives in one household, are now scattered in one-room blocks, that often are not within walking distance of their kin. Those people feel helpless and have caused strain and anxiety for their families.[12]

Many Egyptian Nubians simply chose to abandon their settlements and return to the shores of their now-flooded homelands.

In many senses, the insensitivity with which the new houses had been designed can be seen as a metaphor for the failure of the whole resettlement scheme:

In Old Nubia, the homes were constructed with privacy in mind and were aesthetically very appealing. They were decorated with elaborate, beautifully coloured designs and natural scenes, all of which signified the importance of nature and its beauties to the Nubians. The new structures, however, were designed with modernisation and space efficiency in mind, and were not only displeasing to the Nubians for aesthetic reasons, but offensive in the lack of privacy they afforded.[13]

The design of the new houses in the Upper Volta resettlement scheme in Ghana caused similar social friction. On the face of it, such friction should have been avoided. Indeed, the Volta River Authority is at pains to point out that it made every effort to design the new villages "to maintain the traditional life-style as closely as possible." Toward that end, recalls the former chief executive of the VRA, settlers were housed "in their own tribal or clan groupings . . . with the same neighbours as in their original settlements."[14]

Nonetheless, in the design of the settlers' houses, the VRA made a fatal error. It failed to take into account the size and structure of the traditional family unit. As observed by Stanley Johnson, now a member of the European Parliament:

> Polygamous for the most part, the settlers objected to the concrete houses which had been constructed for them by the Volta River Authority. It was not the concrete they minded. On the contrary, a concrete house back in his "home town" is the average Ghanaian's idea of paradise. . . . No, what bothered them was the size. In the traditional village houses, the wives had separate rooms. The man moved from one room to the other, changing monthly or weekly, depending on taste or circumstances—whether a wife was pregnant or lactating, for instance. *The new houses offered only one room for the man and all the wives.*[15]

The VRA claimed it had always intended that the settlers themselves would expand their houses—and had given them space to do so. Few villagers, however, had the wherewithal even to maintain their houses, let alone enlarge them. Indeed, Akosambo, the model village built to house construction workers at the dam site, has now fallen into such a state of disrepair that it is little more than a slum.

Whatever the prestige value of concrete houses, they are singularly unsuited to Ghana's climate, being hotter during the day and colder at night than traditional mud-and-thatch houses.

That much was admitted by the VRA. In fact, the authority initially considered using traditional building materials but decided against it because "the time required to carry out construction in local materials would have been much too long for the overall project schedule."[16] Expediency was thus allowed to take precedence over the comfort of settlers.

Worse yet, the decision to build in concrete often meant that settlers could no longer undertake their own construction. Once materials had been freely available, but now they had to be bought on the open market. That change had implications far beyond the loss of self-sufficiency—a point well made by Amos Rapoport, senior lecturer in architecture at the University of Sydney. Discussing the general problem of housing design and cultural change, he points out: "The building of houses in a traditional society is more than an economic or technical activity; it is frequently cooperative and this cooperation sets up networks of obligations, solidarity of community, etc. A change to building carried out by experts for cash may lead to disruption of these social arrangements—a substitution of the moral order by a merely technical one with far-ranging consequences."[17]

The Nabdam people of northern Ghana provide a good example of Rapoport's point. Like most of the tribes in the area, the Nabdam are polygamous. They live in family compounds consisting typically of a man, his wives, and their children. As the heads of households die, or men get married, new compounds are built and old ones are expanded. Until recently, such building work was carried out by the men of the compound, with the women taking an active part in the planning and decorating of new houses. Ian Archer, an architect who studied Nabdam settlement patterns extensively, described the building of a new house after a man remarried:

> Traditionally, when a man takes a new wife, the general distribution of the new buildings is discussed by the family and the *Tendaana* [a tribal priest], and marked out on the ground. The buildings are then erected by the men, and rendered and decorated by the women who are to occupy them. The wall paintings are

bold and, within limits, excitingly varied from house to house, so that each woman's domain is physically and stylistically delineated.[18]

Today, much has changed. Many Nabdam now take jobs in the South and return with enough money to employ builders to put up their compounds. The new structures bear little resemblance to traditional Nabdam houses. Archer argues that the introduction of professional builders has meant the end of traditional housing styles; people are no longer able to participate in the "tailoring" of their homes. Certainly, Archer's description of one of the new compounds—belonging, in this instance, to the son of a local chief—highlights the difference between the ancient and the modern in Nabdam:

> Sampana had lived in the South for many years and when he returned North he built a compound closely resembling those built by the Ashanti, with a corrugated aluminum roof. *It is probably significant that this compound was almost always empty of people.* The sharp definition of inside and outside space does not equal the range of environments produced by the screens, walls, and semi-enclosures of the traditional construction, which so aptly accommodates the complex climate and the segmented living pattern of the Nabdam. The traditional form of building can be manipulated to create easily a small environment for each wife. The wife will normally decorate the walls of her area by finger-marking the wet rendering as she applies it. Abstract patterns are then applied with vegetable dyes. Sampana's compound had none of this and one felt that the women had been unable to identify with their homes.[19]

In many respects, the Nabdam are fortunate. At least the changes brought about in their traditional settlement patterns and housing designs have been introduced by fellow Nabdam—not forced upon them by an anonymous bureaucracy. Even so, Archer warns that the subtle social effects of those changes are already making themselves felt, and he makes an important point: "The impact of change in the area is all the more apparent because of *the synthesis of all aspects of Nabdam life.* Time has mellowed and refined their farming techniques, their architecture and their social conduct so that *all are an essential part of total existence.*"[20]

That cultural coherence is by no means unique to the Nabdam. Time and again, anthropologists have noted how in tribal societies, all aspects of daily life, from the religious to the economic, fit together to form a unified whole. With regard to tribal *settlement* patterns, for example, it has long been observed that the arrangement of houses is not random; it reflects a tribe's social structure and in some cases its cosmology. Those same concerns also influence the design of *houses* in traditional societies. Rare, if not unknown, is the house whose design is purely functional.

HOUSING AND THE INTEGRITY
OF TRADITIONAL CULTURE

The connection between a society's settlement pattern and its social organization was first set out by the French sociologists Emile Durkheim and Marcel Mauss. In their now classic monograph *Primitive Classification*, they argued that the way in which tribal societies view the world reflects the way their own societies are organized.[21] If a tribe is organized in moieties—two discrete groups that intermarry—there will be a tendency to see the natural world as also being divided into moieties. If the tribe is further divided into clans and lineages, so too animal species will be seen as being divided into clans and lineages, and so on.

That same principle, argued Durkheim and Mauss, applies to the layout of settlements. When the tribe is divided into moieties, so the camp is divided in two. Thus, when the Omaha tribe of the Sioux settle down to camp, "the encampment is made in circular form; and within this circle, each particular group has a fixed place." Moreover, "within the semicircle occupied by each moiety, the clans in their turn are clearly localized with respect to each other, and the same is the case with the subclans."[22] The camp is thus laid out on exactly the same lines as the tribe is organized.

In some cases, the connection between a tribe's settlement pattern and its social structure is acknowledged explicitly. An-

thropologists who have studied the eastern Bororo Indians of
Matto Grosso, in Brazil, report that when the Bororo are asked
to describe their social organization, they do so by referring to
the plan of an ideal village (see Fig. 1). As with the Omaha, the
village is circular and divided in two, each half being occupied by
a moiety. Within that area, each of the four clans that make up a
moiety has its own discrete territory, and the position of each clan
within the semicircle is determined by its relationship to all the
other clans. As anthropologist Christopher Crocker explains:
"Within moieties, clans immediately adjacent to each other are
considered to be more closely related both socially and ritually
than those distant from each other."[23] Distance is thus a measure
of social relationships.

Today, severe depopulation has made it impossible for the Bororo to follow the village plan as closely as tradition demands.
Nonetheless, as Crocker reports:

> they remain committed to the model's permanent worth as a guide
> for the proper relations of individuals, groups and communities.
> *The village plan is for them a moral plan, establishing the normative or-*
> *der which must regulate their society.* . . . They consider it crucial
> that the house positions in a given village correspond as much as
> possible to those set out in the model, and the most important du-
> ties of the two rival chiefs of the village include establishing the
> huts' location every time the village is moved. Indeed, the clans
> which provide these chiefs are known by the title "Planner of the
> Village" (*Bado Jebage*).[24]

Tragically, but predictably, where the authorities have prevented
the Bororo from following their traditional settlement pattern,
the result has been the rapid and complete destruction of their
society.

That the Bororo could be destroyed by a change in their settlement pattern is in fact a testament to the remarkable coherence of
their culture. Indeed, it is precisely because the culture of a tribal
society forms such an integrated whole that it is so vulnerable to
destruction: change one feature of a tribe's cultural pattern and
inevitably other features change too. The point is well made by

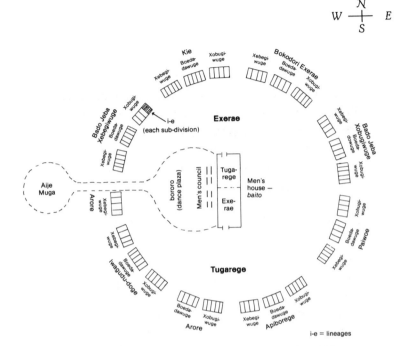

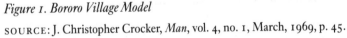

Figure 1. Bororo Village Model

SOURCE: J. Christopher Crocker, *Man*, vol. 4, no. 1, March, 1969, p. 45.

the French anthropologist Robert Jaulin. Discussing the impact of white society on the forest Indians of South America, he writes: "The social structure of a people is not changed by drumming in our ideas, but by altering the everyday details of the Amerindians' life—by modifying their clothing, habitat, cooking, dress, the organisation of their time and their needs, so that family life, consumption, production, all communication, can no longer function other than in the new one-sided relationship with white society."[25] In the case of the Motiline, the Venezuelan tribe Jaulin himself studied, the destruction of their traditional culture was largely ensured by the enforced move from thatched, communal roundhouses to rectangular, corrugated iron sheds.

In Australia, the introduction of electric light sufficed to cause a cultural breakdown. Among one group of Australian Aborigines, electric lighting led to increased violence by undermining the traditional means of resolving conflicts. Before the advent of electricity, those with complaints would air their grievances at night from the safety of their own family camp fire. Although others in the camp could hear the complaints, no one could see who was making them—ensuring an albeit fictitious anonymity. As Rapoport explained: "Only at dusk or later, when visual displays of anger are impossible, does a person give expression to his emotions. It is possible that this is a ritualised way of separating visual and aural aggressive displays and thus avoiding and preventing physical conflict."[26] Physical violence was further kept at a minimum by the belief that to stray too far from the light of one's own family camp fire was to invite being attacked by evil spirits that prowled around under cover of darkness. Inevitably, the introduction of electricity destroyed such traditional means of resolving conflicts. "Now people can see each other and since it is no longer dark they are free to leave their *wiltja* (family fire). The result is a much higher level of physical violence."

Despite the evidence that even the most minor change can spell cultural death for a tribal society, the message has not gotten through. Although the Guyanese authorities stressed the importance of appropriate housing for those Akawaio Indians who were to have been resettled under the Upper Mazaruni Hydroelectric scheme, the planners' idea of what was "appropriate" took little account of what was culturally appropriate. "The architecture within, and the physical layout of the new settlements will, of course, depend on the sociocultural realities which characterise the various communities that have to resettle. With respect to architecture, a competition at the national level involving designs for various types of buildings for the various communities to be resettled has been mooted."[27] It is difficult to imagine how any house designed as a result of a national competition—inevitably open to architects of widely different ethnic backgrounds—could ever be appropriate to the Akawaio's cultural needs.

IS BETTER PLANNING POSSIBLE?

Despite all that has gone wrong, there is still a general belief that through skillful planning and sufficient funding the resettlement schemes of the future can avoid the mistakes of the past. In that respect, Robert Goodland writes:

> It is most encouraging to observe the enormous improvement achieved over the last several decades. . . . Now, it is expected that an acceptable resettlement plan will be made an integral part of all projects where such an action is required. Socio-economic studies of the population to be affected are started as soon as project design starts. It is becoming widely recognised that adequate resettlement can be more complicated than project engineering and more time-consuming than project design and construction. . . . The Bank now has a systematic and detailed policy designed to ensure successful resettlement.[28]

Systematic and detailed as the World Bank's new resettlement policy may be, it is difficult to share Goodland's confidence that it will ensure success. In some cases, the measures proposed for cushioning the social blows of resettlement are woefully inadequate. Take, for instance, Brazil's Tucuruí hydroelectric project, a scheme for which Goodland himself undertook the ecological impact study on behalf of Electronorte, the company that will run the dam. In that study, Goodland recommended that Electronorte set up a full-time competent community sociological unit "responsible for early detection and defusing of social tensions related to all project activities."[29]

On paper, that recommendation made sense enough. But set against the social problems of the area, problems vividly described as follows by Goodland himself, it was clearly unequal to the task in hand: "Irrespective of the Tucuruí project," he writes,

> the region seethes with social problems: land disputes commonly solved by the gun, abject poverty, harsh servitude to the landlords, soaring infant mortality, malaria commonly attacking a full third of the populace, plummeting crop yields and spiraling food prices, combined with inexorable accelerating immigration. These factors engender critically inflammatory social tensions which have already exploded into bloodshed and warfare on several occasions in recent years. The political atmosphere in the area continues to be tense, and an "outside" consultant quickly learns that there are several sensitive topics which one is advised to avoid. The region is now under tight control by the Exercito da Selva—the Jungle

Army—so the guerrilla invasions of 1972 and 1974 are unlikely to be repeated. Such tense social conditions are not propitious for the success of Electronorte. The project will improve to the extent Electronorte decides to ease the tensions and relieve social unrest.[30]

It is difficult to see how Electronorte will succeed in that task by setting up a "competent community sociological unit." Competent or otherwise, such units have yet to win a civil war.

It might be argued that Tucuruí is an exception, and that the hardships incurred at other resettlement schemes could indeed be avoided through better planning and greater generosity on the part of the authorities. To some extent this is undoubtedly true. There is no reason—at least in theory—why those who are resettled should be given insufficient compensation or inferior land. Politically, however, there are many good reasons why this should occur. Put bluntly, few governments are willing to increase the funds allocated for resettlement if doing so threatens the economic viability of a project. And in the majority of cases, that is precisely what would happen.

The point was well made by Professor William Ackermann at a 1971 conference on man-made lakes. Regretting that the implications of resettlement often are not even considered in feasibility studies for dam projects, he went on to tell his audience:

Also seriously underestimated are the financial cost of compensating and physically moving people, the cost of forming new communities and new systems of production, and the time required for essential help. In the major African dams, per capita relocation expenses have varied from approximately $200 per capita to $2,000. In all of these projects the relocation expenses have been at least three times the original estimates and sometimes substantially more. Had planners known from the start that relocation costs would rarely be less than 25 percent of the combined cost of power generation and transmission and dam construction, they would have approached feasibility studies in a rather different way. Sometimes, financial costs of resettlement may be sufficiently great to offset expected benefits of dam construction in comparison to alternate uses of funds.[31]

When the Kaiser Corporation made its 1959 reassessment of the economic viability of the Volta Dam, it arrived at a satisfactory costing only by cutting the estimated costs of roads, railways, land acquisition, and resettlement by 30 percent. The new figures were accepted with alacrity by the Ghanaian government. There is little reason to suppose that other governments today would behave any differently if they, too, saw high resettlement costs as threatening a project. How would Sri Lanka's President Jayewardene react to the idea of increasing the compensation to be paid to the 1.5 million people being resettled under the Mahaweli Scheme? He has staked his political future on the project and millions of dollars have already gone into it. If such an increase undermined the economic viability of the scheme, how probable is it that the president would agree to it?

Indeed, one might ask, just how far are the authorities in *any* country actually concerned about the traumas of resettlement? Consider the testimony of Dr. David Price before the 1983 U.S. House of Representatives subcommittee on International Development Institutions and Finance. An anthropologist, Price had worked as a consultant to the World Bank on Brazil's Polonoreste Project, a $1.25 billion scheme to develop 158,000 square miles of western Brazil, an area equivalent to the entire state of California. The experience was not a happy one.

> My experience as a consultant to the World Bank has led me to question the sincerity of that institution's commitment to safeguarding the welfare of people affected by the projects it supports. . . . I was not asked to come to Washington until June 1980, eight months after the Bank had been informed that there were native peoples in the area of the proposed project. During this time, four anthropologists with experience in other parts of Brazil informed the Bank that I was more familiar with conditions in the project area. . . .
>
> When I went to Washington to explain the complexities of the Brazilian Indian policy as it related to the peoples of Western Matto Grosso, I found that the Bank had already agreed that: (a) any program of assistance to the Indians in the area would be conducted solely by the FUNAI [the Brazilian agency responsible for the

country's Indian population]: (b) the FUNAI would accept no funding from the World Bank for such a program: and (c) the evaluation and monitoring of such a program would be done by full-time staff members of the World Bank and the FUNAI, without the aid of outside authorities such as professional anthropologists.

The Bank renegotiated the third condition and sent me to Brazil to assess the adequacy of the FUNAI's plan of assistance, only after I had learned that it was ignoring the threat to the native people and had begun working to mobilize public opinion. . . .

After returning from Brazil, I prepared and submitted a 48-page document detailing the results of my investigations and making recommendations. *I was surprised to learn, some weeks later, that no one in the World Bank had seen this report except the two staff members who had accompanied me to Brazil and the Chief of the Latin America and Caribbean Regional Office* [emphasis added].

A report of the three-person mission in which I had participated, which was supposed to include my findings and recommendations, *systematically suppressed and distorted them* [emphasis added]. I had been charged with evaluating: (a) the FUNAI's plan to safeguard the Indians of the Polonoreste area, and (b) the agency's competence to carry out this plan. The FUNAI's proposal was completely divorced from reality—so puerile and fanciful that I could not help but wonder whether the agency really intended it to be taken seriously, or simply believed that the World Bank would not care whether it was realistic. As for the FUNAI's competence, available evidence suggested that it recently had been taken over by military men with a background of intelligence and security, and more than 50 staff members who were conscientiously committed to the welfare of the Indians had been systematically weeded out.

The official report of the three-person mission suppressed these strongly negative conclusions, and suggested that a few minor shortcomings should not impede the progress of negotiations. I vigorously protested what I saw as a deliberate distortion of my findings, but nevertheless, this document was made the basis of a section on 'Amerindians' in the World Bank's comprehensive evaluation of the Polonoreste project.[32]

Testifying before the same subcommittee, Bruce M. Rich, of the Natural Resources Defense Council, charged that the World

Bank was not the sole development bank lacking concern for the ecological effects of its projects. "Up to 1981," as he pointed out, "the Inter-American Development Bank (IADB) did not even employ a single full-time, professional forester on its staff, in spite of the fact that it finances substantial projects to exploit industrially forest resources, and a much greater number of projects, such as dams and roads, which are both affected by and affect the ecological balance of adjacent forest resources."[33] Even in 1983, the IADB had only two professional foresters.

Nonetheless, the bank claims to take full account of environmental factors in planning its projects. Such claims, says Rich, "do not reflect reality." One project cited by the IADB as an example of its concern for the environment is Colombia's Sinú River Development Scheme, which involves the building of two large dams, the flooding of 70,000 hectares of tropical forest, and the resettlement of two thousand Indians and thousands of campesinos. "A Colombian environmental organization, the Fundaçion del Caribe, has been monitoring the scheme with increasing concern for over two years," reports Rich. "With the help of a U.S. government aid agency, the Inter-American Foundation, it is preparing a study of the sociological, ecological, and economic impacts of the project to attempt to remedy the inadequacy of existing planning studies. . . . Yet the IADB singles out the Sinú scheme as an example of 'technical cooperation with a decided environmental emphasis,' particularly the IADB financial planning studies."[34]

The record of other development agencies is often worse. The African Development Bank, for example, "has no environmental staff, procedures or guidelines." The Asian Development Bank, which employs more than 1,200 people, has only two people working in its environmental unit—and the unit has "no direct mandate to influence project design." Even the World Bank, with a staff of 5,250, employs only five full-time ecologists. Moreover, as Rich observed: "Full, separate and thorough environmental assessments are not performed by the Bank as a matter of course, even for projects with important negative environmental impacts. In fact, the Bank's sole mandatory environmental procedures call for projects to be reviewed by its Office of Environmental Affairs long after they have been chosen, designed and appraised—just before the initiation of loan negotiations. This is much too late a stage in the World Bank's project cycle to change environmentally destructive projects in any significant way."[35] Such procedures are hardly equipped to ensure better planning of resettlement schemes.

THE ROAD TO THE SLUM

Cultural change is actively sought by the governments of the Third World nations. For them, resettlement and development projects are a vital means of bringing "progress" to the people. Indeed, the aim is quite explicit: to transform traditional lifestyles. Nomads must be settled, pastoralists turned into farmers, subsistence farmers into modern agriculturalists.

Introducing the Mahaweli Scheme to Sri Lanka's Parliament in 1979, for instance, the minister for the Mahaweli made it clear that a major aim of the scheme was to break the mold of traditional farming. The explicit intention was "to enable the peasant colonist farmers to produce a surplus . . . not to create a large body of subsistence farmers." The feasibility study prepared for the government went further: "The objectives of the project are to increase production, productivity and income, to arouse peasant initiative, to integrate the population and to generalise social change."[36]

Even those who argue for better planning of social change, however, are well aware that such planning cannot prevent all adverse cultural change. Discussing the impact of development on tribal peoples, for instance, the World Bank itself makes clear that it sees its task as cushioning the inevitable cultural blow that development will bring:

> It is not the Bank's policy to prevent the development of areas presently occupied by tribal people. The Bank will assist projects within areas used or occupied by such people only if it is satisfied that the best efforts have been made to obtain the voluntary, full

and conscionable agreement of the tribal people. . . . *Assuming that tribal people will either acculturate or disappear* [emphasis added], there are two basic design options: the World Bank can assist the government either with acculturization, or with protection in order to avoid harm.[37]

For those tribal people who will be affected, it is a galling prospect. The World Bank is right to assume that "acculturization" is the inevitable consequence of development. If, as we have seen, even the smallest change can lead to cultural death for traditional society, what will be the impact of the wholesale changes demanded by resettlement? Consider, for example, what being settled could mean for a pastoral society like the Dinka of southern Sudan. Originally, it was intended that the Jonglei Canal Scheme would lead to the development of a 250,000-acre irrigation project alongside the banks of the canal. Under the scheme, the Dinka were to have been forced to abandon their cattle-herding way of life in order to become farmers.

It is inconceivable that the Dinka's traditional culture could have survived such a change. For the Dinka, cattle are the very basis of their culture: everything revolves around them. Godfrey Leinhardt, the anthropologist whose book on Dinka religion is rightly considered a classic, gives some examples.[38] The Dinka perceive color, light, and shade in terms of the colors and markings of their cattle. They imitate cattle in their dances, and it is the height of elegance and grace to stand with one's arms outstretched to look like the curved horns of an ox. When boys reach manhood, they are named after the color of a cow. There is thought to be a binding contract between a man and his beasts, and it is considered outrageous to kill an ox or a cow simply because one has an appetite for meat (as distinct from eating meat in order to survive a famine). Cattle have a prominent place in the Dinka afterlife, and a cow that has been killed without appropriate ceremony is thought to haunt its killers.

Fortunately, the Sudanese government decided against settling the Dinka under the Jonglei scheme. Nonetheless, the point is made. To ask a traditional society to change is in effect to ask its people to abandon their whole way of life. It is not comparable to, let us say, asking a western pig-farmer to go into sheep or cattle; nor is it like asking a man to change his job. It is saying that traditional societies should embrace "modern" values and "modern" lifestyles regardless of what that will do to their own culture. As Stanley Johnson comments of the Volta scheme: "Anyone who has endured the horrors of downtown Accra and witnessed the ultimate consequences of 'modern' sets of values and a 'modern approach to life' may justifiably wonder whether the game is really worth the candle."[39]

Indeed they might. Deprived of their traditional culture and stripped of the support of their communities, many of those who are resettled drift towards the cities. There, a now familiar tragedy repeats itself. The men frequently turn to alcohol, and the women are often forced to prostitute themselves simply to earn the wherewithal to feed themselves and their families. Malnutrition and disease are rife, jobs almost impossible to find. It is a world far removed from the "paradise" offered to them by the authorities. Unfortunately, it is a world in which most of them will spend the rest of their lives.

4. Closing the Dam: Loss of Land and Wildlife Upstream, Loss of Silt and Fertility Downstream

LOSS OF AGRICULTURAL LAND TO FLOODING

When a dam is closed, the waters of its reservoir begin to rise, submerging vast areas of land. Beneath the waters of Lake Nasser, for example, 400,000 hectares disappeared; 848,200 hectares were lost to the Volta River project; 510,000 hectares were flooded by the Kariba Dam; 380,000 hectares by the Cabora Bassa Dam in Mozambique; and 328,000 by the Guri Project in Venezuela (see Table 3).

Often the area flooded contains thousands of acres of good agricultural land. In Sri Lanka, for example, the Victoria Dam (part of the giant Mahaweli Project) will, according to L. Alexis, "destroy 3,000 acres of land cultivated with paddy, tobacco, vegetables, and other food crops; 2,000 acres cultivated with mixed fruit, cocoa, coffee, coconut, spices, tubers, and soft wood in village gardens and homesteads; and 2,000 acres in big and small estates of cocoa, coffee, pepper, rubber, coconut, sugar cane, and soft wood."[1]

Figures are not available for the total worldwide loss of farmland to dam projects, but the number of people who have had to be resettled as a result suggests the productivity of the lands they previously occupied, which have now been flooded. In India, for

51

example, the Srisailam Hydroelectric Scheme near Hyderabad flooded some 107,000 acres of farmland, land which, until the dam was closed, had provided a livelihood for some 100,000 people. Discussing that loss of agricultural land, the Fact-Finding Committee on Srisailam Project Evaluations notes:

> The agricultural economy of the region was considered to be highly prosperous. The lands, both dry and wet, situated along the Tungabhadra and Krishna rivers were highly fertile and the cropping patterns adopted by the farmers were both remunerative and profitable. Not only food crops such as paddy, wheat, and redgram, but also commercial crops such as groundnut, tobacco, chillies, and cotton were grown extensively in the areas which have been submerged. The level of food production in these areas was quite high as the soil and the climate were very favourable to agriculture. Thus, the submersion of 107,000 acres caused an enormous amount of loss and hardship to the local villagers.

LOSS OF FORESTS AND WILDLIFE TO FLOODING

In addition to causing the loss of agricultural land, dams have also caused the drowning of thousands of acres of forest. It is estimated, for example, that between 1950 and 1975, India lost 479,000 hectares of forest land to various river valley projects.

For the promoters of large-scale dams, that loss of forests is generally seen only in economic terms—that is, in terms of the actual market value of the timber submerged. "Officials totally ignore the *intangible* ecological value of such benefits as soil preservation, water replenishment, climatic stabilization, air purification, or wildlife shelter," comment the authors of a recent report on India's giant Narmada Valley Project. This scheme involves the building of thirty major dams and will itself drown some 150,000 acres of forest, including 35,000 acres of teak forest. Indeed, the report goes on to note, if the intangible benefits provided by trees were taken into account, then—in the estimation of India's prestigious Forest Research Institute—every tree should be valued at an economic worth of 100,000 rupees per fifty years of its life.

TABLE 3
Areas Inundated by Selected Dams

Project	Country	Normal area of reservoir, in hectares (one hectare = 2.47 acres)
Paulo Afonso	Brazil	7,520
Sayanskaya	USSR	80,000
Churchill Falls	Canada	66,500
Itaipu	Brazil/Paraguay	135,000
Grand Coulee	USA	32,400
Jupia	Brazil	33,300
São Simão	Brazil	66,000
Tucuruí	Brazil	
	Ultimate	216,000
	Initial	216,000
Ilha Solteira	Brazil	120,000
Mazaruni	Guyana	
	Projected Ultimate	39,000
	Projected Initial	259,000
Guri	Venezuela	328,000
Paredão	Brazil	2,300
Cabora Bassa	Mozambique	380,000
Furnas	Brazil	135,000
Samuel	Brazil	15,000
Kabalebo	Suriname	
	Ultimate	145,000
Aswan High	Egypt	400,000
Curuá-una	Brazil	8,600
Três Marias	Brazil	105,200
Kariba	Zimbabwe/Zambia	510,000
Sobradinho	Brazil	450,000
Baibina	Brazil	124,000
Volta	Ghana	848,200
Brokopondo	Suriname	150,000

SOURCE: Goodland, 1977. (These data are approximate only.)

We are also reminded that forests provide benefits that cannot be given an economic value. "Even if the intangible ecological benefits are quantifiable, the social value of forests is not. Yet, for the [indigenous tribal groups] the forest is of great cultural and psychological importance, and its destruction represents a serious disruptive event. Moreover, there is no way of calculating the loss of the economic and genetic potential of a forest, for there may be dozens or hundreds of species which have not been . . . even identified."

The inevitable loss of wildlife due to the flooding of forests, agricultural land, and bush is rarely cited as a reason for preventing the building of a dam. Indeed, at times, the indifference shown by officials to the fate of those natural species that will be drowned by a dam's reservoir is astounding. We quote again from the report cited above on India's Narmada Valley Project:

> Characteristically, there is no plan to relocate the wildlife [in the threatened area]. When we asked officials about this, they stated that there would be "natural relocation"—that is to say, the animals would move out of the area to be flooded by themselves. Such an assumption, however, seems to us to be more of a sick joke and a convenient excuse than a serious proposition. Other than birds, and possibly a few alert mammals, how many animals really stand a chance of "relocating" themselves when the waters come their way? How much adjoining forest is there, anyway, for them to move into? Will not such a movement increase competition between animals (especially the strongly territorial ones) in the new habitat? And, if one includes wild flora in the category "wildlife," how on earth are all the plants going to "naturally relocate" themselves? Or, for that matter, the microorganisms?
>
> Incredibly enough, for some government departments "wildlife" seems to mean only tigers and deer and other big mammals. In answer to a query from the Department of the Environment, the Government of Gujarat says, "at present, there is no wildlife in the reservoir area of the proposed Sardar Sarovar Dam and its vicinity." The sick joke continues. To the very next question, the reply is: "After construction of the dam and the creation of the reservoir, it will be possible to develop a wildlife sanctuary or Safari Park in the vicinity." Where, pray, is all the wildlife suddenly going

to come from? When it comes to costs, there seems to be none; when it comes to benefits, there are suddenly a lot. And, when asked to specify rare and endangered species, as well as fish and crocodile breeding grounds, in the submergence zone, the Gujarat Government has kept silent. Why?

At a time when experts warn that 20 percent of the world's animals and plants could be extinct by the end of the century as a result of poaching and illegal trading *alone*, the indifference of Third World and industrialized governments alike to the fate of their wildlife is alarming. Underlying that indifference is the widely held view that "conservation" is somehow the concern only of the rich and the indulgent.

To those committed to the idea that industrial development offers the panacea for such ills as poverty and malnutrition, the very thought that the interests of wildlife should take precedence over the requirements of development is inconceivable. Small wonder, then, that proponents of India's controversial Silent Valley Dam (which, if it goes ahead, would flood one of the few remaining tracts of tropical rainforest in India and condemn the last surviving colony of liontailed macaques to extinction) chose to denigrate their opponents as "monkey lovers" who would deny their fellow men the "fruits of progress" for the sake of "a few wild animals."[2]

At best, it is assumed that the interests of wildlife can be protected by striking some sort of balance between conservation and development. Under pressure from environmentalists—and, perhaps more to the point, the tourist industry—many Third World governments have set up national parks and wildlife sanctuaries in order to safeguard the future of their wildlife. Such parks, however, have failed miserably to stem the loss of wildlife to development. Slowly but surely, the enclaves have been whittled down in size as their lands have been encroached upon for "projects in the national interest." Eventually, the parks exist in name only.

The dam-building industry and its government sponsors have shown few qualms about siting projects in "protected" areas. For example, the Thai government insists on its right to build the

Nam Choan Dam on the Kwae Yai River even though the dam will flood approximately 4 percent of the Thung Yai Wildlife Sanctuary. That sanctuary, together with the adjacent Huai Kha Khaeng Sanctuary, makes up a forested area of some 4,800 square kilometers. Today it is the most valuable remaining wildlife park in Thailand, a country which, in recent years, has been subject to devastating deforestation and habitat destruction.

If the dam is built, the whole area will be divided in two. Moreover, warns Philip Round, the staff ornithologist of the Association for the Conservation of Wildlife in Thailand, the resulting "development" will almost certainly bring "a flood of illegal settlers along the access road into the heart of the sanctuary area, which will bring attendant problems of large-scale deforestation and poaching."[3] Such illegal setttlers have already wrought havoc in the Salak Phra Wildlife Sanctuary (downstream from the proposed Nam Choan scheme), where the Srinakarin Dam already stands as a stark reminder of the Thai government's "commitment" to preserving the integrity of its national parks.

If the Nam Choan Dam goes ahead, then the largest population of Asian elephant in Thailand, as well as other threatened species, such as the gaur and the tapir, could face destruction. Flooding the area could also lead to the destruction of the riverine habitat of the rare green pea fowl, a species that has already been eliminated from 95 percent of the country.

In Sri Lanka, the project area for the Mahaweli scheme contains parts of the Pollunnaruwa, Seruwila, and Allai wildlife sanctuaries. Already, the building of the Mahaweli dams has led to the logging of the Somawathie Wildlife Sanctuary (which covers an area of 22,275 hectares) by the State Timber Corporation. A further 30,000 hectares of forest elsewhere have also been earmarked for logging.[4]

The scheme will seriously disturb valuable wetland habitats along the banks of the Mahaweli. More than 50 *villus* (the Sinhalese term for the pools that accumulate in the flood plains of rivers) will be flooded, the affected areas ranging from 10 to 900 hectares in size.[5] Those *villus* are extremely productive biologically and their vegetation provides an important source of grazing for wildlife. During the wet season, wildlife moves from the inundated flood plains to higher ground but returns to the *villus* with the beginning of the dry season.

Not surprisingly, the Mahaweli scheme will seriously affect the habitat of many animals, including the Indian elephant, the leopard, the red-faced malkoha (which is endemic to Sri Lanka), the swan crocodile, the estuarine crocodile, the Bengal monitor, and the python. The project will also seriously reduce the habitat of a number of threatened species, such as the purple-faced langur and the toque macaque, both endemic to Sri Lanka. In particular, the project is likely to prove disastrous for Sri Lanka's dwindling elephant population. Eight hundred elephants are said to inhabit the project area, and an important migratory route will disappear when the dams are closed. In addition, some eight species of fish, four species of amphibians, nineteen species of reptiles, eight species of birds, three species of mammals, and fifty-three species of plant—all endemic to the island—will be threatened by the scheme.[6]

In North Perak, northern Malaysia, the Temenggor Dam has drowned valuable forests, threatening the survival of 100 species of mammals and 300 species of birds. Most of these species are already near extinction. Most severely affected have been the Sumatran rhinoceros, the Malayan tapir, the Malayan elephant, and the flying lemur.

Had it not been for the efforts of local conservationists, the Malaysian government would almost certainly have gone ahead with plans to dam the Tembeling River in the Taman Nagara National Park, the only national park in northern Malaysia. The dam would have created a 130-square-kilometer lake and would have destroyed the habitat of a number of species, including the highly threatened Sumatran rhinoceros, the Malayan tiger, and the Malayan tapir. All this to add a mere 2.9 percent to the country's total energy capacity.[7]

Not only in the Third World have governments been less than receptive to conservation. The Tasmanian government, for instance, was utterly determined to go ahead with its plans to dam the Gordon and Franklin rivers although the area had been declared a heritage site. The proposed dam was halted only after the Australian federal government took the State of Tasmania to court. Peter Thompson, of the Australian Conservation Foundation, describes what would have been lost if the dam had been built:

> The vegetation of the Gordon and Franklin Rivers is a mosaic of rainforest, wet schlerophyll, scrub heathland, sedgeland and bog communities. The rainforests are composed of species such as myrtle (*nothofagus cunninghamii*), sassafras (*Atherosperma moschatum*), leatherwood (*Eucryphia lucida*) and the now rare Huon pine (*Dacrydium franklinii*). Many of these species are loosely related to temperate rainforest species in New Zealand and Chile and it is supposed that they have common origins on the supercontinent of Gondawanaland.

As originally proposed, the dam would have destroyed more than one-third of the Huon pine habitat.

Discussing the general effects of dams on wildlife, Bardach and Dussart note that "most species of large and small game have territories, home ranges and feeding circuits associated with the main stream of a river or its tributaries." It is this habitat, of course, that a dam floods. Since most animals "cling tenaciously to their home grounds, the arrival of [the flood waters] spells death for most territorial creatures."[8]

Unfortunately, where efforts have been made to rescue wildlife before a river is flooded—as was attempted in "Operation Noah," before the closing of the Kariba Dam—they have proved of limited success. Even if individual animals in the area to be flooded are rescued, few will be able to breed since they can do so only in a river valley like the one from which they have been driven. The same is true of those bird species that manage to escape drowning: a few will fly away, but once their natural habitat has been destroyed, their future breeding prospects are slim.

We must also remember that as "development" proceeds, the number of suitable habitats to which wild animals can be transferred is sharply reduced. Eventually, the wildlife has nowhere to go, and game wardens have little option but to slaughter displaced animals in vast numbers. For example, the present plan to build another huge dam on the Zambezi River (this time at Mutapa Gorge) in order to produce 500 megawatts of electricity will drown 130,000 hectares of giant mahoganies, acacia woods, and lush savannah. That land is dotted with perennial watering holes that are vital to local wildlife. Because of the lack of suitable habitats elsewhere, inundation will force game wardens to slaughter at least half of the area's present population of elephant, buffalo, lion, leopard, eland, sable, and other animals.[9]

At present, the argument in favor of conservation that is most likely to make any impression on government planners is an economic one—the claim that wildlife must be preserved for the sake of the tourist industry. That argument is being used by the well-known environmentalist Dick Pitman in his efforts to prevent the flooding of the Mutapa Gorge.[10] Others—notably Bardach, Dussart, and Balon—point out that a large population of herbivores inhabits the savannahs and grasslands that are so often flooded by dams. If ranched, these animals could provide as much food as the fisheries developed in the artificial lakes that will drown them.[11]

Such arguments have so far failed to impress the politicians. Indeed, the idea that the future of man is linked with that of such species as the lion or the elephant—let alone the termite or the snail—is still alien to the most influential of today's development planners. Yet, as Paul and Anne Ehrlich point out in the book *Extinction*, the very subtlety of the relationships among the species in a natural ecosystem makes it impossible to predict whether or not any one species can be lost with impunity.[12] To be sure, throughout history, animals have become extinct, but who knows which new extinction will prove fatal to the survival of life on this planet? To make the point, the Ehrlichs use the analogy of an airline passenger who boards his airplane only to find that engineers are busily removing the rivets from the wings. "Don't worry," they tell him cheerfully, "we've lost numerous rivets in the past— and nothing disastrous has happened." Who, ask the Ehrlichs, would consider traveling on such an airline? Yet, they point out, our indifference to the fate of wildlife suffers from the same

flawed thinking as that of the rivet-poppers. How many more animal "rivets" can be popped without causing the destruction of
"spaceship earth"?

THE REDUCTION OF FERTILITY DOWNSTREAM
DUE TO IMPOUNDMENT

Quite apart from the ecological devastation it causes in the area
drowned by a dam's reservoir, impoundment prevents a river's
silt from being carried to the sea. That silt—which generally contains large quantities of feldspar, clay and organic matter—often
has a high nutrient value.

Before the damming of the Amu Daria River in the Soviet
Union, for instance, an estimated 40 tons of silt were deposited
by the river each year on every hectare of the delta. According to
Victor Kovda, of the University of Moscow, the land thus received 250 kilograms of humus, 200 kilograms of nitrogen, 50
kilograms of available potassium oxide, and 50 kilograms of total
phosphoric oxide.[13]

Before the building of the Aswan Dam, the River Nile deposited 100 million tons of sediment a year on nearly one million
hectares of land in the Nile Valley—that is, about 100 tons of silt
per hectare.[14] Although that silt had a low nitrogen content, it was
rich in silica, aluminum, iron, and other valuable trace elements
whose loss is, according to Waterbury, being increasingly felt (see
Table 4).

Today, the Nile deposits only a few tons of sediment per year
on the delta, and much of that comes as a result of riverbed
scouring. Such scouring occurs in all rivers; as their waters flow
downstream, so the riverbed is eroded. In normal circumstances,
the eroded soils are compensated for by the silt deposited by the
river, but the almost silt-free waters of a river that has been
dammed leave little or no sediment on the riverbed. The result is
a gradual loss of riverbed soils.

With its silt trapped behind the High Dam, the once muddy-
brown waters of the Nile are now green. To compensate—and
very partially at that—for the nutrients previously provided free

TABLE 4

Estimated Amounts of Nile Sediment
and Total Nutrients Deposited Annually by the Nile Flood (in 1,000 tons)

Region	Sediment	Potassium Oxide	Phospheric Oxide	Nitrogen	Organic matter
UPPER EGYPT					
Basin	8,800	94	20	11	218
Perennial	2,900	31	7	4	72
LOWER EGYPT					
Perennial	1,500	16	4	2	37
Total	13,200	141	31	17	327

SOURCE: H. A. El-Tobgy, *Contemporary Egyptian Agriculture*, 2d ed. (Cairo: Ford Foundation, 1976), p. 34; in J. Waterbury, *Hydropolitics of the Nile Valley*, Syracuse University Press, 1979, p. 130.

by the river's annual flood, which are now prevented from flowing down the river, Egypt must apply artificial fertilizers on an ever increasing scale. In terms of its nitrogen content alone, the "fertilizer value" of the Nile's silt has been estimated to be equivalent to 13,000 tons of calcium nitrate fertilizer.[15] The annual cost of the fertilizers now required by Egypt is about $100 million a year—a sum the country can ill afford. Small wonder, perhaps, that one Egyptian agronomist has said he would give his soul to see the waters of the Nile turn muddy-brown again.[16]

LOSS OF SILT AND COASTAL EROSION

When the waters downstream of a dam are deprived of their silt content, this causes the erosion of land in the delta. Again, the Aswan experience provides a case in point. Before the High Dam was built, the Nile deposited vast quantities of alluvia in the Delta at a rate greater than that of coastal erosion by the normal action of the sea. Today, according to Mohammad Kassas, "the Delta shoreline that had obviously been advancing throughout the history of the Delta is now retreating."[17]

Not all of the coastal erosion now being experienced in the Nile Delta can be blamed on the Aswan Dam, but the dam's impact should not be underestimated. As Waterbury observes:

With or without the High Dam, the northern Delta would be under attack. Since Roman times, the level of the Mediterranean has risen some two meters, accompanied by some indication of a tilting of the eastern end of the basin from north to south. Second, under the sheer weight of its sediment, the Delta may be settling or sinking. During the nineteenth century, the Delta held its own against the sea but, probably with the heightening of the Old Aswan Dam, in 1934, the diminution in silt discharge began to shift the balance. Over the past decade, something like 600 million tons of sediment have never reached the sea. The Delta is clearly no longer holding its own.[18]

As a result, "the ecology of the northern lakes may be transformed by sea water invasion. This would jeopardize existing and planned reclamation projects and would also lead to increased sea-water seepage into the northern Delta aquifer." The consequences for Egyptian agriculture could be severe.

Thus we can conclude that right from the outset, the building of a large-scale dam causes irrevocable environmental destruction in several ways. That tragic destruction does not end with the filling of the reservoir and the inevitable loss of land, forests, and wildlife. As we shall see, there is scarcely an aspect of the dam's future operations that will not carry a heavy environmental cost.

5. Water Losses:
Do They Exceed Gains?

IN HOT DRY AREAS, the loss of water from a dam's reservoir and its accompanying channels can be staggering. In many regions—the Colorado River Basin, for example—evaporation alone can result in such high losses that, according to Professor William Ackermann, "increased storage reservoir development may reach a point beyond which the reduction of water yield . . . surpasses the possibility of increasing low-flow discharges from reservoir storage."[1] If that is so, then, in many cases, one of the major benefits claimed for dams—namely, the storage of water against times of low rainfall—is not as clear-cut as it might appear. The more so when one adds to evaporation losses the loss of water through seepage and evapotranspiration. Let us look at those three causes of water loss in more detail. How far do they undermine the benefits of having a permanent store of water available? And how, if at all, can they be avoided?

LOSSES TO EVAPORATION

In arid and semiarid countries, the loss of water to evaporation is—as Mohammed Kassas is quick to tell us—inevitable.[2] That loss can be considerable. In Guyana, for example, evaporation losses from open surfaces reach 139.7 cm a year, and in Burma, 114 to 152 cm; in some regions of India, it is common for up to 300 cm of water to be lost.[3] Indeed, in certain areas of the world, evaporation rates can exceed local rainfall. Such areas are said to suffer from a water deficiency; such a deficiency can be temporary, lasting only a month or two a year, or permanent. More than one-third of India's 160 million hectares of cultivated land, for example, receive less than 750 mm of rainfall annually, and are thus classified by the Ministry of Agriculture as "drought affected."[4]

Building vast reservoirs in areas where evaporation rates are high is thus to invite trouble. In Egypt, Lake Nasser loses a minimum of 15 billion cubic meters a year to evaporation—enough water, as Kassas points out, to irrigate two million acres of farmland.[5] Although, in theory, such evaporation losses can be reduced by spreading a thin film of chemicals over the reservoir's surface, that solution presents insuperable environmental risks. Its cost is also exorbitant. It would seem, therefore, that the loss of water by evaporation from reservoirs is inevitable.

LOSSES TO TRANSPIRATION:
THE PROBLEM OF AQUATIC WEEDS

Creating a vast artificial reservoir inevitably transforms a terrestrial ecosystem into an aquatic one. Inevitably, too, that new aquatic environment will favor the growth of types of vegetation very different from those that existed before the reservoir was filled. Various phytoplankton and aquatic weeds will turn up sooner or later. Those aquatic weeds pose a particular problem where water losses are concerned for they increase dramatically the rate of transpiration. Indeed, several recent studies have shown that such water losses are two, three, or even six times higher in reservoirs covered in weeds than they are in open waters.[6]

Of these aquatic weeds, the most infamous is undoubtedly the water hyacinth (*Eichhornia crasspipes*). Not only does it establish itself very quickly, but it thrives in almost every area into which it has been introduced. Moreover, it spreads at a phenomenal rate: a pond infested with one hectare of water hyacinth will produce up to an estimated 1.8 tons of dry mass a day. That rate of reproduction alone makes the weed almost impossible to control.

Despite the known effects of water weeds on the rate of evapotranspiration, the planners of large dams rarely consider such contributors to water losses. Yet it is now accepted that the invasion of reservoirs and their accompanying water channels is almost inevitable. Indeed, a recent study undertaken as part of UNESCO's Man and the Biosphere (MAB) project noted that canals and distribution systems that "are rich in organic matter and nutrients, but unsatisfactorily maintained, invariably are invaded and sometimes choked by dense growth of algae and aquatic weeds."[7] Since just about all canals and irrigation channels in hot dry areas are rich in organic matter and nutrients (such as soil and vegetation from eroding banks, raw sewage from nearby settlements, and the runoff of artificial fertilizers) the problem of weeds would seem thoroughly foreseeable, especially—as we shall see in chapter 12—given the low standards of maintenance that prevail throughout irrigation schemes in the Third World.

Few reservoirs have escaped the menace of water weeds. In Suriname, for example, in 1964, aquatic weeds invaded the Brokopondo reservoir almost as soon as it was filled. Within two years, more than 50 percent of the surface of the reservoir was infested, an area of some 410 square kilometers.[8] So, too, within three years of the damming of the Congo River, aquatic weeds had spread throughout 1,600 kilometers of the 4,640-kilometer river. Egypt has also suffered from a plague of water weeds; by 1974, a variety of aquatic weeds had infested more than 80 percent of the water courses fed by Lake Nasser, and much of the Nile itself was affected. Meanwhile, in the Sudan, an estimated 3,000 square kilometers are infested with water weeds.

Once established, water weeds are difficult, if not impossible, to eradicate. The Egyptian government has dosed its canals and irrigation drains with massive quantities of herbicides—at unknown ecological cost—in its battle to destroy water weeds. Yet such spraying is admittedly little more than a holding operation: "Because of the viability of the [water hyacinth] and its ability to reproduce sexually and asexually, it is believed that the best that can be hoped for is to strike a balance of control and utilisation methods that will contain the plant and reduce its effects to manageable proportions."[9]

LOSSES DUE TO SEEPAGE AND OVERUSE OF WATER

Water losses do not occur only through evaporation and transpiration; seepage from irrigation canals is also a major contributor to the problem. The extent of seepage varies considerably according to climate, soil, and the length and type of distribution system. Almost always, however, the extent of seepage is underestimated by the planners of large-scale irrigation schemes. Indeed, in some cases, seepage rates have been underestimated by 100 percent.[10] The following examples are indicative of the extent of seepage and its contribution to overall water losses.

—A 1967 study undertaken by the Internation Commission on Irrigation and Drainage (ICID) reported that between 13.1 and 19.15 percent of the water transported along India's Upper Bari Doab Canal was lost to seepage. In the plains of Uttar Pradesh and the Punjab, such losses were as high as 36 percent.[11]

—In Egypt, during the summer, the main irrigation canals lose an estimated 1,500 million cubic meters of water through seepage every year—approximately 10 percent of the water available for irrigation.[12] Over the entire irrigation system, losses due to conveyance, seepage, and extravagance in water utilization equal 17 percent of the water delivered.

—In many areas of the Middle East, between 10 and 70 percent of the total volume of water conveyed through irrigation canals is lost to seepage.[13]

—In Pakistan, conveyance losses in the waterways fed by the massive Tarbala Dam are estimated to be "of a size corresponding to the content of the dam's reservoir"—some 4 to 7 million acre-feet per year.[14]

Other losses are caused by damaged dams and inefficient operation. Water is wasted when too much is applied to the land; the plants cannot use it up and consequently a considerable proportion simply seeps into the subsoil. According to one U.S. General Accounting Office study, for example, half the water used in American agriculture is lost to overwatering and seepage.[15] In Taiwan, the loss is 30 percent; in other countries of South and Southeast Asia, it is said to range from 50 to 80 percent.

Indeed, the overall water use efficiency of modern irrigation schemes is notoriously low. In the United States, for example, it ranges from below 25 percent to 70 percent.[16] In Third World countries, the figures are even worse. For example, the Indus River has a total of 142 million acre-feet of water available for use, of which 86 million acre-feet are diverted into irrigation canals by way of dams and headworks. Of that figure, "some 64 million acre-feet reach the farming areas via some 80,000 separate water courses, serving 3.2 million farms on 32 million acres. At the farm level, an estimated 26 million acre-feet are added by 125,000 private and public tube-wells. Of these 90 million acre-feet, however, 35 million are lost in the poorly maintained earth channels en route from the public distributary to the farmers' fields. 55 million acre-feet, or 1.7 acre-feet per household, are thus left for the farmers. Of these, some 24 million acre-feet are lost due to field application losses."[17] Effectively, therefore, only 31 million acre-feet out of a total supply of 168 million acre-feet are ever really utilized.

Can the losses due to seepage and overwatering be avoided? In theory, the answer is yes. The problem, however, lies in the vast expense involved. Ideally, closed tube conduits should be introduced, thus preventing both seepage and evaporation. Unfortunately, the cost is astronomical—particularly where large amounts of water are being discharged, which, according to Professor Holy, is the main reason why closed conduits have not been used on any appreciable scale in the world's large irrigation systems.[18]

The second best method for avoiding losses from seepage is to line irrigation canals. The most efficient—and expensive—technique is to install a concrete lining. Cheaper methods include the use of plastics, oil films, and even mirrors; and cheapest of all is a process known as "colmation," which involves sealing porous soils with small soil grains that enter the pores during watering.[19] It is by no means clear how effectively those cheaper methods work. What is certain, however, is that few irrigation canals are ever lined. Aside from the expense involved, lined canals frequently suffer from poor management and technical foul-ups that drastically reduce their efficiency.

Overwatering can certainly be reduced by the introduction of sprinkler irrigation, which makes possible very accurate water distribution. Once again, however, the cost of sprinkler irrigation is extremely high and, like lined canals, the sprinklers require frequent maintenance and a high level of skill on the part of their operators. As we shall see in the next chapter, they also introduce other problems of their own making—notably the creation of a permanent, moist ecosystem that favors pest infestations.

6. The Effects of Perennial Irrigation on Pest Populations

To INTRODUCE PERENNIAL IRRIGATION into an arid area is to change the microclimate. Among other things, the moisture level of the atmosphere increases as a result of evaporation from the

newly constructed reservoir, the irrigation canals, and the flooded fields. The moisture level of the soil, too, increases drastically:
in the sandy soils of Egypt, for instance, by something approaching twenty-five times—from 0.7 percent to between 15 and 22
percent.[1] As Professor Uvarov points out, introducing perennial
irrigation into an arid area is like creating an oasis in the desert.[2]
What was previously a hot dry ecosystem, in which moisture was
introduced only temporarily, with the flooding of the river or with
the seasonal rains, is transformed into one that is permanently
moist.

The new moist ecosystem will attract all sorts of microorganisms, insects, and other forms of animal life that are particularly
adapted to the new conditions. Inevitably, their populations build
up at the expense of the species that previously lived there and
cannot adapt to the new moisture levels.

Some of the new species may, of course, be beneficial to agriculture. Earthworms attracted to a moist environment are useful,
among other things, because their excrement contains a great
deal of nitrogen. In experimental conditions, according to Professor S. T. Ghabbour of the University of Cairo, the common
earthworm (*Allolobophora caliginosa*) produces 6.5 percent of its
fresh weight in the form of urine every day.[3]

But many of the forms of life encouraged by the new moist
conditions are highly undesirable. Moreover, where land is irrigated by overhead sprinklers, those undesirable species are provided with a uniformly moist ecosystem in which they may
become permanently established. Indeed, to make that point,
Professor Ezekiel Rivnay, former head of the Plant Protection
Department of Israel's Volcani Institute of Agriculture Research,
actually entitled an article on the problem, "How to provide a
nice wet place where insects you don't want thrive."[4]

It is not, of course, just the undesirability of the newcomers,
but their sheer numbers, that poses the problem. We all know just
how much more attractive an oasis is to living things than a desert. Moreover, many of those living things are likely to be adapted
to living off the very crops that are cultivated in the irrigated
fields of the new oasis.

Thus it is not surprising that the building of the Aswan Dam should have led to an increase in the number of agriculturally harmful insect pests—such as the great moth (*Polychrosis botrana*) and the cotton-leaf worm (*Spodoptera littoralis*), neither one previously known in Upper Egypt and both now common—and also the cornstalk borer (*Chilo agamemnon*).[5]

Nor is it surprising that the introduction of perennial—and, in particular, sprinkler—irrigation in Israel caused, as Rivnay points out, "invasions and an increase in many pests of agricultural importance" that has led to "the destruction of entire fields of crops."[6] For example, until three decades ago, the onion fly (*Hylemyia antiqua* Meigen) was considered by Israelis to be a pest of little importance: no insecticides were used against it "as its damage was hardly felt."[7] Under modern irrigated conditions, however, it has become "conspicuous, thereby necessitating measures of control."

Nor was the seed corn maggot (*Hylemyia cilicrura* Rondani) any problem in Israel until the early 1950s. Under irrigated conditions, it now thrives. Likewise, the red pumpkin beetle (*Rhaphidopalpa foreicollis* Lucchese), which eats the leaves of cucurbit seedlings, now causes so much damage that entire fields must often be reseeded. The reason is clear enough: under dry irrigation, there was not always enough moisture for the beetles' eggs to hatch out but, as Rivnay points out, "with overhead irrigation, the entire area is uniformly watered, offering ideal conditions for the eggs to hatch."[8]

The cultivation of vast stretches of the same crop (monoculture) under perennially irrigated conditions must of course attract pests that are specific to single crops (monophagous). Thus the weevil (*Hypera variabilis*), a pest of alfalfa, "was hardly noticeable in Israel in the early thirties." Today it has become very common and has to be controlled by spraying.[9] The same is true of another weevil that is specific to beet (*Lixus yunci*). Its population expanded considerably once sugar and fodder beets came to be grown under perennial irrigation over large areas.[10]

Unfortunately, insects also seem quick to modify their feeding habits in order to take advantage of the vast new niches created when new crops are introduced as a result of perennial irrigation. Thus the cotton-leaf worm (*Spodoptera littoralis*), which appears to have been present in the region since the 1870s, did not become a serious pest in Egypt until the building of the Aswan Dam. With the extension of irrigation and the introduction of new crops such as peanuts, cotton and sugar beet, which do particularly well under perennial irrigation, its population has radically increased, as has the period during which it does damage and also the number of crops it infests. These now include grape vines and apples, for instance, which it apparently never attacked before.[11]

Because insects can travel great distances, newly irrigated areas are often infested by pests not previously known in the area, as in Egypt since the building of the Aswan Dam, as well as in parts of Israel. An attempt to grow rice under perennial irrigation in the Hula area, for example, proved disastrous because the rice was quickly infested with corn borers, which had never been seen in the area before. The loss of yields in the first year was 10 to 15 percent; by the second year, that figure had risen to 33 percent. Eventually, losses were so high that rice cultivation had to be abandoned.[12]

At Nitzana, an isolated desert area 40 kilometers from the nearest agricultural land, a tract of land was converted to a truck crop farm. This led to an invasion of aphids that frequently reduced the yield of such crops as vetch and beans by as much as 40 percent.[13] Aphids have wings and can be transported by air currents at high altitudes and dropped long distances away. They have been known to infect an area as much as 130 kilometers away from where they previously thrived.

At Avdat, in the middle of the Negev Desert, a small tract of land was irrigated and put under cotton. It was 50 kilometers from the nearest cotton field. This did not prevent it from being attacked by the spiny boll-worm (*Earias insulana* Boisduval), which has been known to reduce yields by as much as 80 percent.

The problem is further compounded by the need to take full advantage of perennial irrigation facilities by growing several annual crops where, under conditions of basin-irrigated or rain-fed agriculture, only one would have been grown. As Rivnay points out, this greatly prolongs the vegetative period of a crop, provides a permanent rather than a temporary niche for pests, and may even increase the number of pests that can live off the crop.

Thus, the oriental cornstalk borer (*Chilo agamemnon*) has become a major pest in Israel and, as we have seen, in Egypt too. Under conditions of dry farming, it could raise only two to three generations because by August the crop had become dry and provided an unsuitable habitat for the development of its larvae. Once perennial irrigation and multicropping were introduced, however, food was provided for the borer all summer. This enabled it to raise six generations between May and early September—with predictably disastrous consequences.

The same thing occurred in Israel with the Spodoptera moth (*Spodoptera littoralis*). Under dry farming conditions it tended not to become active until June, by which time crops such as wheat, chick peas, and lentils, on which it might have lived, had already matured and dried, and those that were still growing, like sesame, had already been watered and did not attract moths. Once perennial irrigation was introduced, new crops were cultivated, in particular peanuts, cotton and sugar beet. This meant "offering food to the polyphagous *Spodoptera* continuously from May until late in November; when one kind of crop dried out, another was still fresh a short distance away."[14] As a result, the cotton-leaf worm became a serious pest.

Rivnay also notes that the tendency of perennial irrigation—and in particular, overhead sprinkler irrigation—to increase pest infestations seems to have attracted very little attention on the part of those concerned with the building of dams and large-scale irrigation works.[15] If the paucity of material on the subject in the currently available literature is anything to go by, then he is clearly right.

7. Dams and Disease

WHEN A RIVER IS DAMMED and a large artificial lake is created, those forms of life adapted to the previous riverine ecosystem are likely to disappear. In their place, other species will emerge that are better adapted to the new environment. Some will thrive in the lake, others in the irrigation channels that it feeds, and still others in the new towns and cities spawned by the "development" the dam brings. Not only will animal and bird life be affected, but also plants, fungi, protozoa, bacteria, and other microorganisms. Many of those species play an integral part in the transmission of infectious diseases. It follows that as the composition of species in the new environment changes, so the pattern of disease will change also. Unfortunately, such change is generally for the worse. Indeed, in most cases, it has led to an upsurge in waterborne and other diseases.

MALARIA

In spite of the efforts of the World Health Organization (WHO), malaria remains one of the most widespread and lethal diseases in the world. At one time, WHO experts were confident that new pesticides would put an end to malaria once and for all by eradicating the mosquitoes that act as its vector. Today that much vaunted malaria eradication program is in tatters. Thousands of tons of pesticides have been sprayed, with disastrous ecological consequences but to little avail: every year, malaria still kills one million people. At any given moment, 160 million people—the equivalent of the entire population of Japan, Malaysia, and the Philippines—suffer from the disease.[1]

In man, malaria is caused by four species of parasite: *Plasmodium malariae, P. vivax, P. ovale* and *P. falciparum*, of which *P. vivax* and *P. falciparum* are the most common. The parasite has a complicated life-cycle. Reproducing only within mosquitoes of the genus *Anopheles*, the parasite must pass an "asexual" phase within humans. When an infected mosquito bites a human, thousands of *Plasmodium* parasites are released into the blood and eventually establish themselves in the human liver. There they incubate and eventually release their offspring into the bloodstream to invade the red corpuscles.

A mosquito that bites a human after the parasite has incubated will inevitably eat a meal of infected blood. The parasites reproduce within the mosquito's gut, where they form a cyst that finally bursts, releasing new parasites into the mosquito's blood-stream. Inevitably some of those parasites make their way to the mosquito's salivary glands, and the cycle repeats itself when the mosquito bites another human.

The role played by the *Plasmodium* parasite and its mosquito vector was not discovered until early in the twentieth century. Previously, the most common theory was that malaria was caused by the stench and fumes from stagnant water. Indeed, the word *malaria* is derived from the Latin *mal aria* ("bad air"), and there is little question that the Romans associated the disease with swamps and marshlands. That association is entirely accurate: swamps, marshes, and stagnant pools are indeed ideal breeding grounds for malaria's mosquito vectors.[2]

Not surprisingly, such areas were generally avoided—and not just by the Romans. Writing of Ceylon in the early nineteenth century, the historian Sir James Emmerson Tennent, for example, tells us:

> Compared with Bengal and the Deccan Plains, the climate of Ceylon presents a striking superiority in mildness and exception from all the extremes of atmospheric disturbance: and except in particular localities all of which are well known and avoided from being liable after the rains from malaria, or infected at particular seasons with agues and fever, a lengthened residence in the island may be completed without the slightest apprehension of prejudicial results.[3]

In those parts of the world where malarial areas have been inhabited, a whole range of cultural strategies has been developed to keep the disease to a minimum. The Montagnards of Vietnam, for example, build their houses on stilts, do not equip them with chimneys, and keep their cows underneath. Since mosquitoes prefer to sting cows rather than people, have an aversion to smoke, and do not fly high off the ground, few Montagnards suffer from the disease. By contrast, the incidence of malaria is high among those immigrants who have come into the area from the coast and who have been housed by the government in modern concrete buildings.[4]

Where people have lived for long periods in malarial areas, genetic adaptations to the disease have occurred. Many Africans, for example, have developed a particular hemoglobin molecule, Hemoglobin S. Those who are homozygous for this molecule suffer from sickle-cell anemia, which is often fatal, but those who are heterozygous for Hemoglobin S have considerable resistance to malaria.

Of some 300 species of *Anopheles* mosquito, an estimated 40 are thought to be important transmitters of malaria.[5] Each has its own breeding, feeding, and daytime resting habits; its own range of flight and dispersal patterns; and its own human biting-rate. There are also many different species of the *Plasmodium* parasite. Like their mosquito vectors, the various *Plasmodium* protozoa have different lifestyles and thrive on different environmental factors, primarily climate and temperature. *P. falciparum*, the parasite responsible for the most lethal form of malaria, requires a summer temperature above 19 degrees centigrade in order to survive. Humidity is also important. If the mosquitoes are to live long enough for the *Plasmodium* parasite to develop within their bodies—that is, until they reach the infective stage—then the relative humidity during the summer months must be maintained at an average of 52 percent.

Because these conditions are rarely satisfied in temperate areas—where *P. vivax* is the parasite—malaria never had more than a tenuous hold in such regions and was easily controlled by such measures as marsh drainage. Even in subtropical climates, the conditions conducive to the disease prevail only during the humid summer months. It is then that transmission occurs. Where "dry farming" is practiced—or where crops are irrigated during the winter, and thus outside the transmission period—the mosquito vectors can find few niches in which to breed. Malaria is thus likely to be absent or, at worst, its incidence will be minimal.[6]

The introduction of modern, perennial irrigation schemes has, however, heightened both the incidence and the lethality of malaria. Not only have such projects created permanent and vastly extended habitats for the mosquito vectors of the disease, they have also created precisely those habitats favored by the most efficient of the vectors. In Africa, water development projects have led to a proliferation of *Anopheles gambiae* and *Anopheles funestas*, the former breeding in flooded rice fields, the latter in drainage and irrigation canals.[7] *A. gambiae* has the reputation of being the most efficient of all the malarial vectors. Not only does it bite man in preference to other animals but it also has a high infectivity rate and is capable of transmitting malaria even when its population density is extremely low (about one mosquito per thirty persons).[8] In South Asia, irrigation schemes have favored the mosquito that acts as the vector for both *P. vivax* and *P. falciparum*.

Because perennial irrigation makes possible two crops a year, it correspondingly increases the period during which mosquitoes have habitats in which to breed. Inevitably, too, by increasing the land area under water, irrigation schemes also increase the total mosquito population, hence too the likelihood of infection. Moreover, the introduction of irrigated agriculture appears to bring changes in the biting habits of mosquitoes. As the human population increases and land use shifts to crops from livestock, so the mosquitoes switch from biting animals to biting humans. In those areas of the Kano plains where herding was still the principal means of livelihood, 70 percent of *A. gambiae* fed on cattle and only 30 percent on man. The reverse is true in the modern irrigated rice-growing areas.

Nor is the risk of infection reduced by the design of irrigation schemes. It is known, for instance, that mosquitoes rarely fly more than one kilometer or so beyond the canals and ricefields in which they live and breed. People living at least one kilometer from the canals will thus be beyond the mosquitoes' reach. In the majority of large-scale irrigation schemes, however, the tendency has been to build the houses much closer to the irrigated fields. Where irrigation schemes have been built in settled areas, or where land has been flooded in order to build a dam, it has often proved difficult to persuade those whose existing houses are now next to the new irrigation schemes to move.[9]

The problem of malaria has been made still worse by the increased mobility that inevitably accompanies development. For malaria to be transmitted, both the vector and the parasite must be present in the same area at the same time. But although the parasite cannot exist without the vector, the opposite is not the case. Thus, many malaria-free areas have populations of the vector but not of the parasite (ironically, the vector may only have become established as a result of an irrigation scheme). Small wonder, then, that the movement of people from infested areas, where the parasite is present, to noninfested areas, where the vector is present but not the parasite, has frequently led to the establishment of disease in areas where it was previously unknown, with the parasite brought to the vector in the blood of the migrants.

It has long been recognized that malaria is particularly lethal among people weakened by malnutrition. Indeed, the French have an old saying, Le traitement du paludisme est dans la marmite ("the cure for malaria lies in the cooking pot"),[10] which is particularly relevant where large-scale water projects are concerned. Inevitably, immigrants are attracted to the area by the prospect of jobs. Those immigrants are often impoverished and undernourished. This point is emphasized by Dr. Robert Goodland, a senior ecologist at the World Bank. Describing the extent of malnutrition in the area around Brazil's Tucuruí Dam, for instance, he writes:

> In general, self-sufficient peasants or tribesmen whose varied diets of fresh foods and whose lifestyle as a whole was perfectly adapted to the conditions in which they lived, are replaced with the water-development scheme by an impoverished proletariat whose members are often employed as casual labor, who suffer from seasonal or permanent unemployment, and whose diet and lifestyle are usually unadapted to local conditions. Not surprisingly, the nutritional status of these people is particularly poor and this makes them particularly vulnerable to infectious diseases.[11]

Sadly, the conditions at Tucuruí are by no means exceptional. Perhaps it is not surprising, then, that wherever large-scale irrigation works have brought a rise in the incidence of malaria, the disease has become a more potent killer.

Unfortunately, once the conditions for malaria have been established, the disease is virtually impossible to control. In the Middle East, for example, successive malaria eradication campaigns have failed to stem malaria either in the Delta region of Egypt (particularly in the rice-growing areas) or in those areas of Iraq, Syria, and Iran that are under perennial irrigation.[12] One major obstacle is the remarkable ability of the mosquito vectors to develop genetic resistance to the insecticides used to destroy them. In 1981, WHO reported that 51 species had developed resistance to one or more insecticides; 34 were resistant to DDT, 47 to Dieldrin, and 30 to both DDT and Dieldrin. Resistance to organophosphate pesticides had been recorded in 10 species and resistance to carbamates in 4 species.

As a result, there has been a resurgence of malaria in many countries in which it was once thought to have been practically eliminated. Discussing the history of WHO's malaria eradication campaign, Georganne Chapin and Robert Wasserstrom of Columbia University write:

> Initially, at least, it seemed that WHO's campaign enjoyed almost unmitigated success. In India, for example, after ten years of anti-malaria efforts [1961] only 50,000 cases of the disease were uncovered by government officials and a number of states had passed from attack to consolidation or maintenance. Similar triumphs were registered in Pakistan, Sri Lanka, Paraguay, Venezuela, Mexico, and Central America, which devoted considerable resources to this task. Moreover, in ten other countries *Plasmodium* infection was completely overcome. But within a short time the campaign began to falter. Between 1961 and 1966, disease rates in India increased threefold; by 1970, half a million people caught malaria each year—many in areas where health authorities had recently scored impressive victories. Much the same course of events took place in Sri Lanka, which in 1968 experienced an epidemic that left 1.5 million people stricken. Around the globe, in El Salvador, Nicaragua, and Honduras (where antimalaria measures began in the late 1960s), the incidence of disease in 1975 was three times higher than it had been a decade earlier, before the program had started.[13]

With success apparently around the corner and with insecticide resistance necessitating the use of more expensive sprays

(sometimes costing ten times as much as the more common insecticides), many governments had abandoned the eradication
program as soon as infection rates dropped. When the mosquitoes returned, they did so with a vengeance. For its part, WHO
accepted defeat: "Faced with problems for which they had no solutions, in 1973 WHO officials reluctantly transformed the Malaria Eradication Division into the Division of Malaria and other
Parasitic Diseases."[14]

Such defeat was predictable. It had always been recognized
that for eradication to succeed, it would be necessary to eliminate
malaria worldwide. Otherwise, areas that had been cleared would
sooner or later become reinfested when people moved in from
areas where the disease was still endemic. Worldwide eradication
of malaria would have entailed the extermination of every single
Anopheles mosquito. The only other option, destroying the *Plasmodium* parasite through drugs, was considered not only too expensive but also almost impossible to achieve—especially in light
of the rate at which the *Plasmodium* parasite reproduces within
the bloodstream of its victims, the staggering logistics of screen-
ing whole populations for the disease, and the problems of resistance that were exacerbated by the use of agricultural chemicals
to which the mosquitoes also developed resistance.

The spraying programs still being carried out by WHO and
other agencies have wrought untold ecological damage in addition to causing numerous pesticide-related deaths and poison-
ings. Many pesticides—particularly DDT and other chlorinated
hydrocarbons—tend to accumulate in the fatty tissues of those
animals that eat them. Moving up the food chain, predators accumulate more and more pesticide in their fat.

The process is well illustrated by the wholesale contamination
of the aquatic food chain in California's Clear Lake after it was
sprayed with DDD, a close chemical cousin of DDT, to control
gnats. Levels of the chemical in the water were as low as 0.02
parts per million. Plankton and other microscopic organisms
feeding in the lake, however, accumulated DDD residues at 4
parts per million; fish eating the plankton concentrated the pesticide still further—to levels as high as 2,000 parts per million;

and birds feeding on the fish were found to be contaminated with 80,000 times the level of DDD present in the lake, and thousands died.[15]

Such "bioaccumulation" can have unforeseen and tragic consequences. Anne and Paul Ehrlich, two of America's most famous biologists, tell of the macabre experience of a village in Borneo:

> Some years ago, large quantities of DDT were used by the World Health Organisation in a programme of mosquito control in Borneo. Soon the local people, spared a mosquito plague, began to suffer a plague of caterpillars, which devoured the thatched roofs of their houses, causing them to fall in. The habits of the caterpillars limited their exposure to DDT, but predatory wasps that had formerly controlled the caterpillars were devastated.
>
> Further spraying was done indoors to get rid of houseflies. The local gecko lizards which previously had controlled the flies, continued to gobble their corpses—now full of DDT. As a result, the geckos were poisoned, and the dying geckos were caught and eaten by house cats. The cats received massive doses of DDT, which had been concentrated as it passed from fly to gecko to cat, and the cats died. This led to another plague, now of rats. They not only devoured the people's food but also threatened them with yet another plague—this time the genuine article, bubonic plague. The government of Borneo became so concerned that cats were parachuted into the area in an attempt to restore the balance.[16]

Many countries are now exploring the possibilities of using "biological control" to keep malaria in check. There is a tragic irony in that development, for the best practitioners of biological control are precisely those traditional societies that have been most disrupted by the introduction of modern agriculture. In Sri Lanka, for instance, traditional farmers knew well the value of the fish that lived in their paddy fields—Lula, Kawaiya, Hadaya and Ara being the most common species. Those fish not only ate mosquito larvae but could also survive in the dried-up ponds where mosquitoes liked to breed. Today, few such fish species remain. Many have been killed by agricultural chemicals, and some have been eaten by tilapia, a fish introduced from Africa by the government for the purposes of fish farming. Unfortunately, tilapia, although it eats mosquito larvae, cannot survive in small puddles during the dry season and does not venture into the paddy fields.[17] Thus malaria has become a major problem in areas where it was previously under control.

Meanwhile, the introduction of perennial irrigation schemes continues apace throughout the world. Despite the serious malaria hazards associated with such schemes, the mistakes of the past seem doomed to be repeated. Some ascribe those past failures to lack of vision on the part of the authorities; others—ourselves included—are less sanguine. The truth is that the totally predictable increase in the incidence of malaria as a result of introducing irrigation into the tropics and arid subtropics is considered an acceptable political price to pay for the political and economic gains to be made from the scheme. Foreign exchange must take priority over health.

SCHISTOSOMIASIS

In 1947, an estimated 114 million people suffered from schistosomiasis;[18] in 1977, 200 million people were affected.[19] Today the disease is widespread in Africa, Japan, the Philippines, Thailand, Laos, and other parts of Asia, the Middle East, the West Indies, and parts of South America. In all, 71 countries are affected.[20]

The disease is caused by parasitic flatworms known as schistosomes. Three common species infect man: *S. haematobium*, *S. mansoni*, and *S. japoni*. The larvae of the schistosomes, the "miracidia" develop within the bodies of freshwater snails; each of the three types requires a different snail host. Within the snail, the miracidia are transformed into a second larval form, the "sporocyst," which in turn produces thousands of larvae of a third type, the "cercaria."

When people swim or wade in water contaminated by infected snails, the cercaria larvae bore through their skin and enter their bloodstream. From there they move to the liver, where they mature in a few weeks and mate. The female adults of *S. mansoni* and *S. japonicum* produce eggs every day during their estimated thirty-five-year life. The *S. haematobium*, however, settles down in the vesical vein, where it spends about eight weeks laying eggs. Its life cycle is so much shorter that it is theoretically much easier to control.[21] The eggs leave the human body via urine or feces. Once back in water, they hatch into miracidia, which to survive must find and penetrate the body of a new snail host. The cycle is then repeated.

The eggs of all three species tend to spread to various organs within the human body. Indeed, they have been recovered from the brain, the spinal cord, the lungs, bladder, appendix, rectum, uterus, spleen, and liver. The eggs occur in such quantities that they tend to damage neighboring tissue, and this process is exacerbated by the toxic chemicals the body produces in order to kill the worms.[22]

If *S. haematobium* develops in the bladder or genitals, the victim is seriously weakened and blood is passed in the urine. If the disease is caused by *S. mansoni* or *S. japonicum*, it leads to diarrhea and enlargement of the lymph glands, the spleen, and the liver. Cirrhosis of the liver may also develop. The form of the disease caused by *S. japonicum* is often fatal.[23]

The dramatic spread of schistosomiasis over the last thirty-five years is now recognized to be largely a result of large-scale water projects. Such projects provide ideal habitats for both freshwater snails and the schistosome parasite. Indeed, the connection is so well established that Gilbert White has claimed: "The invasion by schistosomiasis of irrigation schemes in arid lands is so common that there is no need to give examples. The non-invasion of schemes in a region where the disease exists is exceptional."[24]

Asit Biswas is equally emphatic: "The incidence and extension of schistosomiasis and other waterborne diseases can be directly related to the proliferation of irrigation schemes, the stabilisation of the aquatic biotope and subsequent ecological changes." By contrast, "when agriculture depended primarily on seasonal rainfall, the relationship between snail host, schistosome parasite and human host was somewhat stabilised, and infection rates were low."[25] Under the traditional agricultural pattern, it was principally during the rainy season, when cultivation took place, that the parasite had the opportunity to come into contact with humans. It was then that infections were at their height. During the dry season, on the other hand, little infection took place.

The building of large-scale reservoirs and perennial irrigation schemes changed all that. Not only has the snail's habitat been vastly extended, but also the conditions for much longer breeding periods have been created. Thus, the *Bulinus* and *Biomphalaria* snails that act as intermediary hosts during the schistosomiasis cycle tend to flourish in the habitat provided by the aquatic weeds that invade large man-made lakes. Indeed the submerged weeds in Lake Volta, principally *Ceratophyllum*, harbor more *Bulinus* snails than do any other plant communities.[26] More generally, John Waterbury, discussing the rise of schistosomiasis after the building of the Aswan Dam, comments: "The impact of perennial irrigation is threefold: it eliminates fallows during which the snail host would be killed off as canals dried out; it increases the amount of still or stagnant water and the amount of aquatic weeds to which the snails cling; and it increases the amount of time the fellahin [peasants] spend in the water."[27]

Inevitably, infection rates rise with the numbers of worms per person. According to one study, the building of the Aswan Low Dam caused the schistosomiasis rate among the population in some areas of Egypt to rise from 21 percent to 75 percent. Once the Aswan High Dam had been completed, the comparable figure rose in some communities to an estimated 100 percent.[28]

Elsewhere, the story is the same. Biswas, for example, cites a study undertaken in four selected areas three years after the introduction of perennial irrigation. In one area, the schistosomiasis rate had risen from 10 to 44 percent; in another, from 7 to 50 percent; in a third, from 11 to 64 percent; and in the fourth, from 2 to 75 percent. In Kenya, schistosomiasis now affects almost 100 percent of the schoolchildren in those areas around Lake Victoria that have been irrigated. In the Transvaal, South Africa, the *S. mansoni* infection rate is 68.5 percent among indigenous people working on European farms and only 33.5 percent in the reserves. The reason, of course, is that only the former are irrigated.[29]

In the Sudan, the massive Gezira scheme, which now covers 900,000 hectares, has seen a veritable epidemic of the disease. Before 1925, when the scheme was started, schistosomiasis was practically unknown in the Blue Nile area. As soon as the scheme came into operation, the disease started spreading and continued to do so in spite of all the measures undertaken to control it. In 1958, the Gezira medical officer of health claimed that the campaign to control the disease had been a complete success, an assertion that seems to have been accepted by all the authorities concerned. Indeed, in 1961, it was claimed that the disease was under complete control. Fifteen years later, the infection rate of *S. mansoni* had increased to 70 percent in some villages, although infection with *S. haematobium* had declined.[30] A survey undertaken in 1979 puts the general infection rate at 60 to 70 percent, with the rate among schoolchildren reaching over 90 percent. All in all, nearly 1.4 million people are affected.[31] It is difficult to imagine what economic gains can possibly justify inflicting the terrible miseries of this most pernicious of diseases on such an enormous body of people—especially so many children.

Few doubt that the incidence of schistosomiasis is on the increase—or that it will spread still further throughout the world as new irrigation works are built. Even those areas where the disease is at present unknown may soon succumb. The experience of South America is instructive. For many years, it was claimed that the highly acidic waters of Amazonia, in which the schistosomes' snail vector cannot breed, would keep that region free from the disease.[32] In fact, the experts have now been proved wrong. The construction of large-scale dams and the creation of vast reservoirs has dramatically altered the chemistry of the water in many areas. In the twelve years since Suriname's Brokopondo Dam was closed, for example, the once acid waters of its reservoir have been effectively neutralized. "Acidity can no longer prevent the proliferation of the schistosomiasis snails there," says Robert Goodland.[33]

Elsewhere, Goodland points out that snails capable of acting as the vector for schistosomiasis have already been discovered in rivers near the site of the Itaipu Dam on the Rio Paraná in Brazil. Although the disease is not endemic to the area, cases have been reported among immigrants seeking work at the dam site. "The creation of the reservoir," warns Goodland, "could lead to a great increase in the snail population and the influx of infected construction workers could infect the snail, thus completing the cycle. Once infected, the snails will be extremely difficult to disinfect or to remove. . . . Human medication is difficult, dangerous and ineffective."[34] To combat the spread of the disease, Goodland recommends that great care be taken with the hiring of workers. But how likely is it that the tens of thousands of migrant laborers, drawn to the dam in the search for employment, can be adequately screened? And what of their relatives and friends who may come to visit them, if only for a few days? Will they also be checked? It would seem more probable that the dam will be built with no more than the usual precautions and that the area will fall prey to schistosomiasis.

Perhaps it is not surprising, then, that Letitia Obeng, of the United Nations Environment Program, has warned that the current incidence of schistosomiasis is only the "thin end of the wedge." Indeed, in her opinion, the disease can—and presumably will—establish itself in those other areas "where climatic, ecological, social, cultural, and economic conditions favour its establishment."[35] It is a grim prospect.

FILARIASIS AND ONCHOCERCIASIS

Filariasis is caused by a parasitic worm, the principal species being *Wuchereria bancrofti*, which is transmitted by several species of mosquito. The disease itself can take several forms, most notoriously elephantiasis. The arms, legs, genitals, and breasts of elephantiasis victims swell to monstrous proportions, in some cases retaining as much as 40 pounds of fluid. Men whose genitals are affected frequently have to carry them in wheelbarrows.

There seems to be no remedy other than the surgical removal of the affected parts.

In 1977, over 250 million people—the equivalent of the entire population of the Soviet Union—suffered from filariasis.[36] The incidence of the disease is increased drastically by large-scale irrigation schemes because its mosquito vector tends to breed in water bodies rich in organic matter, such as marshes, sewers, and badly maintained drains.

River blindness, or onchocerciasis, is widespread in the river basins of Central and South America and tropical Africa. In the Volta River basin, 70,000 people are now blind because of it and another million have been weakened by its effects. In some valleys, more than 30 percent of the population is now blind. Other valleys have been abandoned altogether because of the disease.[37] Many of those valleys are particularly fertile and their former inhabitants have now been forced to eke out a living on crowded and less fertile land in other areas. To judge by the increasing rate at which affected areas are being abandoned, the incidence of the disease in the Volta region is not diminishing. In northeastern Ghana, 40 percent of the total land area has been abandoned as a result of river blindness.[38]

The disease is caused by a parasitic worm of the *Filaria* group, *Onchocerca volvulus*, which is carried by the blackflies of the family Simulidae. The vector tends to breed in fast-flowing rivers. For that reason, it was generally thought that the damming of such rivers would actually reduce the incidence of the disease by reducing the vector's breeding grounds. In fact, the spillways of large dams have proved excellent substitutes for the free-flowing rivers. Thus, blackflies have bred successfully at the Volta Dam, the Owen Falls Dam on the Nile, and the Kainji Dam in Nigeria.

River blindness is extremely difficult to both treat and control, and the World Health Organization's attempts to eradicate the blackfly have been singularly disappointing. In 1975, for instance, a control program was initiated in the Volta River basin. It was expected to cost sixty million dollars and to last twenty years—during which time the disease was to be kept in check by the spraying of local waterways with insecticides. Although the program led to an initial reduction in blackfly populations, that reduction proved only temporary. As Professor John Hunter of Michigan State University points out, it has been found that the blackfly is capable of wind-assisted dispersal over vast areas— possibly as much as 500 kilometers.[39] As a result, the area treated with insecticides is constantly invaded by flies from other areas. In such conditions, the program, like others of its type, would appear doomed.

Meanwhile, the constant spraying has caused considerable ecological damage. Nontarget invertebrate organisms in the rivers of the Volta basin have diminished by 25 to 30 percent.[40] Ironically, on at least one recorded instance the spraying program actually increased the population of blackfly larvae; the insecticide had eliminated the larvae's major predators.

DISEASES INTRODUCED AS AN INDIRECT RESULT OF WATER PROJECTS

The building of large-scale irrigation schemes and other water projects frequently creates conditions that favor the transmission of diseases, not all of them waterborne. As we have seen, hundreds of thousands of people may be moved to make way for new water projects. Usually, they are dumped—and *dumped* is literally the word—wherever a large enough uninhabited area can be found. That such areas exist usually attests to their barrenness and inhospitability. Also, frequently disease is rife in these areas, which is one reason why they are uninhabited. In Zambia, those who were resettled to make way for the Kariba Dam—mainly Tonga tribesmen—were relocated in an area infested by the tsetse fly.[41] As a result, the Tonga now suffer from a high incidence of sleeping sickness. In Sri Lanka, many of those being resettled under the Mahaweli scheme are being moved from the highly fertile Dumbala Valley, near Kandy, where the incidence of malaria is low, to the infertile and malaria-infested plains of the dry zone. Inevitably, many will succumb to both malaria and malnutrition.

To make matters worse, the authorities rarely plan for enough facilities to accommodate even a small proportion of those who are resettled, let alone those migrant workers attracted to newly irrigated areas in search of jobs. "Populations relocated as the reservoir is filled are frequently not planned for," write Linney and Harrison. "Thus, they end up in refugee-camp circumstances, which are notorious for causing epidemics. Many of the 50,000 Tonga tribesmen dislocated by the Kariba Dam caught influenza as they queued up for relief supplies."[42] Moreover, unless sanitation is satisfactory, the local water supply quickly becomes contaminated with human feces, and the transmission of roundworm and hookworm—which together affect almost a billion people around the world—will inevitably increase. Bad sanitation and poor-quality water are responsible also for the transmission of dysentery, gastroenteritis, diarrhea, hepatitis, cholera, and guinea worm. Pneumonia, too, is likely to be rife where people are forced to live in overcrowded conditions, as are respiratory infections and tuberculosis. Finally, the predominance of single men among the migrant population has led to prostitution and the rise of venereal diseases, particularly gonorrhea and syphilis.

At a time when twenty-five million people—six million of them children under five years old—die every year from diarrhea alone, the need for better water supplies is clear enough. Indeed, 80 percent of all sickness and disease in the Third World is now attributed to inadequate water supplies or poor sanitation. There is a tragic irony in the spread of the above diseases—particularly those associated with poor-quality water—since it is the proud boast of the dam-building advocates that large-scale dams actually improve water supplies. Yet, in seeking to provide water through the construction of giant reservoirs, the industry has only succeeded in exacerbating the problem.

As Jane Stein points out in *Environment*, "Once the minimum requirements for human needs are satisfied, the *quality* of water is more important than the *quantity*."[43] Where, after all, is the gain in being able to draw water at will, if that water is thoroughly contaminated? In that respect, those with an intermittent supply of water may be better off—a point well made by Professor Gilbert White: "A Lanjo housewife may withdraw abundant supplies of Nile water to use for bathing, but the water may also be so contaminated that her household chronically suffers intestinal diseases. By contrast, a family in the dry areas of Rajasthan may lament the small volume it can draw from the village standpipe during the dry season but enjoys the security of a fully protected supply."[44] This point has obviously been lost in the frenzy for building larger and larger dams.

EFFORTS TO COMBAT DISEASE

In terms of disease and human suffering, the toll exacted by water development projects has been truly appalling. One might therefore expect that every effort would be made to ensure that the tragedies of the past would not be repeated. However, the health hazards of water development projects continue to be either played down or, worse still, ignored. Significantly, we have not come across even a suggestion that a particular dam project should be cancelled because of the diseases it is likely to inflict on the local population. Indeed, even those countries already ravaged by dam-related epidemics appear unable to learn from their past. A case in point is Ghana. Despite the epidemic of schistosomiasis and river blindness that followed the building of the Volta Dam, the Upper Region Agricultural Development Project is planning to build another 120 relatively small dams in its area by 1985, in addition to rehabilitating 100 older ones that have silted up. Those older dams were built as part of a previous program, launched in the late 1950s, which saw the construction of 104 dams in just three years.[45] That program, undertaken without any accompanying measures to prevent waterborne diseases, led to a not-surprising tripling in the rate of schistosomiasis *haematobium* infections in the area.

Neither that experience, nor the experience at Lake Volta, however, appears to have influenced the planning of the new project in the Upper Region. "To the cynic, perhaps sadly but not surprisingly, it would appear that history may be about to repeat itself, even with compounding effect," John Hunter writes of the program. "Once more, as in 1958–68, no integrated or other measures for disease prevention are included in the development plans. It is predictable, therefore, that there will be acute exacerbation of endemic schistosomiasis and of other water-related diseases. Once again, in a typical sectoral dichotomy, the Ministry of Agriculture will leave the Ministry of Health, with its most meagre resources, to cope on a curative basis, if in fact any special action at all will be possible."[46]

The same lack of concern for preventive health measures, notes Hunter, is evident elsewhere in Ghana. At the Navrongo Dam, for instance, "no disease prevention methods are envisaged in the engineering and agronomic management plan." Hunter concludes his study by asking: "Are acute and chronic illness, morbidity and death to be accepted as a necessary and inevitable cost of agricultural development?"

Ghana's experience is by no means unique. In one water project after another, we find that no efforts are made to control disease until too late—until, in fact, the dams and associated irrigation works have been built and all the problems created. The point is well made by Alexis Coumboros of the Faculty of Medicine of the University of Paris. Arguing that health measures must be incorporated into the planning of a water project from its very inception, he comments: "Unfortunately one has to face the fact that this . . . is only done in exceptional cases and that the advice of those concerned with health is only requested once all the options have been closed. Even then it is rare that any money is set aside for dealing with health problems until, of course, health problems start appearing."[47]

That lack of commitment on the part of governments makes it almost impossible to safeguard the health of those whose environment has been transformed by water development schemes. Even if the technology were available to ensure proper standards of health, the political will to implement it is lacking—an approach that seems at least as short-sighted as it does callous. Many writers concerned with the health effects of large water projects stress the economic cost of disease. Thus M. A. Amin of the London-Khartoum Bilharzia Project points to the "absenteeism or the reduction in the work capacity resulting from schistosomiasis as well as the cost of medical care and the cost of control."[48] So too, W. H. Wright has shown that the actual monetary cost of schistosomiasis for Africa as a whole is approximately $212 million, not including the cost of medical treatment and public health programs.[49] Meanwhile, Dr. M. A. Farooq observed, as early as 1963, that the economic losses caused by schistosomiasis in the Philippines alone came to approximately $6.5 million a year—a figure which, in this instance, includes the cost of medical attention and the loss in production. In Egypt, Farooq estimated, schistosomiasis was causing an economic loss of $560 million a year.[50] Given the appalling suffering caused by waterborne diseases, it is a sad commentary on our times that such suffering must be translated into economic terms in the hope of attracting the attention of politicians. Worse still, there is a distasteful tendency on the part of the authorities to blame the increased incidence of waterborne diseases on the victims themselves. It is pointed out how difficult peasants are to "educate" and how they insist on maintaining their traditional patterns of behavior even in their new environment. If only the local people would refrain from using rivers or reservoirs in the way that they do, it is argued, they would not be vulnerable to so many waterborne diseases.

But is such talk realistic? "In theory," writes John Waterbury, "it would be relatively easy to eliminate bilharziasis. All that is required is that people neither urinate nor defecate in the irrigation canals, thus breaking the cycle between hosts. But theory could become reality only if the entire context of rural living in Egypt was completely transformed. When most villages do not yet have electricity, it is ludicrous to talk of modern plumbing."[51] More important still, the authorities appear oblivious to the crucial part played by rivers in the everyday lives of those who live on their banks. Children are constantly in the water; traders swim out to passing boats in order to sell their wares; and men and women rely on the river to wash the family's clothes. In India, the Ganges, a holy river, plays an even more central role in social life; millions make the pilgrimage to Benares in order to submerge themselves in its (spiritually at least) cleansing waters. Can we really ask those people to abandon their ancient customs and transform their whole way of life simply to serve short-term political interests?

8. The Effects of Large-Scale Water Projects on Fisheries

SHORT-TERM SUCCESSES, LONG-TERM FAILURE

Proponents of large dams place considerable emphasis on the potential that a dam's reservoir offers for the setting up—or, indeed, the expansion—of fishing industries. Even those who are critical of many aspects of large dams see such fisheries as providing major benefits. Professor Ackermann, for instance, regards the boost given by dams to fishing as "one of the more gratifying aspects of man-made lakes."[1] Among other things, he sees such fisheries as slowing down the migration of young people to the cities, and considers that the new fishing opportunities may even lure back those who have already left an area.

Undoubtedly, when a large reservoir is filled, there is likely to be a dramatic rise in the population of whatever fish species are favored by the new lacustrine conditions, although those fish that are adapted to a riverine environment will tend to disappear. All in all, however, the actual number of fish is likely to increase quite substantially under the influence of the vastly expanded aquatic environment. So, too, the release of large quantities of nutrients from the rotting vegetation and soils that have been submerged by the reservoir—together with the increased populations of those microorganisms favored by the new conditions—will encourage the expansion of fish populations.

That expansion in fish numbers, however, is likely to prove a short-lived bonanza. The submerged vegetation and soils soon rot down, thus reducing the amount of available nutrients, and competition and predation cut down the inflated populations of those fish species that first dominated the reservoir's ecosystem. As this occurs, the lake environment will become more highly structured, more diverse and more stable.

In the case of Lake Volta, for instance, a very considerable fishing industry was indeed developed immediately after inundation. In fact, at one time there were as many as 20,000 fishermen on the lake, using some 20,000 canoes and catching up to 60,000 metric tonnes of fish a year. But catches fell off rapidly as the submerged vegetation below the lake rotted away and nutrients became scarcer and scarcer.

The experience of fisheries on Lake Kariba was similar. Five years after the lake was formed, some 2,000 fishermen were landing 3,628 tons of fish per annum. A few years later, however, landings had dropped dramatically. Ten years after closure, no more than 907 tons of fish were caught and the number of fishermen declined correspondingly. Efforts to restock the lake with new species proved a dismal failure: 26 tons of juveniles were introduced in the lake but very few survived. By 1978, fish catches had fallen so low that only a small part of the human population along the shores of the lake was engaged in fishing.

DAMS AND THE DESTRUCTION OF FISHERIES

The pattern of fish yields at Lakes Kariba and Volta would appear to be fairly typical of those at all man-made lakes: initial success followed by long-term failure. It is important to realize, however, that a dam's impact on fisheries does not begin and end with the fate of the fish in its reservoir. By disturbing the ecological balance of the rivers it impounds, a dam can have a serious effect on fish life within the river basin itself—and, indeed, within the seas immediately beyond its estuary.

The problem is succinctly put by Dr. David Tolmazin, former head of the Marine Economy Department at the Economics Institute of the Ukrainian Academy of Sciences. "Rivers, sectioned off by dams, are no longer single ecosystems," he points out. "The flow of suspended material and dissolved gases, which previously sustained the life of a river population, is interrupted. Despite the construction of artificial channels for fish and other measures for transporting them, fish migration is disrupted: spawning and fattening conditions deteriorate. The total river population decreases substantially, and some species disappear completely. The restricted storage lake ecosystem cannot ensure the survival of all life in the river."[2]

Indeed, in terms of fish yields, the loss of fish throughout the river basin as a whole can, in most cases, equal—or even exceed—the temporary gains made in a dam's reservoir. At that point, the claim that dams help to boost fish production wears somewhat thin. Let us look at the extent to which dams disrupt river ecosystems—in particular, their effects on fish life.

First, as Tolmazin intimated above, dams tend to reduce the catch of migratory fish by preventing them from reaching their spawning grounds. The higher the dam, the more fish will be lost trying to leap it or to swim through its turbines. Although fish are often, though not always, provided with "ladders" to enable them to swim over the dam, such ladders are expensive and do not always work. Where dams are more than 30 to 40 meters high, for instance, fish cannot move up the ladders without fatally delaying their migration.

In some cases, the resulting decline in certain fish species has been dramatic. In California, for example, catches of salmon have fallen by 90 percent, largely because dams now make it almost impossible for the salmon to travel upstream in order to spawn. So, too, in the Soviet Union, the drastic fall in sturgeon population has been blamed primarily on the dams, which have cut the sturgeon off from their natural spawning grounds in the major rivers entering the Caspian Sea.

Second, the creation of vast storage reservoirs tends to reduce the flow of rivers largely because the waters that are stored are drawn off for domestic, agricultural, or industrial use. The result is a fall in the water levels of those lakes and inland seas fed by rivers—with disastrous consequences for fishlife. Thus, the shrinking of the Caspian and Aral Seas as a result of upstream water abstraction is also cited to explain the reduced catches of sturgeon and other commercial fish. In the United States, according to the U.S. Water Resources Council, the rivers of fourteen states in the Midwest and Southwest are now so overexploited that they have barely enough water to provide for fish and wildlife. If such habitats are to be protected, then, according to a study by the U.S. Department of Agriculture, the agricultural area under irrigation in the United States must be cut by at least one-fifth.[3] At present, however, every effort is being made to expand the amount of land under irrigation.

Third, the building of storage schemes and other water development projects has led to an increase in the salinity of many rivers, due partly to the return of highly saline drainage waters from irrigated land, and partly to the reduced flow of the rivers themselves. Thus, increased water abstraction upstream not only reduces the amount of water available to dissolve the salts coming downstream, but also leads to the intrusion of sea water into the estuaries and deltas of rivers. Indeed, the salt content of the lower reaches of many rivers is now so high that on that count alone, they no longer provide suitable habitats for riverine fish.

Fourth, the building of a dam traps the silt that used to be washed downstream as the river flowed unimpeded to the sea. That silt, which simply builds up behind the dam, contains nutrients that are vital to the survival of fisheries in the lower reaches of a river and in the sea beyond (see chapter 4). Before the building of the Aswan High Dam, for example, the sardine fisheries along the eastern Mediterranean coast yielded some 18,000 tons of fish a year. Deprived of the nutrients in the Nile's silt, however, the sardine population fell dramatically, and by 1969, catches were down to 500 tons a year. This astounding loss was only partly compensated for by the development of a high seas fishing industry, which in 1969 caught some 5,000 tons of fish.[4]

Tolmazin points out, similarly, that the drastic decline in the fish yields of Russia's Azov and Black Seas "coincided with the introduction of schemes to regulate a large number of major rivers." The brackish coastal area was "substantially deprived of the minerals and detritus brought down by the rivers, so necessary for life in the estuaries and the seas." The result, says Tolmazin, was a "piscatorial disaster." Between the late 1940s and the early 1970s, the Black Sea saw the disappearance of the Black Sea mackerel, the large horse mackerel, the palamida, and the bluefish. By 1979, "the only edible fish still being caught were the anchovy, a small type of horse mackerel, and the occasional sprat." In the Azov Sea, the destruction of fisheries was even more pronounced: by the 1970s, the fish catch was only one-third of what it had been in the 1930s. Worse still, it is the most valuable fish that have disappeared: species such as sturgeon, perch, pike, bream and herring, which once made up 70 to 80 percent of the catch, now account for a mere 7 to 8 percent of the fish landed.[5]

Fifth, the invasion of artificial reservoirs and their associated waterways by aquatic weeds has seriously reduced fish yields both upstream and downstream of dams. The weeds, whose proliferation is the direct result of interference with the river ecosystems, affect fish populations in a number of ways. First, they increase water losses to evapotranspiration, thus reducing the water level of the reservoir. Second, by virtue of their sheer mass, they inevitably reduce the effective capacity of the reservoir, hence restricting the habitat available for fish life. In addition, when they rot and die, they use up valuable oxygen, which can therefore result in high fish mortality. Moreover, by diminishing the sunlight both at the surface of a reservoir and in the waters below, weeds reduce the biological productivity of a reservoir, which, in turn, reduces the number of microorganisms on which fish can feed. Certain weeds also produce toxins, and others give rise to rotting scums; both types have been implicated in causing fish kills.

In addition to their adverse effect on fish life, weeds also interfere with fishing activities. When a reservoir is created in a forested area, for instance, and the forest is not cleared before flooding, there tends to be a proliferation of the weed *Salvinia*. Where this occurs, the *Salvinia* frequently forms broad "mats," which find anchorage amongst the partly submerged trees and shrubs. This may not only severely restrict the movement of boats, to the detriment of the local fishing industry, but also block hydroelectric turbines and even harbors. Although these misfortunes can largely be avoided by clearing forested areas before flooding, such clearance is rarely undertaken. Where forests have been cleared, there tends to be a greater diversity of aquatic plants among which fish, such as tilapia, can thrive.

Finally, aquatic weeds lead indirectly to the loss of fish life as a result of the herbicides that are used to eliminate the weeds—albeit temporarily. Such chemicals kill certain species of aquatic life and leave others to proliferate, thus disrupting the aquatic ecosystem still further. Because the weeds reappear soon after spraying, the herbicides must be applied on an almost continuous basis if the lake and its waterways are to be kept weed-free. Over the years, therefore, the active ingredients of the chemicals tend to build up in the water and the sediment, eventually leading to the contamination of the lake and the poisoning of fish.

PESTICIDE POLLUTION
AND THE DESTRUCTION OF FISHERIES

Unfortunately, the herbicides used to control aquatic weeds are not the only chemicals that are likely to pollute a lake and its waterways. As we have seen in chapter 6, large-scale water development projects greatly increase the habitat for the vectors of waterborne disease. To control those vectors, vast quantities of various pesticides are applied every year to both reservoirs and lakes. Herbicides are sprayed to kill the vegetation they feed off, moluscicides to kill the snails that carry schistosomiasis, and insecticides to kill the blackflies that transmit onchocerciasis (river blindness) and the mosquitoes that transmit malaria.

Many of the pesticides currently used in the Third World are known to linger in the environment for long periods and to pose considerable health risks. In 1976, it was estimated that half the pesticides used were organochlorines, a group whose use has been severely restricted in the industrialized world on both health and environmental grounds.[6] Moreover, the use of such pesticides, many of which are suspected carcinogens and mutagens, has often been profligate. In 1966, for instance, large quantities of DDT were poured into the River Niger in order to combat onchocerciasis. In Uganda, the White Nile was sprayed repeatedly with DDT to protect workers working on the Owen Dam. Large quantities of DDT were used for the same purpose during the building of the Volta Dam.[7]

Recently, less poisonous insecticides (such as Abate R) have been employed to combat onchocerciasis, but it is questionable whether one can continue to use them year after year with impunity. Eventually, unacceptable levels of residues are likely to build up in the sediment of the lakes and rivers where they have been sprayed. Indeed, Professor John Hunter expresses the fear that, as a result of spraying programs, Lake Volta may become "an insecticide sink with biological repercussions yet to be determined."[8]

He goes on to point out that very little research has been undertaken on the effects of insecticides on water quality. In the Volta Scheme, for instance, only $162,000 was allocated for such research, no more than 0.9 percent of the total budget for onchocerciasis control in the area. That paltry research budget, says Hunter, clearly reflects "a low priority for ecosystem stability." It also explains why the "biological repercussions" of present and past spraying programs have "yet to be determined"—and suggests, very strongly, that they are unlikely to be understood until it is, quite probably, too late.

Despite the lack of research on specific chemicals, however, we know enough about the long-term ecological effects of biocides in general to state categorically that the systematic spraying of reservoirs, rivers, and irrigation canals with herbicides, molluscicides, and insecticides is quite incompatible with the maintenance of a healthy fishing industry. Commenting on the use of pesticides in Southeast Asia, Professor Jacques Daget of the Museum of Natural History in Paris points out: "Since the effect must be to kill off insects and plant life, they must necessarily reduce the total quantity of natural food available to fish, especially in the paddy fields."[9] A recent report, undertaken as part of UNESCO's Man and the Biosphere project, comes to the same conclusion. In particular, it points to the vulnerability of *Daphnia*, the waterflea that is an essential component of many freshwater ecosystems and is susceptible to a wide range of pesticides. So too, phytoplankton and algae—which, because they are at the bottom of the aquatic food chain, are essential to the maintenance of the various forms of life at other levels of the chain—are rapidly destroyed by pesticides.[10]

The problem is compounded both by industrial pollution (whose effects on fisheries we shall consider in chapter 16) and by the increasing use of agricultural chemicals. With regard to the latter, it is important to note that the land brought under perennial irrigation by water development schemes is invariably turned over to intensive plantation agriculture (see chapter 12). The resulting increase in the use of pesticides and artificial fertilizer—essential to such farming—has led to algae blooms and to the widespread pollution of waterways through chemical runoff.

As a result, many areas have now been rendered unfit for fish life. In India, for example, pesticide use has led to the complete loss of fish life in some rivers, reservoirs, and estuaries.[11] Elsewhere in South and Southeast Asia, the story is the same—particularly in those areas where new "high-response" varieties of rice and other crops have been introduced as part of the Green Revolution. Such crops are extremely vulnerable to insect depredations and therefore require the application of large quantities of pesticides—often with devastating consequences. In 1983, for example, more than a million fish were killed by biocides in Thailand's Suphanburi Province, in what has since been described as "the country's worst man-made ecological disaster."[12] The biocides—notably Paraquat and Dieldrin—had been sprayed to protect rice crops in the region.

Just as it is the deltas of large rivers that suffer most from silt deprivation and increased salinity, so those are the areas hardest hit by pollution of a river's higher reaches. Moreover, the destruction of delta ecosystems poses a particularly serious threat since deltas tend to be extremely rich in fish life. The Mekong Delta, for example, provides its 20 million inhabitants with an estimated 200 million tons of fish a year. Yet such areas are being systematically destroyed. In that respect, the experience of the Delta Lakes of the Nile is eloquent. Dr. Carl George, of Union College, New York, notes how artificial fertilizer runoff "has created areas of anaerobic waters which are becoming an increasing problem in the shallow brackish waters of the Delta Lakes."[13] So too, "periodic massive fish-kills have been reported . . . as a result of runoff from insecticides, herbicides and moluscicides." In addition to enduring that chemical assault on their ecological integrity, the Delta Lakes have also suffered from silt deprivation, reduced flow, and increased salinity. The whole ecosystem is now so seriously disrupted that it can barely provide a suitable habitat for fish life.

In areas where people have traditionally depended on fish for animal protein, the pollution caused by agricultural chemicals has particularly serious implications. In many parts of South and Southeast Asia, for instance, aquaculture is widely practiced and yields large quantities of fish; "cage" culture, in particular, is highly efficient. According to V. R. Pantalu, up to 25,000 kilograms of fish a year can be produced by suspending a single cage, measuring five meters by three meters by forty-five meters, in a river or large stream.[14]

Yet, as Peter Freeman, a freelance consultant and the author of one of the few overviews on the environmental effects of large dams, points out, such methods of aquaculture are "incompatible with the cultivation of high-yielding rice varieties that require pesticides."[15] Unfortunately, the U.N. Food and Agricultural Organization is totally committed to the expansion of such pesticide-dependent agriculture. Indeed, it foresees global pesticide use increasing fivefold between now and the end of the century— with average pesticide use per hectare in the Third World doubling.[16]

DAMS, FISHING, AND THE NET LOSS OF PROTEIN

Even without considering the reduction in fish catches attributable to the various types of ecological disruption we have described above, it would seem doubtful whether the fisheries provided by a man-made lake can compensate for the food resources lost to flooding. In that respect, the work of Eugene Balon is particularly relevant. He points to the protein value of the fish caught in the river before a dam is built; of the crops in the farmland that is flooded; and of the wild game that inhabits the often extensive croplands, rangelands, and forests that are drowned by a reservoir. When those food resources are taken into account, argues Balon, a dam may well be found to cause a net *loss* in available protein.

Of Lake Kariba, he writes: "Wild animals alone, if harvested, could have yielded the same amount of protein as the lake. Their densities, however, were never studied before the filling of the lake and, when revealed during a rescue operation, took everyone by surprise. In addition, there was space along the river for intensive agricultural use and a much higher potential harvest is possible at a lower energy cost in the river alluvium than on the escarpment or plateau."[17]

Balon has also calculated the protein loss likely to result from building the proposed Treng Dam in Cambodia. If it goes ahead, the dam will flood 8,000 square kilometers of the north Cambodian plains. Those plains, which adjoin the Mekong River, are particularly rich in wildlife, supporting populations of ungulates as dense as those in East Africa. Balon insists that game farming on the plains could produce as much animal protein as might fisheries in the dam's reservoir. In fact, he says, "the potential for protein production seems about the same whether or not the dam is built." The key difference, however, is that the dam will silt up in anywhere from 50 to 200 years, but the plains and their river valley would continue to produce game and crops indefinitely. Moreover, the food derived from the river valley is likely to be richer, more diverse, and more dependable than that obtained for a few decades from fishing the reservoir.

When the protein gains of a dam's fisheries are set against the protein losses caused by flooding, the fishing opportunities provided by man-made lakes hardly seem worth seeking. At the very best, they can only offer short-term compensation for the sustainable food-producing capacities of the river valley that a dam will flood. When the loss of fish life in the waters downstream of a dam are also taken into account, the much-vaunted benefits of fishing man-made lakes quickly turn to costs. Indeed, in the long term, the result is a diminution of fish yields and other sources of protein throughout the river basin. Is it really a cost we should be prepared to go on paying?

9. Dams, Failures and Earthquakes

DAM FAILURES

It is only recently that we have started building large dams, so our experience so far has been largely with small ones. Those, however, have not proved particularly reliable; 1 percent of them "fail" every year,[1] often with disastrous consequences. Although the Teton dam was only 95 meters high, its collapse in December 1976 caused the death of fourteen people as well as a billion dollars' worth of damage. The failure of the 23-meter-high Johnstown dam in Pennsylvania in 1889 led to the death of more than 2,000 people.[2]

The incidence of dam failures is, for a number of reasons, likely to increase in the years to come. To begin with, as Ferdinand Budweg, a noted Brazilian engineer, points out, "The number of new dams in countries with little or no experience in the design, construction, and operation of dams, increases from year to year, and lack of experience may lead to repetition of errors and serious mistakes."[3]

Second, as appropriate sites for dams dwindle—and such sites are strictly limited—less and less suitable locations will be chosen. A case in point is the Malpasset dam, near Fréjus in southern France. Consultants pointed out how unsuitable the site was and recommended that the dam be built elsewhere. However, for reasons of engineering convenience, that advice was disregarded—with terrible consequences. The dam failed on December 2, 1959, causing the death of 421 people.[4] Peru's Tablachaca dam provides another example. The dam, which produces one-fourth of the country's electricity, is seriously threatened by a landslide. Indeed, 20 miles upstream of the dam is a fast-moving mass with a volume of one million cubic meters. Over the last ten years, it has moved at the rate of one millimeter a day, increasing to between two and four millimeters a day in the wet season. In 1983, however, the movement increased to seventy millimeters a day, causing serious concern in Lima. All sorts of solutions are at present being considered, one of them involving the complete excavation of about 10 million cubic meters of earth above the dam at a cost of approximately a billion dollars.[5]

A third cause of dam failure, possibly the most common, is "overtopping" during floods. Such overtopping occurred with the Machau II dam in India in 1979 and caused the death of 1,500 people downstream. In that case, the malfunctioning of equipment contributed to the failure, since the spillway gates could not be opened in time.[6] The spillway's failure to function properly also led to the near-failure of the 400-foot Tarbela dam in Pakistan in 1975–76. In this case, design errors and perhaps poor construction materials were also involved.

Shoddy workmanship is fairly common in constructions put up by foreign companies in the Third World. Many of the buildings put up in the oil-rich Gulf States by Western contractors are already beginning to fall apart. Dr. Carl Widstrand, of the Scandinavian Institute of African Studies, quotes two studies—one done by the government of Ethiopia, another by the Republic of Kenya—which suggest that the engineering and construction of water supply schemes have been of low quality. "Many consultants," he writes, "have sold shoddy workmanship, second-rate material and third-rate engineering capacity."[7] The same has also been true in the United States. The failure of the St. Francis dam in California, which led to the death of 300 people, has been attributed to faulty foundations. Design errors were apparently also largely responsible for the collapse of the Teton dam.

A further factor to be taken into account is the complete lack of cooperation among the various organizations involved in putting up a dam. According to Dr. E. G. Giglioli, for instance, the construction of the Mwea water scheme in Kenya "proved a fertile ground for bureaucratic antagonisms." As he notes, "The Department of Agriculture had the financial responsibility and looked after the day-to-day control and contractors and the Provincial Administration dealt with settlement, settlers and labor. All the departments had different objectives: maximum agricultural production, or design for design's sake of irrigation installations, or security. A constant struggle existed between the departments to achieve managerial control of the scheme."[8]

To make matters worse, governments usually insist that the dams be constructed in the shortest period possible—largely because the politicians involved want to ensure that it is they rather than their successors who obtain the credit. Such "empire-building" was apparently overt during the construction of the Mwea scheme, and largely explains why it was so badly built. "The crash nature of the programme," writes Giglioli, "gave all concerned an accelerated course in the wrong ways of going about the job."[9]

So too with Sri Lanka's Mahaweli scheme. The original plan was to build six dams over 30 years; the present government, however, decided to telescope the time-scale and complete the scheme within six years. As a result, the British contractors building the Victoria dam are reported to have cut a lot of corners in order to construct the dam in time. Widstrand points out that such corner cutting is "a common feature of [water development] programmes."[10]

Sabotage is also a factor to take into account. During a civil war, rebel forces can cause great embarrassment to the government by demolishing hydropower installations. During the civil war that led to the independence of Mozambique, the rebels made various attempts to sabotage the Cabora Bassa dam, which was under construction at the time. The rebels in El Salvador today are apparently aiming to sabotage the country's hydroelectric installations.[11] Dams also make good targets for enemy action.

The U.S. Air Force destroyed hydroelectric dams in North Korea in 1953.[12]

Finally, many dams fail as a result of what Widstrand calls the "pilot project" syndrome.[13] This means that engineers assume that the technology used to build small-scale dams can be used, with little or no modification, for putting up large dams. As the hydrologist Philip Williams points out, "The new technology of large dams is only imperfectly understood and largely relies on the extrapolation from the design of smaller dams."[14] Similar problems of "scaling up" have been encountered in the nuclear industry. In fact, Williams regards the technology of large dams as being, in many ways, comparable to that of nuclear power plants: "Both require massive capital expenditures; both are new technologies with limited operating experience; and, for both, the consequences of catastrophic failure are large-scale devastation."

Although the hazards associated with nuclear power are now generally accepted, though such hazards are rarely allowed to interfere with governmental nuclear policies, the perils associated with the building of large dams are usually ignored, despite our knowledge that the "failure of a large dam could cause the loss of hundreds of thousands of lives and billions of dollars' worth of damage." As a result, the safety of large dams is nowhere near as intensively examined as is that of nuclear power plants, for which, as Williams notes, "comprehensive risk analyses identifying all possible failure modes are routinely undertaken." For large dams, on the other hand, "if a safety analysis is carried out at all, it usually focuses solely on the dam embankment."[15]

EARTHQUAKES AND DAMS

Only recently has it been recognized that the pressure applied to often fragile geological structures by the vast mass of water impounded by a big dam can—and often does—give rise to earthquakes. Seismic activity was first imputed to a reservoir in the late 1930s. The reservoir in question was Lake Mead, which was impounded by the Boulder dam when it was closed in 1935. The main shock occurred four years afterward, although it had been preceded by numerous smaller shocks. The incident sparked a heated debate as to whether or not there was any connection between the reservoir and the seismic activity; eventually, the connection was generally accepted. The Lake Mead earthquake, as Dr. David Simpson of the Lamont-Doherty Geological Observatory at Columbia University points out, thus became "the first recognized case of reservoir-induced seismicity."[16]

During the next twenty years or so there were a few isolated cases of earthquakes occurring after the impoundment of a reservoir, but those do not seem to have been given much significance. As late as 1958, Professor Richter felt able to claim that Lake Mead "represents a local condition: similar shocks were not observed in tests at other large reservoirs."[17] Thus, the earthquakes at Lake Mead were seen as being caused by freak conditions that were very unlikely to recur. Within the following decade, earthquakes that measured between 5.8 and 6.5 on the Richter scale, a logarithmic scale of measurement, occurred at four large reservoirs: at Hsinfengkiang, in China, in 1962 (magnitude 6.1); at Kariba, in Zimbabwe, in 1963 (magnitude 5.8); at Kremasta, in Greece, in 1966 (magnitude 6.3); and at Koyna, in India, in 1967 (magnitude 6.5).[18] At least two of those earthquakes caused deaths, injuries, and a vast amount of damage to houses and other structures. At Koyna and Hsinfengkiang, the dams themselves were damaged. In addition, a flood caused by a landslide at the Vaiont dam in Italy in 1963, which was probably triggered by seismic activity, killed 2,000 people.

By 1969 the relationship between large dams and earthquakes came under renewed scrutiny, especially after the Fourth World Congress on Earthquake Engineering, in Santiago, Chile, in January heard a French seismologist, Professor Jean Pierre Rothé, secretary-general of the International Association of Seismology and Physics of the Earth's Interior. In a paper entitled "Man-Made Earthquakes" he showed that the earthquakes mentioned above—and others—were definitely caused by the impoundment of reservoirs.[19] If many geologists and geophysicists refused to accept the connection, argued Rothé, it was because they had considered the different incidents in isolation from one another. If they were studied together, then it would become clear that the occurrence of an earthquake under a large man-made lake or in its immediate vicinity was not purely fortuitous. It is worth considering a few of the case studies presented by Rothé.

The Hoover Dam. The Hoover dam (originally called the Boulder Dam) in the western United States is 221 meters high and the reservoir impounded by it contains a maximum of 35,000 million cubic meters (Mm³) of water. Filling began in 1935. The first shocks were felt in September, 1936. In the following year, as the water height of the lake reached 120 meters, 100 shocks were felt. In 1938, seismological stations set up in the area recorded several thousand shocks that would not otherwise have been perceptible. On May 4, 1939, some ten months after the reservoir had risen to a height of 145 meters, and when the water volume had reached its normal capacity of 40 billion cubic meters, a serious shock (with a magnitude of 5) occurred. Seismic activity further increased in the following years. In all, 6,000 shocks were felt over an area of 8,000 square kilometers within a ten-year period after the filling began. In August and September of 1972, two other serious shocks occurred in the area around Lake Mead. Both were of a magnitude of 4 and occurred during short periods when the volume of water stored in the lake was nearly 40 billion cubic meters. Significantly, there had been no reports of earthquakes in the area for fifteen years prior to the filling of the lake, although the area is geologically complex (being composed of granite and gneiss, pre-Cambrian schist, Paleozoic formations, and tertiary volcanic rocks) and several faults had in fact been identified bordering the lake.[20]

The Kariba Dam. The Kariba dam in southern Africa is 128 meters high; the reservoir impounded by it covers an area of 6,649 square kilometers and contains 160,368 million cubic meters of water. The lake overlies a region formed mainly from sediments of the Karoo and of volcanic lava dating from the Upper Carboniferous and Jurassic eras. On the site, numerous faults dating back to the Mesozoic era have been identified and mapped. The filling of the lake started in December, 1958, and was completed in August, 1963. Twenty-two shocks occurred in 1959 and fifteen in 1961; one of the latter attained a magnitude of 4 on the Richter scale. Thereafter, seismic activity increased rapidly; sixty-three shocks were registered in March, 1962, and sixty-one were felt in the first seven months of 1963. Indeed, as the lake rose, "the frequency and energy of the shocks increased."[21]

When the lake was eventually filled, in 1963, a series of particularly strong shocks occurred. Ten epicenters were calculated by the U.S. Coast and Geodetic Survey, all situated in the deepest part of the lake: the strongest having a magnitude of 6.1, and one of its aftershocks having a magnitude of 6. Several hundred tremors occurred in September, 1963, and seismic activity then decreased—but fifty shocks occurred in 1963, thirty-nine in 1968, and several in 1969 and 1970. Again, it is significant that, prior to the construction of the dam, the Zambezi valley was considered aseismic. Not a single epicenter for the region appears in the relevant UNESCO catalogue, although a few weak shocks did occur upstream of the Victoria Falls before the filling of the reservoir.

The Koyna Dam. The Koyna dam in India is 103 meters high and its reservoir has a maximum volume of 2,780 million cubic meters (Mm³). Filling started in 1962 and ended in 1964, when the reservoir was less than half filled. In 1963, the frequency of the shocks increased greatly, and their epicenters were all found to be either near the dam or under the reservoir. In 1964, the volume of the water in the reservoir was brought up to 2,000 Mm³. In the next few years, there was little seismic activity. Indeed, by the summer of 1967, it was assumed that everything had settled down and that tremors would no longer occur. Thus, P. M. Mane, the chief engineer at Koyna, argued at the Ninth Congress on Large Dams, held that year in Istanbul, that the tremors were probably due to "crustal adjustments" taking place in and around the lake.[22] He went on to tell delegates to the conference: "It is gathered that such tremors gradually decrease over a period of some years and stop completely. It is hoped that it will be so [at Koyna] also."

However, on September 13, 1967, two important shocks were felt; the first caused great damage to the village of Koynanagar, killing 177 people and injuring 2,300 others. There were numerous aftershocks, one of which, with a magnitude of 5.4, had an epicenter calculated either in the vicinity of the dam or directly under the reservoir itself. On December 10, 1967, another shock, with a magnitude of 6.4, occurred. Could that series of shocks—in particular, the two more serious ones—have occurred naturally? Rothé does not think so. The area in which the Koyna dam was built, the Deccan plateau, is uniformly covered by basaltic rock. According to Rothé, "this 'shield' is one of the least seismic of the pre-Cambrian areas of the world, [where] there are no known faults."[23] In spite of that, a number of geologists and geophysicists insist that the earthquakes were unrelated to the building of the dam and reservoir. A UNESCO study also denied that the filling of the reservoir was responsible for the two major shocks of September and December, 1967. Other experts maintained that although the small shocks could be attributed to the reservoir, the two important shocks could not—an argument that does not sound very convincing.

The Vaiont Dam. The Vaiont dam in Italy is 261 meters high and the volume of the water contained in its reservoir is 150 Mm³. Filling of the reservoir was started in February, 1960—causing a small number of shocks—and the water reached its maximum height in August, 1963. The reservoir was partly emptied in 1961 and seismic activity fell to almost zero. Filling was resumed and the water reached 155 meters in April, 1962. Fifteen shocks then occurred, all between April and May of that year. In September, 1963, the lake reached a level of 180 meters; sixty shocks were registered in the first fifteen days of that month, and, at the same time, an earth movement started along the slope of Mont Toce above the lake. That movement accelerated in October and caused a landslide. The landslide gave rise to a giant wave that flooded the valley beneath, wiping out several villages and killing more than 2,000 people. As in the other cases cited by Rothé, there was "a clear relation between the frequency of shocks and the progress of filling the reservoir."

Other Examples. Other dams suspected of causing earthquakes include the Monteynard dam in the French Alps and the Kremasta dam in Greece. In the former case, an earthquake measuring 5 on the Richter scale occurred after the reservoir was filled in April, 1963. At Kremasta the filling of the reservoir in April, 1965, was followed by a series of tremors culminating in a violent earthquake with a magnitude of 6.2. That earthquake destroyed 480 houses, killed one person, and injured sixty others.

DAMS AND EARTHQUAKES: RECENT RESEARCH

By the late sixties, Rothé and others had documented an impressive body of evidence that linked the incidence of earthquakes to the building of large reservoirs. In 1969, the Joint Committee on Seismology and Earthquake Engineering of the International Association of Earthquake Engineering recommended that "UNESCO convene as soon as possible a working group of experts, to review existing information on the seismic phenomena that have been observed to accompany, in some cases, the filling of large reservoirs, and to recommend what action, if any, should be taken by UNESCO in this matter." As a result, a Working Group on Seismic Phenomena Associated with Large Reservoirs was set up. It met for the first time on December 14–16, 1970. After a lengthy discussion, its members unanimously approved the following statement:

> During the past few years, the impounding of certain reservoirs has been found to be responsible for triggering seismic phenomena, irrespective of the seismicity of the region. Characteristic examples are associated not only with recent tectonics and high seismicity but also with older and more stable masses of very early tectonics.
>
> Up to the present time, a small number of these events, some of them with magnitudes close to 6 (Richter), have been strong

enough to cause not only widespread concern but also damage to structures, including in at least one case damage to the dam itself. Nevertheless, in most cases the filling of reservoirs has not been accompanied by any significant increase in local or regional seismicity. It is believed, therefore, that special geotechnic and/or hydrogeological conditions are required for the triggering of earthquakes of engineering importance.[24]

The working party met for a second time in December, 1971. At that meeting, it was concluded: "In the present state of knowledge regarding the seismic effects associated with reservoir loading, it is impossible to predict with certainty whether hazardous earthquakes are likely to be triggered by the filling of a large reservoir."[25] The working party acknowledged that it had no method for estimating the stress to which the earth's crust is subjected; that it did not know the effects on underlying rock masses of injecting fluids under pressure into deep wells; and that it still needed to establish the potential activity of faults. Other questions remained. How, for instance, should the ability of dams to resist earthquakes be judged? What is the seismicity of those ancient geological platforms normally regarded as stable? And what is the ability of the slopes of a reservoir to resist earthquakes?

To answer these questions, the working party recommended that a research program be undertaken. By 1974, however, after just two more meetings and a conference, the working party adjourned. One can only speculate on the reasons for its demise. Certainly the research was far from finished and the incidence of reservoir-related earthquakes had not abated. Perhaps UNESCO simply tired of the project.

In the meantime, further evidence linking reservoirs to earthquakes has come to light. It was originally thought that seismic activity could occur only while a reservoir was being filled, or immediately after it reached its maximum height. It has now been found that earthquakes also occur after a reservoir has been emptied and refilled. A case in point is France's 100-meter Vouglans dam, whose reservoir has a maximum volume of 605 Mm^3 of water. Filling began in April, 1968, and was completed by November, 1969. The reservoir was partially emptied from December, 1970, to March, 1971, and was refilled very rapidly, reaching maximum capacity in June, 1971. Almost immediately—on June 21—an earthquake occurred with a magnitude of 4.5. It was followed by twenty or so tremors between June 21 and July 2. Significantly, the epicenter was situated 5 kilometers to the southeast of the reservoir. Previously, no seismic activity had been known in the region.[26]

So too, seismic activity increased after the refilling of the reservoir behind Corsica's Alensani dam. The reservoir, with a maximum capacity of 11 million cubic meters, was closed in 1971, and on September 29 of that year, there was an earthquake with a magnitude of 2.9. Six and a half years later, in April, 1978, seismic activity resumed and was still occurring at the end of 1980. The main shock, in 1978, was much stronger than those in 1971 and was preceded and followed by more than 150 shocks. Most seismologists at the time failed to relate them to the seismic activity that had occurred in 1971.[27] Rothé pointed out the relationship and showed that the seismic activity of 1978 occurred after the lake had been emptied, been allowed to remain empty for several months, and then been rapidly refilled.

Significantly, the Alensani dam was only 60 meters high. Indeed, prior to the Alensani earthquake, it was always argued—even by Rothé himself—that only dams over 100 meters high were likely to cause seismic shocks. Alensani disproved that theory—a point now fully admitted by Rothé. In fact, as can be seen from Table 5, a number of other earthquakes have also been associated with dams of well under 100 meters—notably Marathon, in Greece; Bajina Basta, in Yugoslovia; Clark Hill, in the United States; and Grandval, in France.

Recently, it has been asserted that earthquakes can also be caused when the water level in a reservoir is *lowered*. The implications are clear. As David Simpson notes: "One of the obvious ways of decreasing danger downstream from the dam—the rapid emptying of the reservoir—may, in fact, increase the danger by triggering a further increase in the level of activity." A case in point is California's Oroville dam. Since the occurrence of an earthquake in 1975, there has been regular seismic activity within a 20-kilometer radius of the dam. That activity, as P. W. Morrison of the California Department of Water Resources observes, in a paper written jointly with T. R. Toppozada of the California Division of Mines and Geology, "decreased markedly during winter and spring filling of the lake and increased during summer and fall drawdown."[28]

Interestingly enough, the 1975 earthquake also occurred during the summer drawdown that followed the refilling of the reservoir. Commenting on that sequence, Morrison and Toppozada say: "These observations suggest that filling Lake Oroville results in fault stability, but that during drawdown, instability occurs when the decrease in load stress significantly exceeds the slower decrease in subsurface pore pressure. Seismicity accompanying the summer drawdowns has decreased steadily since the August 1975 earthquake, suggesting that the rupture zone of this earthquake has been largely relieved of stress."[29]

Mono Lake in California provides another example of the phenomenon. Earthquakes, which tend to be of magnitude 4 or less occur within 15 kilometers of the lake, mainly in the late summer and autumn. In a study of the relationship between those earthquakes and the water levels in the lake, Toppozada and his colleagues at the California Division of Mines note: "We found that the seismicity shows a striking correlation with the seasonal depletion of Mono Lake. Seismicity is minimal when the lake level is stable or recharged slightly by inflows during the winter and spring, but increases markedly during evaporative drawdown of the lake in the summer and fall."[30] They go on to comment: "The relation of the seismicity at Mono Lake to the variation in lake level is remarkably similar to that at Lake Oroville, where earthquakes occur during the annual drawdown of the lake but not during the annual refilling. During the latter half of 1980, six earthquakes of magnitude 5 occurred some 30 kilometers east of Mono Lake. The relation of these larger and more distant earthquakes to the seismicity near Mono Lake is not known."

New information has shown that earthquakes can also be triggered some years after the filling of a reservoir when the water level is allowed to remain relatively stable. Such an earthquake

TABLE 5
Reservoir-Induced Changes in Seismicity

Dam name	Location	Height of dam (m)	Volume of reservoir ($\cdot 10^6 m^3$)	Year of impounding	Year of largest earthquake	Magnitude or intensity
MAJOR INDUCED EARTHQUAKES						
Koyna	India	103	2780	1964	1967	6.5
Kremasta	Greece	165	4750	1965	1966	6.3
Hsinfengkiang	China	105	10500	1959	1962	6.1
Oroville*	U.S.A. (Calif.)	236	4295	1968	1975	5.9
Kariba	Rhodesia	128	160368	1959	1963	5.8
Hoover	U.S.A. (Ariz.)	221	36703	1936	1939	5.0
Marathon	Greece	63	41	1930	1938	5.0

TABLE 5 (continued)
Reservoir-Induced Changes in Seismicity

Dam name	Location	Height of dam (m)	Volume of reservoir ($\cdot 10^6 m^3$)	Year of impounding	Year of largest earthquake	Magnitude or intensity
MINOR INDUCED EARTHQUAKES						
Benmore	New Zealand	118	2100	1965	1966	5.0
Monteynard	France	155	240	1962	1963	4.9
Kurobe	Japan	186	199	1960	1961	4.9
Bajina-Basta	Yugoslavia	89	340	1966	1967	4.5–5.0
Nurek	U.S.S.R.	317	10400	1969	1972	4.5
Clark Hill	U.S.A. (S.C.)	67	2500	1952	1974	4.3
Talbingo	Australia	162	921	1971	1972	3.5
Keban	Turkey	207	31000	1973	1974	3.5
Jocassee	U.S.A. (S.C.)	133	1430	1972	1975	3.2
Vaiont	Italy	261	61	1961	1963	
Grandval	France	88	292	1959	1963	V
Canalles	Spain	150	678	1960	1962	V
CHANGES IN MICRO-EARTHQUAKE ACTIVITY						
Kamafusa	Japan	46	45	1970		<2.5
Pieve de Cadore	Italy	112	68	1949		2.0

Grancarevo	Yugoslavia	123	1280	1967		1.0–2.0
Hendrik-Verwoerd	S. Africa	88	5954	1970		<2.0
Schlegeis	Austria	130	129	1971		<0.0

TRANSIENT CHANGES IN SEISMICITY

Oued Fodda	Algeria	101	228	1932		
Camarilles	Spain	44	40	1960	1961	3.5
Piasta	Italy	93	13	1965	1966	VI–VII
Vouglans	France	130	605	1968	1971	4.5
Contra	Switzerland	220	86	1965	1965	

DECREASED ACTIVITY

Tarbela	Pakistan	143	13687	1974
Flaming Gorge	U.S.A. (Utah)	153	4647	1964
Glen Canyon	U.S.A. (Ariz.)	216	33305	1964
Anderson	U.S.A. (Calif.)	72	110	1950

OTHER POSSIBLE CASES

Height in meters follows dam name (n.a. = not available).
U.S.A.—Shasta (183), Calif.; San Luis (116), Calif.; Palisades (82), Utah; Clark Canyon (40), Mont.; Kerr (n.a.), Mont.; Cabin Creek (n.a.), Colo.; Rocky Reach (n.a.), Wash.

Australia—Eucumbene (116); Warragamba (137)
Pakistan—Mangla (116)
Spain—El Grado (130)
India—Kinnersani, Parambikulam, Sharavathi, Ukai, Ghirni, Mula (all n.a.)

occurred at Lake Nasser, the reservoir behind Egypt's Aswan dam. Filling started in 1964 and the lake reached its maximum water level of 177.8 meters in 1978: since then it has fluctuated between 171 and 177 meters. On November 14, 1981, an earthquake with a magnitude of 5.6 occurred, preceded by three main foreshocks and followed by a "tremendous number of aftershocks."[31] The intensity* of the earthquake was estimated at 8 near the epicenter and dropped to 6 at Aswan where it caused minor damage to old buildings. The earthquake was attributed by Dr. Kebeasey and his colleagues from the Helwan Institute of Astronomy and Geophysics in Egypt to tectonic activity. However, they admit that the lake's effect in triggering the earthquake cannot be ruled out, for a number of reasons, among them the area's long aseismic history and the fact that the epicenter of the earthquake borders a very wide area of the lake.[32]

New information has also cast some light, however hazy, on the nature of the geological conditions under which the building of a dam is likely to trigger seismic activity. Rothé originally suggested that seismicity would occur only when large dams were built in specific geological conditions—such as "diclastic" forma-

---

*"The intensity of an earthquake is a measure of its visible effects on the surface. There is a macroseismic intensity scale which runs from zero to 12. The macroseismic intensity of a specific earthquake will obviously vary at different distances from its epicentre. The 12 degrees of the macroseismic scale are characterised by the following events:

1. An imperceptible disturbance.

2. A disturbance noticed by only a very few people.

3. A disturbance perceptible to a number of people, and sufficiently strong for them to determine the direction and duration.

4. A disturbance felt by a number of people indoors.

5. A disturbance felt by all the inhabitants of the district; at night, sleepers are wakened.

6. People are sufficiently frightened to leave their houses; slight falls of pebble and plaster.

7. Chimneys fall; cracks develop in the walls of houses.

8. Partial destruction of some buildings.

9–12. Severe damage; total destruction of buildings."

('Fill a lake, start an earthquake', Professor J. P. Rothé, *New Scientist*, 11th July 1968, vol. 39, no. 605).

tions, where a high water loss occurs (as in the case of the Hoover dam, the Kariba, the Kremasta, and the Monteynard) or where there is heterogeneity in the underlying strata. Such conditions favor the circulation of water under pressure, which tends to trigger the shocks.[33]

Today, Rothé considers it far more difficult to identify the geological conditions under which induced earthquakes will occur. Simpson agrees. Nonetheless, he argues that on the basis of our limited experience, a general pattern has emerged. Thus, the potential for induced seismicity appears to be highest "in areas of strikeslip or normal faulting." Induced activity has proved to be most common "in areas of high to moderate strain accumulation," and "areas of low strain accumulation" such as "stable interiors or pre-Cambrian shields" appear to carry the lowest risk of induced seismicity.[34] That said, however, it should be noted that the Aswan dam is situated in an area of low strain accumulation—as are the Akosombo and Bratsk dams, both of which have also experienced induced earthquakes. Indeed, our knowledge of induced seismicity is so limited that Simpson concludes: "Since no diagnostic criteria appear to be presently available for determining the risk of triggering induced earthquakes, all 'large reservoirs' must to some extent be considered potential sources of induced activity."[35]

Even the actual mechanism whereby reservoirs trigger earthquakes is not well known. Rothé suggests that "the weight of impounded water may, in some cases, be enough to explain the triggering of the stored strain energy. Such triggering action will be favored by the existence of layers having different deformabilities." On the other hand,

> The raising of the water level in a reservoir may change the field of effective stresses in the rock mass, as a result of the increase in the pore pressures, and failure may occur. Such change will occur especially along joints, faults, or other weaknesses allowing flow of the pore fluid. As a result of the increase of pore pressures, the normal effective stress decreases and this may trigger earthquakes; in such cases the difference between the water level reached in the reservoir and the natural water table level will be an important factor. . . . In both cases [action of water weight or of

pore pressures], an increase in the surface area loaded by a reservoir raises the probability of the occurrence of shocks, by increasing the rock mass subjected to a given condition of stress.[36]

Rothé considers pore-pressure changes to be a more important factor in the triggering of earthquakes than the weight of impounded water. Certainly, where earthquakes have been induced by high-pressure fluid injection into deep wells (a process often undertaken to get rid of toxic wastes), the role of pore-pressure changes was found to be significant. Such earthquakes have occurred near Denver, at Rangely, at Matsushiro, and at Dale. For his part, however, Simpson—along with the British seismologists D. I. Gough and W. I. Gough—argues that pore-pressure changes played only a small part in reservoir-induced earthquakes caused by high-pressure fluid injection. Thus he writes: "It should be noted . . . that the increases in pore pressure involved in the case of fluid injection are very much higher than those created by a deep reservoir."[37] He also notes that those earthquakes caused by fluid injection all took place at, or very near, a fault zone.

Yet another question is whether reservoir-induced earthquakes actually create stresses or simply serve to release existing ones. The British seismologist, Dr. R. D. Adams, regards it as "generally accepted that induced seismicity only releases strains already stored in the region, perhaps bringing forward in time earthquakes which would have occurred in the future. In no cases should reservoirs increase the long-term seismic energy release, and it may be that an episode of induced seismicity will be followed by a compensating period of quiescence."[38] However, there is no reason to suppose that this is so. Simpson, for example, wonders "whether the reservoir changes only the time-scale for the release of stress, triggering earthquakes which would eventually have occurred anyway, or whether it can modify the magnitude of possible earthquakes too."[39] Whatever the answer to that question, it now seems clear beyond any reasonable doubt that reservoirs can trigger earthquakes—sometimes serious ones—even in areas where there has been no previous seismic activity. As Rothé puts it, when he builds dams, "Man plays the role of the sorcerer's apprentice: in trying to control the energy of the rivers, he brings about stresses whose energy can be suddenly and disastrously released."[40]

That knowledge, however, does not seem to have had any influence on current dam-building plans. The Indian government, for instance, is at present constructing a large dam near Tehri on the Bhagirathi river in the mid-Himalayas, an area that has been marked by considerable seismic activity. Indeed, such activity appears to be on the increase: between 1971 and 1973 the yearly average was one or two earthquakes; in 1974, five earthquakes occurred, and in 1975, there were seven. There also appears to be heavy cracking in the rocks of the river gorge where the Tehri dam is to be built. Those rocks, according to V. D. Saklani, president of the Committee Against the Tehri Dam, are "most unlikely to be able to bear the weight of [the] 2.62 million acre-feet of water to be impounded in the lake."[41]

In light of our present knowledge of reservoir-induced seismicity, it is difficult to see how the government of India can justify the construction of the Tehri dam. Nor is Tehri the only dam under construction that is likely to give rise to seismic activity. Worldwide, many other dams are being built—or planned—in areas known to be seismically active. It is surely only a matter of time before one of those dams causes a truly serious earthquake. If that earthquake also destroys the dam structure, thus releasing the massive volume of water impounded in the reservoir behind, it could kill tens, if not hundreds, of thousands of people in the surrounding area.

10. The Myth of Flood Control

FLOODS: AN INCREASING MENACE

Floods are a serious problem in many river basins throughout the world, particularly in the monsoon and typhoon areas of Southeast Asia. In the ESCAP (Economic and Social Council for Asia and the Pacific) region, for example, the damage caused by floods today has been estimated at some $3,000 million per year.[1] In Asia as a whole, floods are said to destroy about four million hectares of crops every year and the lives of some seventeen million people are affected.[2]

In recent years, floods have been exceptionally destructive. In 1978, India was struck by some of the worst floods in its history. Thousands of villages were inundated. Crops were damaged on millions of acres of farmland. Hundreds of people were drowned, millions were made homeless, and damage to property and livestock is said to have run into billions of dollars.

In 1981, China was devastated by record floods. In July and August of that year, 53 cities, 580 towns, 2,600 factories, and vast areas of agricultural land in Sichuan Province were submerged. There were 1.6 million rooms in the houses destroyed; 1,000 people were killed and nearly 30,000 injured; and damage to property was estimated at over a billion dollars. That very same year, floods ravaged neighboring Shaanxi Province, causing the death of 764 people, injuring 5,000 people, destroying 160,000 houses, washing away 230 villages and leaving 200,000 people homeless.[3]

Similar devastation has been caused by floods in many other parts of the world, and all the evidence suggests that such tragedies are becoming ever more frequent as well as destructive. Thus, in India, the National Commission on Flood Control estimates that the area ravaged by floods has almost doubled in the last thirty years (see Table 6).[4]

In the United States, according to Dr. Maurice Arnold, of Philadelphia's Bureau of Outdoor Recreation, floods cost the country some $300 million in 1937. By 1976, the annual damage caused by floods amounted to $3.5 billion. At the time, Arnold calculated that if the current trends continued, then the annual bill due to floods could reach $12 billion by the year 2000.[5] More recently, Dr. Stanley Changnon, Jr., chief of the Illinois State Water Survey, told the 1983 conference of the American Association for the Advancement of Science that flood damage was costing $4 billion annually—and that the cost of such damage was rising at a rate of between 4 and 7 percent a year in real dollars.[6] Although Changnon did not give an estimate of the likely future cost of floods in the United States, his figures suggest that by the turn of the century the cost of floods will have reached $9 billion a year—not quite the sum calculated by Arnold, but staggering all the same.

What, then, has gone wrong? Why, despite massive expenditure worldwide on flood control measures, does the damage done by floods continue to rise?

THE FAILURE OF A STRATEGY

The main technique for "controlling" floods today is the building of embankments to contain flood waters within rivers. Another practice is the construction of reservoirs in which flood waters can be impounded before being released at a slow enough rate to prevent destructive flooding downstream. Embankments, dams, and other similar devices are referred to as "structural" controls.

Experience with such controls has shown repeatedly how ineffective they are. The inhabitants of China's Yellow River Basin, for instance, have since time immemorial built barriers to control the course of the Yellow River and its tributaries. Those barriers, however, have not prevented the Yellow River from flooding surrounding villages and agricultural land at least 1,500 times in the last 3,000 years—nor from changing its course on at least twenty-six occasions, nine times very violently.

Despite the record, the Chinese government, like other governments throughout the world, continues to rely on embankments to control floods—and the floods continue to occur. Indeed, a growing body of evidence now makes it increasingly clear that structural controls do little or nothing to reduce the ravages of floods. On the contrary, they would appear to exacerbate the problem, largely by increasing the severity of those floods that occur.

In India, for example, a National Flood Control program was launched in 1953. By 1979, 9.75 billion rupees (nearly a billion U.S. dollars) had been spent on embankments and other structural controls. Yet, as we have seen, flood damage is increasing

TABLE 6

Annual Damage Caused by Floods in India, 1953 to 1981

Year	Cropped area affected (100,000 hectares)	Total damage (in millions of rupees)	
		At 1982 valuation	At 1952–53 prices
1953	9.3	540	520
1954	26.5	580	590
1955	54.0	1190	1340
1956	21.0	510	510
1957	4.5	240	220
1958	14.9	510	460
1959	15.4	790	680
1960	26.5	670	550
1961	18.3	320	260
1962	35.6	930	750
1963	19.7	380	300
1964	24.7	670	450
1965	2.5	60	30
1966	16.1	650	340
1967	33.0	1370	620

year by year. Significantly, Mr. B. B. Vohra, who is president of the Environmental Planning Commission of the Indian government, warns: "The building of spurs and embankments—which, incidentally, have to be rebuilt or raised every year—is no answer at all to the problems of floods."[7] Rather than offering a solution to the problem of floods, says Vohra, the building of embankments "merely creates the illusion of doing so."

In the United States, apparently, the situation is very similar. As both Arnold and Changnon emphasize, the devastation caused by floods has increased in spite of the vast amount of money that has been spent on flood controls.[8] Since 1937, the year that the structural flood control program was launched, the

TABLE 6, CONTINUED
Annual Damage Caused by Floods in India, 1953 to 1981

| Year | Cropped area affected (100,000 hectares) | Total damage (in millions of rupees) | |
		At 1982 valuation	At 1952–53 prices
1968	26.9	2030	950
1969	43.4	3330	1490
1970	48.5	2870	1210
1971	62.4	6320	2630
1972	24.4	1580	630
1973	76.0	5690	1790
1974	33.0	5690	1400
1975	38.5	4710	1190
1976	76.8	8890	2390
1977	82.5	12000	2820
1978	100.5	14550	3420
1979	20.0	5970	1400
1980	54.1	8300	1950
1981 (as of 19 August)	16.2	2050	480

SOURCES: (a) Report of the National Commission of Floods, vol. 1, Department of Irrigation, New Delhi, 1980; and (b) Replies to Rajya Sabha Unstarred Questions 109 (November 17, 1980), 1906 (March 11, 1981) and 836 (August 26, 1981), in Centre for Science and Environment, *The State of India's Environment 1982*, New Delhi, 1982, p. 62.

federal government has spent over $12,000 million on structural controls as well as massive sums on flood relief. Yet since then, as we have seen, the average annual cost of flood damage has risen from $350 million to between $3.5 billion and $4 billion in 1976,[9] and it seems that much of the devastation can be blamed on the structural controls themselves.

When hurricane Agnes hit the Middle and North Atlantic drainage basins of the Upper Ohio River, it caused $3 billion worth of damage, more than any other single "natural" disaster in the history of the United States. It so happens that those were precisely the areas where the most elaborate structural controls had been put up.[10] So, too, Professor Arthur E. Morgan argues that the runoff that caused the 1967 floods in the Lower Mississippi was no greater than usual; he asserts that it was only because of the levees built to contain the flow of the river that the floods were so destructive.[11] In a similar vein, Professor Charles Belt, Jr., of St. Louis University, points out that the floods that ravaged the Mississippi basin in 1973 contained less water than a previous and less destructive flood; he attributes the amount of damage caused largely to the levees and navigation structures built along the river.[12]

The idea that flood control embankments actually increase the severity of floods must seem paradoxical. It is, however, a paradox that is easily explained. By containing a river within concrete embankments, one does not reduce the total *volume* of flood waters. One does, however, dramatically increase the river's *rate of flow*; embankments tend to eliminate the oxbow bends that previously had slowed the river's waters on their way to the sea. When a flood occurs, therefore, the flood waters are literally propelled downstream and, inevitably, the damage done in the flood plains below is correspondingly increased. Arnold therefore argues that channels or canals—also used as structural flood controls—should not be regarded as flood control mechanisms but, rather, as "flood threat transfer devices."[13] The same can indeed be said for embankments.

DEFORESTATION, EROSION, AND FLOODS

The problem of controlling floods by structural means has undoubtedly been compounded by the widespread deforestation that has occurred almost everywhere in the Third World since the Second World War. Such deforestation appears to be an inevitable concomitant of "development"—largely because it is by cutting down forests and exporting timber (especially tropical hardwoods) that Third World countries earn the foreign exchange to develop. But cutting down forests does more than increase the nation's cash: it also dramatically increases the risk of flooding. Let us see how.

When the catchment area of a river is heavily forested, the elaborate root system of the trees acts as a vast sponge; it soaks up rainfall, releasing it only very slowly to the river below. Once a catchment area has been deforested, however, the runoff (as a proportion of rainfall) is vastly increased. A recent UNESCO study found that, when forested, the watershed of one selected river released not more than 1 to 3 percent of the total rainfall; by contrast, once the area was deforested, between 97 and 99 percent was released to the river. During periods of heavy rainfall, therefore, the volume of water carried by rivers in deforested areas can be massive. Inevitably, the pressure put on existing embankments is tremendous—which increases both the need for repairs and maintenance after each rainy season and the possibility that the embankments will simply collapse.

Deforestation has another serious consequence. In a heavily forested area, the soil's organic content—and hence its structure—is maintained by the decomposition of the forest litter. The soil itself is held together by an elaborate network of roots that underlies the forest floor, and is thus subject to minimum erosion. Once the forest cover has been removed, however, the roots rot away, and there is no longer anything to hold the soil together. In addition, the soil, deprived of the forest litter, rapidly loses its structure and becomes very vulnerable to erosion by wind and water.

A study quoted by Alan Grainger, of the School of Forestry at Oxford University, shows that a natural rain forest lost only one ton of soil per hectare to soil erosion; but soil losses increased to between 20 and 30 tons once the trees had been removed and the land put to cultivation. Another study, conducted in the Ivory Coast, found that soil erosion in a secondary forest with a 7 percent slope was no more than 0.03 ton per hectare per year. Again, once the tree cover had been removed and the area brought under cultivation, soil losses increased—in this instance, to 90 tons per hectare. When the land was left bare, erosion increased still further—with 138 tons of soil being lost per hectare.[14]

Under such conditions, during periods of heavy rainfall, the soil is carried down the denuded mountain slopes into the rivers below. This correspondingly increases their silt load, which, in the tropics, is already likely to be high. In normal circumstances, that silt would be deposited on the flood plains downstream when the rivers flooded their banks during the rainy season. If a river is channeled between embankments, however, such flooding is no longer possible. The silt simply accumulates, raising the height of the river bed until, eventually, it becomes higher than the surrounding land. Indeed, where China's Yellow River crosses the Yellow Plains, the river's bed is now five to ten meters above ground level.

Inevitably, such "silting up" further increases the pressure on embankments, necessitating that their height be continually raised in order to prevent flooding. Raising the height of embankments, however, is only a temporary solution and one that, in the long run, can only increase the severity of floods. The point is well made by Alan Grainger in an article on the problems of flood control in India: "High embankments have served to raise the level of several rivers above that of the surrounding countryside; and when a breach occurs, the result is disaster."[15] Sooner or later, he observes, erosion inevitably "offsets the protective value of embankments." Indeed, the building of such embankments "has proved to be no more than a temporary palliative."

In China, as in India, the terrible floods of the last few years have been attributed to increased runoff and erosion in the catchment area of the large rivers. Dr. Li Jinchang, deputy representative of the Permanent Mission of the People's Republic of China to UNEP (United Nations Environment Programme) in Nairobi, points out that every year, the three major rivers in the province of Sichuan now carry an estimated 250 million tons of silt—equal to a layer of 5 centimeters of topsoil over an area of 166,000 hectares of cultivated land. Much of that silt, says Li Jinchang, has been washed away from land in the upper reaches of the Yangtze and Yellow rivers, which have been deforested in recent years. An expert committee from China's National Science Association points out that it is no coincidence that of the 193 counties in Sichuan Province, "only 12 had forest cover exceeding 30 percent of their land area, while of the 53 counties in Central Sichuan, almost half had forest cover that was less than 3 percent of land area, in some cases, less than 1 percent."[16] Much of that deforestation has occurred in the last thirty years. Wuzeng, one of the areas hardest hit by floods, possessed more than 10,000 hectares of forest in the early 1950s; by 1975, this figure was 56 hectares. Significantly, even the provincial authorities have blamed the recent spate of floods on deforestation.[17]

BUILDING ON THE FLOOD PLAINS

During periods of heavy rainfall, free-flowing rivers regularly burst their banks and inundate their flood plains, and those floods are often extensive. Flood plains occupy between 1 and 20 percent of most countries. In Bangladesh the figure is particularly high, with approximately 66 percent of the country in the flood plains of the Ganges and Brahmaputra rivers. According to Maurice Arnold, 7 percent of the total land area of the United States is subject to some flood risk; 5 percent—known as "hundred years plains"—is classified as having one chance in a hundred of being flooded in any given year.[18]

In times gone by, people very sensibly avoided building permanent settlements on flood plains. Today, however, we live in an age of technological euphoria, in which man's ability to control the forces of nature is taken for granted. People have become accustomed to the idea that—so long as enough money is spent on embankments, dams, and other structural controls—it is comparatively safe to build all the houses, factories, and shops they want on the flood plains of the wildest rivers. Sadly, this belief has been actively encouraged by developers and governments alike—governments being particularly attracted by the prospect of increasing their tax income from new developments.

Yet, the 1969 United Nations Conference on Floods singled out the intensified use of flood plains as a major cause of the increased costs of floods in North America and Western Europe. The conference also argued that building on flood plains had greatly increased the potential for flood damage in Japan, Eastern Europe, South and Southeast Asia, South America, and Africa. Professor D. I. Sikka of the Department of Major Multipurpose Projects, Madhya Pradesh, blames the terrible destruction caused in India by the floods of 1971—and, indeed, by those of more recent years—on the intensified use of flood plains.[19]

OTHER REASONS WHY STRUCTURAL CONTROLS
CANNOT WORK

From the above, it should be clear that on theoretical grounds alone, structural controls are unlikely to solve the problem of floods. For nontheoretical reasons, however, structural controls are even more inappropriate to the task in hand.

To begin with, they are too expensive—especially for those poor countries of the Third World, such as India, Bangladesh, and China, where floods cause the most serious damage. In India, $900 million will be spent in the next few years on flood control measures. Yet, even that vast sum is regarded by many experts as woefully inadequate. Indeed, it is argued, $1,300 million must be spent in the Ganges Basin alone.[20]

As Third World countries sink further into debt, the money required for structural controls is less likely to be available. That squeeze on funds will undoubtedly be compounded by the low priority which politicians give to flood control in general. Even today, very few dams are built specifically in order to combat floods; indeed, out of the 1,554 dams listed in *The International Registry of Large Dams*, only 17 have been built for that sole purpose. More often than not, funds are allocated for flood control only when a disaster looms—a point well made by an editorial in the *Statesman*, one of India's leading newspapers. "Parliamentary indignation is roused only when the waters are at their highest; demands and pledges alike being quietly shelved once the deluge has disappeared."[21] Put bluntly, few politicians see any political capital to be gained from spending money on projects that bring neither visible nor immediate economic benefits. Cynics might argue that political advantage is derived from floods only when they actually occur, and politicians can be seen "doing something" about the situation.

Even if the money is available to build structural controls, there is the additional problem of managing them. Carl Widstrand argues that structural controls have little chance of success unless there is "a highly committed administrative staff, as well as a sound organizational structure" to ensure that they are properly run and maintained.[22] In the Third World in particular, those conditions are rarely met, despite the high-sounding titles of those departments responsible for administering flood control programs. In many instances, such departments exist in little more than name. Thus, according to the *Indian Express*, India's National Commission on Flood Control, set up in the wake of the disastrous 1975 floods, has remained "in a state of suspended animation after the first chairman named for it was moved to a political office." Significantly, no one has been appointed to take his place. The newspaper goes on to brand the commission as "an alibi for evading positive action."[23]

THE TRADE-OFF BETWEEN FLOOD CONTROL, HYDROPOWER, AND IRRIGATION

Where dams are used to "control" floods, the task of management is encumbered by the politicians' desire to make maximum use of the waters in the dam's reservoir. Although for flood-control purposes, the water level in the reservoir must be kept as low as possible, for generating hydroelectricity or for irrigation, the opposite is the case. There is therefore a trade-off between, on the one hand, the containment of floods, and on the other, the provision of electricity and irrigation water. More often than not, the latter uses have priority. As Widstrand puts it, "The high short-term value of water for irrigation or hydropower would be too strong an argument not to sacrifice some flood-mitigation benefits in favor of increased supply benefits."[24]

That trade-off frequently proves disastrous. Dr. A. L. Mukherjee describes how in 1978, operations at a dam in West Bengal led directly to widespread flooding.[25] In their eagerness to generate the maximum amount of hydroelectricity, the dam's authorities kept the reservoir practically full even during the rains of May and June. Those rains were particularly heavy, and as a result, the flow of the river was greatly increased. With the reservoir full, the river's flood waters could not be contained behind the dam. Inevitably, vast areas of West Bengal were flooded.

More recently, we have the example of the 1983 floods that ravaged California.[26] Heavy snowfall, said to be three times the annual average, in the winter of 1983 resulted in greatly increased runoff from the Rocky Mountains during the following spring. The waters of the Colorado River swelled to almost unprecedented levels, quickly filling the reservoirs behind the dams built along the river—and incidentally placing considerable stress on the dams themselves. Although it soon became clear that the water level in the reservoirs would have to be lowered to avoid large-scale floods downstream, the decision to do so was put off repeatedly.

It is now clear that those delays were prompted by purely short-term politicial and economic motives. Worried about its massive budgetary deficit, the U.S. government wanted government agencies throughout the state to increase their incomes as far as possible. Bob Gottlieb of the Los Angeles Metropolitan Water District (MWD) later revealed to William Scobie of the *Observer* that the MWD was under strong pressure from Washington "to squeeze every kilowatt from the river's hydroelectric stations." So, too, says Gottlieb, there was pressure from California's powerful farming lobby to keep the reservoirs as full as possible to provide the maximum amount of water for irrigation. Meanwhile, the tourist industry—which, in California, has an annual turnover of billions of dollars—was also lobbying to keep water levels high so that the reservoirs could still be used for recreation.

When, in the first week of July, 1983, a decision was finally taken to release water from the reservoirs, it was far too late. Officials openly admitted that they were unleashing "a controlled disaster" on the Southwest. Fifty-five thousand acres of farmland were flooded, thousands of people made homeless, an estimated hundred million dollars' worth of property destroyed, and at least five people drowned. Nonetheless, the U.S. government refused to admit that the floods were man-made. For its part, the Bureau of Reclamation attributed the error to faulty computer models—its own and those of the National Weather Service. Local hydrologists, however, were less euphemistic. They told Scobie, "The gates were opened ten weeks too late for basically politico-economic reasons."

DEALING WITH FLOODS: THE ECOLOGICAL APPROACH

Serious floods are not simply acts of God. As Arnold points out: "Too often, flood policies and programs are based on the assumption that flood disasters result from nature's actions, not man's, whereas in actual fact the misery and damage are mostly caused by human error—especially by poor land management and myopic flood-control strategies."[27]

Those myopic flood-control strategies undoubtedly have their roots in the atmosphere of panic that reigns when a serious flood occurs. At such times, writes Arnold, "rationality is difficult to achieve." He goes on to explain why: "People in a trauma want immediate action, which means dealing with the effects rather than the cause—in other words, building structural controls rather than adopting real long-term solutions."[28]

How then should the problem be tackled? Quite obviously, the first task is to prevent any further deforestation in the catchment areas of the world's greatest rivers. The importance of such an antideforestation policy is eloquently stated by B. B. Vohra, president of India's Environment Planning Council, in a recent speech on the subject of land and water management:

The only way to tackle the growing menace of floods is to control deforestation, denudation, and soil erosion in the watersheds of rivers. [Such a task] must be undertaken on the most urgent basis, particularly in the case of the Himalayan rivers, if certain disaster is to be avoided. If this problem is not tackled in time, it is not difficult to imagine a situation in which, thanks to increasingly frequent and intense floods, and the consequent rise in the level of river beds, large portions of the rich flat lands of the Ganga basin may be turned into undrainable swamps. Perhaps it is already too late to save the situation because, while the denudation and erosion of the Himalayas is already far advanced and is growing rapidly, it will be years—even with the best will in the world—before we will be able to control it effectively.[29]

In India, as in many other countries, flood control is the responsibility of the Irrigation Department, whose officials are mostly engineers or people with an engineering mentality. Unfortunately, that department is totally committed to building structural flood controls and is apparently unwilling even to entertain the notion that the solution to the problem of floods is of a nontechnical character. Vohra very sensibly suggests that for that reason, the responsibility for controlling floods should immediately be "handed over to organisations which can control soil erosion in the catchments." The trouble, of course, is that such organizations do not exist. Moreover, were they to be created, it is questionable whether they could survive for long in the present politicoeconomic climate.

Any long-term solution to the problem of floods must undoubtedly go further than simply halting deforestation. Indeed, deforestation is now so far advanced in many areas of the Third World that a massive and systematic program of reforestation is of the utmost urgency. That reforestation is required—and not only for flood control—is generally accepted by both governments and international agencies. The World Bank, in particular, has on occasion made the reforestation of watersheds a condition for the financing of water development schemes. But for the World Bank (and most other aid agencies) reforestation still means the planting of row upon row of fast-growing pine or other exotic trees that often have a very shallow root system and, therefore, a minimal capacity either to retain water or to bind soils within their roots. Furthermore, most varieties chosen for planting are selected because there is a ready market for their timber, and one day they will be cut down. Such trees are therefore of little use in combating erosion or runoff. If those functions are to be performed, reforestation programs must provide a mix of native trees so that the new forests resemble as closely as possible those that previously grew in the area. Only then can we be confident that the trees will be adapted to local geological, biotic, and climatic conditions.

Finally, it is essential to prevent the further appropriation of the flood plains of the great rivers for commercial development—and not only for flood-control purposes. Flood plains, as Arnold points out, "provide key links in many food chains. They are the habitat of numerous birds and other wildlife. They support a vast diversity of plant-life; they also provide some of the most fertile land and best-watered land for growing crops for a society that has mastered the technique of doing so."[30] The last thing one should do with such land is cover it with tract housing and factories.

In a country like Bangladesh, where flood plains make up 66 percent of the land area, it will of course not be possible to preserve all the flood plains. But where floods are a common occurrence, people eventually learn to live with them. Among other things, houses can be designed and built that are able to withstand flooding or that can easily be rebuilt after inundation.

Above all, what is required is a completely new attitude toward the problem of flood control. We must abandon the illusion that floods can actually be eliminated. Regardless of the brilliance of our scientists, the ingenuity of our engineers, and the generosity of the World Bank, floods will continue to occur. But they need not cause disasters. On the contrary, throughout history, floods have been made use of by populations inhabiting river basins to irrigate and fertilize their fields in a perfectly sustainable manner. If floods could be brought once more under the joint control of the forests and the flood plains, we, too, might learn to live with floods and derive from them still more sophisticated benefits.

11. Salting the Earth:
The Problem of Salinization

THE CAUSES OF SALINIZATION

All soils contain salt. That salt is the result of what geologists call "weathering"—the natural chemical, biological, and physical processes that lead to the gradual breakdown of rocks and other geological formations. As those rocks are gradually worn down, their natural salts are released into the soil, generally to be dissolved in rain water. That water either percolates into the underlying groundwater or is washed away into streams and rivers. It follows that all water, like all soil, contains traces of salt. Even a fresh mountain stream will contain up to 50 parts per million (ppm) of salt—admittedly a minute amount compared with the 35,000 ppm found in sea water, but significant nonetheless.[1]

When the concentration of salts in soil reaches a range of 0.5 to 1.0 percent, the land becomes toxic to plant life.[2] In the dry tropics that problem is particularly acute, since there is not enough rainfall to flush out the salts that accumulate in the soil. Soils in those areas can thus have a natural salt content as high as 12 percent. Equally important, groundwater can contain salts at levels approaching the concentration of those in sea water.[3] Although such natural salt levels are the exception rather than the rule, the generally high salt burden of arid and semiarid lands renders them particularly vulnerable to salinization.

As Professor Victor Kovda, of the Soviet Academy of Sciences, emphasizes, groundwater provides "the main reserve and source of salts circulating in the soil profile," and for that reason it is essential that the water table under potentially saline soils should be kept at the appropriate level below the surface.[4] If the water table is permitted to rise to within 2.5 meters of the surface, then the groundwaters are drawn upward by capillary action—and

TABLE 7

The Impact of Waterlogging on Crop Yields, Shaanxi Province, China

Ground water depth (meters)	Harvest as a percentage of normal yield	
	Wheat	Cotton
2–3	100	100
1–2	50	65
0.5–1	20	50
0.5 and higher	0	10–20

SOURCE: Bruce Stokes, "Bread and Water: Growing Tomorrow's Food," Worldwatch Institute, Washington D.C. 1980.

add to their own salt burden on the way by dissolving the salts in the soils near the surface.[5] In effect, the land becomes water-logged with increasingly saline water.

Even before that water reaches the surface, it starts affecting crop yields by interfering with the capacity of plants to take up moisture and oxygen. In China's Shaanxi Province, where the impact of waterlogging on wheat and coffee production has been carefully recorded, it was found that normal yields could still be obtained when the water was 2 to 3 meters below the surface. When it rose to 1 meter below the surface, and hence into the root zone, wheat yields fell to one-fifth of the norm, and cotton yields to one-half. When the water table rose to 0.5 meters and higher, wheat production fell to zero and cotton production fell to between one-fifth and one-twentieth of the norm (see Table 7).[6]

Worse still, once they approach the surface, the by now increasingly saline groundwaters quickly evaporate, and the salts they contain accumulate on the surface. Once again, the dry tropics are particularly vulnerable, since evaporation rates in hot arid and semiarid lands are four to five times higher than those in temperate areas. Under such conditions, it is not long before the whole area becomes covered with a white saline crust.

If the salts in the water contain sodium or sodium bicarbonate—which occurs when sodium aluminosilicate minerals are released by the weathering of volcanic rocks—the destruction goes one step further. The lands become alkaline. "The soil undergoes intensive hydrophilization, losing its structure and permeability," explains Kovda. "An intensive cementation process gets under way in dry conditions. High alkalinity, cementation, and impermeability in the aggregate lead to loss of fertility. The soil turns barren and is very difficult to reclaim."[7] Such alkalinization is already affecting parts of northern India, Pakistan, Armenia, Afghanistan, and Iran. Those lands are now in effect dead forever.

IRRIGATION AND SALINIZATION: THE INTIMATE CONNECTION

If arid lands are not to become salinized, it is clearly essential to maintain the "water-salt balance" of the soil. That is to say, the amount of water leaving the soil must be at least equal to the amount entering it. The water should not be allowed to accumulate. So, too, salt must not be added to the soil—for example, by using irrigation water with a high salt content—unless an equal amount of salt can be flushed out of the land.

Irrigation schemes throw that delicate water-salt balance dangerously out of kilter. First, perennial irrigation invariably raises the water table. According to Professor Gilbert White, of the University of Colorado, there are "numerous cases" throughout the world where the water table under irrigated land "has risen within ten years about 25–30 meters below the soil surface up to 1–2 meters' depth."[8] In some areas, groundwater tables are rising at a rate of three to five meters a year.

That rise in groundwater levels is caused primarily by the water lost through seepage from irrigation channels. As we noted in chapter 5, such losses can be considerable—in some instances, up to 60 percent. Where the irrigation water is provided by large-scale dams, the problem is compounded by the seepage of water from the dam's reservoir; in some cases, such seepage has raised the level of groundwaters up to 20 kilometers away. Finally, the overuse of irrigation water, a common problem the world over, helps to raise the water table and hence further increases water-

logging. As waterlogging sets in, so the inevitable process of salinization begins.

Secondly, irrigation adds directly to the salt load of soils
through increasing the rate of evapotranspiration. As plants
"breathe," much of the water taken up by their roots is lost
through their leaves to the atmosphere in a process known as
transpiration. A large proportion of the water applied to plants is
also lost to direct evaporation. Because it is practically impossible
to measure separately the amounts of water lost in the two processes, they are treated as a single phenomenon, known technically as evapotranspiration. Where land is irrigated, the losses
due to evapotranspiration are particularly high. Not only does irrigation increase the extent of vegetative cover—and, hence, the
rates of transpiration—but it also means water is spread thinly
over a wide area, thus increasing direct evaporation losses.

The inevitable result of high evapotranspiration is that the natural salt in water becomes concentrated in the soil. On that score,
the research of Arthur Pillsbury, professor of engineering and
(until he retired) director of the Water Resources Center at the
University of California, Los Angeles, is particularly relevant.
Writing in *Scientific American*, Professor Pillsbury estimated that
three-quarters of the water applied each year to irrigated land in
the United States is lost to evapotranspiration. "If, as seems reasonable, the average annual amount of water applied in irrigation
in the Western United States is equivalent to 3 feet covering the
area cultivated, about 120 million acre-feet of water is applied
annually to some 40 million acres of land. Roughly 90 million
acre-feet of the total volume are lost by evapo-transpiration. The
remaining 30 million acre-feet hold essentially all the original
salts: a fourfold concentration." Such water frequently contains
more than 2,000 ppm of salt.[9]

That imbalance is even worse when irrigation water is drawn
directly from rivers or from the reservoirs impounded by large
dams. For example, evaporation at Lake Mead (behind the Hoover Dam) and at Lake Powell (behind the Glen Canyon Dam) is
reported to have increased the salinity of the Colorado River by
100 milligrams per liter (mg/l).

John Waterbury reports that high evaporation rates at the Aswan High Dam reservoir "have led to 10 percent increases in salinity: that is, water entering the reservoir has about 200 ppm, and when it leaves, 220 ppm." He goes on to note: "Because Upper and Middle Egyptian lands drain back into the main Nile, salinity around Cairo and in the Delta is in excess of 300 ppm. In itself, this is no cause for alarm, but agricultural intensification in Egypt and the Sudan cannot fail to aggravate the problem. Moreover, in developing new water resources from the equatorial lakes and the Jonglei scheme, the White Nile, with a higher salt content than the Blue Nile, will figure prominently in downstream discharge."[10]

That rising salt burden in the waters of reservoirs and rivers leads Victor Kovda to warn that irrigation water itself is now a significant factor in the spread of salinization. "Precipitation water has 10 to 30 mg/l, and sometimes 50 mg/l, of salts and the water may still be considered practically fresh. The best irrigation water from large rivers contains 200 to 500 mg/l of salts. Supplying 10,000 cubic metres of water on 1 hectare of land during the irrigation season deposits 2 to 5 tons/ha of salts in soils. After 10 to 20 years of irrigation, this amount becomes enormous—amounting to dozens and even hundreds of tons per hectare."[11]

THE EXTENT OF THE PROBLEM

The devastation caused by waterlogging and salinization is hard to quantify—partly because there is no agreement as to when land should be classified as "saline". The Pakistan Department of Power and Irrigation, for example, suggests that land should be regarded as "saline" when crop yields have been reduced by a fifth or more. Nonetheless, various figures have been advanced. The FAO estimates that at least 50 percent of the world's irrigated land now suffers from salinization.[12] Others put the figure even higher. Victor Kovda argues that salinization affects 60 to 80 percent of the world's irrigated land, with between 1 million and 1.5 million hectares succumbing every year. Significantly, much of that land is "in irrigated croplands of high potential production."[13]

In Pakistan, 25 million of the 37 million acres under irrigation are estimated to be salinized, waterlogged, or both.[14] Of that land, 5 million acres are classified as "severely affected" with salinity; 10 million as suffering "patchy salinity"; and 10 million as being "poorly drained."[15] Overall, 23 percent of the country's land suffers to varying degrees from salinization or waterlogging, but that figure reaches 80 percent in the Punjab. In the lower Indus, concentrations of salt in the groundwater have been found to reach 30,000 ppm—almost as salty as sea water. A recent survey reported that the water from 18 percent of the tube-wells in the area was "unfit for use"; that 76 percent of the wells produced water which, if used, might "salinize the soil profile to a depth of 6 feet within 12 years"; and that only 6 percent of the wells had water that could be classified as "of excellent quality."[16] All told, an estimated 100,000 acres are lost annually to waterlogging and salinization in Pakistan, more than 100 hectares a day.[17]

Of the area earmarked to receive water via China's giant Yangtse Diversion scheme (see Table 1), 2.7 million hectares already suffer from salinization. "Slightly and moderately saline soils prevail on 73.7 percent of the affected area," Guo Huancheng and Xu Zhikang, of the Institute of Geography of the Academy Sinica, told a conference on the diversion scheme.

> Here the salt concentration generally ranges between 0.1 percent and 0.7 percent, so it is still possible to grow crops. The remaining 26.3 percent of the affected area has a salt concentration exceeding 1 percent and a seedling retention rate below 30 percent. The land is used mostly for livestock and forestry. The extensive saline area in the region is not only unfavorable to current agricultural production, but is also an important problem which must be taken into account in considering a south-to-north water transfer.[18]

Others expressed similar concern about the extent of salinization in the proposed transfer region. Although salinization levels in the area had fluctuated dramatically over the last thrity years, said Xu Yuexian and Hong Jilian, also of the Institute of Geography, overall, the amount of saline land was increasing. Moreover, much of the increase had taken place during the late 1970s—largely, they suggested, due to a rise in water tables alongside those rivers that have recently been dammed. In addition to the 2.7 million hectares already affected, 4.7 million hectares in the area consist of potentially saline soil "which is most vulnerable to secondary salinization if affected by detrimental factors."[19]

In Egypt, the problems of salinization and waterlogging have been termed grave. "A few years ago, an FAO study contended that 35 percent of Egypt's cultivated surface is afflicted by salinity and 90 percent by waterlogging," writes John Waterbury. "A USAID mission reported in 1976 that 4.2 million feddans [1 feddan is equal to 1.038 acres] were undergoing slight to severe effects from inadequate drainage, and unless something were done, all would be severely affected."[20] Waterlogging alone is estimated to have reduced agricultural productivity by at least 30 percent, although it is claimed, perhaps optimistically, that drainage will restore productivity.

More than 50 percent of the 3.6 million hectares under irrigation in Iraq suffer from salinization and waterlogging.[21] Most severely affected are the middle and lower Rafidain Plains. Indeed, Erik Eckholm—at the time a researcher with the Worldwatch Institute—reports that vast areas of South Iraq now "glisten like fields of freshly fallen snow."[22]

In Syria, 500,000 acres, half of the country's irrigated land, are waterlogged or salinized. According to M. M. El Gabaly, "Due to the aridity of the climate, with evaporation exceeding precipitation in many locations, it is estimated that 70 percent of the soils put under irrigation are potentially saline." Nonetheless, plans are afoot to irrigate a further 1.5 million acres of part of the giant Euphrates Project.[23] Annual crop losses due to salinity and waterlogging in the Euphrates Valley alone already amount to $300 million.

In Iran, 15 percent of the irrigated land is affected to some degree by waterlogging, salinity, and alkalinity. Of the country's 16.8 million hectares of arable land, 7.3 million are estimated to be saline, and 8.2 million waterlogged.[24]

In India, the amount of land devastated by water and salt has been variously estimated at between 6 million and 10 million hectares—almost a quarter of the 43 million hectares under irrigation. In Madhya Pradesh, affected areas are referred to as "wet deserts."[25]

For the Near East as a whole, El Gabaly warns: "In all countries of the region, without exception, salinity is of prime concern in agricultural development."[26] Another source estimates that more than 70 percent of the 30 million hectares of irrigated land in Egypt, Iran, Iraq, and Pakistan is now "moderately to severely affected" by salinization.

In the United States, Jan van Schilgaarde, director of the U. S. Salinity Laboratory, considers that 25 to 35 percent of the country's irrigated land suffers from salinity—and that the problem is getting worse. "Today, about 400,000 acres of irrigated farmland in the San Joaquin Valley are affected by high, brackish water tables."[27] If no remedial measures are taken, the valley could lose over a million acres of farmland in the next hundred years.

Worldwide, the annual losses to salinization and waterlogging are staggering. In a survey conducted for the UN Water Conference, Malin Falkenmark and Gunnar Lindh estimated that between 200,000 and 300,000 hectares of irrigated land are taken out of production every year due to the ravages of water and salt. Harold Dregne of Texas Tech puts the figure at 500,000 hectares.[28] The FAO admits merely that "several hundred thousand hectares are abandoned annually as a result of salinization."[29] Indeed, according to one recent study, as much irrigated land is now being taken out of production due to waterlogging and salinization as is being brought into production by new irrigation schemes. If this is correct, then the rate of salinization is much worse than even Dregne's figures suggest.

CAN SALINIZATION AND WATERLOGGING BE AVOIDED?

It is rare indeed to find irrigated areas unscarred by the ecological devastation normally associated with large-scale perennial irrigation schemes. Only where land is well-drained—as in West Texas, for example, where subsoils are particularly permeable—

can the surplus waters drain away sufficiently fast to prevent waterlogging. Such soils, however, are exceptional. Indeed, in almost all the arid areas of the world where irrigation is practiced— the valleys of the Tigris and Euphrates, the Helmand Valley of Afghanistan, or the Imperial and San Joaquin valleys of California, for example—the subsoil is relatively impermeable and down drainage is thus deficient. Inevitably, the surplus waters accumulate, rise, reach the roots of the crops, and eventually make their way to the surface. There they evaporate, leaving behind their deadly saline burden.

According to Kovda, "during many centuries and even millennia, only areas having a free outflow of groundwaters, as in Tashkent and Samarkand, have not undergone salinization or waterlogging."[30] Indeed, irrigated land has been thus degraded with such regularity that Kovda sees "increasing salinity in irrigated soils of arid lands" as being "practically universal."[31] Aloys Michel, whose experience with irrigation projects the world over is vast, goes a step further. As he writes, "Waterlogging and salinity, or both problems, will inevitably arise in all but the truly exceptional surface-water irrigation schemes."[32]

Nevertheless, governments everywhere insist on expanding the amount of land under irrigation. Those who argue that such an extension can only serve to further degrade the environment are assured that the damage of the past will not be repeated in the future. Indeed, the promoters of large-scale irrigation insist that salinization and waterlogging are not the fault of perennial irrigation per se. On the contrary, they claim, these harms result from technical and administrative "mistakes" that can easily be corrected. But is it really possible to avoid waterlogging and salinization in lands watered by large-scale irrigation schemes? And if so, how?

One possibility is to line the irrigation canals, thereby reducing seepage. Unfortunately, the cost of that procedure is truly prohibitive. Moreover, lining irrigation canals does not necessarily reduce *all* seepage. For one thing, the lining does not last indefinitely. For another, its efficiency is largely dependent on regular and thorough maintenance. As we shall see in chapter 12, the standard of maintenance in existing irrigation schemes is extremely low—largely for social rather than technical reasons—and it is unlikely to improve. To fight salinization and waterlogging with technology that cannot work properly without regular maintenance would thus seem foolhardy in the extreme.

Another strategy is to dig tube wells in order to pump out groundwater and thus lower the water table. A large number of such wells have been sunk in Pakistan, China, and elsewhere. However, this is another very costly procedure. In addition, tube wells have a short life span and, like lined irrigation canals, they require regular maintenance. Moreover, where they have been used, as in China, their successes in bringing down the water table appear short-lived. In the three provinces of Hebei, Henan, and Shandong, tube wells—together with improved drainage—helped to reduce the total area of saline land from 1.9 million hectares in the mid-1950s to 1.4 million hectares in the mid-1970s. Over half a million wells were sunk in Hebei alone. By the end of the 1970s, however, the area of saline land in the three provinces had begun once again to increase. By 1979, 1.9 million hectares were officially classified as saline.

Ironically, the excessive use of tube wells can, in itself, intensify the problem of salinization. If the salt balance of underground aquifers is to be maintained, then an aquifer must have not only an inflow of fresh water to dilute its salts and replenish its waters, but also an outflow through which the salty water can be evacuated. If the water table is lowered too far, as has happened in certain parts of the Southwestern United States, then the aquifers may become so depleted that they are cut off from both their points of inflow and their points of outflow. In such circumstances, the aquifers become closed basins within which used irrigation water simply accumulates.

A third method suggested for reducing the rate of salinization is the introduction of "overhead sprinklers." Such sprinklers are said to minimize water use and thus eliminate overwatering as a cause of waterlogging, but they do cause other problems. Discussing the use of sprinklers in Algeria, for instance, Taghi Farvar, of the Centre for the Biology of Natural Systems, told the

1969 "Careless Technology" conference: "Much of the water immediately evaporates when it is sprinkled even before reaching the ground. So you have an increase in the salinity of the water by the time it hits the earth, then the rest of it evaporates and salinizes the soil."[33] Although it has been suggested that the problem can be overcome by irrigating during the night, as is done in Israel, Farvar does not expect this to make much difference in very hot countries. In Algeria, for instance, "the night is very often quite hot, particularly when the sirocco blows." Sprinkler irrigation has also been found to increase pest outbreaks (see chapter 6).

Perhaps the most effective means of combating waterlogging and salinization, however, is the building of drains to remove the excess water. Indeed, irrigation without drainage is now generally perceived as a prescription for ecological disaster. Aloys Michel, for example, argues that "drainage must go hand-in-hand with irrigation," observing that "the provision of an artificial drainage system is an inescapable concomitant of providing an artificial irrigation system."[34] Likewise, Erik Eckholm of the Worldwatch Institute sees irrigation and drainage as "inseparable components of a single system."[35]

Although the essential nature of drainage is now recognized by most of the leading authorities on salinization, governments throughout the world are still building irrigation schemes without installing drains. For example, drainage was never installed in the various irrigation projects set up in the Chambal area of Rajhastan and Madhya Pradesh in India. The soils of the area consist of heavy clay, so waterlogging has quickly developed. In India as a whole, according to M. C. Chaturvedi, only a very small proportion of irrigated land is properly drained.[36]

In Pakistan, with its acute problems of waterlogging and salinization, the government announced elaborate plans for digging tube wells and installing drains throughout the country's irrigated lands. Some tube wells were sunk in the Indus Valley, but the program as a whole never materialized. In New South Wales, Australia, tiled drains have indeed been installed, but only for those irrigated lands under intensive horticulture. Other irrigated crops go undrained.[37]

Even in the San Joaquin Valley, in California, some 60 percent of farmers do not have adequate drainage facilities. Instead of tackling salinization at the source, many farmers simply grow shallow-rooting salt-tolerant crops. In the long term, however, those crops make matters worse. Salt-tolerant they may be, but they still require irrigation, and the saline groundwaters of the region continue their inexorable rise. In some areas, salinization has progressed so far that farmers have simply taken their salt-encrusted lands out of production and intensified the cultivation and irrigation of their remaining fields to make up their losses. Other farmers have converted their most saline fields to "evaporation basins" where the water from the lands that are drained can be dumped.

WHY NO DRAINAGE?

Undoubtedly, one reason for the reluctance of governments to install drainage lies in the expense involved. The UN Food and Agricultural Organization (FAO), for instance, estimates that the installation of effective drainage costs between $200 and $1,000 per hectare of land irrigated.[38] At present, the amount of land under irrigation in the world totals perhaps a little over 200 million hectares, and is said to be increasing at the rate of 2.9 percent a year. In effect, about 5.8 million hectares of land are brought under irrigation every year, but few see that rate continuing. To install drainage for all that land at $200 per hectare would cost $1,160 million; at $1,000 per hectare, the cost would be an astronomical $5,800 million. In 1978, Egypt's minister of irrigation estimated the cost of installing tiled drains in the heavily salinized lands of Upper Egypt and the Delta area would reach some £(E)700 million by 1985–nearly twice the original cost of the Aswan Dam itself.[39] This represents only part of a long-term program that will not be fully implemented until the year 2000.

Since most of the work would have to be carried out in the

Third World, it is unlikely that the vast funds needed to finance such a program will be available. For one thing, in order to make a proposed dam project appear viable, the cost is invariably underestimated. This means leaving out what—to the uninitiated—do not seem to be essential components of the system: drainage, for example. If the true cost of drainage were included, then many water projects would appear to be wholly uneconomical.

Under these circumstances, when building work nears completion, there is little money left for what to politicians, economists, and engineers often seems an irrelevance. Carl Widstrand makes the point forcefully: "Costs for drainage are always underestimated and when irrigation schemes overrun their budgets—which they always do—there is little money or interest left for drainage."[40] He quotes Erik Eckholm's conclusion that "The legacy of this continued defiance of reality is a stupendous loss of global agricultural output."[41]

That "defiance of reality" by governments and their advisers has been encouraged by what has come to be known as the "anti-drainage" lobby. When Egypt announced in 1958 that it intended to introduce main and field drains to all of Egypt's cultivated land, it was persuaded not to do so. According to Azim Abulata, the program was opposed on the grounds that "the cessation of the flood phenomenon due to the storage by the High Dam would lead to a fall in water levels from Aswan to Cairo," which would thus improve the natural flow of drainage water back to the riverbed.[42] It was also claimed that the "low-lift irrigation system" to be employed "would permit excessive use of water thus reducing the quantity of drainage water."

All this was sheer wishful thinking. To find the real reason why the government was willing to abandon the program, one need only look at the estimates of the cost of the project. It was admitted that funds were not available to cover the massive expense of draining all the lands to be brought under perennial irrigation. Perhaps still more to the point is Waterbury's terse comment: "No one ever built a monument to themselves by installing tile drains."[43] Given their essentially political motives for building the Aswan Dam, Nasser and his fellow government officers must have had that in mind.

The antidrainage lobby has been at work not only in Egypt. For example, I. P. Gerasimov of the Institute of Geography at Moscow University asserts that the same lobby was largely responsible for the failure to install drainage in the irrigation schemes of the Golodnaya Steppe, southwest of Tashkent.[44] So, too, Aloys Michel notes the hand of the lobby in the Irrigation Branch of the Punjab Public Works Department during the heyday of the British Raj. The department's experts insisted that drains were unnecessary in the area because lowering the water table would prove detrimental to the working of hundreds of Persian wheels operating in shallow wells. Moreover, they claimed, high water tables permitted the regeneration of water supplies by seepage during the dry season.[45]

More recently, Victor Kovda has singled out the U.S. Salinity Laboratory, in Riverside, California, for similar criticism. Pointing to the successes of the Soviet Union in restoring salinized lands in Azerbaidzhan, Uzbekistan, Tadzhikistan and Turkmenia, he berates the laboratory for ignoring the Soviet experience.

> For 25 to 30 years, this laboratory has rejected indisputable conclusions of the geochemical theory of salt accumulation. It has underestimated the importance of groundwater level and mineralization of the groundwater and properties of saline soils. The concept of critical level, critical regime, and critical mineralization of groundwater is either rejected or ignored. Secondary salinization of soils is attributed mostly to salts of irrigation water, which, in fact, are of secondary importance. The necessity of leaching salts from salty soils independently of seasonal watering and the necessity of desalinization of salty groundwaters are rejected or even misunderstood. The importance of ionic composition of the soluble soils is ignored and a "cult" of electroconductivity as the way to study soil salinity has been followed. . . . Publications of the Riverside Laboratory bypass all these problems, are actually cultivating the idea of a permanent domination of downward flux and overirrigation in order to suppress ascending capillary solutions, and are supporting the antidrainage assumptions of the ad-

vocates of cheap "drainageless irrigation," which, in fact, leads to waterlogging and salinisation.[46]

Indeed, David Sheridan, writing in *Environment*, warns that one million acres of the San Joaquin Valley could become unproductive by the year 2080 unless subsurface drainage systems are installed.[47]

The activities of the "antidrainage" lobbies in other countries can only lead to similar results unless they are successfully countered.

SALINIZATION: THE HISTORICAL EXPERIENCE

In reality, it has been known for a very long time that large-scale water development schemes such as the building of dams and canals will, in hot countries, lead to the salinization of the soil. To make the point, let us briefly consider the Indian experience with large-scale water schemes during the nineteenth century. Our information is derived from Elizabeth Whitcombe's seminal book, *Agrarian Conditions in Northern India.*[48]

After the Indian Mutiny, there began in India a period of large-scale economic development, an important constituent of which was the construction of the Lower Ganges Canal. It opened in March, 1874, and commanded an area of 375,800 acres. At the same time, however, canals were built commanding smaller acreage. Those water development schemes gave rise to precisely the same problems that have been described in this report. Among these problems was salinization, a problem referred to in India as *Reh*.

The increasing incidence of Reh was reported as early as 1871, even before the Lower Ganges Canal was opened by C. H. T. Croswaithe. At the time, the then officiating commissioner of Agra Division, G. H. M. Ricketts, argued that the evils of salinization demanded an immediate remedy. Seven years later, the Reh problem was carefully examined by Lt. Col. A. F. Corbett. By this time it had become very much more serious, especially in parts of Aligarh and Meerut and throughout the

Kali Nadi Valley. Hundreds of acres had already been put out of cultivation, which, as Whitcombe points out, was particularly serious in the highly populated areas of the Ganges Valley since it affected the livelihood of thousands of people.

In each case the damage was correctly imputed to excessive irrigation by canal water. A Reh committee was set up under Sir Edward Charles Buck, Director of Agriculture in the United Provinces. He warned in his 1878 report that the causes of salinization—in particular, waterlogging—were "the first and earliest outcome of the introduction of a canal system."[49] He also pointed out that the same disturbing influences might be at work in many areas. The Reh committee report confirmed Corbett's earlier statements.

The committee also attributed the increase in the amount of Reh-affected land (referred to as *Usar*) to the swamping of the fields for irrigation. Too much water was available. The remedy was to aim for economy in the distribution of water, which could be achieved only by charging more for it. The Canal department could not adopt this recommendation. Its concern was a purely economic one: the price was already high and to increase it further would reduce the revenue accruing from canal charges. The Reh Committee, realizing that prices would never be increased, therefore recommended that wherever possible "lift irrigation" should be substituted for flush irrigation. This would increase the amount of effort required to obtain water and thus discourage unnecessary consumption.

On the basis of experiments that had started in 1874, the Committee also recommended that Usar tracts be reclaimed by careful watering and intensive manuring. Unfortunately, this solution did not appear to be economically feasible—at least not on any extensive scale—and the problem simply got worse. In 1891, Dr. J. A. Voelker, a chemist appointed by the government to report on India's agrarian conditions, writes of finding "enormous tracts, especially in the plains of Northern India" affected by Reh.[50] In the Northwest Provinces alone, between 4,000 and 5,000 square miles were by this time already salinized.

Significantly, Voelker pointed out that in the midst of this desolation could be seen patches of "valuable crops" (by which was meant cash crops for export including opium, sugar cane, wheat, castor oil plants, and cotton). These stood out "like oases in the salt covered desert around them."[51] Small wonder, perhaps, for the canal-irrigated land was almost invariably used for plantation agriculture rather than for producing crops for local consumption.

The building of the West Jumna Canal created similar problems in the area commanded by it. The chief commissioner of the Punjab, for instance, reported that "for some time past it has been known that many villages on the banks of these canals in the Paneeput, Delhi and Rohtuk Districts have been suffering from a destructive saline efflorescence. The accounts of poverty in some of these villages have been quite distressing." He pointed out that "the mischief is increasing yearly" and that it would "soon attain to very considerable proportions and would entail fiscal loss to the government and suffering to the people."[52]

The causes of salinization were already well understood. In a note prepared for the *Journal of the Royal Asiatic Society*, H. B. Medlicott, then professor of the Geological Survey, pointed out that although the canal waters were themselves a source of trouble, they were not the prime cause. It was the salt in the soil itself that played the key part in salinization. Moreover, he maintained, with inefficient drainage and water accumulation, those salts were dissolved and then rose, through capillary action, to the surface, where they remained after the irrigation waters had evaporated. It was, in fact, a very modern analysis of the process of salinization.[53]

Medlicott went on to suggest that the solution lay in using the canal waters to soak the soil thoroughly in order to wash away the salts and establish a groundwater connection. Although today that solution would be frowned upon for ecological reasons, it was rejected then—despite the urgency of the problem—simply because it would have meant reducing the amount of land under irrigation in order to make more water available for flushing out the salts. As Elizabeth Whitcombe points out, Medlicott's blueprint for desalinizing the area was of little interest to the authorities because it "clearly conflicted with the official canal policy of distributing canal water over an increasingly wide command area for revenue purposes." Indeed, the Jumna experience clearly illustrates a recurring theme in this report: how suicidal it is—ecologically, socially, and indeed economically—to allow short-term economic ends to dominate public policy.

Medlicott's diagnosis of the salinization problem was subsequently confirmed by both T. E. B. Brown, then chemical examiner for the Punjab, and Dr. Thomas Anderson, professor of chemistry at Glasgow University. Anderson reported that the cause of the problem was the presence in the soil of "some minerals rich in alkaline, the decomposition of which is prompted by the irrigation water. . . . A large quantity of these substances are converted into a soluble form, and gradually accumulate until they become so abundant as to become noxious to plants."[54] For Anderson, the solution was drainage.

Those early reports—together with subsequent correspondence—reveal, according to Whitcombe, the first "collected documentation of the problem [of Reh] and its scientific analysis."[55] Copies of the various documents were sent to the secretary of state, and three boxes of Reh-affected soil were sent to be examined in the United Kingdom. A further report on Reh-affected lands was then produced by the officiating superintendent engineer of the Punjab, along with the executive engineer (Delhi Division) of the West Jumna Canal. Specimens collected during the research for that report were examined at the Royal School of Mines by W. J. Ward. Technical reports were also sent to provincial administrations in India, and it was recommended that experiments in leaching out salts by applying sufficient water to "wash" the soils should be undertaken. In addition, it was urged that a drainage scheme in the Jumna area should be initiated forthwith. Unfortunately, the governor general—though apparently in agreement with the thrust of the reports—felt he could do no more than sanction a modest research program. As he put it at the time, "the whole operation must necessarily be of an exceedingly simple character."[56]

Although experiments were duly carried out, it was deemed

"uneconomic" to take any long-term action to reclaim salinized soils—a reminder that no remedial action is ever likely to be taken so long as we adhere to conventional economic dogma. It was already well established that salinization was a serious problem, that it could only get worse, that in the long run it would inevitably affect government revenues and cause increased poverty among the populace, and that its primary cause lay in the development of large-scale irrigation schemes. Nevertheless, the government, no doubt hamstrung by the Exchequer, persuaded itself that money spent on reclaiming salinized lands would be money down the drain—except, of course, that there were no drains, wherein lay the main cause of the Reh crisis.

Although there was no doubt about the role of undrained irrigation schemes in furthering salinization, given the experiments carried out by the most prestigious authorities of the time, the government still embarked on such projects. Thus, the building of the Lower Ganges Canal went ahead, between 1873 and 1878, in the clear knowledge that the canal's command areas were affected or threatened by Usar and Reh. No measures were taken, however, to prevent further salinization, nor does any of the experience with previous schemes appear to have influenced the design of the canal in any way.

The Reh Committee presented its report in 1878, the year that the Lower Ganges Canal was opened. In his contribution as superintendent of the Geological Survey, H. B. Medlicott concluded that the cause of salinization involved the "combination of deforestation and evaporation together with the presence and movement of excessive quantities of moisture in the soil."[57]

Denzil Ibbeston, another contributor, objected that the solutions Medlicott proposed were not practical, especially that it was difficult to restore forest cover. Moreover, he argued, flush irrigation, which Medlicott deplored, was official canal policy. It could not, therefore, be changed.[58]

Like previous government investigations of the problem of salinization, the Reh Committee report concluded with a proposal for a modest series of reclamation experiments. As a result, attempts were made to reclaim Usar patches by planting trees for fuel and fodder. Those experiments were rarely successful. Indeed, since the Reh problem could not be solved without compromising short-term economic priorities, little was done, which left a legacy of salinized land, much of it never to be reclaimed. That legacy is a damning indictment of the economic system that produced it—a system that persists today, albeit in modified form, and is still wreaking havoc in the arid lands of the world.

SALINITY AND DOWNSTREAM AGRICULTURE

Paradoxically, the very means for reducing salinization and waterlogging at a local level is counterproductive for those living downstream of the irrigation schemes. The reason is clear enough. Lining irrigation canals, digging tube wells, and introducing drainage are all undertaken to ensure that salts are flushed away from irrigated land in the water. But that salty water must go somewhere. When, as is generally the case, it is returned to the nearest river, the river's salt content will inevitably increase.

In the past, increased salinity did not pose the problem it does today. "Before man began harnessing the rivers," argues Arthur Pillsbury, "the seasonal floods were highly effective in carrying salts to the ocean and keeping the river basin in reasonable salt balance. Today, with river flow being regulated by storage systems, and with high consumptive use of the released water, there is not enough waste flow left to achieve salt balance. The salt is being stored, in one way or another, within the river basins."[59]

For the downstream farmer, the problem is obvious: he must irrigate his land with increasingly saline water. Moreover, if there are cities upstream of him, the water he uses is likely to be contaminated also with domestic waste and industrial chemicals. Furthermore, in heavily developed river basins, much of the river's water will have been extracted before it even reaches him, and the flow of the river will have been considerably reduced—in many cases to the extent that it can no longer prevent the intrusion of sea water into the delta. Indeed, in some river basins, notably in Bangladesh, sea water has been known to intrude up to

100 kilometers inland. Small wonder, perhaps, that downstream farmers in arid lands everywhere are finding their livelihood increasingly threatened.

Consider, for example, the situation in Mexico. Northern Mexico is partly dependent for its water supply on two "shared" rivers, the Colorado and the Rio Grande, both of which flow first through the southwestern United States. Unfortunately for Mexico, the southwestern United States, in recent years, has seen an enormous expansion in irrigated agriculture. Approximately forty million acres are now under irrigation, and given the high evaporation rates, even good-quality water can be used only twice before it becomes too brackish for agriculture.

Disposing of that brackish water is proving increasingly difficult. One method is to divert excess water into "evaporation basins," where the salts can be left to accumulate. In that respect, the farmers of southern California are particularly fortunate. Much of the saline water from the farms in the Imperial Valley, where more than 500,000 acres are under irrigation, is channeled for eighty miles via the All-American Canal into the naturally salty, inland Salton Sea (see figs. 2 and 3). That sea, whose waters are almost as salty as sea water, also receives water from the 65,000 acres irrigated by the Coachella Canal. All told, 90 percent of the surface water entering the Salton Sea is waste water from agricultural land.

Few agricultural areas have access to a Salton Sea, and where no natural salt "sink" exists, artificial evaporation basins have been built. Those basins, however, do not—and cannot—provide a lasting solution to the salt problem. "Such schemes, designed to store salts in the river basins themselves, may work for a few years or decades but they are bound to be disastrous in the long term," notes Pillsbury.[60] In particular, they are almost certain to result in the contamination of groundwaters.

That problem, says Pillsbury, cannot be avoided. For one thing, saline water rapidly breaks down soils that are impermeable to fresh water, thereby rendering them permeable. Thus, building evaporation basins even on impermeable land will not prevent the long-term contamination of groundwaters. Nor, says

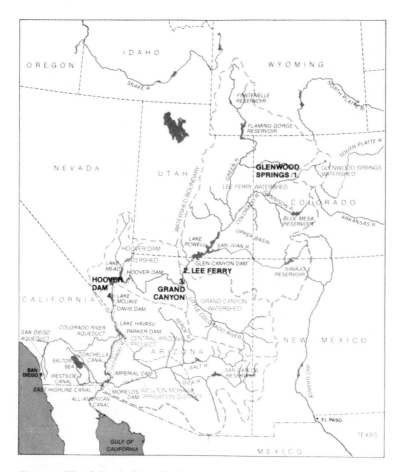

Figure 2. The Colorado River Basin

SOURCE: *Scientific American*, July 1981, p. 40.

Pillsbury, can that problem be circumvented by lining basins with an impervious material such as rubber or plastic, asphalt, or even special concrete. "Conceivably, such linings will be effective for as long as 50 years, but ultimately, one expects them to fail. In all probability, their lifetime when they are exposed to saline water will be shorter than their lifetime is when they are exposed to fresh water, for which they are normally tested."[61] Finally, the damage caused through groundwater contamination cannot—as some have argued—be minimized by placing evaporation basins

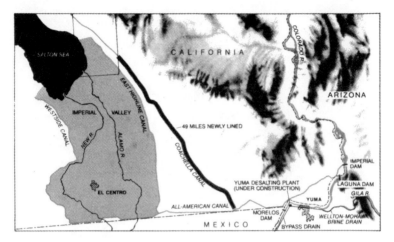

Figure 3. The All-American Canal

SOURCE: *Scientific American*, July 1981, p. 34.

over already saline groundwaters. "Every groundwater basin
with a flow gradient must have an outlet somewhere near its lower
end. The saline water in the evaporation basin will serve to increase the 'head,' or hydraulic pressure, on the saline waters below, and will thereby increase the rate of discharge at the natural
outlet, wreaking havoc in downstream groundwaters and downstream lands."

Apart from evaporation basins, the other principal means of
disposing of waste irrigation waters is via long-distance drainage
canals. Thus, in southern California, a 290-mile-long "master
drain" has been half-built—at an estimated cost of more than
$1.2 billion—in order to take the waste waters from the San Joa-
quin Valley directly to the Pacific. One canal will serve 500,000
acres and will have the capacity to move more than three million
tons of salt every year. Inevitably, the dumping of such massive
quantities of salt will cause untold ecological damage within the
bays and estuaries where the canals meet the sea.

Moreover, we cannot be sure that long-distance drainage canals actually avoid the further salinization of water tables. Indeed,
Pillsbury argues that such salinization is avoidable only where the
water table is semiperched—that is, isolated from the deeper,

main body of groundwater. "Under those conditions there is little opportunity for the irrigation water, enriched in salts, to percolate downward and degrade the deep ground water, which remains available for irrigation or other uses." In the valley lands, however, "the subterranean structure is such that near-surface water cannot be isolated from deeper water, with the result that ditch or tile-drain systems are powerless to preserve the quality of the ground water."

In the meantime, the Colorado River and the Rio Grande—which, between them, receive most of the drainage water from the surrounding agricultural lands—are becoming increasingly saline. Salt concentrations in the Rio Grande, for instance, have increased from 221 to 1,691 ppm in recent years. As for the Colorado, if salinity levels continue to rise at their present rate, by the year 2010 the economic cost in terms of lost production and declining water quality will have exceeded $1.24 billion.[62]

Under the terms of a joint treaty signed in the early 1970s between Mexico and the United States, the U.S. government agreed to reduce the salinity levels of waters entering Mexico. To that end, a massive desalinization plant is being built at Yuma, Arizona, on the Mexican border. The plant is designed to treat 107,000 acre-feet of water (with an average salinity level of 2,800 ppm) a year; 92,000 acre-feet of water with a salinity of less than 800 ppm will thus be provided to Mexico. Originally priced at $300 million, the plant is now expected to cost more than one billion dollars. At that price, irrigation water provided by the plant will cost some $800 per acre-foot—more than thirty-five times the current cost of irrigation water in the Imperial Valley.

It is now quite clear that the Yuma desalinization plant will not by itself even begin to solve the water and salt problems facing the Southwest. Indeed, several other, much more ambitious schemes have been proposed for the area. Although those schemes are certainly intended to provide water for flushing out excess salts from the soil, their primary purpose is undoubtedly to further the extension of irrigated agriculture. All involve importing vast quantities of water from other parts of the United States, and, due largely to the government's concern for its escalating budgetary deficit, all have run up against financial problems. Indeed, with local taxpayers unwilling to meet even a part of the vast costs of the projects—and available federal funds diminishing—two of the schemes have already been vetoed as too expensive. No doubt, however, those vetoes will be reconsidered if and when economic conditions become more propitious.

One proposal is addressed to the Peripheral Canal project, which would bring water from northern California rivers around the San Francisco Bay Delta and down to southern California at an initial cost of between $700 million and $1.3 billion. It was voted down in a statewide referendum in 1982.

Another is the Texas Water System, which is intended to provide water to the arid and semiarid west of Texas. The scheme involves the building of a system of reservoirs and interbasin water transfer facilities in eastern and central Texas; a coastal aqueduct stretching some 400 miles from the Sabine River to the Lower Rio Grande Valley; and a trans-Texas canal stretching mainly uphill from Northeast Texas to the High Plains, with a branch running to New Mexico and another to the trans-Pecos area. Much of the 17.3 million acre-feet of water that would run through those canals annually would come from the Mississippi (some 12 million to 13 million acre-feet per year) and would have to cross Louisiana before entering Texas. Because the course of the canal would be largely uphill, almost two-fifths of the state's total electricity supply (as of 1970) would be needed to pump the water along the canal. Like the Peripheral Canal scheme, the Texas Water System has been vetoed by local taxpayers, who simply refused to finance a $3.5 billion bond issue to fund the project.

Another proposal is the North American Water and Power Alliance (NAWAPA). Proposed by the Ralph M. Parsons Company of Pasadena, California, the NAWAPA scheme is one of the most ambitious of all time (see fig. 4). It would divert water from Alaska and northern Canada to various parts of Canada, the United States, and Mexico. Hydroelectric plants built along the giant canal would provide—over and above what would be required for pumping—a surplus electricity capacity of 70,000 megawatts, output equivalent to that of 70 large nuclear power stations. The drainage area of the scheme would be 1.3 million square miles, and 160 million acre-feet of water would be diverted southward for irrigation and "waterway control." The estimated cost of the project is $200 billion, which suggests that the final cost could well be three to four times higher.

Clearly the environmental destruction that would be caused by the NAWAPA scheme would be enormous. Moreover, the scheme is likely to be strenuously opposed by Alaska and Canada, who do not take kindly to the idea of their waters being diverted to the Southwest. Indeed, it seems that there is little chance of the NAWAPA project ever getting off the drawing board.

Nonetheless—and this is particularly significant—Pillsbury insists that without the NAWAPA scheme, the future of the Southwest is extremely precarious. In his opinion, it is quite simply "the only concept advanced so far that will enable the lower reaches of western rivers to achieve the salt balance necessary for the long-term health of western agriculture, on which the entire United States and indeed the world has much dependence. Unless the lower rivers are allowed to reassert their natural function as exporters of salt to the ocean, today's productive lands will eventually become salt-encrusted and barren."[63]

We should also consider the situation in Sind, Pakistan, condemned by geography to being a "sink" for the whole Indus River valley. As a result of economic development wthin both Afghanistan and the Punjab, the two upstream states that also share it, the Indus is becoming increasingly polluted. Although the Tarbela Dam is intended to ensure a supply of 92 million acre-feet of good-quality water to the Sind, few experts expect the dam to provide a permanent solution to the problem. Indeed, even with the dam, it will be necessary to mine the extensive groundwater reservoirs beneath the Punjab. After the year 2000, however, that supply is likely to start running out, although some twenty million acre-feet per year of groundwater recharge will still be available. At that point, it will be only a question of time before the inevitable happens: "Sooner or later, the concentration of salts, due to repeated capillary rise and evaporation followed by repeated ir-

Figure 4. The North American Water and Power Alliance Proposals

SOURCE: *Scientific American*, July 1981, p. 42.

rigation and leaching, is bound to increase . . . downstream."[64]
The only solution—or, rather, palliative—would be to "export"
that highly saline water directly to the sea or to allow it to accumulate in sinks along the desert margins. The cost of either undertaking would be enormous. Not surprisingly, Aloys Michel
concludes that such wasteways "are likely to be postponed." If so,
it is hard to see how further salinization in the area can be
avoided.

Like Sind Province, Iraq is at the tail-end of a shared water
supply. The River Euphrates must pass through both Turkey and
Syria before it crosses into Iraq. Until the end of the Second
World War, only Iraq abstracted water in any quantity from the
river. Since then, however, both Syria and Turkey have put up
large dams—the Keban Dam in Turkey, for one, and the Taba-
qua Dam in Syria—in order to exploit fully the waters of the Euphrates. In the sixties, both countries together abstracted 16,000
million cubic meters a year, which, at that time, represented 45
percent of the average annual discharge of the Euphrates into
Iraq. Should plans to build new dams in all three riverine states
go ahead, then, according to Professor Peter Beaumont, of Ban-
gor University, "the likely demand for water will be in excess of
the available flow of the river."[65] Inevitably, Iraq will suffer most;
very little water will be left for its use and what water there is will
have high salt and pollution loads. One consequence will be a
corresponding fall in the quantity and quality of food produced
in the area.

This dilemma is not unique to the Middle East. South Australia is one of the driest states in what is probably the driest continent in the world. Sixty-six percent of its water supply is derived
from the Murray River—and that figure rises to approximately
83 percent in a dry season. Before the Murray reaches South
Australia, it flows first through the states of Victoria and New
South Wales, which together contribute 64 percent of the 1.1
million tons of salt carried by the river each year. Thanks to abstraction for irrigation, domestic consumption, and industrial
use, the amount of water reaching South Australia has been
drastically reduced. Moreover, what water does arrive is seriously

polluted with agricultural and industrial wastes. South Australia has no say in controlling that pollution—nor is there any inter-state body that could enforce pollution controls upon the two of-fending upstream states. Thus, the Murray River Committee, to which all three states send representatives, has responsibility only for allocating the amount of water used by each of the river-ine states. It has no power to ensure the quality of the Murray's waters. Indeed, in 1980, the New South Wales representative on the committee officially stated: "Water pollution control in South Australia is a matter for that state alone."[66]

The groundwater in South Australia is naturally saline; in some cases, it is saltier than sea water. Inevitably, as irrigation water seeps back into the Murray, it brings with it much of the salt in that groundwater. In an attempt to overcome that problem, tiled drains were installed underneath irrigated lands, the water being pumped from them into evaporation basins on the river flats. Those basins were not watertight, however, and highly sa-line water is already seeping out of them into the Murray. Fur-thermore, the basins are not large enough to hold all the saline water from the state's irrigation schemes. The rest is thus re-leased directly into the river. Saline water is also reported to be seeping from the basins into the water table, leading to the for-mation of "groundwater mounds" from which there is further seepage into the Murray.

With ever greater demands being made on the waters of the Murray River for domestic, agricultural, and industrial purposes, the river's flow is inevitably being reduced. Since the amount of salt carried by the river tends to remain constant—at about 3,000 tons a day—salinity can only increase. The prospects are grim. "In an uncertain economic climate and in the face of rising sa-linity levels and increasing demand for good water for metro-politan Adelaide, the farmer's future looks decidedly shaky," comments Michael Butler, a geographer at Adelaide College. In-deed, he warns: "Irrigated lands will eventually be abandoned and farmers will lose a way of life."[67]

That last comment could apply to any of the examples we have considered. Indeed, by opting for technological solutions to what are essentially ecological problems, the further salinization of lands throughout the world is ensured. In effect, we have become trapped on a technological treadmill, which can only bring about long-term ecological destruction. The experience of the U.S. Southwest is, as we have seen, particularly eloquent. In their thirst for water, the inhabitants of the Southwest have sunk tube wells and built huge reservoirs. In the fight against salinization, America has spent a fortune on technological measures such as less prosperous countries can ill afford: lined irrigation canals, horizontal drains, and evaporation basins. Now that those measures have failed to solve the Southwest's water and salinization crisis, the search for new "technical" fixes has become more desperate. River basin transfers and the development of genetically engineered salt-tolerant crops have become the order of the day, but at what financial—let alone ecological—cost? Sooner or later, the technical fixes will end; even now, as we have seen, many are proving too costly to implement, especially the massive water transfer schemes proposed for the area. The future is thus bleak for the U.S. Southwest—as, indeed, it is for Sind, Iraq, and South Australia. How long will it be before vast areas of those regions are abandoned, their best farmlands transformed into uninhabited salt-encrusted deserts?

12. Management and Maintenance—Perennial Problems

IT IS GENERALLY AGREED that the performance of most large-scale irrigation schemes in the Third World has been very poor. Dr. Anthony Bottrall, of the Overseas Development Institute, for instance, notes: "Planners' targets are rarely met: the overall productivity of water is much lower than might be expected and, especially on large surface-water delivery systems, the pattern of its distribution is often extremely inequitable, with farmers in the head-reaches receiving far more than those at the tail, whose supplies (if they get any at all) tend to be sparse and unreliable."[1]

So too, Bruce Stokes, then at the Worldwatch Institute, warned, "unless farm-level management improves [in irrigation schemes], efforts to rapidly increase food production by expanding irrigation will founder."[2] Indeed, in India, vast areas of irrigated land lie idle for want of the appropriate management and maintenance.

Asit Biswas also notes the poor performance of irrigation schemes. He quotes the conclusion of a 1981 World Bank study of thirty irrigated projects in fifteen countries:

> Overall, water management . . . was found to have received inadequate attention. Insufficient provisions for the systems' operations and maintenance were made at appraisal, and insufficient action was taken during implementation. Analysis of water management issues in completion and audit reports—as well as in the appraisal reports—tended to be incomplete or superficial; quantitative data were sparse and fragmentary . . . water supply proved inadequate in ten cases, unreliable in six, and inequitable in three; water losses proved excessive in five.[3]

Significantly, Biswas comments, "From my personal experience in the developing countries of Africa, Asia and Latin America, the criticisms leveled by the World Bank study are unfortunately commonplace." Rightly or wrongly, he attributes much of the problem of salinization to poor management.

Likewise, James E. Nickum, professor of Asian studies and agricultural economics at Cornell University, attributes the spread of secondary salinization in China to poor management. He points out that the national press is often critical, that it condemns in particular "emphasizing construction to the neglect of management" and "only grasping construction without regard for effectiveness."[4] Indeed, as early as 1963, an editorial in the *People's Daily* estimated that some 6.7 million hectares of irrigated land were going uncultivated due to poor management.

More recently, the management of the giant Bishihang Irrigation Department in northern China has been taken to task for lax supervision. A report on its performance noted that "there is no unified, authoritative, sound management for the irrigation district as a whole, making it impossible to do a good job of managing this kind of large-scale irrigation district." The report listed some of the more obvious management failures: "Technical personnel are lacking and some canal structures and projects have no one to manage them once they have been brought into service. The people who do manage some of the projects actually damage them because they do not understand their technology."[5]

In a similar vein, agronomists in Henan Province complained that "the necessary ancillary projects had not been added to ten large reservoirs built in the 1950s, or to the recently installed 110,000 tube wells, leaving the province's irrigated acreage 2.7 million hectares below its potential."[6]

Professor Nickum learned from colleagues at a recent symposium on Long-Distance Water Transfer Schemes that poor management in China had led to the following general problems:

1. Farmers in the upper reaches use too much water and those in the lower reaches do not receive enough.

2. Though good results are achieved in experimental areas, they are nothing like as good elsewhere. The peasants do not adopt the methods proposed. They regard drainage as too expensive.

3. Poor management has led to salinization in some parts of the North China Plain—principally through excessive seepage from irrigation canals. That rate is indeed high, reaching 45 percent in the People's Victory Canal system, for instance, and over 50 percent in the channels of the Shijin Canal system.

4. Too little water is used to irrigate too much land. This means that water in the main canals remains there for 300 days a year, keeping the water table high.[7]

That those problems should have been encountered in China is particularly significant, since the Chinese agricultural system has frequently been held up as a model for the rest of the world.

The problem of inefficient management in water development schemes is now so widespread that Dr. Robert Chambers of Sussex University has even talked of the need to "manage those who manage the water."[8] A recent workshop on irrigation management, run by the Overseas Development Institute, also noted the poor management of irrigation schemes. In particular, it was argued that such schemes suffer from "inefficient finance and staffing for operation and maintenance; minimal training of irrigation staff in operational procedures; grossly inadequate provision of agricultural extension staff; and slow uptake of water by farmers, leading to much wastage."[9] Participants in the workshop also reported a high incidence of water disputes in large-scale irrigation schemes. In the Chimborazo irrigation district of Ecuador, where such disputes are common, it was reported that water use efficiency was as low as 27 percent. Similar problems are also evident in the area served by the Ganges-Kobadak project in Bangladesh.

MANAGEMENT AND MAINTENANCE: A LOW-PRIORITY CONCERN

One of the most obvious reasons for the poor performance of water projects is that little attention is ever paid to the problems of management and maintenance by those who design and construct such schemes. Thus Bottrall notes:

> The planning and design process tends to be dominated by technical experts (especially engineers), with economists being called in to calculate the costs and benefits of what is technically (but not necessarily socially or administratively) feasible. [Moreover:] In their justification of a project, planners will assume certain future cropping patterns; but (with a population of numerous independent farm operators) what administrative mechanisms will be used to induce widespread adoption of these cropping patterns? What procedures will be used for allocating water? What specialized staff-training programs will be required to apply these procedures and provide farmers with advice on field-level water

management? Few planning reports supply more than vague or routine answers to these questions.[10]

This does not seem to be unusual. Chambers cites a multivolume planning report for a major irrigation project in Sri Lanka that devotes no more than one and a half pages to organization and management.[11]

Once millions of pounds are spent on constructing an irrigation scheme, surely it makes sense to ensure that it is properly operated and maintained? Why then do the promoters of large-scale irrigation schemes—and the governments that back them—consistenly ignore the problem of management? Are we to conclude that the promoters of such schemes are interested in only the political and economic capital to be derived from actually building a dam or irrigation project? Once the dam has been built, there are few kudos to be gained from seeing it is properly run, and the temptation is thus to view management and maintenance as the responsibility of the next government to come into power.

BUREAUCRATIC IGNORANCE

Poor management and maintenance are also explained in terms of the basic ignorance of the bureaucrats who are called upon to assure the smooth running of irrigation schemes. Carl Widstrand, for instance, points out how the assumptions underlying the administration of large-scale irrigation works "are never based on sound knowledge."[12] He provides an interesting illustration from the Gezira scheme's *Handbook of New Personnel*, published in 1951, which surprisingly enough was still being used in 1980. The *Handbook* recommends:

> Before any irrigation is embarked upon a number of particulars must be ascertained beforehand. Having decided it is possible to grow certain types of crops, the volume of water required to bring these crops to maturity must be determined with due regard to all circumstances; this is known as the water duty. . . . It may be that the precise water duty in the Gezira is not yet unanimously agreed

upon, but an overall figure of 30 cubic meters per feddan per day seems fairly safe for design purposes [of canals].

Broadly speaking, the agriculturalists have found that a volume of 400 cubic meters of water is required in the Gezira on each feddan of cotton every month during the dry season. Also that, on average, each feddan of cotton should be watered every 15 days. Though this applies primarily to cotton, it suffices for other crops such as *dura* and *lubia*.

That quote was first singled out for comment by Tony Barnett in an article on the Gezira scheme in 1977. The operative phrases he singles out are "for design purposes" and "broadly speaking."[13] Widstrand goes even further: "No one obviously knows anything about the known behaviour of cotton and, if they do, it is not put at the service of the cultivators. Irrigation technicalities, rather than agricultural realities, seem to determine decisions about watering."[14]

The contrast between modern methods of "management" and the running of a vernacular irrigation system could not be sharper. Indeed, Widstrand admits, "the peasant has very much more knowledge of local conditions than the local administration." For instance, often the peasant "knows that the new methods will not work" and refuses to accept "recommendations based on the latest scientific knowledge." This "creates an instant conflict between the cultivator, who knows his environment and who knows how to manipulate it, and the government extension, who does not understand that the peasant lives by his wits and not by his hands alone."

The peasant realizes, in particular, that the rules set up by the administration are crude and inflexible—partly so that they can be implemented by distant bureaucrats with no knowledge of local conditions. Again, the Gezira scheme provides a case in point. Water is allocated according to what Widstrand calls the "average" principle, which he defines as meaning "that 'the average' farmer gets an 'average' amount of water for an 'average' crop over the year. Everybody gets water over the year, but not necessarily at the precise or necessary moments. This concept is closely related to the idea of 'normal rainfall' and other peculiarities in the 'Folklore of the Normal' that simplifies administrative thought."

By contrast, in those traditional societies where irrigation is practiced, water tends to be distributed to farmers in accordance with the requirements of the actual land they farm. The system is flexible enough to make sure that their actual crop, not just their average crop over the years, is watered. The irrigation cycle is also carefully synchronized at a village level in such a way that the water is provided exactly when and where it is required, thereby enabling the system to deal with periods of abnormal rainfall. Indeed, a traditional system is above all subtle. Small wonder, perhaps, for it is run by people who have been imbued since childhood with the traditional knowledge required for its operation and maintenance.

LACK OF ACCOUNTABILITY

A further shortcoming is the lack of accountability. If anything goes wrong, excuses are always found; no one in the administration is held responsible. Bruce Stokes of the Worldwatch Institute considers that this failing is particularly apparent where irrigation systems are state-owned. "With no individual accountability," he writes, "those at the head of the canal often withdraw more than their share of water, adversely affecting all the farmers in the system."[15]

That lack of accountability also favors corruption, which unfortunately seems to be a feature of bureaucratically run irrigation systems throughout the whole world. The most readily discernible form of corruption is favoritism toward farmers who are members of the ruling political party to the detriment of those who are not. We have been told locally that this is very much the case, for example, where new land has been brought under irrigation in Sri Lanka.

Such corruption can take many forms. As Bottrall points out:

Even in the best-managed irrigation projects, operating staff are likely to be subjected to strong pressures from farmers to supply them with more water than they are entitled to; and these farmers may often have powerful local political backing. If the operating agency is to meet its objectives, staff must therefore be able and willing to impose discipline on competing pressure groups by applying rules impartially and penalising those who break them. In fact, staff often give way to the pressures placed on them, in the absence of strong commitment at high levels to meet the agency's [stated] objectives, and the result in the worst cases can be a degeneration into "water anarchy," in which disproportionately large amounts of water go to farmers who are more influential and/or favourably located near the head of the system. The staff's difficulties are compounded when controlled operation of the water delivery system is hampered by design deficiencies.[16]

Widstrand notes: "Irrigation staff are . . . subject to strong pressures, threats and inducements. This leads to what we, in our Calvinistic approach to life, call corrupt practices." Indeed, not only is corruption common, it is sometimes so necessary for survival that it has become an accepted part of life. As he describes it:

> The gate keeper may be persuaded to open the gate to let more water through; the gauge reader may underreport the amount of water taken; the overseer may install large watercourse outlets. The assessors [patwaris] in the Pakistani system assess each farmer twice a year for each crop. They are supposed to reduce the possibility of corruption, but as the assessment procedures and the water rates to be paid are so mysterious, the person who cannot fill in the right forms or does not know his rights is very much in the hands of the patwari.[17]

The influence of large landowners over tenants who require water can be considerable. In the Punjab, for instance, according to Ashfag Mizra, farmers are so used to being victimized that they consider fairness in dealings with an official to be a favor in itself.[18]

THE PROBLEMS OF MAINTENANCE

If the management of water development schemes in the Third World is nearly always deficient, so too is the maintenance. It is not easy to find the appropriate technicians or spare parts, as is well illustrated by Tanzania's experience with simple, small-scale water supply schemes.[19] As Widstrand reports, some of those schemes actually came to a complete halt "because the technical advice available could not serve every scheme at the time the service was needed." Thus, "there was only one technician, whose visits were constrained by lack of transport to reach the schemes and to deliver the materials, and by the necessity to spend two or three days with one scheme before entrusting the work to the local mechanics. Also, materials could not reach the scheme in time, because they had to be purchased in Tanga or Dar es Salaam."[20]

It has also been pointed out by Drs. Heijnen and Conyers that pumps are often out of order and repairs are delayed indefinitely because of the shortage of qualified technicians and funds.[21] To overcome that problem, Widstrand suggests, the organization of maintenance work should be decentralized, but it is difficult to see how decentralization will solve the shortage of technicians. It is even less likely to help overcome the problem of finance; funds are less likely to be available at the local level than in the large cities.

Dr. N. A. De Ridder suggests that minor repairs and maintenance work be left to the villagers. Although the villagers will have other preoccupations, De Ridder asserts they must be taught how to use their wells. "Unless this is done and some form of maintenance is organized, there is little hope for a long lifetime for the wells provided by the project."[22]

Outright vandalism has also been a major problem in areas where technology is still a novelty. In East Africa, for example, taps, valves, and pipes are often stolen during construction to be used elsewhere or sold in the market. In India too, reports Salisbury, the brass fittings are often stolen from pumps because they are useful for making pots and pans.[23] Such household items obviously play a more direct role in the lives of the local peasantry than do the largely irrelevant machines from which the brass is removed. The Indian authorities responded by making pumps and other equipment out of cast iron, a material with which local blacksmiths were unacquainted. The result was that 80 percent of the 50,000 cast-iron wells in drought-prone, hard-rock areas broke down and ceased to produce water.[24]

COOPERATION AND MAINTENANCE

The above examples illustrate the basic failure of the authorities to obtain the cooperation of the peasants who must operate water development schemes. This could not contrast more starkly, as we shall see, with the way tribesmen or peasants closely cooperate with one another in the operation and maintenance of traditional irrigation systems.

But why should tribesmen and peasants cooperate with the authorities? In effect, they are being asked to behave in a way that is totally contrary to everything they have learnt since childhood. Indeed, it is only through systematically destroying the cultural pattern of peasants and tribal farmers that traditional cultivators can be introduced—with any success—into the market system.[25] We have already seen, in our chapter on resettlement, how the Sri Lankan government is using the Mahaweli scheme to transform its peasantry from subsistence farmers into "modern agriculturalists."

Another example of the same trend is provided by the plan of the government of Zaire to create a "paysannat indigène." The government was quite explicit about its goals, as George Kay points out:

> It was decided . . . that, in addition to normal extension work, an "impact scheme" should be introduced whereby progresssive individuals could be relieved of the economic and social difficulties of village life and equipped with the land, capital and technical assistance necessary to enable them to become advanced commercial farmers in a very short time. The object of the scheme was to facilitate the development of commercial farming and rural prosperity by creating a nucleus of proficient peasant farmers who would, by their example, inspire others to improve their farming and seek their living from the land.[26]

That undertaking, like many similar ones, failed, the failure being blamed "on the stupidity of the farmers who did not want to become progressive."[27] The peasants were seen as incompetent, lazy and incapable of following government instructions.

In fact, the whole scheme might be said to have been doomed from the start. What the Zairean government referred to so disparagingly as "the economic and social difficulties of village life" were the very mores that for generations had governed local behavior. Those customs were essential for maintaining the integrity and stability of the villagers' society and their environment. To abandon those customs was to violate every law previously enforced by their elders and sanctioned by their community. Small wonder, then, that the tribesmen of the area refused to cooperate. To have done so would have destroyed their culture, their families, and their communities, and would have left them as despised and badly paid members of a depressed rural proletariat. It is regrettable that so many development theorists still look upon the cultural dictates of traditional societies as unfortunate restrictions on individual freedom and impediments to the free interchange of goods and services, with no intrinsic merit.

THE CONFLICT BETWEEN FOOD AND CASH CROPS

In addition to being asked to accept the eradication of their culture, the traditional cultivators uprooted by water development schemes are also being asked to jeopardize their very security. As Widstrand points out, "government is interested in marketable surplus"; farmers, on the other hand, "may be more concerned with survival and thus prefer to grow food crops or pay more attention to other crops than the cash crops of the scheme or program."[28]

In Egypt, for example, a conflict has arisen "between the government's cotton and the farmer's bread."[29] If the peasant cooperates with the government and produces cotton, he will have to sell to the government at a price that is only a fraction of the world market price. How, then, can he acquire food for himself and his family—food that he is no longer allowed to produce by himself? Moreover, to produce cash crops, he needs fertilizer and pesticides and irrigation water, all of which are often beyond his means.

The history of development in the Third World is replete with similar accounts of what happens when villagers and peasant farmers are forced to enter the cash economy. John Gretton of the London-based Earthscan organization describes a large-scale agricultural scheme in Senegal in which the peasants were asked to grow rice under irrigation, rather than the more traditional millet. The scheme failed dismally, and only one-third of the rice fields were harvested. "Though rice is more productive than millet, the peasants were unused to cultivating rice and resented the additional work involved," reports Gretton. "In addition, there were the problems of switching from a subsistence to a cash-crop economy. People found themselves unable to pay even the cost of fuel for the irrigation pumps. They had to borrow money, which could mean an ever-growing debt."[30] This pattern is being repeated throughout the Third World today, wherever the market economy has been imposed on subsistence farmers.

THE ADVANTAGES OF TRADITIONAL IRRIGATION SYSTEMS

Anthony Bottrall, who perhaps more than anyone else has studied the deficiencies of management in water development projects, suggests that the only solution to the problem is to use traditional irrigation systems as a model for new schemes. "In contrast to the large, publicly operated systems," he writes, "the communal systems are generally well organized: man-management is not one of their problems."[31] He cites E. Walter Coward, who points to three important features common to most indigenous communal irrigation systems:

(i) They have an "accountable leadership": leaders of each local group are selected by members of that group, their performance is periodically reviewed by them, and they are compensated for their services directly by the group.

(ii) The systems, although themselves small, are usually subdivided into smaller subunits, each with its own leader: "management intensity" is very high. Moreover, each of these "mini-units" corresponds to a discrete physical subsection of the larger system.

(iii) The systems are rarely coterminous with village boundaries: they are channel-based, not village-based. Attempts by outside agencies to organize local irrigation groups on a village basis may, therefore, often run into difficulties.[32]

Coward admits that indigenous irrigation systems can be improved in many ways, but he observes that "it has been a common experience . . . that governments' attempts to incorporate communal systems into large projects tend to lead to the disintegration of previously dynamic water users' groups, because they lose most of their original responsibilities in the process and are given no new ones to take their place."[33]

In recent times water-user associations have been set up very successfully—in Taiwan, for instance—but efforts to introduce them in Southeast Asia have failed.[34] Nickum claims the Chinese have achieved certain successes in this field, but the most recent book on large-scale water development in China does not seem to bear this out.[35] One of the problems is the difficulty of creating an efficient association of water users out of nothing. Widstrand admits that "groups cannot be conveniently structured or produced, and blanket government decrees to start such groups do not work."[36] He cites as an example "the death rate" of government-introduced cooperatives in East Africa, but such schemes are still being tried out in Bangladesh, India, Indonesia, and Malaysia.

Here we come to the crux of the matter. "To be successful," writes Ian Carruthers, "planned irrigation technology transfer must include not only the hardware but also the software of services, institutions and attitudes."[37] Those attitudes must include the motivation, the ability to cooperate, and the knowhow to manage and maintain an irrigation system—qualities that have, historically, been provided only by the cultural pattern of a traditional society.

Indeed, where no traditional cultural mechanism exists, either to assure cooperation or to provide the knowhow to practice irrigation agriculture, it is very difficult to ensure the smooth running of an irrigation system—let alone its proper maintenance. René Millon points out, for instance, that when in 1927 the Hacienda de Arroyo de Enmedio, near Guadalajara, Mexico, was divided among farmers from a number of different communities, the farmers "were unable to agree to act in concert to keep these lands under irrigation." As a result, "the irrigation system was allowed to fall into disrepair. The villagers involved were unable to cope with the problems posed by the necessity for intervillage cooperation."[38]

There is also the problem of introducing an irrigation system to a society that has no cultural tradition of irrigation, as Wolf Roder points out. When irrigation technology was first introduced to the Shona of Eastern Rhodesia by European settlers at the turn of the century, he notes, "the absence of a tradition of customary concepts of water allocation and of community cooperation in maintaining canals hampered the development of this form of agriculture. As is so often the case, diffusion of technological innovation outran the ability of the social traditions to adjust."[39] Many similar examples can be cited.

The question, then, is how to learn from the experience of traditional irrigation societies. In Part V of this book we look at five such societies. As we shall see, all of them have proved themselves capable not only of managing and maintaining their irrigation works, but, most important of all, of doing so without precipitating the ecological and social destruction caused by most modern water development schemes.

13. Loss of Land and Food to Plantations

THE CASH-CROP ECONOMY

As we have seen, the main justification for building large-scale irrigation projects is to increase food supplies, in light of the world's appalling burden of famine and malnutrition. It may come as something of a surprise, therefore, that the majority of irrigation projects are not used to grow food for local consumption; on the contrary, they are cultivated with cash crops for export.

One reason, undoubtedly, lies in the vast expense of irrigating land. Large-scale irrigation schemes require hundreds, and sometimes thousands, of millions of dollars to set up. Although the initial investment may be borrowed at advantageous rates from the various development banks, it has still been borrowed and must therefore—in theory at least—be paid back. With the average cost of irrigating one hectare of land in 1980 running at between $1,900 and $3,100 (Syria's Balik Basin project faces a bill of $11,000 for each hectare irrigated), governments and development agencies alike claim that cash crops offer the only means of enabling large-scale irrigation schemes to achieve a satisfactory rate of return on investment.

Furthermore, most Third World countries are locked into an economic system that dictates that development can be achieved only through industrialization. To industrialize, however, a country must earn foreign exchange in order to import the technology that will (in theory at least) enable it to achieve what W. W. Rostow calls "economic lift-off." A country with no mineral or oil wealth can earn that foreign exchange only by exporting the produce of its land. Hence the drive to cultivate cash crops.

Vast areas of the Third World have thus been turned over to the production of crops for export. In the Philippines, for instance, over 50 percent of the country's prime agricultural land is now used to grow cash crops.[1] Almost half of all the farmland in Central America and the Caribbean is used to raise cattle or crops for export. In 1977, 66 percent of the arable land in Guadeloupe was cultivated with export crops; in Martinique, 70 percent; and in Barbados 75 percent of the arable land was used solely to grow sugar cane.[2]

Since the end of the Second World War, the increase in cash crops for export has been phenomenal. In just ten years—between 1955 and 1965—the production of export crops worldwide grew two times faster than the total agricultural growth rate in the Third World. And in the last twenty years, the production of coffee in Africa has quadrupled; the output of tea has increased sixfold; that of sugar, threefold; cotton and cocoa production has doubled; and the output of tobacco has risen by 60 percent. "With some exceptions," write Barbara Dinham and Colin Hines in their book *Agribusiness in Africa*, "those increases came from an expansion in the area under cash crops rather than from higher yields. Some new land came into production and some land previously used to grow food was turned over to cash crops."[3]

Today, some twelve African countries "are dependent on just one main crop for over 70 percent of their income," and "a further eleven countries depend on only two crops for well over half their income." Over 70 percent of Gambia's arable land and 55 percent of Senegal's is used to grow groundnuts; in Mauritius, a staggering 90 percent of the country's arable land is under sugar cane.[4]

Initially introduced to the Third World by the colonial powers, the pattern of cash-crop agriculture has been actively encouraged since independence by the major development agencies. Consider, for example, the distribution of loans to Tanzania since 1960. In the 1960s, the World Bank agreed to back a government program to intensify land use. By the end of 1975, the Bank had invested 2,015 million to 2,016 million Tanzanian shillings in the program, of which 40 percent was for agricultural purposes. Not a single project, however, was designed to produce basic foodstuffs for local consumption. Loans from other agencies were also mainly for cash crops. In 1978–79, for example, 61 percent of loans received went toward increasing tobacco production. Somewhat depressingly, Dinham and Hines comment: "The bias in investment toward export crops did little to increase food production and, indeed, tended to push food crops into the more arid parts of the country while good land was turned over to export crops."[5]

For the most part, the cash crops grown in the Third World—in even the poorest nations—are exported to the West. A 1973 report from the U.S. Department of Agriculture reveals that thirty-six nations classified as "most seriously affected" by hunger and malnutrition were nonetheless exporting food to the United States. Moreover, that pattern of diverting food to the already well-fed nations has persisted even during periods of local famine. Indeed, as Lappé and Collins report, "agricultural exports from the Sahelian countries to Europe actually increased during the late sixties and early seventies, in the face of worsening drought and widespread hunger." In fact, "during the drought in Mali, the area planted with the two most important export crops, peanuts and cotton, was expanded by almost 50 percent and over 100 percent respectively between 1965 and 1972."[6]

CASH CROPS AND IRRIGATION PROJECTS

The following examples of how irrigated land is being used in a cross-section of Third World countries make it quite clear that the rural poor have been (and will continue to be) the last people to benefit from large-scale irrigation schemes.

As originally conceived, Iran's Dez dam was intended to provide more than 200,000 acres of irrigated land to small farmers in Khuzestan. However, the irrigated land went almost exclusively to foreign-run, intensive plantations producing crops for export.[7] Until the overthrow of the shah, the agribusiness firms that managed the "farms" in the area included such household names as: Shell, John Deere, Dow Chemical, Chase Manhattan, the Bank of America, Transworld Agricultural Development Corporation, Diamond A. Cattle, and Hawaiian Agronomics. For them, the Shah had made an offer no sane businessman could refuse. As one executive put it: "They develop the water first and we come and farm it."[8] Seventeen thousand peasants were uprooted from their land to make way for the scheme, and many are still landless and jobless.

In Kenya, Pan African Vegetable Products—a company set up by Brueker Werker of West Germany and financed by, among others, Barclays Overseas Development—grows some 18,000 tons of vegetables a year on 800 acres of irrigated land. Five thousand outgrowers supply the company with another 18,000 tons a year. Ninety percent of all those vegetables are dehydrated and exported to West Germany and other European countries.[9]

Elsewhere in Kenya, the Sulmac Company (in which Brooke Bond Liebig Kenya has a 75 percent interest) is growing carnations, ferns, chrysanthemum cuttings, sisal, and vegetables on its acreage. "The flowers and vegetables are for export to Europe, expressed by air-freight, to meet the demand for off-season and exotic vegetables and winter flowers," report Dinham and Hines. They comment:

> Brooke Bond is here contributing to an established trend among agribusiness investors of using scarce land in African countries to grow food to supply a luxury market overseas. The frivolous nature of such market "needs" is illustrated by Sulmac's estate at Masongaleni, which has "the world's biggest production area of *Asparagus plumosus*, a fluffy foliage which is very popular as green support for bouquets." Not only is Kenya encouraged to "develop" its resources to meet the industrialized world's demand for tea and coffee, it is now encouraged to "develop" to meet the demand for fluffy foliage for bouquets.[10]

More than 375,000 hectares are to be irrigated in the Senegal River Valley as a result of an eighty-year plan—to be undertaken by the governments of Senegal, Mali, and Mauritania—to develop the entire river basin. Between 75,000 and 98,000 hectares will be irrigated by the Diama Dam, near the coast, and a future 255,000 hectares by the Manautali Dam 1,000 kilometers upstream. Officially, the scheme is intended to promote "communal rural development." Small-scale village farms are to be set up, the peasant farmers will be allowed to grow traditional crops using traditional methods of farming, and (again "officially") the food needs of the local people are to be met before crops are grown specifically for export.

For all the talk of "rural development," it is now apparent that the local populace will play little part in the project. Discussing the future of the Manautali scheme, the influential French-language magazine *Marchés Tropicaux et Méditerranéens*, for instance, had this to say: "The future does not seem to rest on the extended development of village units. For the moment, such villages provide an excellent means of settling those people living on the river banks, but they do not fit into the development scheme as conceived and planned by the three participating states. Therefore, these village units should not take up more than 20,000 to 25,000 hectares of the land in the scheme."[11]

The governments of the three riparian states are apparently of a like mind. Indeed, one need look no further than the official timetable for irrigating the Manautali project to see what sort of development the authorities intend to introduce. After 1987, for instance, no more small farms will be set up, and all resources are to be devoted to expanding the area under large farms. "In effect," comments Frederick Mounier, of the aid organization *Frères des Hommes, Terres des Hommes*, "the decision has been made to favor large-scale mechanized agriculture, with its imports of fertilizers and pesticides, in order to produce crops for export—at the expense of the individual smallholder."[12]

Plans are already afoot to convert 30,000 hectares in the Casamance region of Senegal into a highly mechanized rice plantation. The aim of the project—which will cost $60 million—is to double rice yields in the area and thus reduce the need to import rice. Local farmers will have little say in the running of the plantation. As Richard Franke and Barbara Chasin of Montclair College, New York, point out: "The Casamance rice scheme is to be a profit-making venture in which the Senegalese farmers will be decertified from the land under Senegal's 'socialist' land reform act of 1964. The land will then be rented or otherwise made available to SODAGRI (the government's agricultural development corporation), which, in turn, will hire the farmer-smallholders or village communal farmers as wage laborers for its operations."[13] Vast areas now under millet will be flooded as a result of the scheme and local vegetable gardens will disappear beneath the waters of the paddies. Moreover, the rice grown on the plantations will not be available for local consumption; instead, it will supply Senegal's urban population—or rather, those who can afford to buy it.

To the extent that the rice grown at Casamance will (in theory) be consumed within Senegal, the project could be said to be of value to the Senegalese. But as for the other plantations being planned for the area, few will even grow food for local consumption. Already, the Sahel region in general—Mali, Mauritania, and Senegal in particular—has been earmarked by development "experts" as a future market garden for Europe. As far back as the early 1970s, a confidential World Bank report noted: "Senegal is the closest country to the European market where vegetables can be cultivated in the open without glass or plastic protection during the Winter."[14] Since then, the bank has been even more specific in its recommendations for developing the area. According to Frances Moore Lappé and Joseph Collins, of the San Francisco–based Institute for Food and Development Policy, "recent World Bank reports on Senegal and Mauritania see the region's future in mango, aubergine, and avocado exports."[15]

Others, too, have perceived the Sahel's agricultural potential—in particular, its potential as Europe's backyard vegetable garden. In some cases, the idea has been embraced with an enthusiasm that borders on the euphoric. Take, for instance, an article entitled "The Sahel: Today's Disaster Area . . . Tomorrow's Glorious Garden?" which appeared in the October 1974 edition of *To the Point International*. It is quoted by Lappé and Collins in their book *Food First: The Myth of Scarcity*.

> Space-age farms, modern cattle ranches and lush market gardens in the middle of the Sahara. . . . This is no mirage. It is what experts from six of the world's most backward nations have conjured up for the future. Their idea is to roll back the desert and turn their drought-ravaged countries into a fertile green belt of productive crop land and pasture. . . . *It could eventually turn the rural subsistence economies of the West African nations of Chad, Mali, Mauritania, Niger, Senegal and Upper Volta into a vegetable garden for Europe and a vast beef belt.*[16]

In fact, this article was outdated even before it was printed. At the height of the appalling 1970–74 drought that ravaged the Sahel, the Sahelian countries were exporting 60 percent of their agricultural produce to feed Europe, North America, and the urban elites of other African countries. One company involved in the production of such cash crops was Bud Senegal, an affiliate of the House of Bud in Brussels. The company—which was nationalized in 1977 amid accusations of financial malpractice—used a highly sophisticated drip-irrigation system to grow vegetables for export on a 450 hectare plantation. "Three times a week, from early December until May, a DC-10 cargo jet would take off from Senegal loaded with green beans, melons, tomatoes, aubergines, strawberries and paprika," report Dinham and Hines. "The destinations were Amsterdam, Paris, and Stockholm."[17]

Even during the months when vegetables were not being grown, the plantation was not allowed to lie fallow. Production continued, but the land was not used to grow crops for local consumption: instead, the company grew feed for livestock. Still more indicative of the priorities of the plantation was Bud's response to the dramatic fall in the price of green beans in Europe. Once it was no longer economical for the company to export the beans it was growing in Senegal, rather than market the produce locally, Bud chose to destroy its entire crop. "Since the Senegalese are not familiar with green beans and do not eat them, we had to destroy them," explained Paul Van Pelt, director of Bud Holland.[18]

PUSHING PEASANTS ONTO MARGINAL LANDS

Export-oriented plantations tend to be set up on the best available land. As a result peasants producing crops for local consumption are invariably pushed onto marginal land which is often unsuitable for farming. The results have frequently been disastrous. For example, Lappé and Collins cite the experience of El Salvador, where plantations now take up half of the total farming area of the country—including all the prime land. "The land left over, mainly barren hills, is all that some 350,000 campesinos have on which to scratch out a subsistence living for their fami-

lies. Much of the land they are forced to cultivate is so steep it has
to be planted with a stick. The erosion can be so devastating—
one study concluded that 77 percent of the nation's land is suffering from accelerated erosion—that the campesinos must abandon a slope after a single year's meager yield."[19]

Elsewhere the story is the same. Indeed, many now explain the
disastrous famines that have ravaged the Sahel since the late
1960s in terms of the expansion of cash crops and the consequent
pressure on local pastoralists to graze the arid and inhospitable
margins of the Sahara desert. Thus, between 1954 and 1957,
Niger—one of the most severely affected countries—saw an expansion in the amount of land under peanuts from 142,000 hectares in 1954 to 304,000 in 1957. Despite warnings that peanut
production was harmful to the cultivation of subsistence crops,
the lure of high profits encouraged many peasant farmers to grow
peanuts. A survey in the late 1950s found that half of the farms
in the Maradi district alone were dependent on peanuts for 50 to
80 percent of their income; another quarter depended on peanuts for 35 percent, and the rest for 25 percent of their incomes.[20]

That dependency, as Franke and Chasin point out, locked the
local peasants onto a familiar treadmill. Declining terms of trade
meant that farmers had to grow more and more peanuts to generate the same amount of income; the advent of new varieties of
"high-yielding" peanut plants put many farmers into debt because they could not afford the fertilizers and other items needed
for the new seeds; and that indebtedness forced a push for higher
and higher levels of production. The results were perhaps predictable. By the mid-sixties, two disastrous trends were already
well-established: first, the peasants had begun to grow peanuts
on village lands that had been allowed to lie fallow as insurance
against periods of crop failure; and, second, they had begun to
move northward in search of new lands on which to cultivate
peanuts.

That northward march of the peanut brought its peasant cultivators into direct conflict with the nomads of northern Niger,
pushing the nomads further and further into the desert. To make

matters worse, the expansion of peanut production came just when the nomads themselves were being encouraged to expand the size of their herds in order to cash in on the export market for meat in Nigeria, the Ivory Coast, and other West African countries where livestock cannot be raised because of the tsetse fly. In effect, "more production was thus occurring on less and less of an available resource base."[21]

Moreover, many of the development programs introduced to help the nomads increase their herds were already placing an undue strain on the fragile environment of northern Niger. Modern veterinary projects, for instance, have permitted the buildup of herds to a size far beyond the carrying capacity of even the existing grazing land. In addition, the digging of thousands of wells throughout the Sahel to supply water—but *not* more pasture—for the cattle had led to severe over-grazing around well sites.*

The authorities now see that over-grazing as the root cause of the famines that decimated the nomads' herds and led to the starvation of at least 100,000 people throughout the Sahel in the early 1970s. However, they blame such over-grazing entirely on the nomads themselves—or, to use the phrase of the International Monetary Fund, their "improper use of pasture."[22]

Franke and Chasin are quick to refute this. "It would be more accurate," they write, "to say that the peanut and the profit system which was pushing it north were the real 'overgrazers,' not the nomads."[23] Indeed, they go on to comment:

> That "improper use of pasture" might be related to an oversupply
> of watering points and an overly expanding livestock and peanut

---

*Lappé and Collins note: "When the rains began to fail, the nomads started to move their cattle en masse to the wells. A well, however, acts as false signal in the traditional culture's communication system. A well *appears* to be a good substitute for rain. Unlike rain, however, it does not make pasture grow. . . . After the cattle ate out the areas around the wells and trampled down the soils, the caked earth could no longer even absorb the scarce rains. One eyewitness reported that each well 'quickly became the centre of its own little desert forty or fifty miles square.'" (F. Moore Lappé and J. Collins, *Food First: The Myth of Scarcity*, Souvenir Press, London, 1980, p. 44.)

production system does not enter into the IMF's thinking. But this seems to be just the point. The wells, the veterinary services, the slaughterhouses, the increased herd sizes are all related to the beginnings of a development plan for commercialized livestock production in the Sahel. At the same time, however, the pastoral regions were being subjected to rapid encroachments by herds-people who were being pushed by the peanut culture into ever more marginal regions. These processes were working together to bring about what might be called the *maximization* of ecological damage, all for the sake of profits to the colonial economy, inter-national businesses, and the commercial African elites. The "overgrazing" of the nomads, such a common phrase in reports on the Sahel famine, can be seen from the example of Niger to be part of a national and international production system which gave them no other alternatives, and then provided them with the necessary technology for environmental destruction.[24]

CASH CROPS AND THE DEGRADATION OF AGRICULTURAL LAND

The intensive nature of plantation agriculture has usually result-ed in the overburdening of the land used to grow cash crops. Vast tracts of land in Africa that are suitable for growing grazing grasses or trees, but little else, have been torn up to make way for cotton or peanut plantations. "The soil becomes rapidly poor in humus and loses its cohesiveness," report Lappé and Collins. "The wind, quite strong in the dry season, then easily erodes the soils. Soil deterioration leads to declining crops and, conse-quently, to an enormous expansion of cultivated land, often onto marginal soils."[25]

In the Sahel region, where land is under peanuts, a minimum *six years* of fallow is recommended if the soil is not to degenerate. Without that fallow, such essential minerals as potassium, phos-phorus, and magnesium do not have sufficient time to build up again in the soil. Indeed, as Franke and Chasin say of the Casa-mance region of Senegal, "it has been estimated that after only two successive years of peanut growing, there is a loss of 30 per-cent of the soil's organic matter and 60 percent of the colloidal humus. In two successive years of peanut planting, the second year's yield will be from 20 to 40 percent lower than the first."

They go on to explain that

As the organic matter diminishes, the soil's capacity to retain water is lessened and there is more susceptibility to drought. Without reserves of moisture, the soil dries out and the harmattan, or desert wind, can blow it away. This is much less of a problem when millet is planted. After harvesting, the stems and roots of millet are left in the ground, acting as a protection against erosion. But the ground on which peanuts are harvested is left completely bare. The shells which are underground are harvested by uprooting. The soil is loosened and the wind will carry away the finest and most important elements.[26]

Unfortunately, the pressure to increase the production of cash crops has led to the widespread violation of fallow periods throughout the Sahel. Moreover, with the nomadic herdsmen of the North now being pushed further and further away from the peanut-growing areas, natural fertilizers in the form of cow dung are becoming increasingly scarce, and artificial fertilizers are too expensive for most farmers to buy. Consequently, many peanut-growing areas are now both overexploited and underfertilized. The result has been a rapid deterioration in the soil quality of the region. The prefect of the Maradi district of Niger says some soils in his area "can be considered totally depleted."

The role of coffee in Brazil has been similar to that of peanuts in the Sahel. It is worth quoting at some length from George Borgstrom's book, *The Hungry Planet.*

The almost predatory exploitations by the coffee planters have ruined a considerable portion of Brazil's soils. In many areas, these abandoned coffee lands are so ruined that they can hardly ever be restored to crop production. In others, a varying portion of the topsoil has been removed, or the humus content of the soil has been seriously reduced. In most regions, a mere one-tenth now remains of the amount of humus present when coffee cultivation was started. Therefore, the coffee plantations have always been on the march, grabbing new land and leaving behind eroded or impoverished soils. Coffee has climbed even higher along the slopes of the Brazilian high plateau and has finally reached up there. In search of new soils to take the place of those that have been destroyed, coffee-growing moved toward the south and west as well as into entirely new states.

Each time, however, the coffee plantations were forced to move to less favorable regions, where especially the frost risks have turned out to be considerable. They have also been compelled to abandon the fertile red soil, *terra rosa*, where uninterrupted production is possible from forty to sixty years. Poor sandy soils have been put under cultivation where the lifespan of the coffee bushes is only half as long. As a last resort, still poorer soils in the state of Espirito Santo have been used, where the bushes render reasonable yields merely for eight years or so.

This march of the coffee plantations over the wide expanses of Brazil has been likened to a giant wave which has now reached the River Paranà, where cultivation takes place under much more unfavorable conditions compared to the time when the coffee bushes flourished in the vast Paraíba Valley, west of Rio de Janeiro. Here, the pioneers burned enormous forests in order to obtain room for the largest possible number of coffee bushes. Behind them, the coffee-thirsty peoples of the world have left poor pastures. Here and there a grove of eucalyptus trees, imported from Australia, may be seen. The humus has not stood up against the strain. The soil has deteriorated and has subsequently been damaged on quite a scale in a man-induced erosion. Centuries of forest growth would be required to restore an adequate humus layer.[27]

What do the rural peasants of the Third World get in return for the food they cultivate and export? Precious little. The bulk of the foreign exchange earned by developing countries goes for luxury items only the elite can afford. With respect to those countries worst hit by the catastrophic Sahelian drought, the point was well made by Lappé and Collins in 1977:

Much of the foreign exchange is used to enable government bureaucrats and other better-off urban workers to live an imported lifestyle—refrigerators, air-conditioners, refined sugar, alcoholic beverages, tobacco and so on. In 1974, about 30 percent of the foreign exchange earned by Senegal went for just such items. The peanut exports annually account for one-third of the national budget of Senegal—but 47.2 percent of the budget goes on the salaries of the government bureaucrats. Between 1961 and the worst drought year, 1971, Niger, a country with marked malnutrition and a life expectancy of only thirty-eight years, quadrupled its cotton production and tripled that of peanuts. But $20 million in foreign exchange was then used up importing clothing, over nine times the amount earned by exporting raw cotton. Over $1 million went for private cars and over $4 million for gasoline and tires. In only three years, 1967–70, the number of private cars increased by over 50 percent, most of them driven by the minuscule elite in the capital. Over $1 million was spent to import alcoholic beverages and tobacco products.[28]

Sadly, that is the typical pattern of consumption in Third World countries that are committed to "Western-style" development.

CASH CROPS AND RISING FOOD PRICES

For the rural poor, the problem is compounded by the tendency of cash-crop cultivation to push up the price of even locally grown foodstuffs, thus widening still further the gap between the peasant and his next meal.

In Brazil, for example, the widespread introduction of soybeans led to a dramatic reduction in the cultivation of such staple food crops as *feijaos* (black beans) and corn. The results? In less than a year, between the end of 1972 and August 1973, black-bean prices rose 275 percent. Furthermore, the growing shortage of corn led to a dramatic rise in the price of animal feedstuffs, so between 1970 and 1972, the price of meat rose by 60 percent and that of chicken by one-third.[29] In most developing countries, such a rise in the price of meat would have affected only the affluent elite. In Brazil, however, meat was—at that time, though no longer—still a staple food for the majority of the population. Summing up the overall effect of the introduction of the soybean, a report by the French government's Center for External Trade concluded: "The consequences were that not only did a great price increase for the principal food products take place, but it also became necessary to import large quantities of foodstuffs."[30]

In the Dominican Republic, reports Susan George, in her book *How the Other Half Dies*, sugar plantations have played a similar role. "In the past twenty years, the amount of land under sugar cane has doubled, and now stands at about 25 percent of the total acreage, while food production per capita has decreased. Food prices are twice as high as ten years ago, and many Dominican families are only eating one meal a day. A 1969 study by a Columbia University doctor showed that over half the sample of 5,500 Dominicans were anaemic, and showed 'chronic malnutrition since birth'."[31]

Behind those price rises lie two trends. First, as we have seen, the increase in the amount of land devoted to cash crops for export has led to a reduction in the cultivation of local foodstuffs, and hence—the law of supply and demand being what it is—to a rise in food prices. Second, the increasing costs of production—an inevitable concomitant of modernizing agriculture—*must* mean that food prices rise to cover those extra costs. As Susan George puts it:

> Expensive technology will produce expensive goods—including higher priced food. This is particularly true when Western-style, highly energy-intensive growing methods are used. *Someone* is going to pay the cost of such items as spare parts, imported fertilizer, sophisticated distribution systems, and just plain energy. If you then want to keep food prices down for the urban consumers, you will have to reduce the prices and wages you pay rural producers and laborers. You can also simply let prices follow "market" forces and fix themselves at the level commensurate with the technology that went into producing the food. If this places the food beyond the reach of the poorest consumers, too bad. You will sell to the upper classes or to foreigners.[32]

Looking toward the future, that second trend is certain to become more and more pronounced—particularly in those areas that have been brought under irrigation. "As farmers are driven up the rising cost curve," writes Bruce Stokes of the Washington-based Worldwatch Institute, "one of the inherent contradictions of large-scale irrigation programs will become apparent. Ultimately, food prices will have to increase to enable farmers to pay for new water projects."[33] In that respect, we would argue, the building of further large-scale irrigation schemes can only serve to intensify the problems of hunger and malnutrition. Undoubtedly, more food will be grown, at least in the short-term, but it will be food that few Third World peasants will be able to afford—assuming, of course, that the food grown is actually intended for local consumption rather than for export.

Indeed, many of the irrigation schemes now being planned will prove economical only if food prices are increased substantially. Thus a recent study undertaken for the U.S. Department of Agriculture estimated that the price of sorghum grown in Texas—where the groundwater reserves are, as we have seen, being rapidly depleted—would have to rise by $2.90 to pay for the increasing cost of pumping water. Since sorghum is largely fed to beef, a rise in the price of meat would follow. Another study concluded that the High Plains Ogallala Aquifer Project in the Southwestern United States could be justified only if the price of grain increased by one-third by the end of the century. At that price, how many more people will join the ranks of those millions who cannot afford to eat?

To conclude, if we conclude that large-scale irrigation schemes in the Third World appear justified, in spite of their terrible consequences for the inhabitants of the area in which they are built, it is surely because we are told that it is the only way, in today's aberrant conditions, that they can possibly be fed.

As we have already seen, however, land that is brought under perennial irrigation in hot dry areas will almost always become waterlogged and salinized, and the reservoirs will rapidly silt up. We have now shown that little of the land that is irrigated will in any case produce food for local inhabitants. On the contrary, most of what is grown will be exported to the already well-fed (if malnourished) peoples of the Industrial World or else made available to local peasants at a price they cannot conceivably afford. Once the land has served that purpose, it is likely to be so degraded that it will be of little use for further food production. On that score alone, further large-scale water development schemes are little more than a recipe for starvation and hunger.

14. The Loss of Land and Water to Industry and Urbanization

IF SETTING UP PLANTATIONS is one means of obtaining the foreign exchange deemed necessary for economic development, providing cheap electricity in order to attract foreign investment in local energy-intensive industries (such as aluminum smelting) is another. As we have seen, dams provide extremely cheap—in the narrowest sense of the word—electricity. Small wonder, then, that "hydroindustrialization" has become something of a buzzword among those who would promote the building of large dams. Their assumption is that by using hydropower to industrialize, Third World countries will increase local standards of living and thus (in theory) eliminate the poverty that is seen as the primary cause of hunger, malnutrition and disease.

Much of this book seems to us to be an implicit refutation of that claim, but we wish also to address it explicitly in the context of one frequent consequence that is particularly relevant to our concerns: namely, the inevitable competition that arises between industry and agriculture for both land and water.

Providing electricity for industrial development inevitably reduces the amount of land available for feeding people. Agricultural land will of necessity be lost to housing developments, factories, shopping centers, office buildings, roads, highways, and the rest of the physical infrastructure of an industrial society.

So too, industrial development will inevitably degrade (for reasons that we shall consider in chapter 15) additional land in the adjacent areas. The net result is a reduction in the amount of land available for growing food—and food, not industrial goods, is the commodity most needed by the rural poor of the Third World.

It is worth considering, then, how far that process of land loss to industry alone—not including erosion and desertification—has gone in a few selected countries—beginning with those in which it is farthest advanced and proceeding to those developing countries where its effects are now beginning to make themselves felt.

THE LOSS OF LAND TO URBANIZATION AND INDUSTRIALIZATION IN SELECTED COUNTRIES

Increasing amounts of agricultural land are being lost in the United States to urban and industrial encroachment. The problem is particularly serious in some eastern states, where farmland is disappearing at phenomenal rates. Indeed, if current trends continue, then, by the year 2000, New Hampshire alone will have lost essentially all its prime farmland to development.[1] Although that might not seem an immediate problem, it poses a long-term threat for future generations. As Carrying Capacity, a Washington-based environmental group, points out, "if lack of energy for transporting food necessitates a return to regionalized food production, highly urbanized areas may find themselves in serious trouble."[2]

Just how much U.S. land is being lost to urbanization is hard to quantify. David Pimentel of Cornell University puts the loss at 2.5 million acres every year.[3] Drs. Brewer and Boxley put the annual figure at 2.9 million acres; of that total, "about 700,000 acres are cropland; 2.2 million acres are pasture, range, and woodland and other lands that also have high and medium potential for conversion to cropland."[4]

In 1981, Dr. Neil Sampson, president of the Soil Conservation Society of America, put the "cropland resource pool" of the

United States at 540 million acres. Of that total, 413 million acres were used for producing crops and 127 million acres were available for conversion to cropland. At the then current rates of conversion to other uses, Sampson estimated that the "pool" would be reduced to 437 million acres by the year 2000 and to 302 million acres by the year 2030.[5]

"Shrinkage at such rates," argued Sampson, "would, of course, result in a serious problem in view of the estimates by the U.S. Department of Agriculture as to the cropland needs in the future." He went on to warn: "The courses we are on today, in terms of energy use, land use, land management, and water use, are simply untenable in the future. And the future is not very far away."[6]

The situation in the United Kingdom is very similar to that in the United States—although perhaps more serious in view of the much more limited amount of agricultural land available per capita. Land is now being lost at such a rapid rate in Britain that, given current trends, the last acre of agricultural land in England and Wales will have been either cemented over or transformed into "tended space," derelict land, or wasteland by the year 2157.[7] Well before then, the world's cereal producers (in particular, Canada and the United States) are likely to have become unable to export food, so it is very difficult to see where the English and the Welsh will get their food from.

As far back as the 1930s, the rate at which valuable agricultural land was being lost to urbanization was already a cause for concern. As a result, a committee (under the chairmanship of the famous geographer, Sir Dudley Stamp) was set up to study the problem and propose measures for solving it. The committee's report, *The First Land Utilisation Survey*, was published in 1933.[8] The report was so alarming that the government decided to set up a special department charged with reversing the trends that the Stamp Committee described.

Whatever else that new department achieved, it clearly failed to stem the loss of agricultural land to urbanization. Indeed, in 1976, the *Second Land Utilisation Survey* (under the chairmanship of Dr. Alice Coleman) reported that since 1933, England

and Wales had lost 1,250,000 acres of farmland—that is, 30,000 acres a year—to urbanization. More serious still, Coleman warned that the rate of farmland loss was increasing and "may accelerate still more with the emphasis on greenfield sites for acquisition under the Community Land Act."[9]

In fact, as Coleman points out, the damage done by recent urban sprawl and industrialization is much worse than official government figures suggest. During the Second World War, the amount of land under cultivation actually increased, and it was not until 1960 that the total cultivated area dropped back below its 1939 level. The net loss of land referred to in the *Second Land Utilisation Survey* is thus the result of the industrialization since 1960. In effect, the real rate at which farmland is being lost is 60,000 acres—not 30,000 acres—a year.

But the figures still do not give an accurate picture of the real loss of productive agricultural land in Great Britain. If, for instance, an acre of good-grade land is lost and an acre of poor-grade land is converted to agricultural use, then the loss and the gain are taken to cancel each other out. The true amount of land lost, in terms of productivity, is therefore much higher than the official figures suggest. They do not reveal, for instance, that the bulk of the land that has been lost since the war lies in the fertile valleys of southern England and the Midlands, and the land gained is largely low-quality scrubland in the Uplands. Fourth- or fifth-grade land has thus replaced high-quality land—a serious qualitative loss that is masked by the official figures.

Finally, the official figures gloss over the amount of land lost to "fragmentation." Anarchic patterns of urban growth have rendered unproductive much land that has not actually been paved over—largely by exposing it to trespassers and to damage by vandals. (We learn, for example, of boys from a housing development at New Addington climbing into an adjacent field and cutting off the tails of all the cows grazing there.) According to Coleman, at least 22 percent of agricultural land in England and Wales is now affected by such fragmentation.[10] The result is not only a reduction in yields but also the abandonment of otherwise good agricultural land in and around towns and cities. Still more land is lost in such areas due to farmers "reclassifying" their holdings in order to get them approved as development sites—a move which, if successful, can earn a farmer more in a single transaction than he could ever have hoped to earn in a lifetime of farming.

The extent to which urban development impinges on agricultural land is well illustrated by Coleman's own study of the pattern of land use in some 850 square miles of the Thames Estuary. She tells us that "for every unit of land used for providing homes and shops, six have been used for factories, sixteen for roads, fifteen have been turned into 'tended space' [i.e., lawns, gardens, and play areas] and nine have become derelict, whilst sixty-one have been turned into wasteland."

Such wasteful patterns of land use are usually attributed to bureaucratic inefficiency. In reality, however, they also reflect the intense pressures applied on local councils by developers and government agencies to obtain what they regard as prime sites for their particular development projects—regardless of the potential of these sites in the context of a sensible policy for preserving as much agricultural land as possible for feeding people. Coleman asserts that if government and local councils had not been subjected to such pressures, much of the building in the area she studied would have been carried out on wasteland—and the loss of agricultural land would thus have been relatively small. Experience suggests that such pressures will be intense in any industrial society, however, whether that society is run on capitalist or communist lines. The apparently avoidable loss of land is not, therefore, in reality avoidable; indeed, it should be regarded as part of the normal cost of economic development.

Despite having less arable land than the United Kingdom and almost twice as many people to feed, Japan sacrificed an average of 50,000 hectares (120,000 acres) a year to urbanization and industrialization between 1968 and 1974—a rate almost twice as high as that in Britain.[11] How long that shrinkage of Japan's agricultural base can continue before her food-producing capacity is reduced to zero is hard to tell—but it cannot be for many decades more.

THE FAILURE TO TAKE LAND LOSSES
INTO ACCOUNT, AS IN EGYPT

One cannot, of course, blame all the loss of fertile land in the United Kingdom, the United States, or Japan on the building of large dams per se. After all, much of the industrial and urban development that has been responsible for that loss of land has been powered by thermal and nuclear energy. The same is not true, however, for many other countries—in particular, for the majority of Third World countries, where the electricity used to power development is largely provided by hydroelectric schemes.

In such countries, the agricultural benefits derived from water development projects—and in particular, the increased yields due to irrigation—should be weighed against the reduction of food supplies as a result of the loss of agricultural land to the development spawned by hydroindustrialization. Unfortunately, such "land loss budgeting" has never been carried out. If it had been, it would have undoubtedly revealed that the net gain in food production due to water development projects is often very slim indeed—and, in some cases, negative. Let us consider the case of the Aswan Dam.

Noting how serious the loss of agricultural land to urbanization has been in Egypt over the last few decades, Asit Biswas writes: "The magnitude of the problem can best be realised by considering the fact that total irrigated land has virtually remained the same in Egypt during the last two decades, in spite of the thousands of hectares of new irrigated land developed due to the building of the Aswan Dam. In other words, Egypt has continued to lose good arable land to urbanisation as fast as she has brought new land under irrigation, at tremendous investment costs."[12]

Dr. Khalil El Mancey emphasizes the widespread loss of land to urbanization. He tells us that the Aswan Dam has made it possible to convert about 293,000 hectares of previously basin-irrigated land to perennial irrigation, permitting three crops a year instead of one. In addition, 526,000 hectares of desert have been reclaimed and are now under perennial irrigation. Unfortunately, however, "about an equal amount of land [presumably 526,000 hectares] has been lost to urban sprawl during the same period."[13]

Mohammed Kassas comes to a similar conclusion—although his figures are different. He writes: "Nationwide programs to re-claim new land [river-control schemes, the irrigation of desert lands, etc.] brought a total area of 372,000 hectares under culti-vation during 1955–1975 but the loss of prime croplands of the fertile Nile Valley and delta due to urban expansion was 400,000 hectares."[14]

In fact, the loss of land to industry and urban sprawl in Egypt is very much worse than suggested by Biswas, El Mancey, or Kassas. One reason is that the official figures for land losses (like those in the United Kingdom) provide only a quantitative com-parison between the amount of land gained and the amount lost. No account is taken of the quality of the land involved. Thus, the greater part of the 526,000 acres reclaimed from the desert is of extremely poor quality. It cannot conceivably compensate for the high-quality land lost in the Nile Valley, where most of the urban-ization in Egypt has taken place. Given that the overt reason for building the Aswan Dam was to relieve Egypt's problem of chronic malnutrition, that loss of good quality land to urban and industrial sprawl is particularly ironic; without the power provid-ed by the High Dam, it would never have occurred.

The issue of land losses has been explored in greatest detail by John Waterbury, and the facts are not reassuring. To begin with, he points out, the amount of land effectively reclaimed has been grossly exaggerated by the government. For some years after the building of the Aswan Dam, we were told that 1.2 million feddans had been reclaimed. In 1972, when reclamation efforts came to a halt, it was admitted that a gross area of only 912,000 feddans had been reclaimed, of which only 770,000 feddans represented a net "cultivable surface."[15]

Even those figures are misleading, however, since they include land reclaimed before the High Dam came into operation. In ad-dition, 80,000 feddans in the New Valley were reclaimed using groundwater for irrigation rather than water from Lake Nasser. Moreover, only 600,000 feddans had actually been brought into production by 1972, and of that area only 345,000 feddans "had reached marginal levels of production."

The poor record of reclaiming land in Egypt is usually attributed to the incompetence of the state bureaucracy. Waterbury, however, considers that the decisive factor must be the low quality of the soil in the areas reclaimed. No serious soil survey was undertaken in the target area prior to the commencement of reclamation work. Indeed, it was only in 1964 that a joint FAO-Egyptian survey analyzed the soils of some 14 million feddans; by that time, Egypt had already begun reclaiming 600,000 feddans.[16]

The soils were classed in six different categories, ranging from excellent (I) to poor (IV) to uncultivable (VI). Significantly, much of Egypt's "old lands," where most of the urban development has occurred, was classified in categories II and III. In the "new lands" surveyed, out of 2,221,552 feddans in categories I–IV, almost two-thirds was in class IV.

More recently, a USAID Mission notes: "Of the 500,000 [reclaimed] feddans now producing crops, about 70 percent are Class IV, 25 percent Class III, and the remaining 5 percent are Class II. Soil Classes III and IV have severe limitations for crop production, particularly Class IV, which requires special soil treatment to obtain moderate yields at relatively high cost."

Because of the low quality of the "new lands," efforts to reclaim them have not only taken longer than expected but have also required very much more water than anticipated—which adds considerably to costs. Moreover, much of the land has—predictably—fallen victim to salinization. As a result, reports Waterbury, "while old lands are going out of cultivation at the rate of at least 20,000 feddans a year, owing to urban and village sprawl, large chunks of the new lands have returned to a state of nature—160,000 feddans, by one observer's estimate."[17]

The implications for further large-scale economic development in Egypt are clear.

TABLE 8

Water Requirements for Selected Industries (USA)

Industry	Unit	Range of water requirements per unit of product
Steel	ton	8,000–61,000
Soap	ton	960–37,000
Gasoline	kiloliter	7,000–34,000
Paperboard	ton	62,000–376,000
Sugar beets	ton	1,800–20,000

SOURCE: Asit K. Biswas et al., eds., *Water Management for Arid Lands in Developing Countries*, Pergamon, Oxford, 1980, p. 18.

LOSS OF WATER TO INDUSTRIAL AND DOMESTIC USES IN THE UNITED STATES, EGYPT, AND ELSEWHERE

Quite apart from paving over agricultural land, the urbanization and industrialization powered by the hydroelectricity a dam provides also leads to a loss of water. Water requirements for different industries are given in Table 8. As will be seen, they vary considerably from one product to the next, but are generally very high.

Although water conservation and the development of recycling technology are likely to bring industrial water use in the United States down to as little as 36 percent of total freshwater consumption, that saving could well be obliterated by increased demand for domestic water. Indeed, it is now estimated that the average U.S. family of four consumes some 126,000 gallons a year (or 340 gallons a day). In the United States as a whole, domestic and municipal water consumption now eats up 8.5 percent of total freshwater supplies—and that figure is expected to rise to 12.1 percent by the year 2000. It would thus seem that in 1975 as much water was used in America to satisfy the requirements of industry and the domestic consumer as was required for agricultural purposes: 52 percent of freshwater supplies going for industrial and domestic consumption as against 47.5 percent for agriculture. By the year 2000, the comparable figures are expected to be 48.1 percent as against 51 percent.[18]

In areas of high rainfall, such high rates of water consumption for industrial and domestic purposes may well be tolerable. In hot areas, where rainfall is low and evaporation rates are high, however, they can prove disastrous—particularly when, as in the American Southwest, water is already proving a limiting factor on food production. In Pinal County, Arizona, for example, 100,000 acres of agricultural land have recently been taken out of production due to a lack of irrigation water.[19] So too, land is steadily being withdrawn from cultivation in the Texas Panhandle as groundwater levels sink lower and lower and the cost of pumping water from ever deeper wells becomes correspondingly more expensive. In Kansas, the situation is particularly severe: at the current rate, 75 percent of existing irrigated cropland will have been taken out of production by the year 2025 due to lack of water.[20]

Under such conditions, the water abstracted to satisfy industrial and domestic requirements can only result in a corresponding decrease in agricultural production. Unfortunately, when such competition occurs, water tends to go to the highest bidder. Invariably, industry wins out for it can afford to pay incomparably higher prices for water than agriculture. Indeed, water charges represent from 0.005 to 2.58 percent—with the average being 1 percent—of total manufacturing costs for the five most water-intensive industries (food and kindred products, pulp and paper, chemicals, petroleum, coal products and primary metals).[21]

Thus it is not really surprising that a California utility should recently have paid $1,750 per acre-foot for water in Utah where local farmers were paying only $25 per acre-foot. As Bruce Stokes notes, "Allocating a scarce resource such as water solely through the marketplace may work against society's broader interests by encouraging some farmers to sell all their water and stop producing food."[22] Apparently some farmers have already made that choice. In certain parts of Arizona, the lack of water is so acute that entrepreneurs wishing to set up new mining enterprises have actually bought up farms solely to have access to their water supply and then closed them down.

That trade-off between development and food production may

make short-term sense in a country like the United States, which still has a considerable food surplus. It is clearly suicidal, however, in the countries of the Third World, where every scrap of food is needed to feed their massive and generally malnourished populations. In such countries, industrialization can be achieved only at the expense of decreased agricultural production. It is a trade-off that cannot be avoided. It is also a trade-off that—despite the denials of Third World governments and international development agencies alike—can only result in the death of many more people through starvation.

By way of example, let us look again at the Egyptian experience.

Despite Egypt's poor economic performance over the last few years, the Egyptian government foresees the economy booming in the decades to come. To that end, there are ambitious plans afoot both to expand industry—in particular, petrochemicals, iron and steel production, aluminum smelting, and fertilizer production—and to set up various large-scale agroindustrial projects such as sugar refineries and canning plants.

The government concedes that those development schemes will increase considerably the demand for electricity. According to 1979 estimates, for instance, industry will require 85 billion kilowatt hours (kwh) by the year 2000—seventeen times the amount consumed in 1973. To provide that power, the government announced plans in 1979 to build a number of nuclear power stations. In addition, a 100-kilometer canal is to be built from the Mediterranean to the Qattara Depression—the plan being to generate 50 billion kwh (five times the output of the Aswan High Dam) as the water flows through a series of turbines on its way down the canal. The Qattara Depression itself will be transformed into a vast salt lake with an area of 19,500 square kilometers.[23]

Despite those plans for industrial expansion, the Egyptian government insists that the rate of industrial water consumption will remain constant at 1 billion cubic meters (m^3) a year until the end of the century—a figure that also includes domestic water consumption.[24] Quite how the government justifies that figure is unclear. If its development plans materialize, then, as Waterbury points out, industrial water consumption is likely to be "far in excess of anything the Ministry of Irrigation is willing to contemplate." Waterbury himself estimates that by 1990 industry alone will consume 3 billion m³. If he is right, then 6.5 billion m³ are likely to be needed by the same date in order to cover all Egypt's nonagricultural water needs.[25] Other estimates are in the range of 4 billion to 4.5 billion m³.

Domestic water consumption too is almost certain to rise dramatically as Egypt's urban elite, who will be the first to benefit from any economic growth, begin to install the trappings of affluence—the dishwashers, washing machines, swimming pools, and other water-intensive symbols of economic success. Nonetheless, the Egyptian Ministry of Irrigation insists that domestic water consumption will remain constant until the end of the century at an unspecified percentage of the 1 billion m³ that the government projects for both domestic and industrial use. It is surely difficult to find a more blatant example of wishful thinking.

That same element of wishful thinking is evident in other official assumptions as to Egypt's future water budget. The government, anxious to allay fears of a trade-off between industry and agriculture, insists that there will be sufficient water available to satisfy the needs of both sectors of the economy. In fact, it claims, there will be enough water for another 4,625,000 feddans to be reclaimed and irrigated by the end of the century.[26] That claim, however, is based on a number of shaky assumptions as to the availability of water.

First, the government takes for granted the "official credo" that the amount of water released at Aswan is 55 billion m³. That figure rests on the questionable premise that water losses to evaporation and seepage at Lake Nasser are as low as 11 billion m³. Waterbury, however, considers that the true rate of water loss is closer to 15 billion m³.[27]

The government's figures are based on the further assumption that an extra 7 billion m³ will be made available by various minor water development projects in Upper Egypt, the Sudan, and Ethiopia. It is also assumed that 4 billion m³ will be provided by the massive water storage scheme being planned on the Upper Baro River in Ethiopia.[28] Those water projects—together with the widening of the Jonglei Canal in order to double its discharge—are expected to increase the water yield at Aswan by 18 billion m³, with half of that yield being made available (in theory at least) by the end of the century.[29] But will the various schemes be built in time to stave off a water shortage in Egypt? Where will the money come from to pay for the projects? And, even if they are built and paid for, will they provide enough water for Egypt's growing needs? The situation is fraught with uncertainties. Indeed, Waterbury argues that of all the proposed projects, only the Jonglei Canal Scheme is likely to be built by the turn of the century.

Third, the government estimates that 12 billion m³ of drainage water can be recovered for agricultural use, as against the 2.5 billion m³ recovered at present. Reusing drainage water, however, poses considerable problems—not least because it is highly saline and must therefore be diluted with fresh water before being applied again on the land. Waterbury estimates that the total amount of water that can be recovered through improved drainage schemes will not exceed 4 billion to 6 billion m³—half, or possibly one-third, of the figure projected by the government.[30]

Furthermore, the government's calculations assume that the lining and covering of irrigation canals will reduce seepage and evaporation losses by 3.5 billion m³—from 11.2 billion m³ to an estimated 7.7 billion m³. Waterbury, however, doubts that such a reduction will be achieved, largely because of the vast expense involved in lining and covering canals. Moreover, if the area under irrigation is expanded—as the government intends—then the losses due to seepage and evaporation are likely to increase still further.

On the demand side, too, the government's figures are questionable. The government foresees having 11.3 million feddans under cultivation by the end of the century, with 39.9 billion m³ of water being required for irrigation. In fact, if the poor record of past reclamation schemes is anything to go by, it would seem probable that the amount of land under cultivation at the end of the century will be far lower. USAID, for example, expects that no more than 6.2 million feddans will be under cultivation and that water requirements will not exceed 26 billion m³. Dr. I. Z. El Kinawy sees 10,837,000 feddans under cultivation.

In any event, the water requirements for irrigating 11.3 million feddans are likely to be far higher than the government forecasts. One reason cited by El Kinawy is that the extent of "on-farm wastage"—and thus the amount of water required per feddan—has been generally underestimated. Waterbury agrees, asserting that if the government's plans to irrigate 11,333,172 feddans come to fruition, then (on the basis of El Kinawy's figures for "on-farm wastage") the total water requirements for Egypt's agricultural sector could be 43.3 billion m³—as against the 39.9 billion m³ projected by the government.[31] It should also be noted that the types of crops the government intends to cultivate (cotton, for example) consume far more water than do traditional subsistence crops.

The Egyptian government's water budget for the next two decades would thus seem wildly optimistic. Put bluntly, Egypt is unlikely to have enough water to pursue its dual program of industrial and agricultural expansion. At the very least, argues Waterbury, the country will be faced with a water deficit of 7.7 billion m³ by 1990. At worst—and Waterbury considers this a more realistic possibility—that deficit is likely to be as high as 14.1 billion m³ in terms of domestic and industrial consumption.[32]

Clearly, the Egyptian government is trying to have its cake and eat it. It is surely only a question of time before the government is brought rudely down to earth by growing water shortages. As Waterbury puts it: "Egypt cannot have it all ways. Cities in the desert, population transfers, millions of new cultivated acres, more intense use of old acres, heavy industrialization, self-sufficiency in basic foodstuffs: all bear water prices in excess of what Egypt can pay." Future plans for industrial development in particular make it almost inconceivable that Egypt will achieve its goal of self-sufficiency in food supplies by the year 2000—a goal that would, according to Mustapha al-Gabali, a former minister of agriculture, require a cropped area of some 22 million feddans.

TABLE 9
*Estimated Water Use and Projected Water Requirements in India,
1973/74 and 2000 (km³/yr)*

	1973/74 (km³/yr)	(%)	2000 (km³/yr)	(%)
Rural domestic	6.7	1.4	16.4	1.1
Urban domestic	5.7	1.2	14.6	1.0
Industrial	4.5	0.9	55.4	3.7
Steam electric power	12.6	2.6	86.8	5.8
Irrigation	452.2	92.9	1,314.0	87.9
Livestock	4.8	1.0	7.0	0.5
Total	487.0	100.0	1,494.0	
% of ultimate utilizable	50%		150%	100.0

SOURCE: Carl Widstrand, ed., *Water Conflicts and Research Priorities*, Pergamon, Oxford, 1980.

"There is simply no way to find fresh water for that kind of acreage [assuming that one could find the acres] at acceptable costs," writes Waterbury. "Egypt must begin to weigh all projects in awareness that water is already a limited resource. That fact has only just begun to sink in, and many misconceived projects may be launched before it influences policies."[33]

Waterbury's point is even more relevant to India. We have already noted that large parts of India are officially labeled by the Ministry of Agriculture as "drought-affected." Those areas, Malin Falkenmark notes, "contain 56 million hectares of cultivated land out of the country's total of 160 million hectares."[34] What is more, they are inhabited by 100 million people, most of whom already suffer from varying degrees of malnutrition.

Unfortunately, current government plans are addressed to a massive increase in water use for wasteful large-scale irrigation projects and, also, for urban and industrial use (see Table 9). Those plans are, of course, totally unrealistic; the water required

TABLE 10

Approximate Year When Water Demand in India
Will Exceed Ultimate Utilizible Resources (by State)

State	1975–80	1980–85	1985–90	1990–95	1995–2000
Punjab				X	
Haryana			X		
Rajasthan			X		
Gujarat		X			
Uttar Pradash		X			
Madhya Pradesh			X		
Bihar					X
Arunachal			X		
West Bengal		X			
Orissa				X	
Andhra Pradesh					X
Tamil Nadu	X				
Kerala			X		
Kamataka			X		
Maharashtra		X			

SOURCE: Carl Widstrand, ed., *Water Conflicts and Research Priorities*, Pergamon, Oxford, 1980, p. 55.

will simply not be available. Indeed, according to Falkenmark, requirements will exceed dependable flow very quickly in some states (Gujarat, Uttar Pradesh, West Bengal, Tamil Nadu, and Maharashtra) and later in others (Arunachal and Andhra Pradesh) but it will do so in all states by the year 2000 (see Table 10).[35]

As this occurs, one can predict that in the ensuing cutthroat competition for ever scarcer supplies, water will be made available (as in the United States) to the highest bidders—to the urban and industrial sector first, to the export-oriented large plantations next, and to the peasants who make up the vast bulk of the population last. The result can only be large-scale famine, a prospect admitted privately by many in government circles.

15. Dams, Pollution, and the Reduction of Food Supplies

SINCE THE EARLY 1960S, environmental pollution has been a topic of increasing concern. Disasters such as Bhopal, Minamata, Love Canal, and Seveso have alerted people to the awesome power of chemicals to cause untold damage to both the environment and human health. Yet, despite the growing realization that pollution and industrialization are two sides of the same coin, cost-benefit analyses for new hydroelectric schemes rarely even mention the pollution that will be caused by the industries a dam makes possible.

Within the context of this study, we cannot examine all the adverse effects of industrial pollution. Setting aside the hazards that pollution poses to human health and to wildlife, hazards well documented in the literature, we will concentrate on the effects of pollution on food supplies, a problem that is particularly relevant to this section. First, however, let us consider what hydroindustrialization has added to the problem of pollution in general.

THE EXPORT OF HAZARDOUS INDUSTRIES

In the Third World, most industries powered by hydroelectric schemes are highly polluting. One reason, undoubtedly, is that pollution controls are almost nonexistent in most developing countries. Indeed, "permission to pollute" is one of the major concessions granted by Third World governments in order to attract foreign industries to their shores.[1]

If developing countries are willing (indeed eager) to accommodate polluting industries, it is largely because they do not see pollution as a problem. On the contrary, pollution is frequently seen as a sign of "progress"—a point well made by the *Oriental Economist* in an article on the general attitude of Asian governments toward pollution. "Such countries," it notes, "are now placing top priority on rapid economic growth and their complaints are not of industrial pollution but rather the lack of it. They want to attain the level of economic growth where they have to worry about industrial pollution."[2]

To that end, Third World governments have been prepared not only to grant foreign industries a license to pollute, but have offered numerous other concessions. Those concessions include: tax exemptions; the freedom to repatriate profits; the right to import from abroad, duty-free, raw materials and components; access to low-cost land; and, where hydroelectric schemes are involved, electricity at a price often below generating costs.[3]

Recently, some Third World countries have gone further still and set up "Free Trade Zones" in which foreign companies are exempted from virtually all fiscal measures or domestic regulations that might impinge on their profitability. Such zones, reports the Republic of Korea's Catholic Committee for Justice and Peace, tend to attract labor-intensive and polluting industries that "depend on having cheap labor and cheap land to exploit without regard to the environment."[4] Something of the spirit behind Free Trade Zones can be gleaned from a recent speech by President Jayewardene to the Sri Lankan Parliament: "I want to say quite frankly that the Free Trade Zone will be like the 'Robber Baron' areas set up in America, Japan and Britain before the industrial revolution. Let them fight each other, compete with each other, destroy each other, and let the fittest survive—all for the benefit of Sri Lanka."

The package of concessions offered by Third World countries—in particular, the license to pollute—is one that many hazardous industries in the industrialized world have found hard to resist. Faced with tougher pollution controls in their home countries, many companies have therefore exported their "dirtier" operations to the developing countries.

The pollution caused by the migration of hazardous industries is intensified by their tendency to be concentrated in a limited area. Where hydroelectric schemes are involved, for example, several industries will often form a consortium in order to guarantee that all the electricity produced is actually used and paid for. Such an assurance is generally required by the major development banks before any loans are forthcoming. In addition, by forming a consortium, the companies involved greatly enhance their bargaining power in negotiations with host governments.

The Amazon Aluminum smelter project (signed in 1976), for example, involves at least thirty-two different corporations, including five aluminum companies and a number of trading companies.[5] The Purari Scheme in New Guinea—as originally conceived by the Industrial Bank of Japan's survey mission—would have involved installing an aluminum reduction plant; factories making ferrous alloys, caustic soda, and electrolytic copper; an electrolytic zinc plant; a silicon carbide plant; a natural gas liquefaction plant; and a urea fertilizer factory. One can easily visualize the pollution that would have resulted from having so many heavy industries concentrated in a single area—particularly when their management had been given carte blanche to pollute.

The trend towards exporting hazardous industries is particularly apparent in Japan. Indeed, as the Australian environmental group International Development Action (IDA) points out, one of the major reasons for Japanese interest in financing the construction of hydroelectric plants in Southeast Asia and Oceania is that conditions within Japan no longer favor the further expansion of energy-intensive heavy industries. The high price of labor has made construction costs uncompetitive; moreover, the small, densely populated, heavily industrialized islands of Japan can accommodate no further pollution.

Japanese industry is fully aware of this problem. In 1973, for instance, the Iron and Steel Committee of the Industrial Structure Council, a governmental advisory body, reported: "The biggest problems faced by the steel industry in the seventies are those of environmental pollution and of energy and raw material resources. In future . . . there should be positive endeavor to locate at overseas sites, with the Government providing the proper legal basis for a system enabling proper control of overseas siting projects."[6]

That strategy has since been followed by numerous Japanese companies—generally with severe ecological consequences for those countries to which polluting industries have been exported. The following two examples make the point.

Some years ago, the Kawasaki Steel Corporation (KSC) announced plans to add a new blast furnace—to be the biggest in the world—at its main factory on Japan's Chiba coast. The project met with widespread local opposition. The Chiba coast, once a beautiful and unspoiled area, dotted with small fishing villages, is now one of the most polluted regions of Japan. Indeed, since the KSC's steel mill began operations just after the war, more than thirty large industrial plants (including oil and chemical factories, shipbuilding yards and power stations) have been established on 4,341 hectares of reclaimed land in the area.

As that industrial complex grew, reports IDA, so the local environment became increasingly blighted. "The sky and land became covered with smoke and wastes . . . crude oil and industrial wastes have turned the sea a coffee color and the air is a reeking, dirty violet haze." Indeed, the area is now so polluted that it is known as "the pollution department store"—a grim reference to the fact that one can find every type of pollution there.

Inevitably, the health of local inhabitants has suffered. By 1977, thirty-nine people had died from diseases associated with pollution and nearly 700 cases of pollution-induced disease had been registered by the Chiba city authorities.

The new development proposed by KSC would in effect have doubled pollution emissions from its steel mill—and the public balked. KSC was forced to compromise and eventually decided to transfer the sinter plant, one of the most highly polluting elements of the proposed development, to Mindanao, in the Philippines. (Using coke and limestone, a sinter plant processes iron ore at very high temperatures, emitting large amounts of noxious gases.) In 1974, the Japanese Prime Minister, Mr. Tanaka, visited Manila and obtained President Marcos's agreement to KSC's plans. "Industrialization is what we are aiming for," announced Marcos. "If it gets difficult to expand plants in Japan, we are willing to accept them."[7]

The plant began operating in 1977, and the surrounding area rapidly became visibly polluted. The government's National Pollution Control Board attempted to monitor that pollution but alleged that its efforts to do so were hampered by the company— apparently intentionally. The Board complained: "By taking samples at thirty places around the factory, continuous investigation of water pollution is carried out. However, you are not allowed to go close to the factory to take the most important samples. It is forbidden to go near the plant and there is heavy surveillance equipment all around it. So the establishment of the National Pollution Control Board is a pure formality as it is impossible to do any real investigations."[8]

Policed by a watchdog without teeth, Kawasaki Steel in effect had obtained a license to pollute. In addition, the company had access to cheap electricity and cheap labor. For KSC, the move to the Philippines could not have been more profitable.

Growing opposition to the pollution also caused by Japan's aluminum industry has forced many companies to site their smelters abroad, and the ecological damage caused by such smelters can indeed be devastating. Thus, according to IDA, Nippon Light Metal's Kanbara plant has proved so polluting that today, no plants grow "within a radius of ten kilometers of the refinery."[9]

Not surprisingly, a proposal to build a similar plant on the island of Okinawa was vetoed in 1973 as a result of local opposition. Five aluminum producers then formed a consortium and began to look for alternative sites outside Japan, sites that came equipped with the requisite license to pollute. They chose Kuala Tanjung, on the eastern coast of Sumatra.

As a result of negotiations with the Indonesian government, it was agreed that a smelter capable of producing 220,000 tons of aluminum a year should be built—and that it should be powered by two 500-megawatt hydroelectric dams on the Asahan River. To finance their share of the project, some $900 million, the five original companies joined forces with seven trading companies and formed the Japan Asahan Aluminum Company (JAAC). The contract for the scheme was signed in 1975.

Under that contract, 80 percent of the electricity produced by the Asahan dams was to be supplied to the smelter at cost price —and that price was to be determined by the JAAC.[10] The consortium thus obtained both cheap electricity and a means of exporting its pollution problems. Subsequently, the chief negotiator for the Indonesian government was heard to admit that "Indonesia is not going to draw any major benefit from the project."[11]

THE EFFECT OF POLLUTION ON CROP GROWTH

Throughout this discussion, it has been our fundamental premise that the commodity the Third World needs most is food. Indeed, we would argue that the desirability of a development project should be assessed in terms of the probable effect it will have on food supplies. Let us therefore consider how the pollution we have described above might affect food production.

The adverse impact of pollution on crop growth is now well documented. In the United States, where much of the relevant research has been undertaken, the National Agricultural Lands Study, for instance, reports that some grape-producing regions have had to be abandoned as a result of photochemical smog.[12] So too, there are cases of spinach production being discontinued near urban centers and of tobacco farms in the eastern United States being abandoned because of air pollution.[13]

In 1975, a study of agricultural production in Michigan found that certain crops (notably beans) were being seriously affected by ozone pollution.[14] In particular, the Bay City-Saginaw region—a major bean-producing region—had suffered major crop losses due to increased ozone levels. More recently, a 1982 study (conducted by the National Crop Loss Assessment Network) sought to establish the effect of ozone pollution on the yields of corn, wheat, soya beans and peanuts. It concluded that ozone caused the loss of between 1.9 and 4.5 billion dollars' worth of such crops each year.[15]

Ozone, which can be linked only indirectly to the industrial process, is clearly not the only pollutant that reduces crop yields.

Researchers in the United Kingdom, for instance, have found that yields of perennial rye grass drop when exposed to sulfur dioxide. So too, yields of plants continuously exposed to air with a sulfur dioxide content of 191 micrograms per cubic meter fell by 50 percent. The researchers—Drs. Brough, Parry, and Whittingham—concluded, "There is a strong indication that pollutants previously regarded as acceptable may be causing significant yield losses in agriculture."[16]

Recently, the Plant Physiology Institute, in Beltsville, Maryland, tried to determine the effect of subjecting crops to various combinations of chemicals—ozone and sulfur dioxide, for instance. Their experiments revealed that when sulfur dioxide is added to air already containing ozone, the yield of snap beans and tomatoes correspondingly decreases. Moreover, it was found that the yield of snap beans fell more dramatically when exposed to the two pollutants simultaneously than when exposed to them separately, which would suggest a synergistic effect of the two substances.[17]

Experiments have also been carried out in the United Kingdom to test the influence of total ambient air pollution on crop growth.[18] In one experiment, plants were grown in plastic-covered hooped channels where they were protected from ambient air pollution. Although those plants were subjected to higher temperatures and lower sunlight levels than those of plants grown out in the open, their yield was significantly higher than that of plants exposed to current levels of air pollution.

Undoubtedly, the total worldwide loss of crops as a result of pollution is very high. In California alone, an estimated one billion dollars' worth of crops is lost each year to pollution.[19] The Washington-based environmental group Carrying Capacity has calculated that industry in the Ohio River basin alone is causing $4.9 billion worth of damage to crops a year.[20]

In the Third World, the extent of crop losses to pollution is less well documented, but some statistics do exist. Professor D. N. Rao, of the Benares Hindu University, estimates that pollution has reduced agricultural yields in India by between 17 and 30 percent. He notes that crops in the Mirzapur district of Uttar

Pradesh in particular have "suffered immensely due to pollution."[21] In other Third World countries, the problem is likely to be found on a similar scale. Where polluting industries have been concentrated in a small area, whether as a result of hydroelectric schemes or the setting up of Free Trade Zones, local crop losses to pollution can be expected to be severe.

POLLUTION AND THE REDUCTION OF FISH YIELDS

As we have already seen in chapter 8, fish stocks throughout the world have been adversely affected by pollution from agricultural chemicals. Equally destructive has been pollution from industrial processes—which, in the Third World, are more often than not powered by large dams. In developed and developing countries alike, rivers have frequently been used as convenient dumping grounds for unwanted toxic chemicals. In Europe, for instance, the Rhône River alone releases some 30,000 tons of oil, 700 tons of phenols, 1,250 tons of detergents and 500 tons of pesticides into the Mediterranean every year.[22]

Similar figures for the Third World are hard to come by; the research has not been done. Indeed, in an overview of the ecological effects of large-scale water projects, Peter Freeman notes, "No survey was found on the quantities and composition of water discharges into the rivers of the world, nor have comprehensive projections been attempted."[23] One reason for that lack of research, argues Freeman, is that "many nations would be reluctant to make public the quantities of waste entering international waters."

Nevertheless, there is every reason to suppose that the pollution of waterways in the Third World is rapidly reaching crisis conditions. In India, according to the National Environmental Engineering and Research Institute (NEERI), as much as 70 percent of available water is polluted. Indeed, the institute tells us, "from the Dal Lake in the North to the Perijar and Chaliyar Rivers in the South, from the Damodar and Hooghly in the East to the Thana creek in the West, the picture of water pollution is uniformly gloomy."[24]

Apart from seriously affecting the health of the population—a recent study estimated that two-thirds of all illnesses in India are caused by contaminated water—the pollution of India's waterways has had a severe impact on fish life. In polluted stretches of the Hooghly River, for instance, the annual fish catch in 1982 was only 129.4 tons; by contrast, in unpolluted stretches, it was 719.25 tons—more than five and a half times higher.[25]

Those figures are drawn from a highly acclaimed report issued by the Delhi-based Centre for Science and the Environment. The report, entitled *The State of India's Environment 1982*, makes depressing reading. Indeed the following extract gives a graphic account of the devastation that untrammeled industrialization has brought to India's rivers and waterways.

High levels of pollution exist along vast stretches of the Yamuna River. Every day, its 48 km portion through Delhi picks up nearly 200 million liters of untreated sewage. Twenty million liters of industrial effluents, including about half a million liters of DDT wastes, enter the Yamuna in this stretch.

From Delhi to Agra, the Yamuna water is unfit for drinking and bathing. A survey by the CBPCWP predicts that if the sewage from Delhi's 17 drains is not treated properly soon, it will be highly polluted from Delhi to Allahabad. At present, the waters of six tributaries dilute the polluted wastes before Allahabad.

One of the major tributaries of the Yamuna is the Chambal River. The latter is Rajasthan's biggest as well as most polluted river. Kota, the site of a fertilizer complex, an atomic power station, a thermal power unit, and other industrial units add toxic effluents, including urea, ammonia, chlorine, lead, mercury, and other metals. Aquatic life has been destroyed. The Chambal's water is unfit for consumption, as is evidenced by the large number of cattle deaths.

A 35 km stretch of the Gomti receives about 180,000 cu. meters of sewage and waste from pulp and paper factories near Lucknow every day. A high count of coliform bacteria, 34,000 to 144,000 per ml, an average BOD count of 160 mg/l (maximum up to 2,000 mg/l) and SS concentrations up to 964 mg/l have been recorded. The recovery is not complete even 65 km downstream from Lucknow, due to the river's low self-purifying capacity.

The Son River suffers heavy pollution near Dalmianagar, where effluents from paper, chemicals, cement and sugar factories are discharged into its waters. Many years ago, carp fish were eliminated here, along a 22 km zone. Discharges from paper mills and chemical units at Mirzapur (Bihar) are so toxic that the fish mortality rate is the highest recorded for an Indian river.

Rising in the Chota Nagpur hills, the Damodar river flows its 540 km course first through the mining belt of Bihar. It then receives effluents from chemical and metallurgical factories between Bokaro and Sindhri, including the Bokaro steel plant, a thermal power station, and the Sindhri fertilizer unit. The lower Damodar Valley from Asansol to Durgapur is one of the most highly industrialized regions in India. Seventy major industries and 250 coal mines are spread around Asansol alone. In terms of oxygen depletion, eight industrial units in Durgapur dump wastes that are equivalent to the sewage from a city of one million population. Fish kills are a common occurrence in summer. "The river is heading towards ecological disaster," predicts A. V. Natarajan and B. B. Gosh of the Central Inland Fisheries Research Institute in Calcutta.[26]

Summarizing the overall ecological state of India's rivers, the CSE report notes: "The occurrence of massive fish kills and the destruction of lower aquatic life forms, due to industrial pollutants, have become a common feature in various parts of the country. Dead fish means the loss of a major source of protein and, worse still, a livelihood for millions of Indians."[27]

In Malaysia, the situation would seem to be almost as bad as in India. Agricultural, domestic, and industrial pollutants have all taken their toll on fish life, and the general decline in riverine fisheries, especially in the western coastal plains, can be attributed at least in part to the resulting decline in water quality. To quote Dr. Alexander J. Jothy, of the Fisheries Research Institute of the Malaysian Ministry of Agriculture:

Incidents of large-scale mortality in streams and rivers have been reported frequently, from such activities as man's deliberate use of poisons to kill fish and the discharge of toxic effluents and effluents creating incredible biological demands of oxygen in the water. Riverine fishermen have reported on the decline of the giant river carp, *Probarus jullieni*, which is known to occur in the rivers Sungai Perak and Sungai Pahang. This fish has now been listed as an endangered species.

Declines in molluscan shell fisheries, particularly oysters (*Crassostrea rivularis*) to a level of almost total eradication in the estuarine areas of two rivers, Sundai Muar and Sungai Perak, have been reported. The oysters, known to be flourishing in both these areas in the early sixties, are believed to have been gradually wiped out by effluents from sawmills, boatyards, and iron foundries.

Another discernible effect is the almost total disappearance of the fish *Clupea macrura*, known to occur seasonally in immense shoals in the inshore coastal areas of the Straits of Malacca during their migration to spawning grounds up-river. It is possible that the increasing pollution load in rivers would have destroyed their traditional spawning grounds.[28]

In Jothy's opinion, if industrial development continues in Malaysia without stricter environmental control, the further deterioration of the aquatic environment is almost certain. Indeed, he warns: "Fish life in the rivers and impoundments may be totally eradicated or decline to irrecoverable levels. Aquaculture will be faced with the situation of acute shortages of good-quality water for successful culture operations. The fate of fisheries in general in the aquatic environment would be rather bleak."[29]

It is a warning that Third World governments throughout the world would do well to heed—particularly in countries that are located in the hot, dry areas of the monsoon zone. In such areas, the flow of rivers is greatly reduced during the dry season and the chemicals they contain become increasingly concentrated. Heightened demand for water only makes matters worse. As Peter Freeman points out, withdrawal of water that "reduced dry season flow could convert rivers into virtual sewers."[30]

For millions of people, the progressive contamination of Third World rivers is a nutritional catastrophe. Unable to afford to buy meat, countless numbers of peasants rely on fish for their animal protein. How many will now die from eating fish contaminated by the chemical wastes dumped indiscriminately into their waterways? And how will they get protein when the aquatic environment of their countries becomes so polluted that it can no longer support fish life?

In sum, building dams to increase the Third World's hydroelectric capacity provides power for further urbanization and industrialization. That consumes land and water desperately needed to produce food. It also generates pollution, which in turn reduces crop growth and annihilates fish stocks, accelerating the ravages of malnutrition and starvation.

16. Sedimentation, the Way of All Dams

IN THE PREVIOUS SECTIONS, we have reviewed the ecological and social problems caused by large-scale water projects. We have seen the ecological havoc that results from salinization, the human suffering inflicted by waterborne diseases, the destruction inflicted on fisheries, and the social upheavals caused by resettlement programs. So too, we have seen how hydroindustrialization has adversely affected food supplies, and how it is rarely the rural population of the Third World that "benefits" from irrigation programs.

In this chapter, we consider the final argument against building large-scale water projects. Even if the above problems could be solved by better management, through agrarian reform, or through a more sensitive approach to development, the "benefits" a dam provides would still be only temporary. Sooner or later, the reservoir of a dam must fill up with the silt and other detritus that the dam prevents from flowing downstream. And when that happens, the dam must be decommissioned; without its reservoir, a dam is a useless slab of concrete.

SEDIMENTATION RATES IN TEMPERATE AREAS

In temperate areas, the sedimentation of a reservoir is usually a slow process. A study by Dr. Cyberski of the State Hydrological-Meteorological Institute, Warsaw, for instance, reviewed sedimentation rates at nineteen reservoirs in Central Europe. Cyberski found that their storage capacity (which ranged between 120,000 and 183,000 acre-feet) was depleted by sedimentation at an average rate of 0.51 percent per year.[1]

A study conducted by Dr. Dendy and his colleagues at the USDA Sedimentation Laboratory looked at the sedimentation rates of small, medium, and large reservoirs in the United States. That study found that the rate of sedimentation in 1,105 reservoirs with a capacity of less than 10 acre-feet was approximately 3.5 percent a year. In the case of medium-sized reservoirs (with a storage capacity of more than 100 acre-feet) the annual storage loss was 2.7 percent per year and the median rate of sedimentation was 1.5 percent. For reservoirs with a storage capacity of more than a million acre-feet, the rate of sedimentation was only 0.16 percent per annum, with the mean rate at 0.11 percent a year.[2]

SEDIMENTATION RATES IN THE TROPICS

If sedimentation rates, particularly for large reservoirs, are low in temperate areas, in the tropics the situation is very different indeed. That difference can be explained, principally, by the devastating effect on tropical soils of deforestation.

Clearly, the rate at which a reservoir "silts up" depends on the amount of silt carried by the river that feeds it—and that, in turn, depends on the rate of soil erosion in the river's catchment area. Where that area is forested, not only is the soil held together by the elaborate network of roots that underlies the forest floor, but it is also protected from the effects of wind and rain erosion by the forest canopy above. Under such conditions, the rate of soil erosion is thus very low; even steep slopes are protected. In those areas where forest cover has been depleted, however, the rate of soil erosion increases dramatically. The organically poor soils of the tropics are particularly vulnerable to erosion, and although the monsoons last for only a short time, they can quickly wash away the soils from deforested slopes (see chapter 10).

Given the present rate of deforestation in the tropics (throughout the world, twenty-five acres of rainforest are lost every minute of the day), it is hardly surprising that rivers in the region carry enormous quantities of silt. Indeed, in many areas, the increased sediment load of rivers is clearly visible to the naked eye. In Sri Lanka, for example, one can literally see the monsoon rains washing away the soil from under the often semiexposed roots of tea bushes on the less well-run tea estates in the Highlands. One can as easily see that soil flowing down the Mahaweli River, whose waters, like those of other rivers whose watersheds have been denuded of trees, are thick, brown, and opaque.

It goes without saying that the more sediment a river carries, the faster the reservoirs on that river will silt up. Predictably, therefore, the rate of sedimentation in the tropics in recent years has been nothing short of disastrous.

In India, the expected siltation rate of the Nizamsagar Dam in Andhra Pradesh was 530 acre-feet a year; the actual rate was closer to 8,700 acre-feet a year. Indeed, the dam's reservoir is already estimated to have lost 60 percent of its storage capacity.[3] As can be seen from Table 11, other reservoirs in India have suffered similarly high siltation rates. In fact, few of the dams now operating in India (in 1978, there were 835, of which 26 provided more than two-thirds of the country's storage capacity) have escaped siltation problems: more important still, many have experienced siltation rates far above those predicted by their planners.

In Haiti, the Peligre Dam on the Artibonite River was completed in 1956 as part of a plan to provide irrigation to the Artibonite River Valley, Haiti's main arable plain. It was built to last fifty years. In fact, its reservoir has silted up so quickly that the dam will probably be decommissioned in 1986, after just thirty years of operation.[4]

In China, the Sanmenxia reservoir, which was completed in 1960, had to be decommissioned in 1964 due to premature sil-

TABLE I I
*Annual Rates of Siltation in Selected Reservoirs
in India (in acre-feet)*

Reservoir	Assumed rate	Observed rate
Bhakra	23,000	33,475
Maithon	684	5,980
Mavurakshi	538	2,000
Nizamsagar	530	8,725
Panchet	1,982	9,533
Ramganga	1,089	4,366
Tungabhadra	9,796	41,058
Ukai	7,448	21,758

SOURCE: Report of the Irrigation Commission; from Centre for Science and Environment, *The State of India's Environment 1982*, New Delhi, 1982, p. 62.

tation. Worse still, the Laoying reservoir actually silted up before its dam was completed.[5]

The Indian government has announced plans for the reforestation of watersheds. This is an encouraging move. Unfortunately, however, such reforestation has—so far—only been carried out on a negligible scale compared to the extent of recent deforestation in critical areas.

The need for reforestation is now generally accepted. The World Bank, for instance, fully realises its importance—although it still seems wedded to the counter-productive policy of planting pines and eucalyptus trees. Recently, in providing finance for a hydroelectric project in Malaysia, it has included money for the purchase in part of the watershed upstream, which it is to turn into a national park. Let us hope that the park will exist in reality as well as in name.

Linney and Harrison asked officials at TRDA and the EEC in Nairobi why funds could not be set aside so that a reforestation program might accompany the building of the Masinga Dam and other dams on Kenya's Tana River. They also suggested that a soil conservation program be set up. "TRDA thought this was a good idea," they report, "but preferred to let the Kenyan government take care of soil conservation and they would take care of the dams. The EEC, a major financier of the Masinga Dam, was very aware of the erosion problem but said that funding for soil conservation was unlikely because: (1) they have never provided money for the watershed of a dam project; (2) the funding of water development and soil conservation were in two different departments so they could not be included in the same project; (3) economically, the dam would still benefit Kenya's development and pay for itself, even if the *dam silted up in twenty years*."[6]

Tragically, the lessons of premature siltation do not appear to have been learned by the governments of those nations to which siltation poses the greatest threat. As we have seen, bigger and bigger dams are being planned in the tropics, and, even today, little regard is paid to the rate at which their reservoirs are likely to silt up.

Clearly, the premature sedimentation of reservoirs seriously affects their economics. Already, as we have seen, the final cost of constructing a large dam is—for various reasons—nearly always far higher than estimated. If, therefore, the dam's reservoir silts up far more rapidly than predicted—or worse still, as at Laoying, before the dam even has a chance to function—the time over which the costs of the dam must be amortized is inevitably decreased, thus making nonsense of the calculations used to justify the dam's construction.

As today's dams silt up, so they will leave behind a vast muddy wasteland. Compacted by the weight of a reservoir's waters, the fine particles of silt that have been deposited in the reservoir form a brick-hard pan as they build up. Even when the last waters of the reservoir have drained away, therefore, the land beneath will not be suitable for basin irrigation or rain-fed agriculture. Only a narrow strip close to the dam, where the coarser and thus less compacted particles of silt are likely to have accumulated, will be suitable for cultivation.

Moreover, as reservoir after reservoir is abandoned, it will become increasingly difficult to find sites for new dams. The number of sites where dams can be built is strictly limited—and, in many parts of the world, those sites have already been exploited. For that reason alone, it seems inevitable that large dams will prove to be a passing phenomenon in the history of human affairs. The devastation they will have caused, however, will be of a very much more permanent nature.

17. Are These Problems Inevitable?

CAN THERE BE SATISFACTORY large-scale water development schemes? The historical experience has unquestionably been disastrous. We have seen the terrible consequences of canal building in India during the British raj and of building vast dams in hot dry areas in recent years. On the basis of the empirical evidence, therefore, the answer to that question is a resounding no. Yet even the most active and outspoken critics of large dams assume, implicitly at least, that if the site is geologically and ecologically appropriate and if sufficient precautions are taken, it is possible to put up a large water development scheme with relative impunity.

Four such critics are: Brent Blackwelder, of the Washington-based Environmental Policy Institute; Philip Williams, a hydrologist and principal of Philip Williams and Associates, San Francisco; Barbara Bramble, of the National Wildlife Federation, Washington, D.C.; and Bruce M. Rich, of the Natural Resources Defense Council, also in Washington, D.C. It is possible to distill from the statements of those critics more than a dozen closely related recommendations as to the conditions that should be satisfied before a dam is authorized. Those recommendations are all very sensible, but they raise a fundamental—and as yet unanswered—question; namely, how would their adoption affect the world's increasingly ambitious dam-building program? Let us try and answer that question by considering the recommendations separately.

The first recommendation—made by Bramble,[1] Blackwelder,[2] and Rich[3]—is that no dam should be built until an adequate assessment of its probable environmental effects has been completed and made available to the public. Clearly, such an assessment would be of use only if it could be made by an objective body. But can an objective body really be found? And would such a body have the courage to advise the government, if need be, not to build a particular dam?

Countless environmental assessments have been made of water development schemes—but usually not before the governments concerned have become committed politically and economically to building them. Not surprisingly, very few, if any, such assessments have actually concluded that a scheme should not be built at all. Indeed, it appears that the main motivation for commissioning environmental assessments has been to rationalize decisions already made. Those decisions are based not on a scheme's capacity to achieve its overt goals but rather on political and economic considerations of an often dubious nature.

The second recommendation, this one by Williams, is that water development projects should only be undertaken if they can be shown "to benefit large sectors of the population instead of the urban elite."[4] That condition is extremely unlikely to be satisfied—particularly in the Third World. Such projects cannot benefit the people whose homes and land are flooded to create a dam's reservoir; nor those in the immediate vicinity of a dam, most of whom will see their land taken over by plantations and eventually degraded into little more than a salt desert; nor those who will fall victim to the inevitable outbreak of waterborne diseases. Nor will it be the rural peasants of the Third World who benefit from the manufactured goods produced by the industries that a dam powers. Not only are peasants unable to afford such goods but, once in the cash economy, they are often unable even to buy the food they so desperately need to survive.

The people who benefit from major water development projects are those who have the proper connections and can afford to obtain water for domestic use, those industrialists who obtain water and electricity at cost for their factories, those plantation owners who get much of the irrigation water, the donor governments abroad whose industries put up the dams and ancillary installations and provide most of the equipment used, and, finally, those local politicians who reap the short-term political capital to be gained from the project—not to mention whatever may come their way under the table.

The third recommendation, made by Williams, is that the scheme should favor labor-intensive rather than capital-intensive economic activities.[5] If this recommendation were followed, then all large-scale water development projects would have to be abandoned. Labor-intensive agriculture does not require water from large-scale irrigation works, nor does labor-intensive manufacturing require hydroelectricity from large dams. Moreover, large-scale water development projects are economical only if they are farmed by capital-intensive agricultural enterprises that are fully competitive on the world market. Large-scale dams are thus quite incompatible with labor-intensive development projects.

The fourth recommendation, also proposed by Williams, is that future water development schemes should permit the production of food crops for feeding the local population rather than for growing export crops.[6] This is not possible for very much the same reasons that giving a preference to labor-intensive farming is not possible. First, peasants producing food for local consumption cannot afford to farm land irrigated by massive water development schemes; it is simply too expensive. Second, the foreign exchange needed to pay the interest on the loans contracted to finance a dam (and, more important still, to finance further development projects) can be earned only by exporting crops, not by consuming them. To observe this fourth recommendation would thus mean forgoing nearly all future large-scale water development schemes, as well as any other form of capital-intensive agriculture. For this reason alone, the Green Revolution, which involves substituting modern technological agriculture for traditional labor-intensive agriculture, cannot conceivably provide a means of feeding the poor of the Third World.

The fifth recommendation, made by Rich,[7] is to avoid schemes that "would compromise public health and safety in ways that would be viewed as unacceptable by the people affected." Similarly, Blackwelder[8] recommends that dams should not be built if they "significantly increase the spread of diseases such as schistosomiasis, malaria or onchocerciasis." Our chapter on the health effects of water development projects makes it clear that this recommendation cannot conceivably be observed. An increase in the incidence of waterborne diseases appears an inevitable concomitant of such schemes. Indeed, the title of a talk by Letitia Obeng of UNEP, "Starvation or Bilharzia," is indicative of the view held by many authorities that bilharzia (or schistosomiasis) is an unavoidable consequence of putting up vast irrigation schemes. As Gilbert White tells us, the "noninvasion of schistosomiasis in a region where the disease exists is exceptional."[9] Efforts to control such diseases by the use of molluscicides, nematocides, insecticides, and other biocides, have, as we have noted, been singularly unsuccessful. Moreover, since many of those biocides are either known or suspected carcinogens and mutagens, their routine use over a long period will almost certainly give rise to other equally serious health problems.

The sixth recommendation—made by Bramble,[10] Rich,[11] and Blackwelder[12]—is to avoid building dams and other water development schemes that adversely affect national parks, heritage sites, areas of scientific and educational importance, tropical rainforests, or areas inhabited by wild animals threatened with extinction. As we have seen, however, the destruction of such assets is almost inevitable where dams are concerned. Moreover, since the number of suitable sites for building dams is limited—and can only become more so as the most obvious sites are used up—dams will be built in areas that are less and less suitable. Sooner or later, one of the areas blacklisted by Bramble and her colleagues will be selected as a dam site.

The seventh recommendation, Blackwelder's, is that dams should be built only where they will not silt up within a hundred years.[13] It is possible to observe that recommendation in temperate areas, but not in the tropics, where rivers carry high quantities of silt. Indeed, given the experience of the last thirty years, it would seem almost impossible in the tropics to build dams whose reservoirs did not silt up prematurely. It would mean, at the very least, the reforestation of the whole catchment area of those rivers to be dammed—and not with shallow-rooting pines, but with trees that reconstitute, as closely as possible, the original native forests. As we have seen, the World Bank is beginning to insist on the reforestation of watersheds. To date, however, the bank has recommended only the planting of pine and eucalyptus: never, to our knowledge, native trees. We see little reason to suppose, therefore, that this condition will ever be met.

The eighth recommendation, by Blackwelder[14] and Rich,[15] is that dams should not be built if their associated irrigation schemes are likely to lead to the salinization of agricultural land. Unfortunately, the building of large dams in hot dry areas almost invariably leads to waterlogging and salinization. Aloys Michel, for example, concluded that "waterlogging or salinization, or both problems, will inevitably arise in all but the truly exceptional surface water irrigation system."[16]

Victor Kovda feels the same way. "During many centuries, and even millennia," he writes, "only areas having a free outflow of groundwater, as in Tashkent and Samarkand, have not undergone salinization or waterlogging." In other words, "increasing salinity in irrigated soils on arid lands is practically universal."[17] As salinization inevitably builds up, almost all the land put under irrigated agriculture since the war will have to be abandoned, possibly in the next decades. Effective methods for inhibiting the process, such as the lining of irrigation canals and building horizontal drains, are too expensive and are rarely adopted, even on a small scale. Others, such as reducing the amount of land under irrigation to make water available for flushing out salts, or observing long periods of fallow, would so reduce economic output as to be impractical in the context of capital-intensive, market-oriented agriculture.

This brings us to the ninth recommendation, proposed by Williams, that the emphasis of funding should be "towards sustainable long-term resource enhancement rather than short-term resource exploitation."[18] Simply on the basis of the predictable premature siltation of reservoirs and the salinization of the land that dams serve to irrigate, large water development schemes cannot by any stretch of the imagination be regarded as sustainable. In fact, it would be difficult to imagine any development schemes that more clearly involve "short-term resource exploitation."

The tenth recommendation—by Blackwelder[19] and Rich[20]—is that dams should not be built "if they displace indigenous peoples from their homes and destroy their cultures"—or at least, as Rich puts it, where they "would displace or strongly disadvantage indigenous peoples or other vulnerable social minorities unless compensation is provided to ensure that the affected people are made no worse off, and preferably better off, than before the project." We have seen how the cultural pattern of indigenous people is highly adapted to survival in their natural environment. To flood that environment and force them to live elsewhere—generally, as we have seen, in degraded (and degrading) conditions—is to subject them to an environment in which they are not equipped for survival. Inevitably, their society disintegrates; invariably, too, they become part of an aimless and rootless proletariat. To observe this eleventh recommendation would thus mean to desist from building dams in areas inhabited by indigenous peoples.

A further recommendation by Blackwelder, the eleventh in our list, warns against building dams that "have significant engineering or safety problems."[21] This, of course, would rule out building dams in areas with any sort of seismic activity or in areas subject to landslides. Even then, however, as we have seen, the safety of a dam could not be guaranteed. Both Rothé and Simpson agree that it is impossible to identify the exact conditions under which large dams can trigger off earthquakes; indeed, it appears that dams can cause earthquakes even in areas where no seismic activity has ever been recorded.

The twelfth recommendation, also by Blackwelder, is that dams should not be built where they are likely to inflict significant damage on estuarine or ocean fisheries.[22] All dams, however, affect estuarine nurseries and fisheries by depriving them of the nutrients contained in the silt that the dams prevent from flowing downstream. Moreover, the upstream abstraction of water for irrigation and urban and industrial uses also increases the salinity of the water flowing into estuaries. That water is also invariably contaminated by the toxic wastes—in the form of fertilizer and pesticide runoff and industrial effluent—that inevitably accompany both modern intensive agriculture and modern industry. It follows that this twelfth recommendation is also unlikely to be observed.

Finally, it is recommended by Rich that dams should not be built if they are likely to harm "significantly" the environment of a neighboring country, without its full consent.[23] Unfortunately, no fewer than 214 rivers or lake basins in the world are shared by more than one country; 57 in Africa, 40 in Asia, 48 in Europe, 33 in North and Central America, and 36 in South America. Moreover, much of the total area of many countries falls within such international basins: 80 percent of more than ten African countries and 100 percent of another ten, for instance, and over 80 percent of at least five Asian countries and 100 percent of another two. Whenever several countries are situated along the same river basin, the water that reaches the population living downstream becomes scarce, salty, and contaminated. To observe Rich's recommendation would thus mean desisting from building dams on any of the world's large international rivers.

If water schemes were built only if they satisfied the above conditions—if, in other words, they could definitely provide water on a sustainable basis without disastrous social and ecological costs—then very few, if any, would be built.

18. Social and Environmental Impact Studies

BY THIS TIME, the reader will probably be asking why people continue to build dams, especially bigger and bigger ones. It might be argued, of course, that the governments, development banks, and international agencies engaged in promoting and financing large dam projects are genuinely unaware of the probable social and ecological consequences. We ourselves do not accept that view. We find repeatedly that dams and other large-scale water projects have been given the go-ahead on the basis of the most cursory ecological appraisals. In some cases, the appropriate studies have been undertaken only *after* building work has begun. This suggests to us that governments and international development agencies alike attach little importance to the ecological and social problems caused by large dams. The following examples underscore the point.

James Bay, Canada. Approval for Quebec's giant James Bay scheme was given in 1971 before *any* ecological or economic cost-benefit studies had been undertaken. As planned, the project involves: "The building of ten of the world's largest dams, two new airports, a new ocean port, 60 miles of dikes, eleven or more electrical generating stations, 500 miles of new roads into the wilderness, the diversion of the Nottaway and Broadback rivers into the Rupert River through an elaborate tunnel system, and the 'development' of the Eastmain and La Grande still farther to the north."[1] Despite the scale of the operation and its potential environmental impact, the government of Quebec based the decision to push ahead with the project on just two engineering reports. Those reports, claims the Committee for the Defense of James Bay, "did not mention social or ecological considerations—not even in passing—and provided only a crude 'guestimate' of costs and benefits."[2]

A subsequent report by a joint federal and provincial government Task Force set up to advise on the project was similarly narrow. Indeed, the Task Force was at pains to distance itself from the ecological and economic issues, observing:

> It is understood that the decision to proceed has been taken. This report, therefore, does not reflect any personal or collective reservations held by the Task Force members as to whether society really needs the project, whether there are more economical or less environmentally disturbing ways of harnessing energy resources to meet Quebec's future needs, or whether society should strive to restrain its electrical demands rather than increase its supply. It was assumed that these fundamental questions had been adequately considered by the authorities prior to making the decision to proceed.[3]

It is hard to know how the Task Force could make that assumption. Only a year before the Task Force reported, and only a few months before the James Bay decision was taken, the provincial government's own economic planning board had argued that the feasibility of the scheme had yet to be proved and that millions of dollars' worth of studies would be needed before work could begin. There is no evidence that such millions were in fact spent. Moreover, the assurances of government ministers that ecological studies had been undertaken prior to the James Bay decision are hard to reconcile with subsequent studies—notably one by Quebec-Hydro, which admitted that little was known about the ecology of the 144,000 square miles to be developed under the scheme. Indeed, Dr. K. A. Kershaw, a plant biologist at Mc-

Master University, was subsequently to tell the Committee for the Defense of James Bay: "I have no hesitation in saying that we do not have any biological knowledge of this area worth a damn and I would be prepared to go into court and swear it under oath."[4]

Tana River, Kenya. No studies were undertaken on the ecological effects of the Kindaruma and Kamburu dams on Kenya's Tana River before construction work began. The feasibility studies for the dams only mentioned the likely ecological effects. By the time studies were commissioned—under the auspices of Dr. B. Lundholm of Sweden's Secretariat for International Ecology and R. S. Odingo of the University of Nairobi—work on the dam had progressed to such an extent that it "was impossible to establish a baseline study of the area."[5] Indeed, the Kamburu construction site was already populated by some 2,000 permanent residents and an estimated 2,000 migratory workers.

Anchicaya, Colombia. In what has been called an "unpardonable lack of foresight," the planners of Colombia's Anchicaya hydroelectric project failed totally to assess likely sedimentation rates at the dam. According to Robert N. Allen, a construction engineer who worked on the project, the problem of sedimentation and accumulation of debris due to deforestation was "completely ignored by the originators of the project and the consultants in their review of the project."[6] When the first signs of sedimentation appeared, "a letter from the [dam's] manager to the consultants, noting the sedimentation and requesting information on possible sedimentation rates, brought the reply that tropical rivers carry little sediment and that there would be no sediment problems at Anchicaya." Later, when Allen submitted a report to the consultants in which he argued that the reservoir would be lost to sedimentation earlier than expected, he received the following replies: "We do not believe that the estimates as to the possible rate of annual accumulation of deposits in the reservoir are justified"; and, "We are of the opinion that the Anchicaya watershed is such that the deposits will not accumulate to a serious extent within the economic life of the plant."[7] Twenty-one months after the dam was first closed, 23.4 percent of the reservoir's volume had been lost to sedimentation.

Skagit Valley, Canada. Permission to build the High Ross Dam on British Columbia's Skagit River was originally granted to the Seattle City Department of Lighting after a single public hearing lasting just two hours. Because the High Ross Dam would impound water belonging to both the United States and Canada, permission to build the dam first had to be sought from an international commission set up under the Canada-U.S. Boundary Waters Treaty. That commission, the International Joint Commission (IJC), held its hearings in Seattle on September 12, 1941. Thomas I. Perry describes the meeting:

> Of the six Commission members, three were absent, including the Chairman of the Canadian section. Most of the hearing time was consumed by Seattle Light's technical presentation, while discussion of environmental effects of the dam was limited to a one-minute statement by the British Columbia Game Commissioner. Having never before heard of the project, he was unable to comment on the effects of flooding except to note the inevitable loss of one of the best fly-fishing streams in the whole of British Columbia.[8]

Wrangling over the amount of money to be paid to the government of British Columbia for flooding the Skagit Valley meant that Seattle Light did not obtain full permission to build the dam until 1967. It was not until 1970, when Seattle Light sought U.S. permission for the dam, that the first hearings on the environmental effects of the dam were held. Despite the evidence presented at those hearings, the government of British Columbia remained intransigent: the dam would go ahead. In 1971, under increasing pressure from the public, the federal government of Canada intervened in the controversy and referred the Skagit Valley decision back to the IJC, and the provincial government expressly forbade its scientists to give evidence before the commission.

No evidence, however damning to Seattle Light's case, would have made much difference, though, for the IJC's hands were tied. Its task was solely to "make recommendations for the protection and enhancement of the environment and the ecology of the Skagit Valley not inconsistent with the Commission's Order of Approval dated 27 January 1942."[9] Whatever conclusion it reached—and in fact, it came out guardedly against the dam—the commission was still bound by the decision it had taken some thirty years earlier.

Helmand, Afghanistan. The introduction of modern canal irrigation to the Helmand Valley of Afghanistan was undertaken without any consideration of the possibility that the land might become salinized. Ten years after the start of the project, 5 million acres out of 23 million had been lost to salinization and waterlogging, with a further 50,000 to 100,000 acres passing out of production annually for the same reason. Commenting on that loss of land, Aloys Michel, then professor of geography at the University of Rhode Island, had the following to say: "The only remarkable points in the Helmand experience are that disaster struck so quickly and that the reasons for it were so obvious. Any engineer or planner should have seen them from the design stage, and some did. But, instead of redesigning the project . . . or substantially increasing the size of individual holdings or lowering the water allowances from the start, the project was implemented in defiance of reality."[10]

Teton Dam, United States. Idaho's Teton Dam collapsed on June 5, 1976, causing $1 billion worth of damage. The dam was under construction even though the final feasibility study and design study (the so-called "definitive plan report") was not finished. According to Rosaleen Bertolino of the Sierra Club, a geological survey of the dam site had been "watered down" and thus failed to indicate the "severity of the instability of soil materials in the area."[11] Ironically, one of the major purposes of the $85 million project was flood control. In fact, as we have seen, it is a characteristic of flood control dams that they tend to increase the severity—while decreasing the frequency—of floods (see chapter 9).

Jonglei Canal, Sudan. Twice as long as Suez and carrying one-quarter of the Nile, the Jonglei Canal is intended "to enable the Nile to bypass the huge papyrus swamps of Sudan's Southern Sudd region, where half the flow of the White Nile is otherwise lost to evaporation."[12] Although the scheme—which was to have been completed in 1983 but at the time of writing is still under construction—has less than half the capacity of the version proposed in 1954, there are still major doubts about its ecological effects. Those doubts are heightened by the general lack of data available to the Sudanese authorities. Indeed, Dr. C. E. Gischeller told a 1975 UNESCO/ROSTAS conference: "With respect to the construction of the proposed Jonglei Canal, it is certain that presently existing data are largely insufficient to estimate even approximately the consequences of such a canal. This means that action without accompanying studies would reduce the entire enterprise to an adventurous undertaking for which no technician can take responsibility."[13] Gischeller's remarks were reinforced in 1977 when the Nairobi-based Environment Liaison Centre produced a report highlighting some of the areas where insufficient data existed to predict the environmental consequences of the Jonglei scheme. In particular, the report stressed that no one even knew the exact size of the swamp; that the social effects of the scheme had not been studied; and that there was considerable controversy over the possible climatic consequences of depriving the Sudd of its annual flood.[14]

Selingue, Mali/Guinea. According to Brian Johnson, of the International Institute for Environment and Development (IIED), the sole environmental study on West Africa's Selingue Dam, which was closed in 1980, "deals briefly with the tourist potential of the reservoir, its possible harm to water quality in the region and seismic stability."[15] A report prepared for the London-based Commonwealth Secretariat noted that the dam authorities were

unable to answer such fundamental questions as how they intended to inhibit siltration, whether there were plans to clear the
forest in the area prior to flooding, what would be the ecological
consequences of not undertaking such clearance, and what measures were being taken to provide for the resettlement of the
9,500 people who would be displaced by the dam. The report also
noted that the feasibility study prepared for the dam gave no
back-up information to support the "brief assertions" it made as
to possible environmental effects.

A more serious charge was that a warning that the growth of
marsh plants and algae might have a detrimental effect on fisheries was "apparently struck out." The author of the report comments: "It appeared that, because of the immense pressure from
the Government of Mali to have the dam closed and the first
turbine operating by August, 1980, various corners (especially
those affecting the environment) were being cut."[16] In particular, the report observed that "massive eutrophication of parts of
the lake appears to be a possibility," but that studies on the
growth of algae had simply been ignored; that "little was being
done to inform the villagers of the plans for the area"; and that,
despite evidence that the fish in the lake would need to be able to
travel upstream in order to spawn, "no provision was being made
for a fish ladder or elevator." Small wonder Brian Johnson warns
that "portents of environmental disaster still hang heavy over
Selingue."[17]

Kariba, Zambia. Following the disastrous resettlement program
at Zambia's Kariba Dam, it emerged that no detailed study had
ever been undertaken to assess the best areas for resettlement. As
Professor Theo Scudder reports: "Though the local district
commissioner and his immediate superiors were much concerned about the impact of resettlement on the Tonga . . . no
positive action was taken on their request for an accurate ecological survey which could serve as the basis for the selection of resettlement areas and the intensification of agriculture following
resettlement. Action was delayed until after the 1955 decision to

proceed with the dam, and by then it was too late to undertake the type of detailed surveys required."[18]

Volta, Ghana. Here, too, no studies were carried out on the resettlement scheme until it was too late. According to Sir Robert Jackson, a noted Foreign Office civil servant, the lack of studies resulted largely from the protracted negotiations over the financing of the dam. Indeed, he says, "we always assumed that during the interval during which final negotiation would be carried out, [the] final planning [on resettlement] would be refined in a great many ways."[19] It wasn't, however, and it was not until two years after preparatory work on the dam had been started that the director and staff of the Resettlement Unit were even recruited.

Chico, Philippines. Funding for the four dams on the Philippines's Chico River was approved by the World Bank on the basis of a feasibility study carried out by a firm of West German consultants. That study, critics claim, "misinterpreted the area, making it out to be a wilderness with only a few scattered families."[20] In fact, the area is the homeland of 90,000 Kalinga and Bontoc tribesmen. In any case, the project was cancelled after intense opposition from the Kalingas and Bontocs led to a state of virtual civil war.

Mesopotamia. Although water projects in the Mesopotamian Plains have resulted in the overirrigation and consequent salinization of both groundwater and soils, plans are afoot to "develop" the region still further. That development, however, is not contingent upon the appropriate studies being completed beforehand. Instead, the search for suitable water distribution and water-control methods to prevent overwatering and salinization will be undertaken as the projects proceed.[21] Whatever is found, the likelihood of the project's being halted is negligible.

The Texas Water Plan. In the United States, few of the environmental implications of the giant Texas Water Plan have been studied in depth. In the first 1968 proposal, the increased salinity of the water to be transported under the plan to West Texas was looked at, as was the quality of the water to be imported from the Mississippi, but not in any detailed way. Charles Greer of Indiana University reports that mention was also made of "the recreational and scientific significance of impacts on freshwater fish, waterfowl, and other wildlife habitats which would be affected by reservoir development in the exporting basins of East Texas."[22] Beyond this, however, "none of the major changes in hydrobiology of these basins which could result from the proposed development were reported as having been studied." When, in 1977, a revised version of the scheme was proposed, environmental considerations remained "very much secondary to the plan's main considerations of engineering and economic feasibility." Indeed, environmental problems were perceived largely "as political obstacles to the plan's adoption," rather than as "geographic realities in which the development is to be carried out."

19. The Politics of Damming

POLITICS OR OVERSIGHT?

The examples discussed in Chapter 18 clearly demand an explanation. One plausible but platitudinous view is that we cannot reasonably expect full and detailed studies for every dam—at least partly because we can never know enough about probable ecological and social effects to resolve every uncertainty. As Professor Barton Worthington put it in 1970 at the "Careless Technology" conference: "In developing countries, at least, there will never be enough funds or enough scientists to cover all aspects of information needed for thorough prediction."[1]

In some situations, Worthington clearly has a case. But lack of funds hardly explains the James Bay example. There, after all, we are not talking about research that has been overlooked or short-changed for financial reasons; we are talking about a vast project that was sanctioned and constructed with little or no research into possible ecological and social effects.

What, then, of the second school of thought, namely, that misplaced optimism and wishful thinking lead government and industry alike into minimizing the problems they are likely to encounter? Here, again, the facts suggest otherwise, given the clear evidence that industry is often unwilling to learn from the past and, indeed, is quite prepared to ignore the advice of its own experts if that is contrary to what it wants to hear.

In this vein Aloys Michel remarks, "The saddest thing about the Helmand experience is that it will probably be repeated, if not in Afghanistan, then in Iran or Iraq. . . ."[2] He goes on to explain his despair:

> Many irrigation engineers have had the wisdom to recognize, and the courage to state, that provision of an artificial drainage system is an inescapable concomitant of providing an artificial irrigation system. But the time dimension of irrigation usually acts to ensure that only the storage and distribution components are initially provided. . . . Ingrained optimism and the tendency to procrastinate make yielding to this temptation all the easier, as does the fact that system designers are often driven to underestimate costs or to include disposable items in order to obtain administrative, legislative, or voter approval for their schemes on the proven theory that once ground is broken the project will have to be completed. Furthermore, the engineer, planner, contractor, bureaucrat, or politician may be looking for a short-term personal or professional gain. By the time the omission of a drainage system begins to damage crops, he has usually moved on to another project or another constituency or has retired. These factors would seem to apply in all modern societies regardless of their ideological orientation.[3]

Michel's views are echoed by John Waterbury, who argues in his book *The Hydropolitics of the Nile Valley* that "policy-making groups and external creditors prefer an incomplete picture, for then the unanticipated can be written off to incomplete information and poorly defined responsibilities."[4] He goes so far as to suggest that "the process of resource planning in developing countries is wilfully fragmented"—precisely because planners wish to avoid future responsibility for any disasters. Thus he writes:

> Planners and policy makers limit their responsibility by limiting their range of vision and by retreating into narrowly defined competences. Sectoral and time horizons are constricted as far as possible. Each specialized agency seeks a closely defined mission and relies upon the information of other relevant agencies in designating targets. If the information is erroneous or not forthcoming and if targets are missed, the blame can be shifted on to other quarters.
>
> Similarly, to launch a project at time X is relatively costless, for its benefits or shortcomings will not accrue until time Y, well after its originators have passed from the scene. When the shortcomings do become apparent, the incumbent policy makers can justifiably place the blame upon their predecessors. Short of criminal neglect no one is held to account except the society itself.
>
> All too often, bilateral and multilateral aid-granting bodies comply with this pattern of "planning" for roughly similar motives. Their raison d'être is to move funds, and prudent inactivity will not win their administrators any plaudits or promotions. Thus they operate with the information provided them or seek to supplement it on the strength of lightning surveys whose conclusions are—not infrequently—foregone. Here again, fragmentation of the field of analysis serves as a defense mechanism to limit responsibility for what may or will go wrong. A top-ranking official in the UN World Food Council commented on this, saying, "there is a lot to be gained from not knowing what is going on." There is, then, a natural collusion between the administrators of aid programs and the formulators of programs and projects they wish to aid. Developing societies are alone held responsible for the inefficiencies engendered by this collusion.[5]

Waterbury's observation that "prudent inactivity will not win . . . any plaudits or promotions" raises a problem frequently glossed over in the literature: no dam is built in a political vacuum. On the one hand, there are those who must design, plan, and construct the dam; and, on the other, there are the politicians who must approve its construction. Both are as subject to the psychological pressures of their jobs as the rest of us: the desire to impress colleagues, the fear of "rocking the boat," and the urge to win promotion and recognition—all these are important influences.

Politicians are also keenly aware of the need to cater to their power base—be it the electorate, in democratic countries, or the party, in nondemocratic states—and the large dam-building agencies are likewise aware of the need to lobby for future projects in order to increase their own power and prestige. To some extent, those "political" pressures are openly acknowledged. What is adamantly denied, however, is that the actual decision to build a dam is ever determined by such considerations.

Waterbury, however, is quite explicit in his view that political considerations are generally paramount when it comes to approving dam projects: "The fact is, that as a rule, the politically determined decision comes first and it is exceedingly difficult thereafter to nurture the informed and dispassionate debate requisite to assessing long-term costs."[6]

On what evidence does Waterbury base that conclusion? In the next section we consider in more detail his study of the political decisions that led to the building of the Aswan Dam.

THE ASWAN EXPERIENCE

Had it not been for the success of the Free Officers' coup in 1955, which ousted King Farouk of Egypt and brought Colonel Gamal Abdel Nasser to power, it is arguable that the Aswan High Dam would never have been built. Although the idea of the dam had been touted around Egypt's ministries since 1948, its originator, an engineer of Greek and Egyptian parentage named Adrien Daninos, had generated little support for the scheme. Not that the Egyptian government was averse to the idea of providing year-round storage of the Nile's flood waters; rather, the enormity of the proposal—a reservoir capable of storing the entire annual flood of the Nile—was what provoked skepticism.

Even Daninos himself admitted to having fears that the reservoir would silt up before its time. Others, notably the irrigation expert H. E. Hurst (whom Waterbury calls "the Nile's most authoritative twentieth-century student"), were deeply concerned that evaporation rates would be so high that any potential storage gain from such a large reservoir would quickly be cancelled out. Still others warned that if the Nile's silt was impounded along with its waters, the result would be riverbed erosion on a dramatic—and disastrous—scale.

In the years after Nasser seized power, however, the mood was solidly pro-Aswan. Few dared to voice such comments, and some who did paid a high price. Even Hurst, by then a member of the committee that reviewed the Aswan scheme for the new regime, was soon insisting that the problems of evaporation could be overcome by proper design. Nor did the mood change when the side effects of the dam became apparent. As Professor Ali Fathy, one of the few who stood their ground over the dam, was to comment: "It became clear that competent technicians in government circles were collectively determined to overlook any signs of the deterioration of soil fertility . . . even as a hypothesis. This was the result of what might be called 'the High Dam Covenant,' a psychological state born of political and other circumstances, which has cloaked the project from its very inception."[7] Indeed, one senior official explained the atmosphere by quoting from the *Rubaiyat of Omar Khayyam*: "When the king says it is midnight at noon, the wise man says, behold the moon."[8]

What then had caused the new king to see the moon at midday? And why had his courtiers opted so decisively for the Aswan High Dam? Although a degree of perennial agriculture was known in Egypt even in the Ptolemaic period, it was not until the early nineteenth century that there was a widespread switch from seasonal to year-round farming. Until then, the pattern of agriculture in the Nile Delta remained much as it had been for the previous 6,000 years. Every summer, as the Nile's waters began to rise, channels were dug in the fields to take the waters into large basins, some as big as 80,000 feddans. Once these basins were filled, the water would be allowed to stand for up to 60 days, soaking deep into the earth and depositing the layer of silt that would replenish the alluvial soils. Excess water was then drained back into the Nile and cultivation began, with the harvest taking place in May and the land then fallow again until the next flood in September.

The switch to perennial agriculture radically changed that cycle. With two crops a year being grown, the problems of water-logging and salinity soon became apparent. To a degree, those problems were alleviated by the introduction of new cropping patterns (in particular, a longer fallow period) and by complex networks of drainage. Even so, in 1882, MacKenzie Wallace was to record "white nitrous salts covering the soil and glistening in the sun like untrodden snow."[9] Indeed, by 1908, the problem had become so acute that the first of many committees set up to study the effects of salinity of Egypt's soils concluded that areas then under cotton should be reduced by two-thirds to minimize further destruction.

Perennial agriculture brought with it not only the twin evils of salinity and waterlogging, but also a new fear, a fear of uncertainty that was to become almost an obsession as the century wore on. Waterbury points out: "As the economy moved beyond subsistence and into production for world markets, it lost its tolerance for poor agricultural performance and its capacity to absorb bad years. Some time after World War I, the need for predictability in all elements of the Nile ecosystem became of paramount concern."[10] A low flood could cut Egypt's agricultural production by half; a high flood could "destroy the basins and leave the flood-plain pockmarked with pestilential swamps."

In 1902, therefore, Sir William Garstin, of the Egyptian Public Works Department, first proposed the idea of year-round storage of the Nile's flood waters. His scheme, the Century Storage Scheme, was grandiose in the extreme. "The essential elements of the strategy," writes Waterbury, "were to increase seasonal storage capacity at Aswan, to utilize the Wadi Rayyan depression of Fayyum [formerly ancient Lake Moeris] to siphon and store excess flood waters downstream from Aswan, to build a discharge regulator at the outlet of Lake Mobutu in order to use it for overyear storage and release, and most important, to cut down the water losses through evaporation in the Sudd swamps."[11]

Before Nasser, Garstin's scheme was preferred by the Egyptian authorities. But Nasser and his Free Officers saw an obvious drawback: the scheme left Egypt at the mercy of those states that controlled the Nile upstream. Moreover, three of those states—Kenya, Uganda, and the Sudan—were under the direct rule of Britain, a country with whom relations were extremely strained (recall that this was the time of Suez). The fear, of course, was that Britain would attempt to put pressure on Egypt by interfering with its water supplies.[12]

Not surprisingly, Waterbury considers the "sense of vulnerability and the attendant fears of the downstream states [in the Nile Valley]" to be central to "all the decisions affecting the choice of projects and technology used to master the river."[13] Thus he writes: "No other major river valley is shared by so many autonomous actors, and no other downstream state is so utterly dependent for its livelihood as Egypt is upon its river. The acute awareness of the juxtaposition of these geopolitical factors is at the heart of Egypt's psychological response to all that goes on upstream."

In that context the decision to opt for Aswan is perhaps understandable. Here, after all, was a scheme that (in theory at least) would provide year-round storage within Egypt's borders. To Nasser and the Free Officers, the opportunity was irresistible. The extent to which Egypt felt threatened by the vulnerability of its water supplies is made clear in a speech given years later by President Anwar Sadat. In 1978, he warned: "We depend upon the Nile 100 percent in our life, so if anyone at any moment thinks to deprive us of our life we shall never hesitate [to go to war] because it is a matter of life or death."[14]

The desire to secure Egypt's water supplies was certainly one political motive for building the Aswan High Dam. Another was the sheer prestige of embarking on such a grandiose scheme. As Waterbury puts it:

> The specific decision regarding the High Dam must . . . be set in the general context of a new and unknown regime seeking to establish its credibility and to signal its citizens, and make known to the nations abroad, that it was prepared to do what no previous regime had dared contemplate or advocate to promote the country's well-being. . . .
>
> There is no evidence that the conspirators had given any consideration to the High Dam Scheme before coming to power. Indeed, it is unlikely that they had even heard of it before it fell, somewhat fortuitously, into their laps. But once before them, the project's political advantages, as well as its economic strengths, became immediately apparent. Politically, it had the advantage of being gigantic and daring, thrusting Egypt into the vanguard of modern hydraulic engineering. Moreover, during its construction and after its completion, it would be highly visible and fittingly monumental.[15]

Those motives were to become increasingly dominant in the early years of the dam, particularly as relations between Nasser and Britain deteriorated. Indeed, after Suez—and with it the end of any hope of British financing for the project—"Nasser and his associates could no longer regard the dam as simply a big engineering project, but rather came to hold it up as the symbol of Egypt's will to resist imperialist endeavors to destroy the revolution."[16]

The mood became one of almost millennial fervor. Crowds would run through the streets of Cairo, chanting, "Nasser, Nasser, we come to salute you; after the Dam our land will be paradise."[17] As for Nasser, he promised that the "largest lake ever shaped by human kind" would prove "a source of everlasting prosperity." He talked glowingly of the achievement that the dam represented: "Here are joined the political, social, national and military battles of the Egyptian people, welded together like the gigantic mass of rock that has blocked the course of the ancient Nile."[18]

In such an atmosphere, Waterbury notes, it was not surprising that the dam "came to symbolize a national patriotism, and therefore any criticism of it was thought of as subversive or even treasonous. . . . Technical criticism—at least in public—became tantamount to aiding and abetting the enemy."[19]

Nonetheless, some critics were brave enough to speak out. The most notable of these was undoubtedly Dr. Abd al-Aziz Ahmad, a past chairman of the State Hydroelectric Power Commission and a technical consultant to the Ministry of Public Works. Ahmad's chief concern was that evaporation and seepage losses at Aswan would be far greater than predicted and would in effect cancel out any gains from storing such a large volume of water. He calculated that high winds at the reservoir site could increase annual evaporation losses by as much as 4 billion m^3. In addition, Ahmad argued that seepage losses—if they followed the same pattern as at the Old Aswan Dam—would be considerable. "Assuming the reservoir's life storage capacity to be 100 billion m^3," reports Waterbury, "Ahmad estimated that for the first twenty years, total losses due especially to seepage and the long period of rock saturation, and to evaporation, would be 124 percent of reservoir capacity. . . . After thirty years, losses would reach a stable state of 17 percent a year. At that level, losses would cancel out all the High Dam's expected gains."[20]

Clearly, Ahmad's views were not ones that the authorities wanted to hear—or to be heard. One can imagine the anger, therefore, when it was learned that Ahmad had presented his findings to a meeting of the British Institute of Civil Engineers. This disclosure, says Waterbury, led the regime to see Ahmad "as being in league with its enemies." Ahmad was never forgiven for his indiscretion. In 1964, when a committee voted to award him the State Prize for Outstanding Achievement, the decision was vetoed from on high. Three years later Ahmad died, still in disgrace.

Ahmad's death, however, did not put an end to the argument over seepage and evaporation losses; that argument still rages today. Although it appears likely that Ahmad's figures were on the high side, it is widely accepted that official estimates of evaporation losses were (and still are) far too low. The official claim is that, on average, nine billion m³ are lost annually to evaporation, and a further two billion m³ lost to seepage. In reality, evaporation losses could be as high as fifteen billion m³, and seepage losses could reach five billion m³ a year. That last figure is based on the calculations of two Egyptian engineers, Taher Abu Wafa and Aziz Hanna Labib. Such is the discrepancy between their figures and those put out by the Egyptian government that Waterbury is led to comment: "Either they are wrong [and both gentlemen were top officials in the High Dam Authority] or the figures released for public consumption are being doctored."[21]

Ahmad was not the only critic whose fears have been largely vindicated; Professor Ali Fathy is another. Although Fathy was never ostracized, the authorities showed themselves singularly unwilling to take his criticisms seriously. When he warned of the dangers of riverbed scouring, a committee set up to study the problem dismissed his fears as exaggerated. His warnings about the effect on soil fertility of depriving the Delta of the Nile's silt were also ignored.

In raising such issues, Fathy was not putting forward any new theory. The dangers of both riverbed scouring and silt deprivation had been known for many years. In 1908, for instance, Sir William Willcocks wisely remarked: "It will be an evil day for Egypt if she forgets that, though basin irrigation with its harvest of corn has given way to perennial irrigation with its cotton fields, the lessons which basin irrigation has taught for 7,000 years cannot be unlearned with impunity. The rich muddy water of the Nile flood has been the mainstay of Egypt for many generations, and it can be no more dispensed with today than in the past."[22]

That, however, was not the view of the authorities. From the very outset, it was argued that the benefits of the silt previously deposited by the Nile's flood could easily be matched by chemical fertilizers. The result has been a dramatic—and now crippling—rise in Egypt's fertilizer bill. From 1952 to 1964, consumption of nitrogenous fertilizer rose from 648,000 tons to 1.2 million tons, and phosphate consumption soared from 92,000 tons to 322,000 tons.[23] What those fertilizers cannot replace, however, are the other trace elements in the silt and the organic matter it contains; nor, more important still, can they replace the soil being lost to the more intensive agricultural practices rendered possible by perennial irrigation. Indeed, in 1974, Sayyid Marei, who had been minister of agriculture since 1952 and was chairman of the 1974 World Food Conference, told a parliamentary committee, "I say in all candour, as loudly as possible, I am worried, extremely worried, because of the threat to the fertility of our soils."[24]

One thing that particularly alarmed Marei was the lack of drainage at sites where land had been reclaimed. Marei says he warned his colleagues that the only possible result of reclamation without drainage would be increased salinization—but, he claims, his warnings went unheeded. In any case, those reclamation schemes that lacked drainage proved disastrous for Egypt. A recent FAO study found that more than one-third of Egypt's agricultural land is now afflicted with salinity and some 90 percent of cultivated land is afflicted with waterlogging. Hardly surprising, perhaps, for in 1975 not even three million feddans had drainage of any kind.

That the Egyptian government could ignore such advice from one of its most prominent politicians confirms its capacity for self-deception. Just as it did not wish to hear about the problems of soil fertility, evaporation, riverbed scouring, or seepage, so it was quite unwilling to listen to talk of waterlogging and salinization. Waterbury ends his study of the hydropolitics of the Nile Valley with the following observation:

> The political decision [to build a dam] frequently embodies a symbolic package that is designed to catch people's imagination at home and abroad, to arouse the populace, to set collective goals and thus to find in motivational terms a substitute for war. This is an atmosphere fundamentally inhospitable to the niggling of conscientious technocrats who may be seen as frontmen, witting or unwitting, for the regime's enemies. Their sincerity will be in question. This has been the case in Egypt, where the sense of national cohesion and even consensus about national goals and leadership is far more pronounced than in many, if not most, Third

World countries. But who would publicly stand up today to question the wisdom of sowing the desert with new cities or trying to make the Sinai green and populous?[25]

It is a good question for, as we shall see in the next section, the political motives that led to the building of Aswan are symptomatic of most dam building projects.

POWER BROKERS, PORK BARRELS, AND CORRUPTION

From the Aswan example, we can identify three general factors that dominated the dam's history: first, the political and psychological fears that were the initial spur to seeking year-round storage in Egypt itself; second, the messianic fervor that motivated both the Nasser regime and the general public; and, third, the unwillingness to countenance criticism.

Although the details are specific to Aswan, those three features are common to many other dams around the world. The millennial element, for instance, is clearly evident in the James Bay project, launched under the slogan "The World Begins Tomorrow." So too, President Kwame Nkrumah of Ghana promised that the Volta dam would rescue the Ghanaians from being "hewers of wood and drawers of water for the West" and lead them instead into a new industrial age where "economic modernization relieves the working man . . . of some of the less necessary forms of drudgery."[26]

Millenarianism may be a constant theme of many large-scale dam projects, but the political motives behind them are many and varied—and sometimes starkly obvious. One reason for the eagerness of the Guyanese government to promote the Upper Mazaruni Dam was that a complex border dispute between Guyana and Venezuela centered on the Mazaruni Basin. In a 1970 moratorium it was agreed that neither party would take unilateral action to strengthen its claim. The hypothesis is that by developing the area, Guyana hoped to establish a presence strong enough to undermine Venezuela's position in any future negotiations.[27]

Nor is there much doubt that the Sudanese government pushed ahead with the building of the Jonglei Canal after the ending of the civil war in the southern Sudan in order to consolidate its victory and complete the integration of the North and South. Indeed, the commissioner for the project was quite specific as to the canal's political advantages: "Historically, the rift between north and south has increased in the past because of the lack of communications. The Sudd has always been a barrier. And that is why the Sudanese in the northern part tend towards the Middle East rather than Africa. Our link with Africa and with the south in particular was weakened because of the difficulty of communication."[28] The commissioner saw the Jonglei Canal as an instrument of reconciliation, but others, fearing it would encourage an influx of Northerners, and particularly Egyptians, rioted in the streets in protest.

Political goals must also explain the inordinately long transmission lines being built to supply Zaire's Shaba mines with electricity. At present, the mines are run on electricity imported from neighbouring Zambia. Plans are afoot, however, to supply power from dams on the Zaire (Congo) River, some 1,700 kilometers away. Once the necessary transmission line is completed, the government's control over the rich and independently minded Shaba province will be considerably increased. As Warren Linney and Susan Harrison point out, "If Shaba tries for independence, the electricity can be cut off."[29]

Such overt machinations are by no means confined to developing countries. In the industrialized world, too, political considerations provide the rationale for many dams. For the most part, those considerations are eminently parochial: dam projects win votes. In the first place, any new project automatically thrusts the sitting member of Congress or Parliament into the limelight. As George Pring, then a researcher at the Washington-based Environmental Defense Fund, points out: "The average congressman can rededicate the same dam for four or five consecutive elections. First, he dedicates the groundbreaking. Then he dedicates the land purchases. Then he comes back and dedicates the flood abutments. And then he dedicates the flagpoles. A congressman's future in many parts of the country, as the saying goes, is written in concrete."[30]

Acquiring a dam for one's home district is the essence of what has become known in U.S. politics as the "pork barrel," derived from the custom among slavers of occasionally providing their slaves with a barrel of preserved pork. Those with the longest reach and the most determined approach inevitably had the most to eat. The handing out of choice federal contracts is now seen by many to operate on the same principles. This is described by George Laycock in *The Diligent Destroyers*:

> The pork barrel has become a way of political life. Politicians . . . often believe they can equate their worth to their home districts with the amount of money they send back from the federal treasury. Although there are other cuts of pork, such as post office buildings, the choice ones are the impressive big water projects scattered from Maine to Hawaii. The individual congressman has his eye on the project closest to his heart, which is to say, nearest to his voting booth. He might sense that projects within the bill are a waste of federal funds, but he is reluctant to argue against his fellow-congressmen's favorite dam or canal. To do so is to jeopardize the other's support for his own pet project.[31]

The key to understanding why the pork-barrel system is so fundamental is that the bits of "pork" being doled out are in effect free gifts from the federal government—vast sums of money to generate localized economic growth. For farmers, the prospect is of cheap supplies of water; for local real estate agents, there is the vision of new housing developments; for the unemployed, there is the possibility of new jobs. That those benefits are often not forthcoming is irrelevant; what is important is that each new project brings with it the promise of an economic bonanza.

The wheeling and dealing that go with pork-barrel politics—and with the influence it brings—inevitably breed corruption. In that respect, it is worth noting a remark made by Representative Michael Meyers, one of those U.S. congressmen involved in the so-called Abscam scandal. In conversation with a group of businessmen whom he assumed to be representatives of an interested foreign power—but who were, in fact, FBI undercover agents—Meyers was asked about his influence with the State Department. Though poorly expressed, his reply (taped by the FBI) was explicit enough: "There's a million deals. It's a trading game down in Washington. . . . Going onto the Appropriations Committee in January, this makes me a very important guy."[32] In particular, Meyers mentioned that some congressional committees "who have key members who are involved in State are interested in something from the Appropriations Committee, where they need funding for a dam." The implication was clear: if Meyers played the game, he could win the necessary influence at the State Department.

The extent to which the U.S. Congress is beset by such corruption is hard to gauge. Direct bribery is probably the exception: more commonly, agribusiness, engineering consultants, and construction unions make campaign contributions to representatives seeking reelection, thereby hoping to secure a dam project.

In the Third World, the role of bribery and corruption is acknowledged more openly. One informed source who has had dealings with certain West African governments, reports that in order to even see a cabinet minister, it is necessary to deposit a briefcase full of money with the appropriate secretary. Another source reports that in Sri Lanka, one-third of the aid money intended for the Mahaweli scheme has gone in bribes.

It need hardly be said, however, that neither overt bribery nor pork-barrel politics makes for a wise decision. Take, for example, the plans to bring water to the western and southwestern United States. The massive demand for water in the area has already led to a precipitous fall in groundwater reserves, rivers running dry, and widespread salinization. David Sheridan claims that "Present rates of irrigation in some parts of southwestern Nebraska will cause water level declines of almost 50 percent between 1978 and the year 2000. In Nebraska, an average of over 300,000 acres of irrigated corn has been established each year since 1973. Half of all the existing irrigation projects in the western part of the state are expected to experience water shortages in 20 to 25 years."[33]

Indeed, Sheridan argues that in many areas of the arid western United States, "human systems are exceeding the carrying capacity of their natural life support systems." Nonetheless, it is unlikely that any sensible conservation measures will be introduced voluntarily, given the availability of federal largesse. No one, least of all the farmers in the area, wants to be told to limit their use of water. They see the solution lying in the massive water projects the politicians promise to build with federal funds. Sheridan cites the city of Tucson's response to its dwindling groundwater supply as typical of the problem.

> Limiting water consumption . . . would seem to be the logical solution, but it apparently has not been politically feasible. Many of the people have moved to this desert oasis from parts of the country with much wetter climates and have brought with them water-consuming habits such as lawn watering that are ill-suited to the desert. More importantly, to limit water use is to limit economic growth, and many vested interests in the area—developers, construction companies, financial institutions—have a big stake in continued economic growth. So, instead of conserving water or doing without more water, cities such as Tucson look to the federal government to provide inexpensive water.[34]

STATES WITHIN STATES

If the eagerness of politicians to bring home the pork is one half of the answer to the question that opened Part 4, the power of the institutions that plan and build dams and other water projects is the other. Handling vast budgets and exercising considerable political power themselves, they are well versed in the art of lobbying. For example, George Laycock recalls how one civil servant who worked for the U.S. Army Corps of Engineers went about handling a congressman he wished to interest in a project. The civil servant told a biologist from the U.S. Fish and Wildlife

Service: "We maintain dossiers on each member of the Appropriations Committee. When one of these congressmen came to New Orleans recently, we were ready for him. One of our people took a friend of his to dinner in Washington just to learn more about him. We found out that he was a diabetic. So, when he arrived in New Orleans, his air-conditioned limousine was already equipped with a refrigerator stocked with everything he might need, including insulin."[35]

Whatever the sources of its influence, the U.S. Army Corps of Engineers—together with the Bureau of Reclamation—wields considerable power on Capitol Hill. When President Carter tried to put through a bill in 1979 that would have created a new department, the Department of Natural Resources, and made it responsible for—among other things—reviewing water projects, his efforts were stymied by the corps and its allies. A year later, Carter was forced to withdraw his presidential veto of a proposed bill that would have sanctioned $4.2 billion worth of water projects—a bill he had previously called "a travesty, wasteful, destructive and expensive."[36]

Other countries have agencies that are equally powerful. In Australia, Tasmania's Hydro-Electric Commission (HEC) has been accused of being a state within a state. "For more than fifty years," writes Peter Thompson, of the Australian Conservation Foundation, "the commission has played a virtually unchallenged role as Tasmania's economic, social and land-use planner. It has been an organization operating in a power vacuum, created by a succession of parliaments which have never insisted on the public accountability of the HEC."[37]

Thompson is not alone in his view of the commission. Other, more official bodies have also voiced growing concern about the power now enjoyed by the HEC. Tasmania's own Directorate of Energy noted with alarm in 1980 that the commission was sounding out potential customers for its hydroelectric power without referring to other government departments. "It would seem that the Hydro-Electric Commission has been permitted, in the absence of adequate policy guidance, to act as a de facto, and largely autonomous, economic planning agency. This is indisputably not its role."

In 1974, a Committee of Inquiry into the HEC's plans to flood Tasmania's Lake Pedder had expressed harsh criticism of "the limited scope of the Commission's planning objectives and evaluation criteria . . . and the narrow scope of the Commission's professional expertise." Indeed, the Committee of Inquiry argued:

> It appears to be a close knit and tightly disciplined organization and might be considered the archetype of the kind of government instrumentality described as a "guild authority" by John Power of the Canberra CAE. Such organizations are common among public works agencies in Australia, particularly in the water resources field. They tend to internalize expertise to avoid independent review of their proposals, to discourage public knowledge of their activities, and to have limited [generally single-purpose] objectives.
>
> Because of their staffing structure and the nature of their charter, such organizations are ill equipped to handle problems which involve multiobjective planning, environmental considerations, or interdisciplinary cooperation. [Some organizations react] by drawing within themselves and refusing to acknowledge that problems outside their own field or expertise exist. The Hydro-Electric Commission was one such organization in 1967. The experience of this Committee suggests that it is still very much so.[38]

That view of the HEC has been amply reinforced in the ten years since the Committee of Inquiry sat, especially by the commission's reaction to the international outcry over its plans to dam the Franklin River. Not until the High Court of Australia ruled that the area, which had been included in the World Heritage List as a site of outstanding natural beauty, should be preserved did the HEC agree to halt work on the dam.

Such outright disregard for international opinion is exceptional. The determination shown by the HEC to build the Franklin River Dam is symptomatic of a more general tendency within the industry to push ahead with projects apparently regardless of the case against them. Indeed, the record makes it quite apparent that figures have frequently been falsified in order to win approval for projects that on the basis of any objective analysis would never be sanctioned, let alone constructed. In the next chapter, we shall consider that allegation in more detail.

20. Fudging the Books

COST-BENEFIT STUDIES:
THE PATTERN OF FALSIFICATION

The old adage that he who pays the piper calls the tune is as apt today as when it was first coined. The record of industry is littered with examples of cover-ups to justify the marketing of products that are unsafe or suspected of causing harm.[1] Invariably an "independent" expert is on hand to tell the public what industry would like heard. That should not surprise us. Scientists and consultants in industry are ruled by everyday concerns—the mortgage, the need to provide for a family, the fear of failure and criticism. They know they were not hired to rock the boat and that trouble-makers do not get promotions. Is it any wonder, then, that many are tempted to cut corners and see things in the best light for the sake of their companies and their careers?

That is not to say that all studies undertaken by a vested interest are suspect. It is to suggest, however, the importance of skepticism. Indeed, it is always wise to ask who funded a study when assessing its objectivity. In the case of large-scale water projects, the point was well made by Jimmy Carter when he was running for president. He told a rally held to oppose plans to build a dam at Melones in California:

In many of the Corps of Engineers' dam projects around the nation, the benefit/cost ratios have been grossly distorted. Data and promises on which project approvals are sought are erroneous and outdated. False justifications of projects are attempted.

Every corps project that was initiated many years ago should be thoroughly evaluated and computations should be confirmed by the General Accounting Office (GAO). This would ensure the saving of billions of dollars in taxpayers' money and hundreds of miles of irreplaceable and precious wild rivers.

A recent GAO analysis of the Sprewell Bluff dam project on the Flint River in Georgia indicated vividly the fallacies in existing Corps of Engineers analysis procedures. Construction costs were underestimated, extremely low interest rates were assumed, nearby lakes were ignored, population projections were exaggerated, environmental damage was concealed, power production estimates were based on overloaded generator ratings, no archaeological losses are included, and major recreation benefits were claimed in spite of official opposition from state and federal recreation agencies. Similar distortions exist in the New Melones project.[2]

The GAO report referred to by Carter was the result of an independent audit by Congress's watchdog agency of a cross section of seven dam projects then being undertaken in the United States.[3] It contained some stinging criticisms of the major dam-building agencies. Thus, as Julian McCaull, former editor of *Environment*, reports: "The study shows many specific instances in which sponsoring agencies, intent on having the projects authorized, overstated expected annual monetary gains to be realized from water management activities such as flood control, irrigation, generation of electricity, and outdoor recreation. At the same time, estimated costs were sharply underestimated for annual operation and maintenance of the projects, reservoir-flooding of productive land, and loss of outdoor recreation sites."[4]

In one case, the U.S. Army Corps of Engineers claimed that Missouri's Pattonsburg Lake project would bring $1.1 million a year in agricultural benefits. In sharp contrast, the U.S. Department of Agriculture estimated that the project would result in an annual *loss* of $1 million a year through the destruction of exist-

ing agricultural land and the loss of business to local farm industries. Typically, the corps chose its own figures for the purpose of
its cost-benefit analysis. It also claimed $198,700 worth of flood
control benefits and $413,000 worth of water supply benefits
without any documented evidence to support either claim.[5]

In another instance, the corps claimed $65,000 worth of ben-
efits a year in irrigation from the Lost Creek Lake project on Or-
egon's Rogue River. Yet, as McCaull reports, those irrigation
facilities would have had to be provided "by a separate project,
the proposal for which was subsequently shelved without ever
being presented to Congress."[6] In a similar vein, the corps boost-
ed the project's hydroelectric potential by including "not only the
economic value of on-site generating capacity of 14,100 kilowatts, but also the value of 10,500 kilowatts which might be
added in the future [but which had not been formally proposed
to Congress] at some other site in the Rogue River Basin, and
which might then be used to supplement the Lost Creek capacity." Furthermore, the "fishing use" benefits for the project were
overestimated by some $22,500 a year because no account was
taken of the economic loss that would be incurred by local fishermen when Lost Creek was flooded. In total, the GAO estimated that the value of expected annual benefits for the seven
projects reviewed had been inflated by $12,607,080.[7]

It is worth putting those figures in perspective. In the case of
the Pattonsburg Lake project, the "claimed annual benefits" that
could not be justified were valued at $873,000; "unsubstantiat-
ed" claims (those benefits that had been overestimated but were
in part justified) at $413,000 a year; and costs were found to have
been underestimated by $446,000 a year. As McCaull points
out—on the basis of the first item alone—"Over the 100-year period used to predict the economic future for the project, this
yearly overstatement would total $87,300,000, or 52 percent of
the entire estimated cost of the project."[8]

Among other water projects around the world whose cost-benefit figures are now open to doubt we find the following examples:

Reviewing the Final Environmental Statement (FES) submitted by the U.S. Bureau of Reclamation in support of its *Garrison*

Diversion Project, the Washington-based Institute of Ecology concluded that the project had "no economic justification."[9] Under
its provisions, a 77-mile open channel and a string of dams are
being built in order to channel the waters of the Missouri River
into a massive reservoir to irrigate some 250,000 acres. Yet, as
Onno Kremer, vice-chairman of the Manitoba Environmental
Council, reports in the Canadian journal *Alternatives*, those
250,000 acres already "support a prosperous agriculture," and to
irrigate them it will be necessary to "convert 220,000 acres of
farmland and wetlands to drains, ditches, service roads and other
facilities."[10] The Institute of Ecology estimated that the project
would in fact "reduce cropland by 8,148 acres, grassland by
39,172 acres, and woods by 6,276 acres." Moreover, the irrigation costs were likely to be so high that they would "amount to a
subsidy of $122,000 per person, or $469,771 per farm."

The Institute of Ecology also pointed out that: "Energy consumption per acre for the Garrison Diversion Unit is nearly nine
times the national average for irrigation agriculture"; the "degradation of water quality by the project will be far greater than
indicated in the FES"; that "the destruction of family farms, the
uprooting of entire families, and the concentration of land ownership due to the project are inadequately discussed"; and that "a
disregard for potential effects on complex ecosystems is a basic
fault of the FES."

The institute reached a devastating conclusion:

> The FES prepared by the Bureau of Reclamation for their Gar-
> rison Diversion Unit in North Dakota does not represent a com-
> prehensive and objective examination of the complete impacts of
> the Garrison Diversion Unit. The FES is final for the principal
> supply works only and not for the total authorized project. Infor-
> mation included in the FES is grossly inadequate and defies ob-
> jective evaluation. Further, the Bureau of Land Reclamation's
> analysis of its own data is often inaccurate, insufficient, or mis-
> leading. The project is described in very general and frequently
> tentative terms and the existing environment is considered in a
> cursory manner. Major adverse impacts are ignored and alterna-
> tives to the project are not considered. It appears . . . that the FES

was prepared as a justification for the Garrison Diversion Project rather than a detailed analysis of its environmental impacts.[11]

Authorized in 1946, the *Tenn-Tom Canal* was intended to link the Tennessee and Tombigbee rivers at a cost of $316 million. "When the calculations were completed, the cost-benefit ratio came out at 1.24 to 1," reports George Laycock. "To reach that profit-making conclusion, the engineers had tossed in all the benefit ingredients they could justify from among those allowed by Congress, including several million dollars for recreation, fish, and wildlife 'enhancement' and wage payments to those employed to work on the canal."[12]

By 1976, however, the benefit-cost ratio had fallen to 1.08 to 1—and even that ratio, claim critics, was achieved only by underestimating costs and overestimating benefits. Thus, in 1981, R. Jeffery Smith reported in *Science*:

In 1976 . . . the Corps and its economic consultant, A. T. Kearney of Chicago, found several dozen firms in the region of the waterway who said they planned to use it after it was completed. Early in 1981, the General Accounting Office contacted 17 of these firms—representing the bulk of the predicted shipments—and discovered that only about half were still interested. The GAO found that some of the predictions "were not based on 'definite' company plans." In other instances, the GAO said, Kearney's estimating practices "may have been too liberal."[13]

By 1981, the cost of the project had jumped to $1 billion, and a further $960 million was estimated to be necessary to straighten and widen the third leg of the canal in order to avoid bottlenecks.

Other hidden federal project costs detected by the GAO could include as much as $31.5 million to soften the waterway's impact on fish and wildlife; $360 million to deepen and widen the port of Mobile where barges will enter the Gulf; and $48 million to construct waterway-related recreational facilities. Mississippi and Alabama, which are obligated under federal water project rules to spend $170 million for highway and bridge relocations, are actually receiving $90 million of this amount from the federal Department of Transportation. . . . *None of these costs are included in the Corps's cost-benefit calculations.*[14]

Despite such criticisms, however, Congress voted in 1981 to continue with the project—at a cost of $10 million a month—on the grounds that construction work on the canal had proceeded too far to be terminated. To do so, commented one of the Tenn-Tom backers, would leave behind "the largest swamp in America."[15]

Early estimates of the cost of the power generated by Kentucky's Devil's Jump Dam made it clear that the price per unit of electricity would be eight to ten times as high as that produced by the Tennessee Valley Authority, the dam's major anticipated customer. With other dams already built upstream at Lake Cumberland, flood control benefits were seen to be negligible. Unable to offer cheap power or flood control benefits, the dam seemed likely to be canceled. The Corps of Engineers, however, was not to be deterred. As George Laycock reports:

> Its solution was simply not to drain Lake Cumberland as low as usual for the winter. Automatically, this would mean that Lake Cumberland no longer had storage capacity to hold back as much water during periods of high runoff. Then these waters, for which there had been no room left in Lake Cumberland, could be accommodated in the proposed Devil's Jump Reservoir. This, at least in theory, would enable the Corps to claim that Devil's Jump would hold back 256,000 acre-feet of water for flood control in spite of the fact that it offered no such benefits in any real sense.[16]

The dam was approved by Congress but was subsequently halted as a result of public protest.

Such blatant falsification occurs by no means only in the United States. Indeed, it would appear to be typical of the industry worldwide. When the Indian economist Vijay Paranjpye reviewed the cost-benefit analyses for numerous dams submitted by India's hydroelectric authorities, he found them so consistently wrong that he concluded: "The estimates had very little to do with the realistic assessment of costs. . . . [Their] sole purpose was, and still is, to get the approval of the Planning Commission and obtain the necessary financial sanction."[17] To support that allegation, Paranjpye cited the findings of an Indian government committee that had analyzed 64 dam projects and found that "the percentage rise in revised costs over initially estimated costs turned out to be an average of 108 per cent."

More specifically, Paranjpye took a detailed look at the figures submitted by the Karnataka Power Corporation in support of its Bedti dam. On the basis of his own calculations, Paranjpye argued: "Even if the most obvious and direct costs of the project are taken into account, the project is economically nonviable. The government of Karnataka will be experiencing an annual loss of over Rs 3 crores [30 million rupees, or £2 million] due to this project throughout the lifetime of the dam, unless the Karnataka Power Corporation raises the average price of power to well over 80 paise [100 paise = one rupee] per unit, so as to derive a reasonable rate of return which could cover the social and economic cost."[18] At that price, the power from the dam would be selling at almost five times the amount that Karnataka Power had forecast.

Paranjpye calculates that the benefit-cost ratio for the project is 0.8 to 1. He concludes: "It is reasonable to presume that if the true costs had been revealed, the Planning Commission would never have sanctioned the project." Karnataka Power had obviously juggled the figures by underestimating the costs of resettlement and compensation, by totally ignoring the cost of transmission lines, by failing to take account of the revenue from the forests that would be lost to the dam, and by allocating trivial sums for such vital measures as soil conservation.

Karnataka Power was eventually forced to recalculate at least the cost of resettlement. Even then, however, the figures were underestimated. Karnataka Power upped the number of people whose land would be flooded from 1,500 to 3,706 (an increase of 147 percent), but Paranjpye put the true figure at 5,193. So, too, the true figure he estimated for submerged paddy land was 1,429 hectares, as against Karnataka Power's revised figure of 459 hectares; for dry land lost, 384.2 hectares as against 201.6 hectares; for gardens, 190 hectares as against 36.4 hectares; and, for the number of houses and hamlets to be submerged, 741 as against Karnataka Power's figure of 50. Indeed, Paranjpye agreed with the authorities on only one set of figures: the amount of forest that would be lost—some 10,000 hectares.

OVERESTIMATING BENEFITS, UNDERESTIMATING COSTS

The above examples highlight just a few of the means used to manipulate cost-benefit ratios in favor of projects that, under any realistic appraisal, would never have had a chance of even getting off the drawing board. Other techniques used to "massage" the figures in order to give a favorable economic assessment of a project include the following:

Using unrealistically low discount rates. Until 1971, the discount rate* used to evaluate U.S. water projects was often as low as 3.125 percent.[19] That level was set in Senate Document 97, in 1962, and bore no relation to then current interest rates, let alone future rates. In 1971, the U.S. Water Resources Council, "recognizing both the objectives of subsidizing water resource projects and the objectives of an efficient combination among and between federal and nonfederal investment activities," set the new rate at 7 percent, rather than the 10 percent it acknowledged to be the rate of return of nonfederal investments.[20] In 1973, the council reduced the rate to 6⅞ percent.

---

*The discount rate is described by Parry and Norgaard: "The discount rate is the rate of interest used to convert future dollar values to present dollar values, and depending on the discount rate assigned to a benefit-cost analysis, it can have a significant influence on the outcome of the analysis. To illustrate what we mean by discount rate, a capital investment which will yield you $10 one year from now really is not worth $10 to you today because you have to wait a year to get the money. If the interest rate in society is 5 per cent, that $10 is only worth about $9.50 to you today since you could be receiving regular interest money at the 5 per cent rate on the $10, and thus have 10.50 rather than just $10.00 at the end of the year." (B. T. Parry and R. B. Norgaard, "Wasting a River," *Environment*, Jan./Feb. 1978, Vol. 17, No. 1, p. 25.)

Even so, in its 1973 cost-benefit analysis for California's New Melones Dam, the Corps of Engineers still insisted on using a discount rate of 3⅛ percent. As Dr. Thomas Parry and Professor Richard Norgaard assert:

> The reason is clear when benefits and costs are examined in the light of the effect of a 6⅞ or 7 percent discount rate. Using the 6⅞ percent figure, the interest forgone would be approximately $13,500,000 annually [as opposed to $5,700,000 at 3⅛ percent]. Adding figures for amortization, maintenance, and operation, and taxes forgone, the total annual costs become about $15,400,000, or significantly more than the $13,500,000 which the corps estimated to be the annual benefit. This disparity, of course, would make the benefit-cost ratio less than one-to-one and, consequently, would make the entire project economically unfeasible.[21]

In other cases, not even a low discount rate can save a project. Idaho's Teton Dam, which impounded 17 miles of river in a massive irrigation and flood control project, is a case in point. Even using the Bureau of Reclamation's own figures and its chosen discount rate of 3.5 percent, a group of environmentalists found that the claimed benefit-cost ratio of 1.2 to 1 was in reality only 0.73 to 1; that is, just 73 cents' worth of benefits for every dollar spent. Using an interest rate of 6 percent, the ratio tumbled to a dismal 0.4 to 1.[22]

It is also important to recognize that although unrealistically low discount rates are used for the costs of the water projects themselves, unrealistically high discount rates are employed to evaluate the ecological benefits that will be destroyed. This is of particular relevance in the Third World. Indeed, as the Nairobi-based Environment Liaison Centre points out:

> The use of a discount rate over time seems unrealistic for such rehabilitative projects as timber and food production or the conservation of wildlife and scenic areas. These resources carry only a slight risk of becoming worthless or obsolescent through technological advancement, changes in the weather, or fashion—in contrast to machinery, chemical factories, or dam projects. With a growing world population, the risk that soil, water, and air will be

valued any less in 50 years is almost zero. Their value can only go up, unless we colonize other planets. Yet, if a figure of 10 percent is adopted as a discount rate, which is a much lower figure than in most cost-benefit analyses, it would appear "uneconomic" to plant trees for fuelwood production. If it takes £100 and 50 years to produce a crop worth £2,000 [at 1975 prices], it would not appear "economic" to do so because interest charges would amount to $10,000. With this analysis, our future generations may have to do without basic requirements of survival, such as forests, fertile soils, clean water and scenic areas. Clearly a new method of evaluating protective measures is needed.[23]

Overestimating job-creation potential. One of the major stated reasons for building the James Bay Project was that it would create 125,000 jobs—at an admitted cost, incidentally, of $80,000 a job. However, only 22,000 jobs were created during the busiest period of construction in 1977, and by 1978 there were only 12,000 to 13,000 on-site jobs available, most of them unskilled. "Indirect jobs will be created as well, of course, but as the project moves toward completion, workers will be laid off, boom towns will become ghost towns, and the economic benefits will evaporate," comments the Committee for the Defence of James Bay. "A completed dam requires very few maintenance personnel. This fact is especially important to the native population, which might find themselves permanently unemployed after working for a few years—having lost their land and their livelihood in the process."[24]

The potential for job creation was similarly overestimated at the Tenn-Tom Canal. As Fred Powledge points out:

Ordinarily, redevelopment benefits are calculated on the basis of hiring local workers who are otherwise unemployed; the assumption is that hiring these people does not reduce productivity anywhere else in the nation, and so wages paid to such workers are not included as project costs. The Corps avoided even these questionable procedures and made three insupportable assumptions: that a "local" worker was one who had been in the area for more than one day; that 80 percent of the work force was "local"; and that 100 percent of the local workers hired by the project were unemployed.[25]

Failing to account for the energy costs of building the dam. Cost-benefit analysis rarely takes account of the actual energy required to build and operate a dam. Where such "energy accounting" has been carried out, however, the results are often surprising. Linney and Harrison point out:

> Blocking a river's course requires that an enormous amount of earth must be moved and a structure raised, either out of landfill and rock or concrete. Access roads must be built, often over long distances and steep terrain, as dam sites are usually isolated. If the dam is constructed of concrete, more petrol will be used to power the mixing plant on the site. Heavy earth-moving equipment will be run during the two to six years of construction. With the exception of the use of dynamite in blasting, all these construction activities will require fossil fuel. Given the increasing cost of fossil fuel and its scarcity in developing countries due to foreign exchange constraints, the influence of fuel consumption should be evaluated. Some dams built in the past create a questionable net gain in energy [energy used in construction minus power generated] due to construction in isolated energy-intensive sites, and a short life from sedimentation.[26]

When Dr. Philip Williams studied the energy accounts of the New Melones Dam in California, he found that the dam would result in a net loss of energy. As Tim Palmer notes in *Stanislaus: The Struggle for a River*: "From the projected average year's 430 million kilowatt hours of electricity, Williams subtracted the energy costs of construction and maintenance; the loss of an existing power plant; energy for irrigation and pumping; and the energy costs of reservoir recreation. Williams's bottom line? A net loss of 39 million kwh per year."[27]

Overestimating the benefits of flood control. As we have seen in chapter 10, the flood control benefits of large dams are frequently overstated. No dam has yet been built to take account of the worst possible flood; the cost of doing so would be prohibitive. The problem, as Grant Ash, the Corps of Engineers's own officer, points out, is that dams give people a false sense of security, tempting them to build on flood plains that common sense might tell them to avoid.

Although the Corps of Engineers is clearly aware of the dangers of building on flood plains, it nonetheless chooses to include the value of the property built there among the benefits claimed for a dam. Such a statistical sleight-of-hand, argues Brent Blackwelder of the Environmental Policy Institute, allows the Corps to justify almost any project: "Many of the structures now protected by upstream dams and levees were not in place and would not have been built were it not for the dam or levee. Using the Corps's argument, almost any dam could be justified provided enough expensive developments were located in the flood-plain downstream from the dam."[28]

In many cases, the claimed flood control benefits of a dam often benefit only a tiny minority. That point was clearly documented in a GAO study entitled *Congressional Guidance Needed on Federal Cost Share of Water Resource Projects When Project Benefits Are Not Widespread.*[29] Among the examples given in the report, the following stand out as particularly profligate:

A planned $17.7 million flood control scheme in Hendry County, Florida, will benefit just twenty-one farmers. Thirteen of them will receive most of the benefits, and four of those are large corporations, owning 61 percent of the 34 square miles to be protected. Moreover, two landowners have expressly stated that "they are against the current project because it would overdrain their land and they would rather have their land in its present state." Ironically, the project is considered necessary in order to mitigate the flood damage caused by an earlier corps scheme. As the GAO explains: "Four levees were constructed in the mid-1950s to prevent floodwaters originating on the then sparsely developed land west of the levees from flooding the agricultural lands to the east. This construction and the subsequent increased development have aggravated flood problems on the lands west of the levees. The Hendry County project, authorized in 1965, provides additional flood protection west of the levees."[30]

The South Sumter flood prevention scheme, costing some $2,742,610, is intended to reduce the damage of local floods with a 47-mile network of drains and channels. Although the original plans estimated that 300 people would benefit, it is clear that the major beneficiary has in fact been T. G. Lee Dairies, the largest landowner in the area. Indeed, "according to the district conservationist, T. G. Lee purchased the land because of the benefits that would accrue from the project." As a result of the project, the company has been able to upgrade 2,390 acres from unimproved pasture to 1,405 acres of cropland and 985 acres of pastureland, bringing annual benefits worth $25,095. Moreover, the scheme has also raised the value of the company's land by $1,195,000. Nonetheless, neither T. G. Lee or any other of the beneficiaries of the scheme has had to make any contribution to the costs of the project.[31]

Underestimating the costs of decommissioning. The cost of decommissioning a dam is rarely taken into account among the costs and benefits of a project. If the dam has served flood control purposes, that is particularly relevant. Indeed, as Dr. Philip Williams points out: "Decommissioning costs may be extremely large if development has occurred in the floodplain downstream and is then exposed to flood damage."[32]

Overestimating the life of dams. Sedimentation significantly reduces the projected useful life of a dam (see chapter 16). In India, for example, dams are known to silt up between three—and in the case of the Nizamgara dam, 17—times faster than expected. Nonetheless, it is clearly in the interest of a dam builder to estimate the longest life possible for a dam, thus spreading the initial high construction costs over a longer period, and hence reducing the proportion of those costs which are charged annually. Indeed, by extending the claimed useful life of a dam, a poor cost-benefit ratio can be transformed into a more favorable one. In its 1961 analysis of the benefits and costs for the New Melones dam in California, the Corps of Engineers estimated a 50-year lifespan. On the basis of that figure, it arrived at a benefit-cost ratio of 1.6 to 1. "The very next year," report Parry and Norgaard, "the Corps decided to increase the period of analysis to 100 years. With other factors, such as increasing prices, the Corps derived a new and much more favorable benefit-cost ratio of 2.5 to 1. The change to the 100-year period obviously was of great advantage in promoting the New Melones Project."[33]

Underestimating construction costs. Sri Lanka's Kotmale dam, part of the Mahaweli Scheme, had to be moved from its original site due to geological problems, a move not contemplated or budgeted at the outset. All too often the estimates of construction are based on what can only be described as "wishful thinking." In the case of Papua New Guinea's Purari project, the government claimed that a feasibility study, undertaken jointly by the Snowy Mountains Engineering Corporation and Nippon Koei, gave the project an all-clear at least as far as its economic viability was concerned. Nothing, however, could have been further from the truth. As the Purari Action Group points out, some of the assumptions used to estimate construction costs were "highly tentative."

> A feature of the feasibility study is its vagueness in costing a number of key elements in the dam construction. This vagueness is mainly to do with assumptions about material availability and suitability. As the area is so remote and there is so little background data on soils, geology, and hydrology, and negligible construction experience, more than the normal amount of care in evaluation should be expected. However, the study reveals that only a relatively small amount of testing of materials has been carried out. In some important areas it recommends that further testing and analysis should be done before the study is formally adopted—an indication that the authors themselves feel that the amount of materials testing had been inadequate.[34]

In particular, the Purari Action Group pointed out that the costs of stripping away landslide debris in order to construct a proposed saddle dam were uncertain, and that it was not known whether suitable earthfill was available locally.

Failing to count land flooded as a cost. Writing in the *Annals of the Oklahoma Academy of Science*, biologists Dr. R. John Taylor and Dr. Constance Taylor note: "Paradoxically, there are about as many acres inundated in a reservoir [in Oklahoma water projects] as are protected downstream. In most cases the potential agribusiness yield of an entire floodplain, even receiving periodic flooding, and its adjacent uplands exceeds the yield of the land protected on a floodplain below the dam."[35] It is rare, however, for such agricultural losses to be accounted for in cost-benefit analyses. The House Committee on Government Operations of the U.S. Congress learned in 1980 that 27,500 acres of farmland would be lost in flooding the Tennessee Valley Authority's Columbia Dam Reservoir; in exchange, flood control would be provided for a mere 9,000 acres downstream. Yet, according to Powledge, the project's original planning documents "made no mention of the multimillion-dollar loss of farm production and farm-related business."[36] He also points out that "The builders like to forget that private land that is inundated by a federal project is, by definition, taken off the local tax rolls."[37]

That cost, too, is frequently ignored. In New Zealand, a local electricity authority tried to procure planning permission for a dam without discussing the land that would be flooded. The land in question was, in fact, a substantial proportion of the district's fertile farmland. In other cases—particularly in the tropics— there have been few attempts to put a value on the thousands of acres of natural forest destroyed to create the reservoir for a dam.

Overestimating the benefits of irrigation. Irrigation is one of the major benefits claimed for large-scale water projects. In some American irrigation schemes, however, as few as 100 farms have benefitted from projects costing as much as $100,000,000.[38] That is, one million dollars has been spent per farm irrigated. Indeed, a 1981 GAO audit of six federal irrigation schemes found that the dollar value of the crops to be grown could never equal the costs of irrigation: between $54 and $130 per acre-foot of water.[39]

Overestimating the value of the crops that will be grown on the irrigated land is a device commonly used by the corps of engineers and other large dam-building agencies to justify these extravaganzas. Once again, the New Melones dam provides an example. The Bureau of Reclamation estimated net irrigation benefits for the dam at $3,610,000 annually, with costs at $1,987,000. When Parry and Norgaard analyzed the figures, however, they pointed out:

> The Bureau of Reclamation predicted irrigation benefits for specialty crops, such as grapes, deciduous fruits, oranges, and vegetables—and cotton—and feed grains. The Bureau estimated that the price of specialty crops would be the same during the lifetime of a 100 year project as they were in 1961. However, a 1970 study by Gerald Dean and Gordon King of the Department of Agricultural Economics, University of California, Davis, indicates that if present trends and plans continue, the specialty crop supply will increase, and, as a result of the inevitable effect of supply and demand, real grape prices will correspondingly decline 17 percent; orange prices will decline 4 percent; deciduous fruit prices will decline 7 percent; and potato prices will decline 43 percent between 1970 and 1980.[40]

As a result, argue Parry and Norgaard, the irrigation benefits from the complex of dams and levees of which New Melones is a part had been overestimated by $12 million to $24 million—at 1974 prices. Annual irrigation benefits from New Melones alone, they claim, should be "adjusted downward by at least $2,200,000 and possibly by as much as $4,403,000. When overestimates for cotton production and sales are adjusted ($2,103,950 for the New Melones project), Parry and Norgaard found that there were "no, or even negative" benefits for irrigation from the dam.

Overestimating the benefits of recreation. In calculating the recreational benefits of a dam, the number of possible visits to the dam and its reservoir by holiday makers, fishermen, schoolchildren, and the like are estimated and then multiplied by a dollar value per head. However, as Powledge points out: "The arithmetic generally overlooks the facts that reservoirs tend to get built in places [such as the Tennessee Valley] where there are many *other* reservoirs, that the *other* reservoirs were justified in part on the number of projected recreational visits, and that a recreational visit to New Reservoir A means one less recreational visit to Old Reservoir B or C."[41] Indeed, in the case of Tennessee's Columbia Dam, whose major stated benefit is recreation, there are nine other reservoirs within fifty miles.

It is also difficult to square the benefits claimed from recreation with the more utilitarian demands that a dam itself makes upon its reservoir in order to generate hydroelectricity and fulfill its role in controlling floods. Again, Powledge makes the point: "A controlled reservoir is not like a natural lake, with a fairly predictable waterline. Its water level fluctuates, sometimes wildly, and when it is down, the recreation-seeking public is treated to the spectacle of boat docks and launching ramps separated from the water by a hundred yards or so of impassable red mud." In its report on the Columbia River Dam,

> the Government Operations Committee . . . found that in the summer the reservoir would be held at 630 feet above sea level, creating an artificial lake 12,600 acres in size. After October 15, the level would drop to 603 feet above sea level to leave more room for storage in the event of winter flooding. The Winter Lake would only be 4,300 acres in size. Between it and the normal shoreline would be more than 8,000 acres of mud flats, hardly a modern version of Walden Pond. And, said the congressional report, it was estimated that during one summer out of every four, the lake would not be able to make it back to its desired level because of lack of rain.[42]

Overestimating the economic benefits. Clearly, if a dam brings industrial growth into a region, the benefits rise correspondingly. Frequently, however, those anticipated industrial spinoffs are chimeras. In the case of Ghana's Volta dam, it was argued that the new lake would augment dramatically the business of the Volta Lake Transport Company (VLTC). Indeed, in 1961 it was estimated that the company would be carrying 150,000 tons of cargo a year by 1970; in 1964, more optimistically still, a figure of 453,000 tons was predicted. In fact, the company's fortunes took a nose-dive. As the Volta River Authority reported in 1976, "the VLTC continued to be faced with an acute shortage of cargo capacity, lack of spare parts and maintenance facilities, and inadequate cargo-handling equipment."[43]

Industrial benefits claimed often turn out to be debatable. The U.S. General Accounting Office points out that many of the industries that supposedly were to be set up as a direct result of the Blue River flood control project in Kansas would in fact have "been realized elsewhere, even without the project."[44] It is doubtful, then, that they should have been included in the cost-benefit analysis.

Perhaps the most spectacularly overoptimistic claim was made on behalf of the Tennessee Valley's Tellico Dam. A major justification for building the dam was that it would power a new industrial city to be built as a company town for Boeing Aerospace. When the dam was three-quarters complete, Boeing withdrew from the scheme. By then the dam had already cost over $100,000,000. Indeed, so small were the other benefits claimed for the dam that when a government committee reviewed the economic justification, it concluded: "The interesting phenomenon is that here is a project that is 95 percent complete, and if one takes just the cost of finishing it against the total benefits . . . it doesn't pay, which says something about the original design."[45]

Not only the United States builds dams that cannot possibly recoup their costs. The modern era of environmental awareness in New Zealand is usually seen as having begun with the controversy over the Manipouri Power Scheme. After years of official secrecy, it was revealed that the price paid by the aluminum smelting consortium for the electricity from this wholly publicly funded project was two cents per kwh, and a later government raised the price about sixfold. Despite continuing secrecy on the costs of the project, it is doubtful whether even the new price recovers costs. No cost-benefit analysis was ever published.[46]

So, too, the Indonesian government agreed to supply Japan's Asahan Aluminum Company with 80 percent of the hydroelectricity from the Asahan Dam. The electricity was to be supplied at cost. As the Purari Action Group reports: "Even after the power plants are transferred to Indonesia in 30 years, the electricity is still to be provided for the company at cost. The Japanese company will determine for itself the cost of the power."[47]

Underestimating the costs to the environment of irrigation. More generally, the disastrous environmental effects of perennial irrigation are rarely taken into account in cost-benefit analyses. On the contrary, where dams provide irrigation, that irrigation is almost always counted as a "benefit." Yet, few perennial irrigation schemes can avoid the twin evils of salinization and waterlogging, especially when there is such clear reluctance on the part of the authorities to earmark any funds for drainage or other remedial measures.

Inevitably, the ecological costs come home to roost. In the United States, the cost of building a master drain to the sea in order to remove the accumulated salts from the San Joaquin Valley has been estimated at a minimum of $1.2 billion.[48] In order to remove the salt from the Colorado River before it enters Mexico, the United States has had to commission a desalinization plant at Yuma—at a cost expected to exceed one billion dollars. Yet, despite such expenditure, the problem of salinization is far from solved. Indeed, according to Arthur Pillsbury, only the construction of the NAWAPA scheme can prevent southern California from becoming a salt-encrusted desert. That scheme is expected to cost two trillion dollars—at 1973 prices.[49] Had those costs of establishing perennial irrigation been taken into account, would the dams that provided the irrigation water have seemed so attractive? And could they ever have been justified on economic, let alone ecological, grounds? In almost every case, the answer is undoubtedly no.

CONCLUSION

It thus seems that those who stand to gain politically and financially from the building of a large dam are willing to go to inordinate lengths to ensure that it will be built. Among other things, they are willing purposefully to mislead those who must be per-suaded of the dam's desirability and viability before the go-ahead to build it will actually be given. This they do by grossly exagger-ating the dam's likely benefits and seriously underestimating its probable costs—in particular its social and ecological costs, which, as we have seen, are often totally ignored.

The power, prestige, and financial resources of the politicians, bureaucrats, and industrialists involved in dam projects greatly facilitate that deceit. So do the credulity and apathy of the public. Moreover, unlike the authorities, those who oppose dams—mostly local tribal or peasant leaders, obscure academics, or youthful environmentalists—have meager financial resources and little credibility. Furthermore, they must confront the en-trenched belief that large-scale water development schemes are an essential part of the process of economic development—and we have been taught to see that process as the only means of com-bating poverty and malnutrition and assuring health, longevity, and prosperity for all. To challenge dams is thus to challenge a fundamental tenet of our civilization.

But enough of criticism. As we have already mentioned, the problems that dog modern irrigation schemes have not, histori-cally, affected the irrigation systems of traditional societies. It is clear, therefore, that we have much to learn from the traditional irrigation societies of both the past and the present. In the next section we shall see how, in five such societies, all the problems associated with modern irrigation agriculture have been avoid-ed—and why.

PART V

TRADITIONAL IRRIGATION: LEARNING FROM THE PAST

21. The Qanats of Iran

PERHAPS ONE OF THE MOST SOPHISTICATED SYSTEMS of traditional irrigation known to us is that associated with the qanats of Iran. A qanat is a conduit that collects the water from an aquifer on the slope of a hill and exploits the natural gradient of the land to transport the water underground to the agricultural areas below. The conduits, which are usually 50 cm to 80 cm wide and 90 cm to 150 cm high, range from 1 km to 70 km in length. Their rate of discharge is between 1 liter per second and 500 liters per second.[1]

Qanats were first developed in Iran but their use spread to India, Arabia, Egypt, North Africa, Spain, and even to the New World. They are referred to by different names in different areas: in Afghanistan and Pakistan, they are known as Karezes; in North Africa, as Foggaras; and in the United Arab Emirates, as Falaj.[2]

What is astonishing is the number and length of these qanats. There are some 22,000 of them in Iran, comprising more than 170,000 miles of underground channels.[3] Equally astonishing, much of that network is still functioning, and some of those channels were built thousands of years ago. Until recently, qanats still supplied 75 percent of the water used in Iran, for both irrigation and household purposes.

277

Most of the area irrigated by qanats is arid and rainless. Without an effective and sustainable form of irrigation, agriculture in those regions would have been impossible. For that reason, one cannot overestimate the importance of the role the qanats have played in Iran. To quote H. E. Wulff: "They have made a garden of what otherwise would have become an uninhabitable desert."[4]

What's more, this incredible network of underground conduits was built entirely by hand, and the method of construction used today is still much the same as that used two thousand years ago. A series of manholes is sunk along the proposed route of the qanat, which is then dug to connect them. Figure 5 shows a cross section of a completed qanat.

The great advantages of transporting water underground in this way are obvious. Since the qanats are often dug into hard subsoil and, when necessary, lined with relatively impermeable clay hoops, there is little seepage, no raising of the water table, no waterlogging, no evaporation during transit—and hence no salinization or alkalization in the area surrounding the conduits. Nor do they provide a niche for the vectors that transmit the waterborne diseases that devastate the population of areas irrigated by modern technological means.

What is particularly important, as H. Pazwash points out in *Civil Engineering*, is that the discharge from qanats "is fixed by nature."[5] They can only provide water produced naturally by a spring in a mountain area and then transport it by the force of gravity. As a result, the aquifer is not depleted and the quality of its water is maintained. By contrast, the amount of water extracted in a modern irrigation system by pumps and other technological means "is determined by man, who, in a modern economy, will be under pressure to extract the maximum amount possible, thereby depleting the aquifer and reducing the quality of the water."[6]

Gunter Garbrecht, chairman of the Working Party on History of the International Commission for Irrigation and Drainage, makes the same point. Qanats "tap the groundwater potential only up to and never beyond the limits of natural replenishment and, as a consequence, do not unbalance the hydrological and

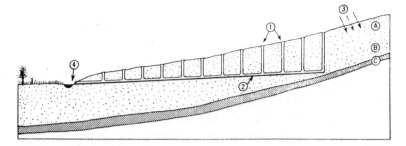

Figure 5. A Qanat. A qanat exploits the natural terrain to transfer water by gravity from the mountains (right) to the plains (left). A series of vertical shafts (1) is dug down to the aquifer (B), and joined by a horizontal canal, the qanat (2). Water falling in the hills (3) passes through the surface soil (A) into the aquifer (B), until stopped by the impermeable layer (C). Water flows down the qanat (2) to a well or canal at the surface (4).

SOURCE: Earthscan, Press Briefing Document No. 22, 1980, p. 55.

ecological equilibrium of the region."[7] Qanats, like the irrigation system of ancient Egypt, were successful because they were self-regulating and "functioned within the limits set by nature." In a sense, modern irrigation technology is a scam. It provides far more water but only at the cost of depleting supplies in the long term. To achieve a short-term supply of water is, of course, very easy. "If water can be withdrawn at will," Garbrecht notes, "regardless of the limits of natural recharge, a water supply can certainly be increased for a period of time. But sooner or later, the water potential will become exhausted and agriculture and economy will have to fall back to their original level, a process that inevitably carries serious socio-economic consequences for the society."

Until recently, the majority of qanats were under the control of local feudal landlords. Each landlord would appoint a bailiff to supervise the allocation of water to tenants in accordance with the size of the tenant's farm and the nature of the crop he was growing.[8] Where the peasants owned the qanats, they themselves elected a trustworthy water bailiff who made sure that each family had an equitable share of the water at the time it needed it. The water bailiff received a free share for his services. Wulff knows of "three hamlets in the region of Sehdeh in western Iran that still receive the shares that were allocated to them in the seventeenth century . . . in the reign of Shah Abbas the Great."[9]

Using the qanats, the peasants also developed "jar" irrigation—a system that reduced water wastage to a minimum. A slim-necked jar filled with water was buried close to a plant's roots whenever required, on average once every two weeks. The seepage through the permeable wall of the clay jar was sufficient to keep the moisture level of the soil constant at a little less than the "field capacity," which is the amount of water the soil could retain against the force of gravity. "In this way no excess water is lost to percolation. Also the conveyance loss, which is inevitable with channel and furrow irrigation, is altogether eliminated."[10]

Because of the introduction of machinery and the increasing price of labor, the cost of building qanats has risen sharply. In 1983, Pazwash estimated that it would cost about one million dollars to build an 8 km qanat with an average tunnel depth of 15 meters. That high capital cost, however, is amply compensated by the low cost of the water delivered—about 75 cents per 100 cubic meters. At that price, the qanat would be paid for in some thirty years—and would, of course, be operative for centuries.

Since qanats make use of the force of gravity only, they are obviously economical to operate. Pump wells, on the other hand, need a continuous energy supply, and also require much more maintenance. Pazwash estimates that if Iran's water were provided only by qanats, there would be an energy saving of 100 kwh per capita. If one takes into account the costs of energy and maintenance, pumped well water would cost a dollar or two per 100 cubic meters—twice as expensive as water provided by qanats.[11]

As part of the developmental process, qanats have had to give way to a more modern system for providing water to the cities. The 36 qanats in Tehran, some of them built more than 250 years ago, were quite capable of satisfying the domestic needs of a city of 1.5 million—as well as irrigating neighboring gardens and farmlands. Unfortunately, in 1955, piped water was introduced, supplied from Amir Kabir reservoir in Karaj, forty miles away.

When this was done, Tehran's existing qanat system was completely ignored by the builders.[12]

Qanats were also abandoned following the 1962 Land Reform Act, which broke up the large estates and redistributed land to the peasants. Such reform might sound like a step forward, but it created problems, too. To begin with, the traditional system of land tenure was well adapted to the optimum use of the qanat system. For instance, traditional landowners not only provided credits to peasants to help them maintain the qanats and irrigation channels, but also coordinated the maintenance work. Once the landlords were ousted, there was no longer a mechanism for assuring the maintenance of the qanats. Moreover, the land holdings given to the peasants were too small—less than 10 acres (2.5 hectares) per family. On such an acreage, it was impossible to finance the maintenance of the qanats and the irrigation channels. Since the 1962 act, there has been a rapid substitution of wells for qanats. With the consequent depletion of groundwater, many of the wells have dried up. Also many of the peasants, who found they could not survive on their small acreage, moved to the cities in search of work. Suddenly the countryside was depopulated and a vast, depressed urban proletariat appeared. Fritz Schumacher referred to this process as "mutual poisoning."

Modern irrigation systems, totally unsuited to local conditions and built without regard to their impact on society, are now replacing the qanats. Many of those irrigation projects are supplied by large dams, of which the most notorious are Sefid Rud and Dez. The former, designed to last 100 years, was finished in 1962. Already, 21 years later, it is half silted up, the sedimentation rate having proved to be three times higher than expected. The Dez dam, known to have had an extremely unfavorable impact on traditional farming, has led to the setting up of three types of experimental schemes—agroindustrial companies, agribusiness enterprises, and farm corporations—that cover 96,000 hectares. Throughout the area, peasants have been forced off their land. Pazwash blames the authorities who planned the dam; they were, he says, "concerned only with the technical aspects of the plan." He also cites the Khuzistan Water and Power Authority as, apparently, concerned only with "economic criteria without regard to the living conditions of the peasants whom they regarded as instruments in this experiment."[13]

22. Two Traditional Irrigation Systems in Tanzania

IRRIGATION AS A SACRED RITUAL AMONG THE SONJO

The Sonjo, a North Tanzanian tribe of some 4,500, have practiced irrigation agriculture from time immemorial. Indeed, their whole way of life, from their worldview to their social and cultural organization, reflects their preoccupation with irrigation. Robert Gray, who made a detailed study of Kheri, a Sonjo village, writes in his book *The Sonjo of Tanganyika*: "Irrigation is a central theme in Sonjo religion as well as in agriculture,"[1] and rainfall, for instance, is thought of as "the overflow from a celestial irrigation system." The tribe's formal prayer for rain is "started in a hydraulic metaphor, 'Open the sluices of Belwa'"—Belwa being the mythical home of the Sonjo.[2]

Natural springs, too, are sacred. "The springs are treated as sanctuaries and may not be approached by ordinary people who are involved in sexual activities and the passions of everyday life. . . . Thus, [the springs] are effectively insulated against contact with the profane world, which might contaminate and weaken their sanctity and introduce disastrous change."[3] For the Sonjo, proof of the sacredness of the springs lies in their very predictability; they have never been known to fail, and are thus "conceived of in a different category from unpredictable blessings such as rain or health." Should the springs fail, however, the results "would be more catastrophic than in the case of drought."

Quite sensibly, therefore, "the basic policy with regard to springs is directed at maintaining the unchanging state of affairs that has prevailed in the past." In fact, one could argue that it is only because the springs are sanctified that they remain productive. In a more materialistic world—Texas, for example—they would undoubtedly have run dry.

With regard to rain, the Sonjo believe that as long as the appropriate rituals are performed, and the traditional moral code upheld, then their god, Khambageu, will protect them. If rain does not fall, that means that some basic rule of conduct has been violated—and that Khambageu has been angered.

The Sonjo cultivate three types of land, which they refer to as *hura*, *magare* and *isirene* land:

> The *hura* land, which is the most important, is situated in the flat alluvial river valley. Every year, during the rainy season, it is flooded by the river, which deposits on it a thick layer of silt. During the dry season, however, it must be cultivated entirely by irrigation, the water being derived from springs and from the river itself. There is clearly no fertility problem, since the land is fertilized annually by the silt deposited on it by the river, nor is there likely to be a salinity problem, since the salts are washed out by the flood waters.
>
> The *magare* lands are located on the sloping lands above the water, which makes them very vulnerable to erosion. Moreover, since no silt is deposited on them by the river, their continued fertility is not assured by natural means. In addition, they are more prone to salinity since the salt in the soil is not washed out by the annual flood waters. The Sonjo have adapted to these ecological constraints by dividing their *magare* land into two different categories, which are cultivated in alternate years—just as did the inhabitants of the Euphrates River. The exact amount of *magare* land actually under irrigation at any one time depends on the amount of water available for irrigating it. Tenure of the *magare* fields gives certain rights to irrigation water, since without the water the plots would be worthless. In a very bad year—when there is very little rain, or when the rain falls at the wrong time—the *magare* land may produce no crops at all, but the *hura* fields will always produce enough food to avert famine.

The *isirene* land is situated on several natural terraces downstream from the *hura* valley. It consists, in all, of thirty acres. A very elaborate irrigation system is required to cultivate the *isirene* land because the different elevations of the terraces make it necessary, in several places, to build aqueducts—hollowed-out logs which bridge the irrigation furrows—so as to bring water to inconveniently situated plots. When there is a shortage of water, the *hura* plots are given priority, and not occasionally there is not enough left to irrigate the *isirene* land. Not surprisingly, individual Sonjo people do not depend entirely for their livelihood on *isirene* plots; they also own *hura* and *magare* plots. In order to adapt to water shortages later in the year, the *isirene* plots are planted very early, in the hope that crops will mature before irrigation water becomes scarce. Nowadays, cassava—a recently introduced crop which requires little irrigation—tends to be grown on the *isirene* plots.[4]

The agricultural system itself is very simple. The water is controlled by means of sluices and is channeled through furrows to wherever it is needed. The system itself is best seen as "a fine network of small channels reinforced by a superimposed coarser network of larger channels."[5] That network is tilted toward the lower end of the valley, effectively ensuring that when there is too much moisture, the surplus drains away and rejoins the mainstream as it leaves the valley. However, water does not enter the irrigated area unless it is strictly required, nor is it allowed to pass through the *hura* plots during the rainy season. The furrow that takes water to the *magare* plots is opened only after the annual rains and once the ground starts to dry out. That furrow is then kept open only until the grain is ripe, after which it is closed off and remains idle for the rest of the year. There is thus no overirrigation, salinity is reduced, and the spread of waterborne diseases is avoided.

According to Sonjo mythology, this irrigation system dates from the founding of the tribe's six villages by semimythical heroes. It is thus considered the sacred duty of each generation of Sonjo to ensure that the system is kept in good repair, and the Council of Elders, or *wenamiji*, is responsible for organizing the necessary maintenance work. After the flood waters have subsided, for instance, it is the elders who organize the repair of any damage done by the rains. All able-bodied men in the village (other than blacksmiths, who are excluded for ritualistic reasons) are expected to take part—largely to desilt channels and to rebuild dikes that may have been washed away. If, during the year, further damage is done by unexpected rain, the village men are called out again to make repairs. The annual maintenance work generally takes about three days, but before the introduction of the iron hoe, it took much longer. The work was done with a digging stick, considered "primitive" by many but, in fact, quite adequate for the task at hand.[6]

The cooperation shown by the Sonjo in keeping their irrigation works in good repair is by no means atypical. Indeed, such cooperation is a feature of all the traditional systems we have studied—and with good reason. The fact that maintenance work is done voluntarily and with the help of minimum technology is of critical importance. It means the endeavor is not hindered by financial constraints, nor by a lack of technicians or a shortage of spare parts. Furthermore, farmers do not have to be charged for water, which could cause serious problems for some.

During the fourteen-day irrigation cycle, all the plots are supposed to be soaked once. The length of the cycle is determined by the need to water the *hura* crops at least once a fortnight. The system is also under the control of the Council of Elders, whose members have first call on irrigation water. The rest of the people are organized into several categories, each having different water rights.

Each day is divided into four periods of about six hours each. Primary rights over water are allocated to each farmer for a six-hour period. The first six-hour periods are allocated to the seventeen *wenamiji* who, all told, use up four days of the cycle. The privileges of the *wenamiji* are respected by all, as derived directly from Khambageu, the Sonjo deity—and by enhancing the status of the *wenamiji* they help to maintain the tribal social structure.

After the *wenamiji*, the next group to have access to the irrigation water is the *wenamiji barirage*, or eighteen "minor" *wenamiji*.

They are followed by the *wakiama*, a group of twenty to twenty-five elders (known individually as *mokiama*) who have no hereditary rights to the water. They must therefore pay "tribute" (usually in the form of goats or produce) to the *wenamiji*.[7]

The number of watering periods assigned to the *wakiama* varies—largely to keep the length of the irrigation cycle down to fourteen days. The water "bought" by the *wakiama*—who are all members of established families and can thus usually afford to pay—is not negotiated with an individual *wenamiji*. The price to be paid is set by the Council of Elders itself. Significantly, where the tribute is paid in the form of a goat, it is usually used in ritual sacrifices, and indeed, such sacrifices are considered essential for the smooth running of the irrigation system. The tribute thus benefits the whole community and not just the individual *wenamiji* to whom it is paid. Because of the limited number of irrigation periods available, the number of *wakiama* members is restricted: even so, when there is a real water shortage, some *mokiama* may not be granted any rights of water to ensure that at least some crops are properly irrigated.[8]

Fewer than half of the farmers in the village that Gray studied fall into the above three categories. The rest are "clients" who have to obtain their water from "patrons" among the *wenamiji*, the minor *wenamiji* or the *wakiama*. That is usually relatively easy, since the patrons themselves can normally soak their plots in two hours rather than six, and are thus likely to have surplus water. Moreover, most clients have a close relative—a father or brother, for instance—within one of the privileged groups, and will seek that person as a patron. A client who does not have any such relative has to depend on his own honey, grain, or money to obtain water. If he cannot succeed by these means, he can still obtain water illegally by making a break in a channel near his plots and flooding them at night. This is not considered a serious crime; the penalty imposed, one goat, is considered relatively small and suggests there is little moral stigma attached to the offense. The system seems to want even the least privileged always to have access to water.

Because, as Gray points out, the *wenamiji* have "the power of depriving individuals of the water which is an absolute necessity for raising crops," they are in a position to apply "an effective sanction for enforcing obedience to tribal laws and their own administrative orders."[9] Indeed, the whole system seems geared to maintaining the authority of the *wenamiji*. This could be a disadvantage if the *wenamiji* were politicians or bureaucrats whose interests were not those of the tribe. But on the contrary, the *wenamiji*, like all tribal elders, act as custodians and interpreters of the tribal wisdom, preserving the society's traditional way of life. In light of this, a system that maintains the authority of the *wenamiji* also ensures the cohesion of the social group and the stability of its relationship with its natural environment.

THE TRADITIONAL IRRIGATION SYSTEM OF THE CHAGGA

Like the Sonjo, the Chagga of Kilimanjaro, in Tanzania, have also practiced irrigation agriculture since time immemorial. Early European travelers who visited the area were vastly impressed by the complicated network of irrigation furrows (*mfongo*) that collect water from the mountain's streams and transport it over long distances to the fields below. Indeed, according to Fidelis T. Masao, even modern engineers have marveled at the sophistication of the Chagga's irrigation works, admitting that they themselves would require highly complicated equipment to achieve the results that the Chagga have achieved with the simplest technology.[10]

As with the Sonjo, it is only possible to understand the success of the Chagga's irrigation system, as Masao points out, through "an understanding of their sociopolitical organization and their rituals." The Chagga are organized into clans, which are powerful and cohesive social units, highly capable of cooperative action. There is considerable division of labor among the clans. Some, like the Wako-Makundi, in Mamba, specialize in making iron tools. The Wamasi specialize in cattle herding and beekeeping. Not surprisingly, some clans specialize in the arts of irrigation. In one area, Siha, we find the Kileo, a clan specialized in surveying furrows. In Uru East, another area of Chaggaland, the Temba, Ngowi, and Njau clans also specialize in furrow surveying.

Like those of the Sonjo, the myths and rituals of the Chagga reflect the priorities of a society committed to irrigation agriculture. Consider, for example, their procedure for deciding on the building of a new furrow and for implementing the decision. Traditionally, a man of the appropriate clan would have a dream in which he conceived a plan to dig an irrigation canal, or else a number of farmers would decide to build a new canal and would then elect a member of the appropriate clan to direct the work. In both cases, the approval of the *Mangi*, or chief, had to be obtained. After that—in the Uru district at least—the head of the clan or the director of the project had to pray for a specific period until a sign was made that the prayer had been answered. Prayers were addressed to the most recently deceased elder; offerings were then made to him and to other important ancestral spirits whose assistance was thought necessary for the success of the project.

During this period, the members of the clan had to observe various taboos, including abstinence from sexual activity. If the sign that the prayers had been answered did not appear, the scheme was postponed until the shaman could be approached. The shaman would then arrange for the ancestral spirits to be placated with offerings of beer, goats, or sheep. If the ancestral spirits were then appeased, certain members of the clan would have a vision in which they would see a large number of red ants marching in single file from the hut of the elder of the furrow-owning clan (or the hut of the project initiator) to the river from which the water was to be drawn. The implication, as Masao points out, "is that deceased members of the clan have the power to demarcate the course of the furrow by sending red ants, which made the surveying work unnecessary."[11]

Chagga myths and legends also reflect the tribe's preoccupation with irrigation. Thus, an important hero is Mlatie of Mbokomu, a famous surveyor who is believed to have been responsible for the most elaborate irrigation works. From him the people of Mbokomu, who are noted for their expertise in building such works, are supposed to have derived much of their knowledge.

The sophistication of Chagga irrigation is also praised by K. M. Stahl and H. M. Johnstone, who stress the degree to which that sophistication contrasts with the simplicity of the Chagga's tools. The surveyor plots the intended course of the furrow using nothing more elaborate than small sticks. The Chagga had no instruments for grading: their knowledge and skill apparently sufficed. Masao describes how they built their furrows. "The alignment," he writes, "was done purely by eye. Here and there, the furrow was excavated under a rock or banked up."[12] He goes on to note:

> Sometimes the furrows were six feet deep. The [Chagga] of those days knew the precise point of the river from which to take the furrow, selecting a spot where the flow was least turbulent, and the current was directed so that it would not eat away the inlet. A favorable point was the tail end of a pond caused by a waterfall on the headwaters. From the main furrow, many branches were led off; these were further subdivided, and eventually the field to be irrigated was flooded by innumerable grooves. Very often, a banked-up pond of considerable size was constructed and filled with water to enable one person to irrigate from this source while another used the main furrow; the water was then let out of the pond through a sluice into another furrow. Lately these ponds have been left to fall into disrepair.[13]

As for the operation and maintenance of the irrigation works, those Chagga who wished to use water had to join a furrow board run by furrow elders. Everyone had to take turns in repairing and cleaning the furrows. Those who failed to do so had to pay a heavy fine, several barrels of beer. The furrow was owned by the clan and most of the members of a furrow board would be members of that clan; others, who were admitted as auxiliaries, had to pay prescribed contributions. Nonmembers could use the water by paying so many barrels of beer a year. If a furrow was damaged accidentally, one of the elders would sound a horn in the evening. This was known as *Ole lo mfongo*, the call to the furrows. The next morning, everyone would leave their normal work and set about repairing the damage. Anyone who did not take part without good reason was fined.

Sir Charles Dundas, who visited the Chagga more than sixty years ago, was impressed by the way they organized the maintenance and operation of the irrigation system. "No small degree of regulation is necessitated and, moreover, within the course of the furrow, order must prevail," he wrote in his book, *Kilimanjaro and Its Peoples*. He went on to surmise: "It is to these circumstances that we may attribute, in a great measure, the early institution of chiefship with the consequent development of a stable organization."[14] Whatever the truth of that statement, there is little question that without the stability of its social organization, Chagga society would not have been able to operate its highly complex irrigation system.

Masao is also impressed by the operation of the furrows and, in particular, by the absence of conflict over the use of water. "So well are matters run by the furrow elders that the number of cases arising out of disputes over water rights are exceedingly few." The normal procedure for regulating water supplies was for the person whose turn it was to use the water to do so from dawn until noon. He then had to turn back the water so that other people could use it for their daily needs—be it cooking, washing, brewing beer or peeling coffee. If the user was unable to finish irrigating his plot, he could do so the next day. Anybody could use the water at night—so long as the water was back in the furrow by four o'clock the next morning.

As Masao notes, irrigation "more than anything shaped the life patterns of the [Chagga]."[15] Elspeth Huxley also stresses the link between the cooperative nature of Chagga society and the need to keep the irrigation furrows in good order, to maintain maximum water flow, to repair the banks, and to regulate the use of the furrow.[16]

Unfortunately, as with so many tribal societies today, the traditional Chagga way of life—and with it, the survival of their irrigation system—is threatened by development. Piped water has been introduced and the people are becoming lax in the maintenance of the furrows. Indeed, the furrows are already falling into disrepair. The result, as Masao points out, can only be a lower agricultural output.

In some parts of Kilimanjaro, efforts are being made to strengthen the furrow banks with concrete—a sign, perhaps, that all is not yet lost. Nevertheless, the shortage of land in the area has forced people to cultivate the ravines down to the rivers. Trees required for preserving the catchment area have been cut down and, as a result, some feeder springs have dried up and rivers have ceased to flow. That trend will undoubtedly get worse unless action is taken soon. If it is not, less water will be available for the furrows and their maintenance will quickly become uneconomical. When that happens, the Chagga's highly efficient irrigation system will sadly, but inevitably, fall into disuse.

23. Traditional Irrigation in the Dry Zone of Sri Lanka

SRI LANKA'S TANKS

Sri Lanka is covered with a network of thousands of man-made lakes and ponds known locally as *tanks* (after *tanque*, the Portuguese word for *reservoir*). Some are truly massive, many are thousands of years old, and almost all show a high degree of sophistication in their construction and design. Sir James Emmerson Tennent, the nineteenth-century historian, marveled in particular at the numerous channels that were dug underneath the bed of each lake in order to ensure that the flow of water was "constant and equal as long as any water remained in the tank." Frequently, he noted, those channels had to be cut through solid granite with the most rudimentary of tools: "Their ruins present illustrations of determined perseverance, undeterred by the most discouraging of difficulties and unrelieved by the slightest appliance of ingenuity to diminish the toil of excavation."[1]

Today, most of the tanks that so impressed Tennent have either totally or partially silted up. Numerous smaller tanks still survive and continue to provide the basis for irrigation agriculture in the dry zone of the island, but many of these, too, are now partially silted up.

Large or small, the tanks are generally assumed to be the work of a centralized state bureaucracy—and, hence, it is argued, their silting up and subsequent abandonment can be explained by the breakdown of the state. Indeed, historians of the Wittfogel school sought to explain the rise of the state in early "hydraulic" societies by the need for a centralized bureaucracy to run their irrigation works. Without such a bureaucracy, it was argued, irrigation agriculture could not have been practiced. That view, however, is not shared by Sir Edmund A. Leach, professor of anthropology at the University of Cambridge and a leading authority on irrigation agriculture in Sri Lanka. Leach argues that although the large tanks may have been the work of a bureaucracy, the small village tanks most decidedly were not. Not only did villages run their own irrigation systems quite independently of the state but—and this is critical—they continued to do so even after the state effectively collapsed. Indeed, his own research leads him to conclude that the Wittfogel hypothesis is quite inapplicable to Sri Lanka. The more that one learns about traditional systems, the less the Wittfogel thesis seems justified. It has also been pointed out that all the societies that practice irrigation in East Africa are democratic to the point of not even having a chief. Instead, their system is run by a council of elders independent of the main political structures.

Leach cites three critical considerations in his refutation. He argues that the primary function of the large tanks was not to provide water for agriculture—certainly not for traditional subsistence agriculture. To be sure, the large tanks were used to irrigate farmland in the immediate vicinity of Sri Lanka's two historical capitals, first Anuradhapura, and later Pollonaruwa— but it was not the peasants who benefited from such irrigation.

The land was used principally to grow crops for urban consumption, to supply water to the capital, or for purely ornamental purposes.[2]

As evidence, Leach cites the massive building program undertaken by Parakrama Bahu, the megalomaniac king who reigned in Pollonaruwa from 1164 to 1197. Quite apart from building 101 temples and statues, Bahu also constructed numerous tanks. Those tanks, says Leach, were clearly built for the king's personal aggrandisement, and had nothing whatsoever to do with satisfying the food needs of his subjects. "They are monuments, not utilitarian structures."

Given the essentially ornamental nature of the large tanks, it follows—Leach's second point—that Sri Lanka's rural villages never actually depended upon the large tanks for their survival. "When the central government was disrupted and the major works fell into disrepair, village life could carry on quite adequately. Each village still possessed its own small-scale irrigation system, which was maintained by the villagers themselves."[3]

Leach's third—and most telling—point is that despite extensive research, he could find no evidence that a centralized bureaucracy ever existed to run the country's irrigation works. "On the contrary, the fact that, in the chronicles of the kings, the various monarchs receive praise for their munificence in repairing village tanks suggests that there was no routine procedure for carrying out such work on a national scale."[4]

That is not to say that the village tanks were neglected. Far from it. The crucial point, however, is that the necessary maintenance work was organized by the villagers themselves; there was never a centralized bureaucracy to direct such work. "From time immemorial, normal repair work to the village tanks has been the ordinary work of ordinary people," writes Leach. "Major repairs and new constructions were traditionally undertaken by a specialized caste group of Tamil laborers—the Kulankatti—but these people worked for the villagers on direct contract; they were not employees of the state." The running of the village irrigation system was thus firmly in the hands of the local community. Indeed, according to Leach, "it is only since about 1860 that a centralized Irrigation Department has had the right to interfere on matters relating to the maintenance and use of village tanks."[5]

Traditionally, much of the maintenance work on the tanks was carried out during the *Rajakariya*, the forty-day period when every Sinhalese villager was required to work free for the king, but the *Rajakariya* should not be seen as a state-run maintenance program. The villagers were not indentured laborers—a point that was lost on the British, who abolished *Rajakariya* service as a distasteful relic of feudalism—nor were they employed by the state. On the contrary, the work was organized at the local level. Moreover, the villagers had a considerable say in the work they undertook. On one occasion, they refused to dig an artificial lake outside the king's palace in Kandy on the grounds that it was an ornamental showpiece and should not, therefore, be built with *Rajakariya* labor.[6]

If, therefore, there is any connection between the practice of irrigation agriculture and the rise of the state, the explanation must lie somewhere other than in the need to have a bureaucracy to run the irrigation works. "Could it be," asks Leach, "that the sociological explanation of why so many of the ancient societies were 'hydraulic' is that, in a wide variety of circumstances, hydraulic society lends itself very readily to the development of specialized labor on a nonmonetary basis?"[7]

Even that interpretation, however, has its problems. For "specialized" work to be undertaken "on a nonmonetary basis" implies—at the very least—the existence of a cohesive community bound together by reciprocal rights and duties. It also implies a common cultural pattern, adapted exclusively to the practice of irrigation agriculture. Such a community is the very antithesis of a state. If, therefore, a state were to arise from it—through the increasing division of labor—then one would have to posit the breakdown of the very communal ties which had previously held it together.

The importance of those communal ties has been stressed by almost all the authors who have studied the traditional practice of irrigation in Sri Lanka. As Sir James Emmerson Tennent wrote:

Cultivation, as it existed in the north of Ceylon, could only be carried on by the combined labor of the whole local community, applied in the first instance to collect and secure the requisite [water] supply for irrigation and afterwards to distribute it to the rice lands which were tilled by the united exertions of the inhabitants, among whom the crop was divided in due proportions. So indispensable were concord and union in such operations that injunctions for their maintenance were sometimes engraved on the rocks, as an imperishable exhortation to forbearance and harmony.[8]

Significantly, Tennent rejects the suggestion that Sri Lanka's irrigation works broke down as a result of faulty construction and, in particular, the absence of spillways for draining off surplus water during the rainy season. "For upward of fifteen centuries," he points out, "the reservoirs, when duly attended to, successfully defied all the dangers to be apprehended from inundation." Besides, "vast numbers of these tanks, though utterly deserted, remain in this respect, almost uninjured to the present day."[9]

Instead, insists Tennent, the destruction and final abandonment of the tanks should be seen as the inevitable outcome of social decay—in particular, "the disruption of the local communities by whom they were so long maintained." With that disruption came an end to the "concord and union" that Tennent held to be so critical to the running of the irrigation works. The consequences were inevitably disastrous:

The ruin of a reservoir when neglected and permitted to fall into decay was speedy and inevitable; and as the destruction of the village tank involved the flight of all dependent upon it, the water, once permitted to escape, carried pestilence and miasma over the plains they had previously covered with plenty. After such a calamity, any partial return of the villagers, even where it was not prevented by the dread of malaria, would have been impracticable; for the obvious reason, that where the whole combined labor of the community was not more than sufficient to carry on the work of conservancy and cultivation, the diminished force of the few would have been utterly unavailing, either to effect the reparation of the watercourse, or to restore the system on which the culture of rice depends. Thus the process of decay, instead of a gradual decline as in other countries, became sudden and utter desolation in Ceylon.[10]

It is a warning that the government of modern Sri Lanka would have done well to ponder before it embarked on the giant Mahaweli scheme.

IRRIGATION AS A WAY OF LIFE

The traditional Ceylonese village was dominated by three features: the temple (*dagoba*), the tank (*wewa*), and the paddy field (*ketha*), and according to the late Upalli Senanayake, "one could not imagine a village in the dry zone without a tank any more than one could imagine it without a temple or a rice paddy."[11] Indeed, the tank was judged to be so vital to village life that the term *wewa* was frequently used synonymously with the term *gama*, or village. As R. H. Brohier, one of the foremost authorities on Sri Lanka's ancient irrigation system, puts it: "People say they belong to *Siyambalagaha-Wewa*, 'the Tamarind tree tank,' and not to *Siyambalagaha-gama*, 'the Tamarind tree village.'"[12]

Several types of tank were built, some of which had nothing to do with irrigation *per se* but all of which were essential to the practice of irrigation agriculture. It was, for example, traditional to build a "forest tank" in the jungle above the village, but not for irrigating land. Its purpose was to provide water to wild animals, to deter them from descending into the paddy fields in search of water and destroying the crops. Other types included:

The Mountain Tank, which was built to provide water for *chena* or slash-and-burn agriculture, a vernacular form of farming now frowned upon (if not actually discouraged) by the authorities.

The Erosion Control Tank, or *Pota Wetiye*, which was so designed that any silt was deposited in it before entering the main water storage tanks. Several erosion control tanks were associated with each village irrigation system. All were built in such a way that they could easily be desilted.

The Storage Tank, of which, traditionally, there were two, one to be used while the other was being repaired. Therefore they were known as "twin tanks."

The Village Tank, of which there was one for each village that depended upon a particular irrigation system. All such tanks were connected by canals to the twin tanks.[13]

Obviously paddy growing was not just an occupation; it was a way of life, closely interwoven with other social activities. Each stage in the agricultural cycle—from weeding, to ploughing, to transplanting the paddy and, finally, to harvesting it—was accompanied by special ceremonies involving song, music, and dance. Indeed, those traditional dances that still survive clearly originated in such ceremonies. They incorporate rhythmic movements that visibly symbolize reaping, ploughing, and digging.

Significantly, it was the priest who initiated the most important agricultural activities. When the time was deemed auspicious for ploughing, for instance, the temple bell would ring and the whole village would stream out into the fields. The king himself would participate in the ploughing ceremonies that took place near the ancient capitals.

As in all peasant societies, agriculture was very much a family affair. Everyone, including the children, had specific responsibilities. One child's job, for instance, was to drive away any marauding monkeys from the paddy fields; another's was to look after the cattle and water buffalo. One or two children would help their father in the fields; the rest would help their mother to harvest firewood, to prepare food, and to milk the cows and buffalo. The girls were specifically responsible for weeding and for making mats. And there was a tradition of mutual help, *attama*, within the village. Neighbors could be relied upon to help with pressing, day-to-day chores and, most important, with the more onerous agricultural tasks.[14]

THE SURVIVAL OF THE TRADITIONAL SYSTEM

Leach points to the great stability of the village and its irrigation system. Whereas governments rose and fell, the village and its tanks remained the same for thousands of years. "Under Ceylon dry zone conditions, once a village and its irrigation tank have been constructed, it is there forever and since the irrigation area must always remain the same size, the population of the village itself can only vary between very narrow limits."[15]

The Sinhalese, like other traditional societies, justifiably regarded their institutions as permanent. Old inscriptions recording donations of land to various temples state that they would be valid *ira handa pavathina thuru* ("so long as the sun and the moon are there").[16] As a traditional peasant society, they had an agriculture geared to minimizing risks rather than to maximizing yields. Thus, in order to guard against the upheavals of drought, pests, floods, and similar agricultural disasters, farmers planted a wide variety of different strains of the same crop. Indeed, Mudyanse Tenakoon, a local farmer and philosopher whom we interviewed in 1982, recalls that more than 280 different varieties of rice were in common usage during his youth; today, however, only 15 survive. Each variety had different characteristics and each was capable of surviving in conditions that would threaten the other varieties.[17]

Other changes have come in recent years. Custom once prohibited the construction of permanent buildings on prime agricultural land. Only the king and the priests, for instance, were entitled to build brick and tiled houses; everybody else lived in mud huts. That custom was founded on sound ecological principles. Brick houses, when they collapse, sterilize the soil. Mud houses, on the other hand, quickly return to the soil, providing valuable organic matter for the fields. Significantly, Tenakoon still refuses to live in a brick house.

The most significant change, however, is that the civilizations of ancient Sri Lanka protected their forests. If we are to believe Robert Knox, the sixteenth-century freebooter who was shipwrecked on the island and spent fifteen years as a captive of the king of Kandy, it was religious beliefs, rather than government ordinances, that prevented the forests from being cut down. According to Knox, the Sinhalese believed that when their ancestors first invaded Sri Lanka, the hostile spirits of the island's original inhabitants sought refuge in the jungles of the highlands. To enter those jungles was thus considered singularly unwise.

Whatever the truth of that explanation, it is certain that the protection of the highland forests played a vital role in ensuring the sustainability of agriculture in the dry zone. Indeed, it might even be argued that adequate forest cover in the highlands was crucial to a healthy irrigation system. Not only did the mountain jungles intercept and store the monsoon rains, but they also regulated the flow of water to the island's rivers. Without them, a perennial and certain supply of water was by no means certain. The point is well made by Brohier:

> The central mountain region . . . consists of hill piled over hill, and mountain range over mountain range, on a succession of ledges of great extent, at various elevations. . . .
>
> Ravines of various depths which form conduits for the mountain torrents lead from each one of these mountain ledges to the other. On the comparatively level tracts they form large swamps. All but two of the larger rivers of Ceylon collect their waters from these swamps in the mountain ledges. Rushing down from the mountains and following the grain of the country between the foothills, they meander sluggishly over the rest of their course, which lies in the maritime plains. It is easy, therefore, to realize that the first principle behind the whole system of water storage and carriage which in ancient times helped in irrigating the low country is centered on the natural reservoirs up in the mountains.
>
> A thousand years ago, as much as today, these centrally situated mountain heights of the island no doubt served to intercept the monsoon currents: but, whereas in the centuries gone, these primeval forests . . . helped to condense the vapor-laden clouds, conditions today tend to dissipate them. We may therefore assume, leaving little room to doubt, that in the past, when large river-fed works of irrigation functioned over the plains, there were influences which induced a much more abundant and liberal rainfall over the mountain zone.
>
> Then, again, the wooded slopes, with foliage acting as a parasol to the ground, served to break the force of the rainfall, to retain the surface soil and to help the ground to absorb some of the moisture.

In this last respect, it exercises an important influence in forming subsoil springs, which afforded the rivers a means of maintaining a perennial flow.[18]

DEFORESTATION: JEOPARDIZING THE FUTURE

After the fall of the ancient kingdoms, the seat of Sinhalese civilization moved to Kandy, in the uplands. Probably some deforestation was necessary to accommodate the city and its surrounding agricultural areas. Deforestation began in earnest, however, with the arrival of the British—in particular, with the setting up of coffee (and later tea) plantations in the mountains. Even so, at the time of independence, Sri Lanka was still 40 percent forested. Since then, whole areas of jungle have been cut down in order to earn foreign currency from the sale of timber. Today, forests cover a mere 4 or 5 percent of the island.

The ecological consequences of such deforestation have proved devastating. Indeed, it would be no exaggeration to say that the virtual disappearance of the country's jungle cover has cast serious doubts on the viability of agriculture in many areas of the island. As Brohier reports:

> Today, streams which were once perennial expose dry and stony beds. As a result of the short, swift descent from the mountain zone, the monsoon torrents, which are no longer restrained, sweep down the rivers carrying debris, earth, and sand. This tendency to sudden flooding in the plains has gradually increased the marshes. It has changed the physiography of many a region which was described in ancient history as proverbially fertile. The effect of denudation has, in fact, been transmitted throughout the entire course of the rivers. This is indicated by the shoals and sand banks and sandbars at the river mouths.[19]

He goes on to comment: "It will be safe to assume that this analysis of altered conditions will come as a revelation to many who proclaim that every ancient tank and channel system is capable, if restored, of fertilizing vast areas that are barren and unproductive."[20] Certainly, it will come as a revelation to the unfortunate bureaucrats who have been called upon to run the massive complex of dams and irrigation works at present being constructed on the Mahaweli River.

LAND TENURE: TRADITIONAL VERSUS MODERN

Under British colonial rule, all land whose ownership could not be firmly established was confiscated, designated "crown land," and then sold off in five-acre plots. Land thus became a marketable commodity in a country where, previously, the only items permissible to trade were salt, salted fish, and clothing. (And even then, the profit from such trade was limited by law to one-fourth of the value of the produce sold.)

Five acres is a large tract of land for a villager in Sri Lanka. Poor peasants were thus excluded from buying the new plots and, inevitably, the pattern of land tenure changed dramatically. Those changes are eloquently described by Edmund A. Leach in *Pul Eliya*, his classic 1953 study of a dry zone village.[21] As he notes, land in Pul Eliya is now divided into two categories: the "Old Field" (the 40 or so acres that had escaped confiscation) and the "New Lands" (land, in other words, that had been sold by the colonial authorities).

The Old Field is divided into two sections, the "upper field" and the "lower field." Those sections are divided into more than one hundred strips of land, which are farmed by different families. The distribution of those holdings is, as it always was, strictly egalitarian. Those "who own land in the lowest and least advantageous portion of the upper fields also own land in the highest and most advantageous portion of the lower field," the latter having first access to irrigation water.[22]

By contrast, land holdings in the New Lands are distributed according to the strict laws of the market. Here, the rich control the best land, and the poor make do with the marginal land. This situation, as Leach says, "is bound to have very drastic implications for the village considered as a social entity."[23] Nevertheless, those who farm the New Lands have done their utmost to reproduce the fragmented pattern of land holdings that characterizes the Old Field system. For instance, when the government put up the land for sale, many villagers formed syndicates to buy land and then divided it up among themselves. Large plots were thus broken down into smaller, individual, holdings. Other groups, in other countries, have handled such situations similarly.

Such syndicates, however, reveal a tension between two patterns. As Leach points out, "the most likely group of people to operate and maintain an irrigation system is a group of kinsmen who are capable of cooperating in a way that people unrelated by family bonds cannot."[24] No such bonds exist between the members of many of the syndicates that have bought the New Lands, and cooperation between them has been difficult. Clearly, the villagers are well aware of the problem. Indeed, Leach notes that they have sought "to reestablish the old form of cooperation among the owners of the New Lands by means of kinship alliances." In some cases, kinsmen themselves have formed syndicates in order to buy plots in the New Lands and work on common irrigation channels.

Finally, the New Lands have been dogged by problems of allocation of water. In the Old Field, water is allocated on the basis of a time-honored rota system that ensures that everyone receives their fair share at the right time. The system—which Leach regards as so highly "traditionalized" that it cannot be changed—is supervised by the *vel vigane* ("irrigation headman"), who also oversees the maintenance of the tanks and channels. Although the allocation of water in the New Lands is also assured by the *vel vigane*, he is not subject to the social constraints that operate in the Old Field—nor is the traditional method of allocating water used in the New Lands. As a result, writes Leach, the *vel vigane* and his friends now have "a dominating economic position in the village," and presumably the allocation of water in the New Lands has become both inequitable and arbitrary.[25]

That problem is compounded by the use of three irrigation channels in the New Lands, each one separately owned and managed. Thus, as Leach notes, "the control of the channels corresponds very closely to the general pattern of factionalism" that now divides the village. The New Lands suffer from chronic water shortages and are able to grow only one crop a year. By contrast, the Old Field had just one irrigation channel, operated and maintained by the whole community, and two crops were grown each year. Perhaps that difference can be explained by the increased acreage under cultivation: there simply is not enough water to irrigate the whole area twice a year. Far more fundamental, however, is the factionalism that plagues the New Lands; in an agricultural system built on cooperation, such strife can produce only disaster.

With the development of the market economy came a rapid expansion of the powers of the state. One of the first steps taken by the British colonial administration was to transfer the responsibility for maintaining the tanks from the villagers to a central irrigation department. The results were catastrophic. As one official reported to a select committee of the House of Commons in 1849, "What was everybody's business has become nobody's business."[26]

Today, the irrigation system of most dry zone villages is crude in comparison with what existed many centuries ago. Rare indeed is the village that still has its full complement of operational tanks. Recently, some work has been done to desilt the larger tanks, but the government has not seen fit to clean out the smaller ones. Nor should that surprise us. To the Irrigation Department, the smaller tanks are ancient relics whose use cannot possibly be justified by a conventional cost-benefit analysis. How, after all, could the government sanction the maintenance (let alone the construction) of a tank purely for the benefit of wild animals? On what economic grounds could it justify the building of two storage tanks, doubling the cost of both construction and maintenance? And who would pay for the bulldozers and other capital-intensive equipment to desilt the smaller tanks?

The sophisticated traditional irrigation has thus been sacrificed to economic expediency, and with it has gone a whole way of life. The tradition of mutual help has all but disappeared, and many essential agricultural tasks—in particular, weeding—are no longer properly carried out. It would seem that history is repeating itself. Just as the irrigation system of the ancient civilization fell apart when the communities that maintained it were disrupted, so today we have a new wave of disintegration. It remains to be seen whether Colombo will go the same way as Anuradhapura and Pollonaruwa.

24. Traditional Irrigation in Mesopotamia

MINIMIZING THE EFFECTS OF SALINIZATION

Irrigation has been practiced along the banks of the Euphrates for thousands of years, in conditions that are far less favorable than in the valley of the Nile. As Professor Gunter Garbrecht, professor of hydraulics and hydraulic engineering at the Technical University of Braunschweig, in West Germany, notes:

> First, the floods of the Tigris and Euphrates were very erratic and occurred at the "wrong time," the period April–June being too late for the summer crops and too early for the winter crops. Secondly, the two rivers carried a much greater amount of sediment than the Nile River. And, finally, the very small incline of the alluvial plain [1:26,000] and the fine texture of the soil easily gave way to waterlogging and salinization [lack of natural drainage].[1]

In spite of this, the inhabitants practiced irrigated basin agriculture as successfully as possible throughout much of the turbulent history of the area. Their principal weapon against salinization was alternate-year fallowing. Such fallowing allows the water table to fall after harvest, a process encouraged by evapotranspiration from the wild plants that take over once the land is temporarily abandoned. The mechanism is succinctly described by Professor McGuire Gibson, of the University of Chicago:

> As a result of irrigation, the water table in a field approaching harvest lies about half a meter below the surface. After the harvest the field turns green with Shok [*Proserpina stephanis*] and Agul [camelthorn, or *Alhagi maurorum*]. These wild plants draw moisture from the water table and gradually dry out the subsoil until winter, when they go dormant. In the spring, since the field is not being irrigated, the plants continue to dry out the subsoil to a depth of two meters, thus preventing the water from rising and bringing salt to the surface. Since they are legumes, the plants also replenish the land with nitrogen, and retard wind erosion of the topsoil. In the autumn, when the field is once again to be cultivated, the dryness of the subsoil allows the irrigation water to leach salt from the surface and carry it below, where it is normally "trapped and harmless."[2]

There is probably no better means of preventing soil salinization in the area. Indeed, J. C. Russell has described the traditional fallowing system as "a beautiful procedure for living with salinity." What is more, he points out, "the rural villagers understand it in that they know it works, and they know how to do it and they insist on it."[3] Sadly, this does not apply to the modern technological methods of irrigation that are being imposed on the peasants today.

Richard Adams and McGuire Gibson, who have both made special studies of the history of irrigation in Mesopotamia, seem to agree that fallowing is the best, if not the only, way of combating salinization in the area. But in the long run, it still does not prevent salty water from being slowly brought up to the surface. As this happens, the Shok and Agul roots slowly lose their capacity to "deep-dry" the land, and as a result, the topsoil becomes increasingly saline. Such soil can, of course, be removed by the farmers, who can then work the deeper layers until they too grow unproductive. Eventually, however, the land must be abandoned—often for 50 to 100 years or more—as indeed it has been during the long history of vernacular irrigation in Mesopotamia.

THE EL SHABANA

Short-term and long-term fallowing were only two elements in a complex cultural behavior pattern adapted perfectly to local ecological demands. The details of that pattern have been lost to history, but we can reconstitute many of its elements from studies of those groups that—at least until recently—practiced traditional irrigation in the region. The work of Robert Fernea, an anthropologist who has studied the social organization and irrigation system of the El Shabana of Daghara, is particularly relevant, especially because Fernea sees the El Shabana's social system as one that must once have been typical of all the tribal groups in Southern Iraq.[4]

The technology employed by the El Shabana was very simple, and their land tenure system was perfectly adapted to their agricultural practices. Joint ownership of land, for instance, was fairly common; this, Fernea considers, helped avoid "plots without access to irrigation water."[5] It also meant plots were large enough so that half of them could be allowed to go fallow at the same time. In addition, the El Shabana established a symbiotic relationship with local nomadic groups—through marriage ties, economic interests, and agreements to allow animals to pasture on fallow fields. When farming became particularly difficult, the farmers could thus revert to pastoral nomadism. The livestock they kept on their farms was, therefore, not only a source of income "but an ultimate insurance against drought, loss of land, or other crisis."[6]

The El Shabana emphasized a tradition of hospitality and the existence of mutual obligations among its members. This made it possible to spread the risks of farming, and strengthened the sense of cooperation essential to cleaning and maintaining the irrigation canals and digging new ones. The group could also subdivide when necessary, which, as McGuire Gibson notes, "removes the necessity for sustaining a large number of laborers and for them being forced or tempted to make work for them."[7] In more general terms, it enabled the tribesmen to keep their impact on their environment in proportion. McGuire Gibson considers the land tenure system of the El Shabana to have been so well suited to their traditional methods of extensive cultivation that "*the two aspects of agriculture must have evolved together in this region.*"[8]

Fernea asserts that the most adaptive feature of the El Shabana social organization was the ability to prevent the concentration of wealth and power. The society was egalitarian; its ruling sheikh, or chief, was no more than "the first among equals." The sheikh had no real political power. His main function was to lead his people into battle and to act "as a reservoir of tribal law and an astute judge . . . enforcing culturally defined and traditional norms."[9] Indeed, as Fernea points out, the segmentary lineage structure of the tribe had an almost "decentralizing tendency," one that was accentuated by the frequent revolutions that would replace "a sheikh from one lineage with a man from another section of the tribe." Furthermore, the sheikh had no incentive to build up large landholdings; his prime interest was in acquiring prestige. For that reason, if for no other, sheikhs did not invest in new irrigation schemes for personal gains and aggrandisement. Instead, what wealth they acquired was plowed back into the social group "in the form of hospitality, help in crisis and the like."[10]

THE EARLIEST HISTORICAL EXPERIENCE IN MESOPOTAMIA

Irrigated agriculture in Mesopotamia was carried out as far back as the fifth or fourth millennium B.C., by communities that were probably very similar to the El Shabana—both in their social structure and in their irrigation methods. However, some time during the third millennium, there seems to have been a massive increase in irrigation works in the Euphrates Valley. These do not seem to have been designed to improve the irrigation system of the local tribesmen, but rather to satisfy the requirements of a burgeoning urban society. "It is noteworthy," Adams writes, "that the objective of urban supply, rather than irrigation, is stressed in the few early royal inscriptions dealing with watercourse maintenance, and that the principal terminological distinction is between navigable and nonnavigable channels rather than between rivers and artificially constructed canals."[11]

Particularly significant was the building in southern Iraq (in the basin of the lower Diyala River, which occupies about 8,000 square kilometers along the northeastern margin of the lower Mesopotamian Plains) of a vast canal by King Entemenak of Girsu around 2400 B.C.[12] The canal was intended to supply water from the Tigris in order to irrigate an area east of Girsu that formerly had been watered by the Euphrates. The canal, which was so large that it was simply referred to as "the Tigris," led to seepage, flooding, and overirrigation, and a rise in the groundwater level.[13] Indeed, shortly after the reign of Entemenak, saline land "is attested in records of ancient temple surveyors."[14]

We also learn that during the same period, there was a gradual but marked reduction in the cultivation of salt-sensitive wheat, which was replaced by salt-tolerant barley. It appears that around 3500 B.C., as much wheat as barley was grown in southern Iraq. By the reign of Entemenak of Girsu (2500 B.C.), wheat accounted for only one-sixth of production; by about 2100 B.C. it accounted for no more than 2 percent of crops; and by 1700 B.C. no wheat was grown at all. Soil fertility also declined dramatically, largely as a result of salinity. In 2400 B.C. the average yield of barley per hectare in Girsu appears to have been 2,537 liters. By 2100 B.C., that yield had declined to 1,460 liters; and by 1700 B.C., the yield at Larsa, nearby, had fallen to an average of 897 liters per hectare. Indeed, the southern part of the alluvial plain "appears never to have recovered fully from the disastrous general decline which accompanied the salinization process." As a result, many of the great Sumerian cities "dwindled to villages or were left in ruins."[15] By the twentieth century the "former Garden of Eden had become a region of poverty and misery."[16] Adams and Jacobsen argue that there is probably "no historical event of this magnitude for which a single explanation is adequate." Nevertheless, it seems certain "that growing soil salinity played an important part in the breakup of Sumerian civilization."[17]

Stanley Walters, who has made a meticulous study of a large number of cuneiform inscriptions, many of which refer to the administration of irrigation works in South Mesopotamia, thinks that the spread of salinization as far as the Larsa area cannot be blamed on the building of Entemenak's canal alone. He postulates that similar large-scale water projects were undertaken around Larsa itself, and in the archives, he found a reference, dating from 1881 B.C., to a major project involving "the building of a wall above a reservoir at the mouth of the Isin Canal."[18] That wall was big enough "to require an inventory of at least 1.3 million bricks" as well as the dispatch of many workers and much material. The project appears to have been the work of Sumuel, king of Larsa; its object was to divert water for Larsa's own agricultural needs from a canal serving the territory of the rival city of Isin. A vast bureaucracy was created to administer and maintain the Larsa canal and many of the tablets studied by Walters clearly illustrate the inefficiency and corruption of the bureaucrats involved.

From 1200 to 100 B.C., and intermittently until the end of the Assyrian empire in the late seventh century, the Diyala area was a "disputed borderland," marched over and sacked by armies of rival empires.[19] A measure of order seems to have been established by Alexander the Great and his heirs, who encouraged urbanization on the Greek model. As a result, the population increased and agriculture was intensified. Those trends continued during the Sassanian period (A.D. 226–637). In the sixth century, probably during the reign of King Chosroes the First, the giant Nahrawan Canal system was built to supplement "the limited and fluctuating supplies of the Diyala River with almost unlimited water from the Tigris."[20]

The construction of the Nahrawan Canal made it necessary "to crisscross formerly unused desert and depression areas with a complex—and entirely artificial—brachiating system of branch canals."[21] That expansion depended also "on the construction of a large supplementary feeder canal from the Tigris, which, with technical proficiency that still excites admiration, and without apparent regard for cost, brought the indispensable additional water through a hard, conglomerate headland, across two rivers, and thence down the wide level left by the Dabban River of antiquity." Three hundred kilometers of the canal still remain. They illustrate "not only . . . the size of the system but also the attention lavished on such ancillary works as thousands of brick sluice gates along its branches." As Jacobsen and Adams point out, "we are dealing here with a whole new conception of irrigation which undertook bodily to reshape the physical environment at a cost which could be met only with the full resources of a powerful and highly centralized state."[22]

From a study of land-tax receipts—which reached a level they have never equaled at any other time—and from our knowledge of the distribution of settlements, we can now conclude that the Nahrawan Canal and its associated works brought the entire surface of the Euphrates plain under cultivation. This led to still more urban growth, and "Ctesiphon, the Sassanian capital, contained a larger urbanized area within its walls alone than the total area of all occupied sites within the 8,000 sq. km composing the lower Diyala basin at the period of the greatest ascendancy of Eshnunna around 2000 B.C."[23] The result was an increased dependence on outside markets, and also the takeover of the irrigation system by the state bureaucracy.

Like other irrigation works of the period, the Nahrawan Canal served principally to supply water to the new royal cities and the agricultural areas on which they depended for their food. Because the Sassanian empire, like the British raj in India, depended for much of its income on an agricultural tax, the canal also served to finance the state bureaucracy and the dynasty's costly imperial policy. The canal may also have served to reduce the power of the landed nobility and otherwise to enhance the power of the central government. The Sassanian empire was thus funded, in effect, by pillaging the alluvial soils of Mesopotamia and by destroying the social and cultural pattern of the communities they sustained.

Indeed, the building of such massive water development schemes caused numerous social and ecological problems. To begin with, there was a steep increase in population—probably as a result of the increased economic activity brought about by the new water works. "Quite possibly," Adams writes, "this led for the first time to a condition of general water shortage rather than local shortages based on uneven distribution."[24] Social disintegration quickly followed, and with it, slippage in the maintenance of the irrigation works (which Jacobsen rather superficially attributes to the breakdown of the central administration). The final stage in the drama, to quote Jacobsen and Adams, "assumes in retrospect a kind of historical inevitability." The area was virtually abandoned.

By the twelfth century, "Only a trickle passed through the upper section of the main canal to supply a few dying towns in the now hostile desert,"[25] and a dramatic increase in soil salinization led to the abandonment of whole areas. Forty percent of the Sassanian settlements became ghost towns, and major canal branches and their adjoining cultivated districts were permanently abandoned. Therefore, Islamic tax collections were never nearly as high as under the Sassanians, and "the prosperity of Baghdad as the seat of the Abbasid caliphate had to rest more on foreign conquests and tribute than on a secure economy in the city's immediate ruralities."[26]

Inevitably, the large-scale, centralized irrigation system broke down under the strain of social upheaval. "What replaced it, at catastrophically lower levels of population and economic interchange, was the first, simplest, and most resilient of configurations . . . which had been antecedent to cities and hence would survive their destruction."[27] In other words, those small-scale, communally managed, traditional systems that alone were adapted to the social and ecological requirements of the area.

THE MODERN EXPERIENCE

Today, history is repeating itself. Once again, the traditional irrigation system is breaking down under the pressures of centralization and agricultural intensification. The recent breakdown began under Turkish rule and was accelerated by the British.

Both colonial administrations increased the power of the local sheikhs to transform them into their own agents within the tribal areas. The sheikhs were thereby "forced to assume roles that they either did not wish to perform or [which were] carried out to the detriment of their people."[28] This radically altered their relationship with the other members of their tribe. No longer "first among equals," they instead became landlords, and their fellow tribesmen were reduced to mere tenants. Tribal land, which previously had been held communally, thus became private property, and many sheikhs simply sold their land to speculators. Others moved to the cities and became absentee landlords.

The story is a familiar one. Ester Boserup, for instance, notes: "When [large-scale irrigation] regions are left in the uncontrolled possession of a landlord class, which is either of foreign origin or partner in a precarious alliance with a foreign conqueror, rural investments are in danger of being neglected, because the landlords inevitably go for quick profits and liquid assets. In extreme cases, the result is starvation and depopulation."[29] As we shall see, this may also occur when the central government is an indigenous one.

As the power of the landlords increased, more and more peasants were drawn into the market economy. They were forced to pay rents, taxes, and interest on loans, which they found increasingly difficult to meet. Fallow periods were violated, and eventually only the large landowners had "sufficient acreage to shift tenants around in order to reduce losses due to poor land fallowing."[30] The reduction in fallow also meant a reduction in pasturage and hence a decrease in livestock. Moreover, the introduction of the new system of land tenure, together with the gradual disintegration of the tribal system, meant that the sheikhs ceased to observe their traditional obligations. Instead of acting as custodians of the tribes' lands, they acted "increasingly in their own family interests."[31]

Discussing the overall effects of government policy under British and Turkish rule, McGuire Gibson has few good words to say. Thus he writes: "By supporting and keeping one family in a position of power; by changing a chief to a landlord; by concentrating wealth while inducing individuals to take up small, fixed plots; by imposing yearly taxes and encouraging rents and debts, the central authority brought about widespread violation of fallow. Eventual selling out by small holders to large landowners did not lead to a reversal of agricultural decline because debt-ridden farmers often did not stay on the land as sharecroppers, but became nomads or fled to the cities."[32] To alleviate the labor shortage, the landlords were forced to obtain tenants elsewhere. Since the newcomers were unfamiliar with the area, they were far less capable than the tribesmen whom they superseded.

Those problems were further compounded by the water development projects initiated by both colonial regimes. Here the experience of the tribes in the Daghara region—where the Turks never exerted effective control—is instructive. In 1870, Midhat Pasha, the progressive Turkish governor, ordered the construction of a dam across the Saqlawiyah canal at its source on the Euphrates, near Felluja. The object was to prevent the flooding of Baghdad. The effect, however, was to impose "a much greater burden of water upon the barrage at Hindiyah," which was "the critical divisor of water allowing a flow to go into the Hilla channel and thence into the Daghara canal."[33] The Saqlawiyah dam eventually gave way; it was repaired but continued to function badly. As a result, "in the last part of the nineteenth century the Daghara area suffered crises of water shortage."

In 1903 the dam collapsed again. H. W. Cadoux, who traveled by stagecoach down the middle of the dry Hilla bed, saw whole sections of the countryside deserted, the former residents having been forced to move to the area around the Hidiyah channel. Only a few forts, deriving their water from wells sunk in the middle of the canal beds, were still inhabited. All the vegetation except palm trees had withered.[34] The dam was restored in 1914.

Elsewhere, other water projects were initiated. The British administration embarked on a vast scheme to build a major new canal in addition to upstream storage basins and dams designed to store the water throughout the dry season. The effect of those developments was perhaps predictable: soil salinity was increased and agricultural yields fell dramatically. Indeed, Mc-

Guire Gibson notes, somewhat sardonically, "Directly, through engineering that promoted waterlogging and salinity, the central government acted to undermine agricultural productivity."[35]

The end of colonial rule brought no improvement to the slow decline of Mesopotamia's irrigation agriculture. In the last twenty years, more and more smallholders have sold their land to the sheikhs and have sought work elsewhere. The waterways are now administered nationally, and the water is supplied by pipe from a government canal. Waterlogging and salinity have rendered one-third to one-half of the land of the El Shabana uncultivable.[36]

THE LESSONS OF MESOPOTAMIA

For many years, historians of irrigation agriculture in Mesopotamia explained the rise and fall of state-run irrigation schemes in terms of Wittfogel's argument—cited in chapter 23—that irrigation agriculture is possible only when run by a centralized bureaucracy, and, consequently, that the collapse of irrigation agriculture results from the breakdown of that bureaucracy. "When government controls weaken," writes Jacobsen, a well-known adherent of the Wittfogel thesis, "and disturbed conditions come to prevail, the great disastrous abandonments of land take place."[37]

Our brief review of the Mesopotamian experience argues for a very different interpretation. To be sure, a state bureaucracy is undoubtedly necessary in order to administer a vast centralized irrigation system. But we are convinced that the collapse of that system comes about as a result of the inevitable social and ecological destruction it causes. Small wonder that the great survivors in the history of irrigation agriculture in Mesopotamia are precisely those societies that have escaped being drawn into the orbit of the state. The fact is that irrigation agriculture does not decline when bureaucratic controls relax; quite the opposite. As McGuire Gibson puts it, "In Mesopotamia, the intervention of state government has tended to weaken and ultimately destroy the agricultural basis of the country."[38]

Another perspective is that of Fernea, who does not regard a tribal society as the only type of society capable of managing an irrigation system.

> If a landlord with a large holding were to allow fallowing [as he could afford to do with that much land] and be satisfied with the yield, without pressing his tenants for greater production; if an external government were to refrain from excessive taxing of the tenants; or if the landlord, pressed for taxes by the government, were not to squeeze his tenants; if the landlord with restraint were to reinvest his return only in his land, canals, and the like; if he were, in short, to be a good landlord and act like a sheikh, it would be possible to carry on productive agriculture without violating fallow and causing increased salinisation.[39]

Nonetheless, Fernea asserts that, historically, irrigation agriculture has been most successful in tribal societies—which he explains in terms of "the congruence of fit between tribal methods of cultivation and land tenure and the nature of land, water and climate."[40] This brings us to the crux of the matter. Throughout history, state-mandated methods of cultivation and systems of land tenure arrogantly defy "the nature of land, water and climate." Indeed, they are based on the illusion that there are no natural constraints on man's activities. As we have seen, the results have been catastrophic.

Experience makes it seem almost inevitable that the pattern of the past will be repeated. Already, the large-scale irrigation schemes of modern Mesopotamia are causing untold ecological and social damage. Catastrophe can undoubtedly be postponed, but it cannot be averted. Presumably, we will then see the reemergence of a traditional irrigation agriculture. As Adams puts it: "An extensive system, whose cultivated areas and balance with animal husbandry have been continually adjusted as salinity and other conditions make necessary, has repeatedly confirmed its viability over a span of more than six millennia. It would require not an act of judgment but of faith to proclaim, on the basis of the very brief, recent experience to date, that this oldest and most flexible of the agricultural configurations that Mesopotamia has known will shortly disappear without a trace."[41]

25. The Lessons of Traditional Irrigation Agriculture: Learning to Live with Nature

AT A RECENT MEETING on water development schemes, Dr. Raymond Nace, a hydrologist, issued a stern rebuke to his colleagues. "Three sins beset water planners and their advisors: faith in science and technology, worship of bigness, and arrogance towards the landscape. . . . The belief that technology can solve any water problem . . . is wrong. It seems essential that a new frame of mind, some new perspective be applied to water planning."[1]

Strong words indeed—and ones with which we would not disagree. But how best to define the "new frame of mind" that Nace calls for? We should examine not only what has caused modern irrigation schemes to *fail*; it is much more important to understand what has made traditional irrigation societies *succeed*. Why, for example, have the El Shabana, the Sonjo, or the Chagga been able to practice sustainable irrigation agriculture over thousands of years, although modern irrigation schemes rarely last more than a few decades? Is it, as Fernea suggests, because tribal societies have achieved a "congruence of fit" between their methods of cultivation, their land tenure systems, and "the nature of land, water, and climate"?[2] And, if so, what is the basis of that congruence?

SIZE: A CRITICAL FACTOR?

Most traditional irrigation systems operate on a very small scale. By contrast, most modern irrigation schemes cover large areas of land and are geared toward maximum production. Obviously, their ecological impact is greater than that of traditional systems. As summed up by Dr. Desmond Anthony, "Experience has shown . . . that the extent and degree of modification [of ecological systems] and the magnitude of the resultant impact are usually directly proportional to the size of the project, and are related to the nature of the environment and its sensitivity to modifications of the kind brought about by construction, operation, and maintenance of such projects."[3]

Or, in the words of Robert Goodland, "the size of hydro projects is almost exponentially related to environmental impact."[4] That general rule, says Goodland, is true of "the area of fertile soil removed from annual production by flooding; the number of people displaced, and houses, infrastructure lost to the reservoir; and the opportunities for proliferation of aquatic disease vectors [e.g., malarial mosquito, schistosomiasis snail] and nuisance organisms [e.g., water hyacinth, gnats]." He goes on to point out that large reservoirs "trigger or exacerbate the perils of induced seismicity" and "produce less fish per unit volume than small reservoirs." Moreover, "water quality deteriorates gravely in large reservoirs while remaining acceptable in small ones."

Therefore, says Goodland, dams should be as small as possible. Better still, tube turbines should be installed: "These cheap, low-maintenance, sparkless sources of power are easy to manufacture in the 100 kw to 1,000 kw range, and 20 mw to 100 mw sizes also can be feasible with minor environmental impact." Indeed, Goodland claims, the smaller turbines cause "practically no environmental problems since little or no reservoir is created."

Despite the environmental virtues of building small dams, small-scale irrigation and hydropower schemes are rarely favored over large-scale schemes. One reason, undoubtedly, is prestige. The more grandiose the scheme, the more credit accrues to the politicians and engineers involved in building it. Also, as William Ackermann points out, small-scale dams are frequently seen as being uneconomical. As he writes:

From the viewpoint of power generation and large-scale water storage, only relatively large and deep reservoirs are economically attractive. One horsepower is generated by dropping 1 cubic foot of water per second through a height of 3.34 meters. Thus there are obvious advantages to constructing power dams with as much "head" as possible. Similarly, for water storage, the approximately parabolic shape of most lake basins ensures that each increase in the height of a dam progressively increases the storage benefits. In consequence, major reservoirs are usually made as extensive as possible, and thus they tend to be in the large-scale range.[5]

WHY SMALL IS NOT ENOUGH

Suppose that, in the future, only small-scale dams were to be built. Would that enable us to avoid the problems associated with today's superdams? Probably not. Small is certainly preferable to big—and on that point we should be quite emphatic—but small is not necessarily safe when it comes to ecological damage. Indeed, even small-scale projects can cause significant ecological and social harm. In some cases, the damage is the result of poor design. In others—as in the first of the following examples—it arises from the very size of the project.

The small dams that have been built in the Volta Valley, for example, provide a more suitable niche for the vector of onchocerciasis than large dams, according to John Hunter. "In many areas," he reports, "the construction of small dams has already augmented the spread of river blindness rather than the reverse."[6] The reason is clear: the more dams there are, the more spillways there will be—and hence, the more breeding places for the blackflies that carry the disease.

In Jamaica, bad design led to the failure of a series of small dams that had been built across various shallow valleys in order to make reservoirs for irrigation from modest creeks. Because the subsoil of the region is particularly porous, which the dams' promoters failed to take into account, the water simply leaked away from the reservoirs. As a result, reports Brian Johnson of I.I.E.D., the dams now "sit high and dry, a series of embarrassing embankments."[7]

Meanwhile, in eastern Nepal, a small hydro dam silted up so quickly that the turbines stopped functioning. According to "faraway economic experts," the dam was supposed to have repaid its initial investment within fifteen years; in just five years, however, it had become "a millstone of modernity around the Nepalese neck."

Even the small-scale irrigation schemes built today aim at replacing seasonal irrigation with perennial irrigation. The latter, however, invariably entails higher social and ecological costs—whatever the size of the scheme. For one thing, perennial irrigation schemes create a permanent (rather than a temporary) niche for the vectors of waterborne diseases, which causes a rise in the incidence of those diseases. The impact is compounded by the fact that perennial irrigation drastically increases the amount of time that farmers must spend in the irrigation waters—and, hence, the amount of time they are exposed to the hazards in those waters. It also increases the moisture level of the atmosphere and the soil, and the vegetative period of crops, thus providing a permanent breeding ground for pests.

Although perennial irrigation makes possible several harvests a year, that is not much of a boon if the soil is too poor to support the extra demands being made upon it. Very few soils—especially among the organically poor soils of the tropics—can be used to produce two or three identical crops a year for very long. Indeed, if multicropping is carried out over any significant period of time in such regions, it must lead to the degradation of agricultural land—which in turn must lead to a reduction rather than an increase in agricultural yield.

Furthermore, multicropping and perennial irrigation tend to raise the water table, which gives rise to all the attendant problems of waterlogging and salinization. Multicropping also increases the work load of local farmers, to the detriment of their social lives. People do not have time to interact in traditional ways—such as singing or dancing or feasting—which would normally create a climate for the co-operation that is so vital to the sound management and maintenance of a viable irrigation system.

For the above reasons, the very notion of perennial irrigation is unacceptable—on whatever scale it is carried out. For traditional irrigation agriculturalists, irrigation is not only seasonal but is limited to the shortest possible period. In most of those societies, half the potential agricultural land is allowed to lie fallow on alternate years, which means that irrigation is carried out for a short season every *other* year.

Such an apparent "waste" of good land must seem intolerable to those who manage today's modern irrigation systems. Indeed, the very ideas of fallow lands and alternate-year irrigation go against all the canons of the modern market system, geared as it is toward increasing production apparently regardless of long-term ecological costs.

THE PRESERVATION OF FORESTS

Traditional irrigation agriculture is also noteworthy in that it is practiced in areas where at least part of the natural forest cover has been allowed to remain intact. Such forests are particularly important in the uplands and in the watersheds of the river whose waters are abstracted, and their destruction is by far the most important cause of the droughts that relentlessly afflict vast areas of the Third World today.

Deforestation makes its mark in a number of ways. For one, it reduces rainfall. In Amazonia, 75 percent of the precipitation is estimated to be derived from the transpiration of trees in the area. Cutting down the Amazon forest will significantly reduce rainfall throughout the region—and increase temperatures. A preliminary mathematical model developed by one group of researchers suggests that the destruction of Amazonia should increase the mean temperature in the tropics to something like 50° centigrade—making them virtually uninhabitable. It would, in fact, seriously affect climate throughout the world, since the vast volume of water now being continuously exchanged between the forest and the atmosphere would no longer exert its massive cooling effect. It appears that the Harappan Desert in Pakistan was also once a vast rainforest whose rainfall was largely self-generated, and once the trees were cut down, rainfall was reduced to near zero.[8]

But the recurrent droughts are not necessarily the result of reduced rainfall. Droughts are regularly reported in areas where there has been no recent reduction in rainfall. Such droughts are the result of a lowered water table caused by deforestation or excessive water abstraction, or else they are due to the reduced water-retaining capacity of an overtaxed soil.

The general desiccation caused by deforestation in India was eloquently described by E. Washburn Hopkins eighty years ago:

> All that great bare belt of country which now stretches south of the Ganges—that vast waste where drought seems to be perennial and famine is as much at home as is Civa in a graveyard—was once an almost impenetrable wood.
>
> Luxuriant growth filled it: self-irrigated, it kept the fruit of the summer's rain till winter, while the light winter rains were treasured there till the June monsoon came again. Even as late as the epic period, it was a hero's derring-do to wander through that forest-world south of the Nerbudda, which at that time was a great inexhaustible river, its springs conserved by the forest. Now the forest is gone, the hills are bare, the valley is unprotected, and the Nerbudda dries up like a brook, while starved cattle lie down to die on the parched clay that should be a river's bed.[9]

The deforestation of upland areas is even less tolerable, since forested uplands attract a great deal of rain, and it is in the uplands that the sources of the rivers that water the plains beneath are situated. We have seen how this is so in Sri Lanka, and how the water required for the vast water development schemes being built today is unlikely to be available now that the uplands have been deforested. Already, the autumn monsoon—which blows from the southwest and used to collect moisture from the forest uplands and deposit it on the dry zone beyond—falls on denuded mountains, and the autumn rains have largely vanished from the northeast of the island.

Such deforested slopes as we have noted, are, in the tropics in particular, very rapidly eroded. The soil that is washed off them raises the river beds, causing floods that can be as devastating to agricultural production as are the droughts to which the same areas have become so prone during the dry season. Ironically, deforestation is the cause of both the floods and the droughts that annually deprive the inhabitants of vast areas of the Third World of more food than could conceivably be provided by the implementation of FAO's plans to increase by 50 percent or so the agricultural area at present under irrigation.

What is more, the forests can provide water in perpetuity, not just temporarily, at no social or ecological cost, and they provide other benefits equally precious. They harbor a wealth of wildlife. They are a source of all sorts of wild fruit and berries, of humus for the fields and of timber for building houses. In a broader context, they generate oxygen and absorb carbon dioxide and generally exert a stabilizing influence on climate. All these benefits are *free* and available to all, not just the urban elite.

BALANCING WATER CONSUMPTION WITH WATER AVAILABILITY

There is also an equilibrium in sound irrigation systems: those who operate them do not draw off more water than is guaranteed by the natural rate at which their water supplies are replenished. They do not try to extract more than the "safe yield" of their aquifers and surface waters.

Traditional societies have historically sought to prevent any increase in the demand for water. In his study of irrigation agriculture in medieval Valencia, for example, Thomas Glick shows how all new developments that might have placed a strain on the region's water budget were strenuously resisted.[10] Hunt and Hunt note the general tendency within traditional irrigation societies "to resist new [water] uses"—even where that entails refusing to open up new lands or to plant new crops.[11]

In arid lands, the need for such restraint is axiomatic if the long-term availability of water is to be assured. That simple axiom, however, is one that modern industrial society has preferred to ignore. The modern belief is that water should not—and, indeed, *does* not—place a constraint on human activities. If water is not available locally, the theory goes, human ingenuity will ensure that it is supplied from elsewhere.

In that respect, it is worth considering the history of agricultural development in the U.S. Southwest, a history that illustrates perfectly the conflict between what might be called the "ecological" and the "industrial" views of water demand and supply. In the late 1880s, ecologically minded people—notably John Wesley Powell, who later became the director of the U.S. Geological Survey—began to warn that the arid West must learn to live within its water budget if future shortages were to be avoided. Emphasizing the natural limits of the West's water resources, Powell wrote: "Only a small portion of the country is irrigable. The irrigable tracts are lowlands lying along the stream. These lands will maintain but a scanty population."[12]

That eminently ecological view of water supplies was not to the liking of Powell's contemporaries. Indeed, as the historian Henry Nash Smith observes, Powell "was asking a great deal; he was suggesting that the West should submit to rational and scientific revision of its central myth"—the myth, that is, that there was enough land and water available for everyone's needs.[13]

Perhaps it was inevitable, then, that Powell lost his battle to make the farmers of the West see sense. His recommendation that the area should tailor its development plans "to fit the limits of its natural resources" was rejected by the U.S. Congress, "with senators and congressmen from the region itself providing the stiffest opposition."[14] At the 1893 International Irrigation Congress, held in Los Angeles, Powell was greeted with catcalls and boos. "I tell you, gentlemen," he persisted, "you are piling up a heritage of conflict and litigation over water rights, for there is not sufficient water to supply the land."[15]

By rejecting Powell's advice, the American establishment ignored the actuality of the "nature of land, water, and climate" in the West. For them, the natural world was something to be shaped at whim to satisfy man's immediate requirements, and that attitude has since become increasingly well entrenched. Some twenty years ago, for example, the U.S. Geological Survey (USGS) simply dropped the notion of "safe yield," declaring that

"Wholesale depletion [of groundwater] may be economically feasible in the long view if it results in building up an economy that can afford to pay for water from a more expensive source."[16]

Does anyone ask what happens when the "more expensive source" is depleted? Even supposing that another—presumably even more expensive—source of water is available, it can surely be only a question of time before the economy becomes dependent on a source that is so expensive that no one can afford to buy water—at which point the whole economy simply collapses. As we have noted, this impasse has already almost been reached in the American West. Thus, even though billions of dollars have been spent on numerous water development schemes in the area (California possesses almost one-tenth of the world's large dams) irrigation agriculture in the West can—in the view of many experts—continue on any significant scale only if the federal government is willing to subsidize such mammoth schemes as the Peripheral Canal and the North American Water and Power Alliance. Already the former has been vetoed at the state level as being too expensive. Even if the money were available from the federal coffers, who would be able to afford the water?

DESIGN AND MANAGEMENT: VILLAGE ELDERS VERSUS DISTANT BUREAUCRATS

If traditional irrigation systems run so smoothly, it is often because they are managed not by members of a network of outsiders imposed upon local farmers by the state, but rather by members of the very community that farms the land. Their values, their mores, and their own personal interests largely coincide with those of their fellow farmers. The knowledge with which they design and operate their local irrigation system has been handed down from generation to generation. It reflects centuries of specific local geological, biotic, and climatic experience. And those who manage a traditional irrigation system have an added reason to want success: if they fail to do their job properly, then it will be not only their neighbors who suffer but their own families as well.

Modern irrigation schemes are invariably run by distant bureaucracies whose officials are not interested in the daily life of the communities they oversee. In the pursuit of long-term personal gains, such as a promotion or an enlarged staff, senior officials tend to ride roughshod over local ecological and social considerations. In the pursuit of short-term political gains, and to expand the influence of their departments, those officials have also shown themselves susceptible to lobbying by powerful commercial pressure groups. The interests of the community usually come last.

This same lack of commitment to the community is visible at the local or regional level. As we have seen, local bureaucrats cannot manage irrigation works with the same degree of equitability and efficiency displayed by traditional irrigation societies. And is there any wonder? The bureaucrats in charge of a modern irrigation scheme are unlikely to have any practical experience of agriculture in the region—or elsewhere. Nor can they draw on the storehouse of information that a traditional society builds up by farming the same land year after year. Instead, they must rely on the few vague generalities which they gleaned from textbooks written by academics who rarely have any knowledge of local conditions. Even where that textbook knowledge is supplemented by feasibility studies carried out prior to the setting up of a scheme, the hapless bureaucrat is still in an unenviable position, for few such studies give any real indication of the problems involved in irrigation agriculture. Their primary function seems to be to justify decisions already taken at a higher political level. The result is frequently a cynical charade in which bureaucrats pass the buck for failures from one department to another, and do their utmost to claim credit for any successes. Unlike the peasants who must make their livelihood from the land they farm, the bureaucrat has an assurance of income—and with it, sustenance.

FOOD FOR LOCAL CONSUMPTION
RATHER THAN FOR EXPORT

What is perhaps most distinctive about traditional irrigation agriculture is that it is geared to producing food for local consumption. Indeed, it is only by ignoring the export market that irrigation schemes can fulfill their intended purpose, which is to serve the interests of the local population.

It is also the only way irrigation agriculture can live with nature on the terms we have enumerated. These are essential if an irrigation scheme is to satisfy the requirements set out in chapter 17, based on recommendations by Brent Blackwelder, Philip Williams, Barbara Bramble and Bruce Rich—in other words, if the scheme is to be effective and sustainable.

To produce enough food to feed itself, a society need not ravage its own environment. Once, however, it becomes geared to producing food for export to a highly competitive—and, at times, seemingly insatiable—world market, such devastation is unavoidable. Indeed, to achieve success in exporting, agricultural activities must be undertaken by vast, capital-intensive enterprises, and society must be willing to subordinate long-term social and ecological considerations to the demands of short-term economic competitiveness.

Under such circumstances, the dams that store the water for irrigation schemes cannot be small. Everything conspires to make them bigger and bigger. Nor can irrigation systems possibly be seasonal. Perennial irrigation is essential if vast stretches of water-intensive monocultures are to be multicropped year after year.

Nor can forests be preserved. Put bluntly, there is no room for them. Moreover, exporting their timber provides an essential source of the foreign exchange needed to finance capital-intensive development systems.

Nor can the overuse of water be avoided. All the water that can be made available must be abstracted in the interests of economic competitiveness and of maximizing economic activity.

Nor, finally, can export-oriented irrigation schemes be managed by local communities. Widstrand, for example, notes the failure of water-users' associations in the Third World and the high death rate of government-introduced cooperatives in East Africa. Why should we ever have expected such schemes to succeed? Why should farmers willingly participate in projects designed to raise food for export on the only land available to them for meeting the needs of their own families, in exchange for money that will be spent by an urban elite on expensive imported goods?

THE NEED FOR A NEW WORLDVIEW: THE ECOLOGICAL APPROACH

Inevitably, the conflict between the "ecological" and "industrial" views of water supplies in the western United States raises questions more generally about our attitudes toward both nature and economics. Can we really take the view that it is justifiable to jeopardize future water supplies in the interests of economic growth? Is it really "economical" to expose vast numbers of people to malaria or schistosomiasis in exchange for the hydroelectricity or irrigation water that a dam provides? What is "economical" about transforming good agricultural land into a salt desert for short-term increases in agricultural yields?

Clearly, our ideas of what is "economical" need serious reconsideration. The point is well made by Robert Goodland: "Economics excludes consideration of . . . adverse consequences—frequently referred to as 'externalities'—from customary evaluations. The time frame of economic thinking is so shortsighted, and the perspective of economic vision is so narrow, that such criteria frequently act to the detriment of the environment." He concludes that "In the final analysis, anything environmentally unsound can never be economically healthy."[17]

Sooner or later, all social and ecological costs must be translated into economic costs—be it in terms of higher medical bills or diminishing agricultural returns. By incurring such costs, we are in effect signing postdated checks against future generations. When those checks are presented for payment, we will probably not have enough money set aside, or we will have forgotten ever incurring the debts in the first place. The only outcome of such shortsighted behavior is ecological and social bankruptcy, and such must eventually be the fate of all countries that place day-to-day economic and political considerations above the survival of our physical and social environment.

To emphasize this message, we need look no farther than to the Dustbowl years in the United States. The fragile soils of the southern plains should never have been put under the plow. This was recognized by the Mexican government, which had decreed as far back as 1823 that its plains should be used only for ranching. John Wesley Powell (who in 1881 became head of the U.S. Geological Survey) also thought ranching was the only suitable use of the southern plains. To the American governments, however, ranching suggested an "undemocratic" policy that would create "great landowning barons" whose interests could only conflict with those of the small homesteader. Even religion was used to justify the popular view that the plains should be cultivated: God, it was claimed, intended "not cattle, but wheat" to be raised on the plains.

The plains were thus cultivated—and the great dustbowls of the 1890s and 1930s were the inevitable consequence. When, in 1936, the Great Plains Committee (under the chairmanship of Maurice Cooke) reported on the tragedy, it vindicated the warnings of Powell. "Nature," the committee wrote, "has established a balance by what, in human terms, would be called the method of trial and error. The white man has disturbed this balance— he must restore it or devise a new one of his own." The Great Dustbowl, the committee insisted, was a wholly man-made disaster, the result of a series of misguided efforts "to impose upon the region a system of agriculture to which the plains are not adapted."[18]

Cooke and his colleagues went on to criticize the prevailing attitude "that nature is something of which to take advantage and to exploit—that Nature can be shaped at will to Man's convenience." They observed:

> In a superficial sense, this is true—felling of trees will clear land for cultivation, planting of seeds will yield crops, and applications of water where natural precipitation is low will increase yields. However, in a deeper sense, modern science had disclosed that fundamentally Nature is inflexible and demands conformity. . . .

We know now, for instance, that it is essential to adjust agricultural economy on the Plains to periods of deficient rather than of abundant rainfall, and to the destructive influence of wind blowing over dry loose soil rather than primarily to a temporary high price for wheat or beef—that it is our way, not Nature's, which can be changed.

This is the heart of the matter. Living things are not arranged in a random manner. Nature is not totally malleable, as those who wish to transform it would have us believe. It is, on the contrary, highly organized—and that rigid order must be maintained. Once degraded by overexploitation and pollution, nature cannot hold its own. Cut down forests and overtax the land, and soils will become eroded. Pollute rivers, and fish will die. Upset the natural balance between pest and predator, and pestilence will be epidemic. Destroy the habitat of wildlife, and species will become extinct. Indeed, the whole gamut of ills that now beset the earth are merely the symptoms of a degraded ecosystem which, under pressure from Homo sapiens, can no longer continue to function properly. Historically, it has been mainly traditional societies that demonstrated an awareness that "it is our way, not Nature's, which can be changed."

PART VI
WHAT SHOULD BE DONE?

26. Recommendations

THERE IS CLEAR EVIDENCE, unpalatable as it must be to some, that building large dams is *not* an appropriate means of feeding the world's hungry, of providing energy, or of reducing flood damage. To conclude otherwise would be to accept as largely expendable the flora, the fauna, the population, and the land itself—the whole area affected by the dam—simply to further the political and financial interests of a very small minority.

In light of today's knowledge, it is clear that the building of large-scale water development schemes can be justified to an electorate and to the world at large only by systematically covering up—as governments and their advisers have shown themselves adept at doing—their true implications.

To persuade Third World governments to abandon plans to build water development schemes to which they are often totally committed is very difficult. Nevertheless, every effort must be made by local environmental groups to do so. If necessary, they should resort to nonviolent direct action at the dam site. We in the West can best prevent the construction of further dams by systematically lobbying donor governments, development banks, and international agencies, without whose financial help such schemes could not be built.

We thereby call upon those organizations, forthwith, to cut off funds from all large-scale water development schemes that they may be planning to finance, or are involved in financing, regardless of how far those schemes have progressed.

The vast concrete hulk of a three-quarters finished dam may not provide irrigation water or electricity—but neither will it drown ancient villages, precious forests, or stretches of fertile bottomland.

Nor will it uproot tens, if not hundreds, of thousands of rural people, condemning them to eke out a miserable existence in the degraded and unfamiliar environment to which they have been consigned.

Nor will it condemn those inhabiting the irrigated areas to seeing their children ravaged by malaria and schistosomiasis.

Nor will it systematically transform much of the remaining agricultural land into a waterlogged and salt-encrusted desert, nor cause arable land to be gradually transformed into large plantations for growing food to export to foreign lands, or into large factories manufacturing goods the local population cannot afford.

Nor will it deprive local inhabitants of their water supply in order to satisfy the unquenchable thirst of the plantations, the factories, and the new conurbations that dams support.

If they insist on completing the project, and all this destruction occurs, we will eventually be left with a silted-up reservoir and the vast concrete hulk of an abandoned dam. Those ruins can serve but one salutary purpose: as a permanent monument to the folly, or the cynicism, of those who now direct the organizations that have financed so much destruction and so much misery throughout the world, a monument set in a vast muddy wasteland where once the fertile soil nourished happy and sustainable communities.

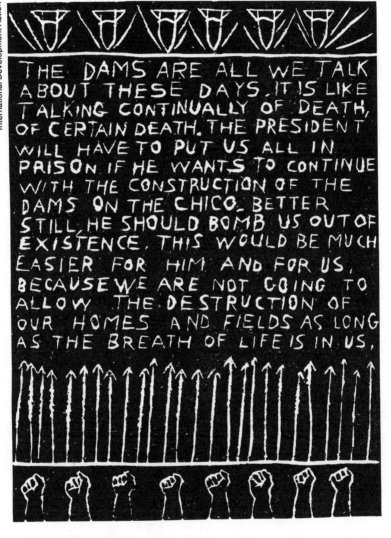

THE DAMS ARE ALL WE TALK
ABOUT THESE DAYS. IT IS LIKE
TALKING CONTINUALLY OF DEATH,
OF CERTAIN DEATH. THE PRESIDENT
WILL HAVE TO PUT US ALL IN
PRISON IF HE WANTS TO CONTINUE
WITH THE CONSTRUCTION OF THE
DAMS ON THE CHICO. BETTER
STILL, HE SHOULD BOMB US OUT OF
EXISTENCE. THIS WOULD BE MUCH
EASIER FOR HIM AND FOR US,
BECAUSE WE ARE NOT GOING TO
ALLOW THE DESTRUCTION OF
OUR HOMES AND FIELDS AS LONG
AS THE BREATH OF LIFE IS IN US,

Appendix One

Major Dams of the World—1984

Name	Date Completed	River or Basin	Location	Dam Type	Dam Height (m)	Dam Volume $(m^3 \times 10^3)$	Reservoir Capacity $(m^3 \times 10^6)$
A							
Afsluitdijk	1932	Zuiderzee	Netherlands	E	19	63,430	6000
Agua Vermelha	1975	Grande	Brazil	E/G	67	13,600	11,100
Akosombo	1966	Volta	Ghana	R	141	7890	148,000
Aldeadavila	1963	Duero	Spain	A	140	848	115
Alicura	1978	Limay	Argentina	E	130	12,900	3250
Almendra	1970	Tormes-Duero	Spain	A	202	1673	2649
Alpe-Gera	1965	Comor	Italy	G	178	1722	65
Altinkaya	(1986)	Kizilirmak	Turkey	R	195	15,310	5763
Amaluza	1982	Paute	Ecuadór	A	170	1157	120
Amir Kabir (Karadj)	1962	Karadj	Iran	A	178	705	205

Name	Year	River	Country	Type			
Angostura	1974	Grijalva	Mexico	R	146	4400	9200
Aswan, High	1970	Nile	Egypt	E/R	111	42,620	164,000
Atatürk	(1990)	Euphrates	Turkey	E/R	179	84,500	48,700
B							
Bad Creek	(1991)	Bad Creek	USA	R	108	28,520	41
Bagdad Tailings	1973	Maroney Gulch	USA	E	37	1663	49
Baishan	1983	Songhuajiang	P.R. of China	G	150	19,096	900
Balimela	1978	Sileru	India	E	75	17,400	3610
Bath County	(1985)	Back Creek	USA	E/R	146	35,500	45
Beas	1974	Beas-Indus	India	G	133		8570
Beauharnois	1960	St. Lawrence	Canada	G			
Bennett, W.A.C. (Portage Mt.)	1967	Peace	Canada	E	183	43,700	74,250
Bersimis No. 1	1959	Bersimis	Canada	R	84	779	11,595
Bhakra	1963	Sutlej	India	G	226	4130	9621
Bhumibol (Yanhee)	1964	Ping-Chao Phraya	Thailand	G/A	154	997	13,462
Big Horn	1972	N. Saskatchewan	Canada	E	150	4300	1768
Bilanadi Tank	1973	Bilanadi	India	E/G	32	2057	63
Blacktail			USA	A	102		
Blenheim-Gilboa (Upper)	1974	Schohari Creek	USA	E	34	3976	21

Major Dams of the World—1984 (continued)

Name	Date Completed	River or Basin	Location	Dam Type	Dam Height (m)	Dam Volume $(m^3 \times 10^3)$	Reservoir Capacity $(m^3 \times 10^6)$
Bonneville	1981	Columbia	USA	G	60	893	662
Boruca	(1990)	Terraba	Costa Rica	R	267	43,000	14,960
Boyd County			USA				
Bratsk	1964	Angara	USSR	E/G	125	4415	169,270
Brouwersha-vense Gat	1972	Brouwershavense Gat	Netherlands	E	36	27,000	575
Brumley Gap	1973		USA		78	28,800	21,166
Bukhtarma	1960	Irtysh	USSR	G	90	1170	49,800
Bureya	–	Bureya	USSR	G	139	3561	20,900
C							
Cabora Bassa	1974	Zambesi	Mozambique	A	171	510	64,000
Canales	1983	Genil	Spain	R	156	4733	7070
Canelles	1960	Noguera	Spain	A	150	380	678
Caniapiscau (KA-3, KA-4 & KA-5)	1981	Caniapiscau	Canada	R	56	11,810	53,800
Castaic	1973	Castaic Creek	USA	E	104	33,642	533

336

Name	Year	River	Country	Type		Reservoir	Output
Cerros Colorados	1973	Neuquén	Argentina	G/E	15		48,000
Chapetón	(1996)	Paraná	Argentina	E/G	35	290,000(T) 6200(G)	60,600
Charvak	1977	Chirchik	USSR	R	168	21,600	2000
Cheboksary	1972	Volga	USSR	G	42	2	12,800
Chicoasén	1981	Grijalva	Mexico	R	245	14,510	1680
Chief Joseph	1955	Columbia	USA	G	70	1381	731
Chirkey	1978	Sulak	USSR	A	233	1358	2780
Chivor	1975	Bata	Colombia	R	237	10,800	815
Churchill Falls	1971	Churchill	Canada	E	32	1658	32,317
Cochiti	1975	Grande	USA	E	77	50,230	743
Contra	1965	Verzasca	Switzerland	A	220	658	86
Coo-Trois Ponts			Belgium				
Copper Cities Tailings 2	1973	Tinhorn Wash	USA	E	99	22,938	5
Corpus Posadas	(1988)	Paraná	Argentina/Paraguay		65	10,000	13,000
Cougar	1964	S.F. McKenzie	USA	R	158	9940	270
Curnera	1967	Rein de Curnera	Switzerland	A	153	562	41

D

| Dabaklamm | (1989) | Dorferbach Matrei | Austria | A | 220 | 1000 | 235 |

Major Dams of the World—1984 (continued)

Name	Date Completed	River or Basin	Location	Dam Type	Dam Height (m)	Dam Volume ($m^3 \times 10^3$)	Reservoir Capacity ($m^3 \times 10^6$)
Daniel Johnson	1968	Manicouagan	Canada	M	214	2255	141,852
Dantiwada	1965	Banas	India	E/G	61	6232	464
Dartmouth	1979	Mitta–Mitta	Australia	R	180	14,100	4000
Davis	1953	Colorado	USA	E	61	2784	2242
Davis-Lower	(1989)	Blackwater	USA	R	23	216	118
Davis-Upper			USA	R	27	2017	37
Dinorwic	1982		Great Britain				
Dneprodzerzhinsk	1964	Dnieper	USSR	E/G	34	21,791	2460
Dongjiang	(1984)	Laishui	P.R. of China	A	157	1389	8120
Don Pedro	1971	Toulumne	USA	R	178	12,815	2504
Drakensburg	1982		South Africa				
Dry Creek	1982	Dry Creek	USA	E	110	23,000	310
Dworshak	1974	Clearwater N. Fork	USA	G	219	4970	4249

	Year	River	Country	Type			
E							
El Cajón	(1985)	Humuya	Honduras	A	226	1480	5650
El Chocón	1974	Limay	Argentina	E	86	13,000	21,000
El M'Jara	(1987)	Ouergha	Morocco	E	87	25,000	4000
Emboração	1982	Paranaíba	Brazil	E/R	158	25,000	17,600
Emosson	1974	Barberine	Switzerland	A	180	1090	225
Esperanza Tailings	1973	Santa Cruz	USA	E	37	30,355	6
Estreito	1969	Grande	Brazil	R	92	4290	1418
F							
Fierze	1978	Drin	Albania	R	158	700	2620
Finstertal	1980	Nederbach	Austria	R	150	4500	60
Flaming Gorge	1964	Green	USA	A	153	754	4647
Fort Peck	1940	Missouri	USA	E	76	96,049	23,560
Fort Randall	1956	Missouri	USA	E	49	38,380	7524
Foz Do Areia	1980	Iguaçu	Brazil	R	153	13,700	6100
Furnas	1963	Grande	Brazil	R/PG	127	9450	22,950
G							
Gardiner	1968	South Saskatchewan	Canada	E	68	65,440	9868
Garrison	1956	Missouri	USA	E	62	50,845	30,097

339

Major Dams of the World—1984 (continued)

Name	Date Completed	River or Basin	Location	Dam Type	Dam Height (m)	Dam Volume ($m^3 \times 10^3$)	Reservoir Capacity ($m^3 \times 10^6$)
Gepatsch	1965	Faggenbach	Austria	R	153	7100	140
Gezhouba	1982	Changjiang	P.R. of China	G	47	5530	1580
Gilboa			USA	G	55		86
Glen Canyon	1964	Colorado	USA	A	216	3747	33,305
Gökçekaya	1973	Sakarya	Turkey	A	160	783	910
Göscheneralp	1960	Göschenerreuss	Switzerland	E	155	9350	75
Grand Coulee	1942	Columbia	USA	G	168	8093	11,795
Grand Dixence	1962	Dixence	Switzerland	G	285	5957	400
Grand Maison	(1985)	Eau d'Olle	France	E/R	160	18,450	140
Guavio	(1986)	Orinoco	Colombia	R	250	17,000	1000
Gura Apelor Retezat	1983	Riul Mare	Romania	R	168	9000	225
Guri (Raul Leoni) (final stage)	(1986)	Caroni	Venezuela	E/G/R	162	75,700	136,335
H							
Haringvliet	1970	Haringvliet	Netherlands	E	24	20,000	650

Hasan Ugurlu (Ayvacik)	1980	Yesilirmak	Turkey	E/R	175	9042	1000
Helms/Courtright	1958	Kings River	USA	R	98	1193	152
Hirakud	1956	Mahanadi	India	E/G	59	25,100	8105
Hoover	1936	Colorado	USA	A/G	221	3364	36,703
Hungry Horse	1953	S. Fork Flathead	USA	A/G	172	2359	4278
I							
Idukki	1974	Periyar	India	A	169	460	1996
Ilha Grande	(1986)	Paraná	Brazil	R/G	29	11,573	30,000
Ilha Solteira	1973	Paraná	Brazil	R/G/E	74	26,276	21,166
Inga II	1979	Zaire	Zaire	B	34		
Inguri	1984	Inguri	USSR	A	272	3960	2500
Irkutsk	1956	Angara	USSR	E/G	44	11,560	46,000
Iron Gates	1971	Danube	Romania/Yugoslavia	G	60	3160	2400
Iroquois (Lake St. Lawrence)	1958	St. Lawrence	USA/Canada	G	20	134	29,960
Itaipú	1983	Paraná	Brazil/Paraguay	G/E/R	185	27,000	29,000
Itaparica	(1986)	São Francisco	Brazil	E/R	105	16,530	10,700
Itumbiara	1980	Paranaíba	Brazil	E/G	106	37,000	17,030
Ivankovo	1937	Volga	USSR	E/G	23	15,200	1120

Major Dams of the World—1984 (continued)

Name	Date Completed	River or Basin	Location	Dam Type	Dam Height (m)	Dam Volume (m³ × 10³)	Reservoir Capacity (m³ × 10⁶)
J							
Jari	1967	Jari	Pakistan	E	71	32,400	494
John Day	1968	Columbia	USA	E/G	71	2650	3256
Jupía	1968	Paraná	Brazil	E/R/G	43	7300	3680
K							
Kainji	1968	Niger	Nigeria	P/E/T	71.5	7510	15,000
Kakhovskaya	1955	Dnieper	USSR	G	37	35,640	182,000
Kanev	1976	Dnieper	USSR	G/E	25	37,860	2620
Kapchagay	1970	Ili	USSR	E	52	6220	28,100
Karakaya	(1986)	Euphrates	Turkey	A/G	180	2000	9580
Kariba	1959	Zambezi	Zimbabwe/Zambia	A	131	1032	160,368
Karun River	1976	Karun	Iran	A	200	1200	2900
Kassa	1978	Kassa	Japan	R	90	4500	13,500
Keban	1974	Euphrates	Turkey	E/R/G	207	15,000	31,000
Kemano	1952	Nechako	Canada	R	104	3071	32,700

Name	Year	River	Country	Type			
Kenyir	(1986)	Trengganu	Malaysia	R	150	15,900	13,600
Kettle Rapids	1970	Nelson	Canada	G/R/E	61	3448	2529
Khakora	1955	Dnieper	USSR	E/G	37	35,640	18,200
Khudoni	(1989)	Inguri	USSR	A	197	1475	365
Kiev	1964	Dnieper	USSR	E	22	42,400	3730
Kingsley	1942	N. Platte	USA	E	52	24,450	2467
Kishau	(1985)	Tons	India	E/R	253		2400
Kölnbrein	1978	Malta	Austria	A	200	1580	205
Kolyma	1978	Kolyma	USSR	R	126	12,550	14,600
Kopperston No. 3 Tailings	1963	Jones Branch	USA	E	177		
Kossou	1972	Bandama	Ivory Coast	R	57	5400	28,750
Krasnoyarsk	1972	Yenisei	USSR	G	124	5580	73,300
Kremasta (King Paul)	1965	Achelos	Greece	E	165	8170	4750
Kremenchug	1960	Dnieper	USSR	G	33	193	13,500
Kurobe No. 4	1964	Kurobe	Japan	A	186	1598	199
Kurokawa	1974	Ichi	Japan	R	98	3590	33,390
Kvilldal	1981	Ulladalsåna	Norway				

L

| La Honda | (1987) | Uribante | Venezuela | E | 150 | 10,500 | 775 |

Major Dams of the World—1984 (continued)

Name	Date Completed	River or Basin	Location	Dam Type	Dam Height (m)	Dam Volume ($m^3 \times 10^3$)	Reservoir Capacity ($m^3 \times 10^6$)
Lago Delio			Italy				
La Grande 2	1982	La Grande	Canada	R	160	22,937	61,720
La Grande 3	1982	La Grande	Canada	R	100	22,187	60,020
La Grande 4	1984	La Grande	Canada	R	125	20,000	19,390
Lakhwar	(1985)	Yamuna	India	G	192	2000	580
Lauwerszee	1969	Lauwerszee	Netherlands	E	23	35,575	50
Liujiaxia	1969	Hwanghe	P.R. of China	G	147	760	5700
Long Spruce	1976	Nelson	Canada	E/R	42	2940	277
Longyangxia	1983	Hwanghe	P.R. of China	G	172	1300	24,700
Los Leones	(1992)	Los Leones	Chile	E	179	9200	106
Ludington	1973	Lake Michigan	USA	E	52	28,825	102
Luzzone	1963	Brenno di Luzzone	Switzerland	A	208	1330	87
M							
Malpaso	1964	Grijalva	Mexico	R	138	5100	1300
Mangla	1967	Jhelum	Pakistan	E	115	65,651	6358

Name	Year	River	Country	Type			
Manicouagan 2	1964	Manicouagan	Canada	G	91	745	4248
Manicouagan 3	1975	Manicouagan	Canada	E	108	9175	10,423
Mantaro			Peru				
Maqarin	(1987)	Yarmuk	Jordan	R	164	21,000	486
Marimbondo	1975	Grande	Brazil	E/G	90	14,500	6150
Mauvoisin	1957	Drange de Bagnes	Switzerland	A	237	2030	180
McNary	1953	Columbia	USA	E/G	67	3668	1100
Menzelet	(1986)	Ceyhan	Turkey	R	150	7000	19,500
Mica	1973	Columbia	Canada	E/R	245	32,112	24,670
Michihuao	(1992)	Limay	Argentina	T	70	29,840	5860
Mihoesti	1983	Aries	Romania	E/R	242	180	6
Mingechaur	1953	Kura	USSR	E	80	15,600	16,000
Mission Tailings No. 1	1973	Santa Cruz	USA	E	39	40,088	57
Mont-Cenis	1968	Cenis	France	E/R	120	15,000	315
Monteynard	1962	Drac	France	A	155	455	240
Mornos	1977	Mornos	Greece	E	126	17,000	780
Mossyrock	1969	Cowlitz	USA	A	185	980	1380
Mosul	1982	Tigris	Iraq	E	100	36,000	11,100
Mratinje	1975	Piva	Yugoslavia	A	220	742	880

Major Dams of the World—1984 (continued)

Name	Date Completed	River or Basin	Location	Dam Type	Dam Height (m)	Dam Volume ($m^3 \times 10^3$)	Reservoir Capacity ($m^3 \times 10^6$)
N							
Nader Shah	1978	Marun	Iran	E	175	7200	1620
Nagawada	1969	Azusa	Japan	A	155	660	123
Naramata	1984	Naramata	Japan	R	158	12,000	90
Navajo	1963	San Juan	USA	E	123	20,523	2108
New Bullard's Bar	1968	N. Yuba	USA	A	194	1064	1184
New Cornelia Tailings	1973	Ten Mile Wash	USA	E	30	209,500	25
New Melones	1975	Stanislaus	USA	R	191	12,211	2960
Northfield	1973		USA	R	44		21
Nurek	1980	Vakhsh	USSR	E	300	42,670	10,500
O							
Oahe Tailings	1960	Missouri	USA	E	75	70,339	29,111
Oak Creek		Yampa	USA	A	118		123
Okutadami	1961	Tadami	Japan	G	157	1640	601
Oosterschelde	(1986)	Vense Gat Oosterschelde	Netherlands	E/G	45	35,000	2000

346

Name	Year	River	Country	Type			
Oroville	1968	Feather	USA	E	235	59,639	4299
Ouchi	1981	Ono	Japan	R	102	3400	19,100
Owen Falls	1954	Lake Victoria/Nile	Uganda	G	31		204,800
Oymapinar	1983	Manavgat	Turkey	A	185	575	310
Özköy	1983	Gediz	Turkey	E/R	180	11,251	940
P							
Pati		Paraná	Argentina	E/G	35.5	230	180
Paulo Afonso I	1955	São Francisco	Brazil	G	19	216	33
Paulo Afonso IV	1979	São Francisco	Brazil	R	30	10,000	50
Piedra del Aquila	(1990)	Limay	Argentina	G	174	2764	12,800
Place Moulin	1965	Buthier	Italy	A/G	153	1500	100
Poechos	1977	Chira	Peru	E	49	18,480	880
Porto Primavera	(1986)	Paraná	Brazil	E/G	38	8441	18,500
Prattsville	(1991)	Schoharie Creek	USA	E	46	10,093	38
Priest Rapids	1959	Columbia	USA	E	55	2520	180
R							
Racoon Mountain	1979	Tennessee	USA	R/E	70		47
Revelstoke	1984	Columbia	Canada	G/E	175	8900	5310

Major Dams of the World—1984 (continued)

Name	Date Completed	River or Basin	Location	Dam Type	Dam Height (m)	Dam Volume ($m^3 \times 10^3$)	Reservoir Capacity ($m^3 \times 10^6$)
Rocky Reach	1962	Columbia	USA	G	57	3570	1100
Rogun	(1985)	Vakhsh	USSR	E/R	335	71,100	13,300
Roncador	(1985)	Uruguay	Brazil/ Argentina	E/R	78	6500	33,580
Roseland	1961	Doronde Beaufort	France	M/B	150	945	187
Ross	1949	Skagit	USA	A	165	695	1770
Rybinsk	1941	Volga	USSR	G	30	2345	25,400
S							
Sakuma	1956	Tenryu	Japan	G	156	1094	327
Salto Grande	1980	Uruguay	Argentina/ Uruguay	E/G	47	3965	5000
Salto Osório	1975	Iguaçu	Brazil	R/G	67	4280	1240
Salto Santiago	1980	Iguaçu	Brazil	R	80	9860	6750
Salvajina	(1985)	Cauca	Colombia	R	154	4000	773
San Luis	1967	San Luis	USA	E	116	59,382	2518
Sanmenxia	1979	Huang He	P.R. of China	G	115	1630	35,400

Santa Guistina	1950	Noce-Adigo	Italy	A	153	112	183
São Simão	1978	Paranaíba	Brazil	E/R/G	120	27,378	12,540
Saratov	1967	Volga	USSR	E	40	40,400	58,500
Sardar Sarovar	(1991)	Narmada	India	G	155	6100	9492
Saunders-F.D. Roosevelt	1958	St. Lawrence	Canada/USA	G	47	826	808
Sayano-Shushensk	1980	Yenisei	USSR	A/G	245	9075	31,300
Seto	1978	Setodani	Japan	R	111	3740	16,850
Sima	1980	Bjoreia	Norway	R			
Shasta	1945	Sacramento	USA	A/G	183	6445	5615
Shintoyone	1973	Onyu	Japan	A	117	345	53,500
Sir Adam Beck	1954	Niagara	Canada	G	17	23	50
Sobradinho	1979	São Francisco	Brazil	E/G/R	43	11,067	34,100
Speccheri	1957	Leno di Vallarsa	Italy	A	157	117	10
Sterkfontein	(1986)	Nuwejaar-spruit	South Africa	E	93	19,800	2656
Stirrat No. 15 Tailings	1976	Rockhouse	USA	E	152	8411	16
Swift	1958	Lewis	USA	E	186	12,081	932

T

Tabqua (Thawra)	1976	Euphrates	Syria	E	60	46,000	14,000

Major Dams of the World—1984 (continued)

Name	Date Completed	River or Basin	Location	Dam Type	Dam Height (m)	Dam Volume (m³ × 10³)	Reservoir Capacity (m³ × 10⁶)
Takase	1978	Takase	Japan	R	176	11,600	76
Talbingo	1971	Tamut	Australia	R	162	14,488	921
Tamahara	1982	Haachi	Japan	R	116	5130	14,800
Tarbela	1976	Indus	Pakistan	E/R	143	121,720	13,690
Tedorigawa	1979	Tedori	Japan	R	153	10,120	231
Tehchi (Tachiero)	1974	Tachia	Taiwan	A	180	430	175
Tehri	(1990)	Bhagirathi	India	E/R	261	25,200	3539
Thein	1982	Ravi	India	R	47	21,920	3670
Thomson	(1985)	Thomson	Australia	R	165	13,200	1100
Tignes	1952	Isère	France	A	180	635	230
Toktogul	1978	Naryn	USSR	G	215	3345	19,500
Tokuyama	(1987)	Ibi	Japan	R	161	10,600	660
Tres Irmãos	(1986)	Tiete	Brazil	E/G	90	15,000	14,200
Trinity	1962	Trinity	USA	E	164	22,485	3020
Tsimlyansk	1952	Don	USSR	E/G	41	33,891	1700
Tucuruí	1984	Tocantins	Brazil	E/G	106	6800	43,000
Tumut 3			Australia				

Name	Year	River	Country	Type			
Tuttle Creek	1962	Big Blue	USA	E	47	17,536	509
Twin Buttes	1963	Concho	USA	E	41	16,393	791
Twin Buttes Tailings	1973	Santa Cruz	USA	E	73	29,514	258
U							
Ukai	1977	Tapi	India	E/G	81	23,240	8511
Upper Wainganga	(1987)	Wainganga	India	E	43		50,700
Ust-Ilim	1977	Angara	USSR	G/R	102	3800	59,300
V							
Vaiont	1961	Vaiont	Italy	A	262	352	169
Vianden			Luxemburg				
Vidraru	1965	Arges-Danube	Romania	A	167	480	465
Vilyui	1967	Vilyui	USSR	R	75	2900	35,900
Volga-V. I. Lenin (Kuibyshev)	1955	Volga	USSR	E/G	45	33,869	58,000
Volgograd 22nd Congress	1958	Volga	USSR	E/R/G	47	1452	31,500
W							
Wajiangdu	1981	Wujiang	P.R. of China	G	165	1930	2300
Wanapum	1963	Columbia	USA	E	59	3570	1100

Major Dams of the World—1984 (continued)

Name	Date Completed	River or Basin	Location	Dam Type	Dam Height (m)	Dam Volume (m$^3 \times 10^3$)	Reservoir Capacity (m$^3 \times 10^6$)
Y							
Yacambu	1982	Yacambu	Venezuela	E/R	158	3400	427
Yacyreta-Apipe	(1988)	Paraná	Paraguay/ Argentina	E/G	41	81,000	21,000
Yellowtail	1966	Bighorn	USA	G/A	160	1182	1696
Z							
Zervreila	1957	Valerrhein	Switzerland	A	151	626	100
Zeuzier	1957	Lienna	Switzerland	A	156	300	50
Zeya	1978	Zeya	USSR	B	115	2160	68,400
Zillergrüdl	(1987)	Ziller	Austria	A	180	980	90

Appendix Two

Total Distribution of Saline and Alkaline Lands by Country
(Areas in 1000 hectares, based on Soil Map of the World at 1:5 million)

Country	Total	Country	Total
NORTH AMERICA		**AFRICA**	
Canada	7,238	Algeria	3,150
USA	8,517	Angola	526
		Botswana	5,679
MEXICO AND CENTRAL AMERICA		Cameroon	671
		Chad	8,267
Cuba	316	Djibouti	1,741
Mexico	1,649	Egypt	7,360
		Ethiopia	11,033
SOUTH AMERICA		Gambia	150
Argentina	85,612	Ghana	318
Bolivia	5,949	Guinea	525
Brazil	4,503	Kenya	4,858
Chile	8,642	Liberia	362
Colombia	907	Libya	2,457
Ecuador	387	Madagascar	1,324
Paraguay	21,902	Mali	2,770
Peru	21	Mauritania	640
Venezuela	1,240		

Total Distribution of Saline and Alkaline Lands (continued)
(Areas in 1000 hectares, based on Soil Map of the World at 1:5 million)

Country	Total	Country	Total
AFRICA *(continued)*		Saudi Arabia	6,002
Morocco	1,148	Sri Lanka	200
Niger	1,489	Syria	532
Nigeria	6,502	Trucial States	1,089
Portuguese Guinea	194		
Senegal	765	**NORTH AND CENTRAL ASIA**	
Sierra Leone	307	China	36,658
Somalia	5,602	Mongolia	4,070
South West Africa	2,313	USSR	170,720
Sudan	4,874		
Tanzania	3,537	**SOUTH EAST ASIA**	
Tunisia	990	Indonesia	13,213
Zaire	53	Khmer Republic	1,291
Zambia	863	Malaysia	3,040
Zimbabwe	26	Thailand	1,456
		Viet Nam D.R.	39
SOUTH ASIA		Viet Nam R.	944
Afghanistan	3,101		
Bangladesh	3,017	**AUSTRALASIA**	
Burma	634	Australia	357,340
India	23,796	Fiji	90
Iran	27,085	Solomon Islands	238
Iraq	6,726		
Israel	28	**EUROPE**	
Jordan	180	Bulgaria	Are not
Kuwait	209	Czechoslovakia	registered
Muscat and Oman	290	France	but frequently observed
Pakistan	10,456	Hungary	
Qatar	225	Italy	
Sarawak	1,538	Spain	
		Turkey	
		Yugoslavia	

SOURCE: V. A. Kooda, *World Soil Map*

Notes

CHAPTER 1. THE REASONS GIVEN FOR BUILDING DAMS

1. Daniel Deudney, *Rivers of Energy: The Hydropower Potential*, Worldwatch Paper 44, Worldwatch Institute, Washington D.C., June 1981, p. 13.

2. Ralph E. Hamil, "Macroengineering: Big is Beautiful," *The Futurist*, October 1980, pp. 27–28.

3. A. K. Biswas, "Foreword" in A. K. Biswas et al., eds. *Long Distance Water Transfers: A Chinese Case Study and International Experiences*, Tycooly International, Dublin, 1983, p. xii.

4. T. W. Mermel, "Major Dams of the World," *Water Power and Dam Construction* 5, 1982. Quoted by Philip Williams, *Planning Problems in Irrigation Water Development*, Philip Williams & Associates, Pier 33 North, The Embarcadero, San Francisco, CA 94111.

5. John M. Hunter, Luis Rey, and David Scott, "Man-Made Lakes: Man-made diseases," *Social Science and Medicine*, vol. 16, 1982, p. 1134.

6. Daniel Deudney, op. cit. 1981, p. 13.

7. Bruce Stokes, "Bread and Water: Growing Tomorrow's Food," unpublished manuscript, *circa* 1980, sec. 6, p. 7.

8. B. Stone, "The Chiang Jing Diversion Project: An Overview of Economic and Environmental Issues," in A. K. Biswas et al., eds., op. cit. 1983, pp. 194–95.

9. Y. Bangyi and Chen Qinglian, "South-North Water Transfer Project Plans," in A. K. Biswas et al., eds., op. cit. 1983, p. 145.

10. Ibid., p. 148.

11. Stokes, op. cit. 1980, sec. 6, p. 12.

12. Arthur Pillsbury, "The Salinity of Rivers," *Scientific American*. See also F. Powledge, *Water: The Nature, Uses and Future of Our Most Precious and Abused Resource*, Farrar, Straus & Giroux, New York, 1982, pp. 277–78.

355

13. Charles Greer, "The Texas Water System: Implications for Environmental Assessment in Planning for Interbasin Water Transfers," in A. K. Biswas et al., eds. op. cit. 1983, pp. 79–81.

14. Gilbert G. Stamm, quoted in Powledge, op. cit. 1982, p. 272.

15. U.S. Army Corps of Engineers, quoted in Powledge, op. cit. 1982, p. 273.

16. "Dams and the Environment," *ICOLD Bulletin* no. 34, 1982, p. 63.

17. Daniel Deudney, op. cit. 1981, p. 12.

18. Ibid., p. 8.

19. Robin Wright, "The Great Carajas: Brazil's Mega-Program for the 80s," *The Global Reporter*, vol. 1, no. 1, March, 1983. See also Elizabeth Monosowski on Grande Carajas in Vol. II: *Case Studies*, available from *The Ecologist*, Worthyvale Manor, Camelford, Cornwall, U.K., price £25.00.

20. M. Gaertner and S. Morariu, *Electricity Masterplan for Guatemala* (Part I), Report published by ZIPC, 1977.

21. Bruce Stokes, op. cit. 1980, sec. 6, p. 5.

22. Robert P. Ambroggi, "Water," *Scientific American*, September 1980, p. 94.

23. Gilbert F. White, "The Main Effects and Problems of Irrigation," in E. Barton Worthington, ed. *Arid Land Irrigation in Developing Countries: Environmental Problems and Effects*, Pergamon, Oxford, 1977, p. 71.

24. M. Holy, *Water and Environment*, FAO, Rome, 1971. Figures quoted by Gilbert F. White in E. Barton Worthington, ed., op. cit. 1977, p. 3.

25. Roger Revelle, SCOPE 1976. Quoted by Peter Freeman, "Environmental Considerations in the Management of International Rivers: A Review," Threshold International Center for Environmental Renewal, Washington D.C., March 1978, p. 18.

26. Victor A. Kovda, "Arid Land Irrigation and Soil Fertility, Problems of Salinization, Alkalinity and Compaction," in Worthington, ed. op. cit. 1977, pp. 213 and 215.

27. M. M. El Gabaly, "Salinization and Waterlogging in the Near East Region," *Water Supply and Management*, vol. 13, no. 1, 1980, p. 48.

28. FAO, *Agriculture: Toward 2000*, (Economic and Social Development Series, no. 23), Rome, 1982.

29. Bruce Stokes, op. cit. 1980, sec. 2, p. 1.

30. Ibid., sec. 6, p. 9.

CHAPTER 2. DAMS AND SOCIETY: THE PROBLEMS OF RESETTLEMENT

1. M. Kassas, "Environmental Aspects of Water Resources Development," in A. K. Biswas et al., eds., *Water Management for Arid Lands in Developing Countries*, Pergamon, Oxford, 1980, p. 73.

P. Freeman, "Environmental Considerations in the Management of International Rivers; A Review," unpublished manuscript, Threshold, Washington, D.C., March 1978, pp. 10–11.

A. K. Biswas, "Environmental Implications of Water Development for Developing Countries," in Carl Widstrand, ed. *The Social and Ecological Effects of Water Development in Developing Countries*, Pergamon, Oxford, 1978, p. 295.

2. Philip B. Williams, "Damming the World," *Not Man Apart*, October 1983, p. 10. Daniel Deudney gives a higher figure still—some 2,000,000,000,000 people. See D. Deudney, *Rivers of Energy: The Hydropower Potential*, Worldwatch Paper 44, Washington D.C., June 1981, p. 18.

3. R. Wright, *International Dams: The Impact on Native Peoples—Background Paper*, (undated), Anthropology Resource Center, p. 2.

4. R. Goodland, *Environmental Assessment of the Tucuruí Hydroproject*, Electronorte, Brasilia, Brazil, 1978, p. 45. See also: Paul L. Aspelin and Silvio Coelho dos Santos, *Indian Areas Threatened by Hydroelectric Projects in Brazil*, IWGIA Document 44, Copenhagen, October 1981, pp. 52–53, 57.

5. R. Wright, op. cit. (undated), p. 6.

6. Ibid., p. 3.

7. Ibid., p. 6.

8. NEDECO, *Mahaweli Ganga Development Program; Implementation Strategy Study*, September, 1979.

9. R. Goodland, Personal Communication.

10. W. Ackermann, "Summary and Recommendations," in W. Ackermann et al., eds. *Man-Made Lakes: Their Problems and Environmental Effects*, American Geophysical Union, Washington, D.C., 1973, p. 28.

11. Abel Alier, *Statement to the People's Regional Assembly on the Proposed Jonglei Canal*, Authority for the Development of the Jonglei Area, Khartoum. Quoted by J. Waterbury, *The Hydropolitics of the Nile Valley*, Syracuse University Press, 1979, p. 77.

12. R. Wright, op. cit. (undated), p. 6.

13. "New Life for Guyana's 4000 Akawaios," *Development Philosophy*, Georgetown, Guyana. Quoted in Gordon Bennett et al., eds. *The*

Dammed: The Plight of the Akawaio Indians of Guyana, Survival International Document VI, London, 1978, p. 2.

14. Stewart Wavell, *The Guardian* (London), March 21, 1975.

15. Survival International, *The Legal Position*, Draft document, London, 1977, p. 1.

16. R. Goodland, op. cit. 1978, p. 38.

17. Ceres P. Doya, "Was Macli-ing killed because he dammed the Chico Dam?" *Panorama* (Sunday Magazine of *The Bulletin Today*), Manila, June 29, 1980.

18. Rob Pardy et al. *Purari: Overpowering PNG?* International Development Action for Purari Action Group, Victoria, Australia, 1978, p. 161.

19. Ibid., p. 178.

20. J. Madeley, "Leaks and Landslide Loom in Sri Lanka," *New Scientist*, April 7, 1983, p. 8.

21. R. Goodland, op. cit. 1978, pp. 39–40.

22. Rob Pardy et al., op. cit. 1978, p. 163.

23. W. Linney and S. Harrison, *Large Dams and the Developing World: Social and Ecological Costs and Benefits—A Look at Africa*, Environment Liaison Centre, P.O. Box 72461, Nairobi, Kenya, 1981, p. 7.

24. Rob Pardy et al., op. cit. 1978, p. 49.

25. Quoted in Gordon Bennett et al., op. cit. 1978, p. 8.

26. Quoted in P. Bunyard, *Brazil: Path to Paradise or Way to Dusty Death?* Wadebridge Ecological Centre, Wadebridge, 1975, p. 9.

27. H. Fahim, *Dams, People and Development: The Aswan High Dam Case*, Pergamon, Oxford, 1981, p. 62.

28. T. Scudder, "Ecological Bottlenecks and the Development of the Kariba Lake Basin," in T. Farvar and J. Milton, eds. *The Careless Technology*, Tom Stacey, London, 1973, p. 232.

29. Ibid., p. 231.

30. Ibid., p. 233.

31. Ibid., p. 225.

32. Ibid., p. 226.

33. F. Powledge, *Water: The Nature, Uses and Future of our Most Precious and Abused Resource*, Farrar, Straus & Giroux, New York, 1982, p. 295.

CHAPTER 3. SOCIAL AND CULTURAL DESTRUCTION

1. Quoted by Rob Pardy et al., *Purari: Overpowering PNG?* International Development Action for Purari Action Group, Victoria, Australia, 1978, p. 103.

2. *Statement of the Akawaio Indians*, Upper Mazaruni District, Guyana, 1977.

3. Gordon Bennett et al. *The Dammed: The Plight of the Akawaio Indians of Guyana*, Survival International Document VI, London, 1978, p. 2.

4. Boyd Richardson, quoted by Walter Taylor, "James Bay; Continental Crisis," *Survival* (North American edition), March 1973, p. 3.

5. T. Scudder, quoted by Pardy et al., op. cit. 1978, p. 105.

6. Quoted by Ceres P. Doya, "Was Macl-ing killed because he damned the Chico Dam?" *Panorama* (Sunday Magazine of *The Bulletin Today*), Manila, June 29, 1980.

7. Anon., "Historical Background on the Chico Dam Controversy." Condensed from: *The Chico River Basin Development Project: A Case Study in National Development*, Paper presented at the 3rd National Annual Conference of the Ugnayang Pang-Aghamtao, Inc. (Anthropological Association of the Philippines), Cebu City, April 1980, p. 3.

8. A.K. Biswas, "A Perspective on Global Issues and Politics," in A.K. Biswas et al., eds. *Water Management for Arid Lands in Developing Countries*, Pergamon, Oxford, 1980, p. 22.

9. Hussein Fahim, *Dams, People and Development*, Pergamon, Oxford, 1981, p. 74.

10. Ibid., p. 74.

11. Ibid., p. 67.

12. Ibid., p. 61.

13. Ibid., p. 92.

14. E.L. Quartey and L. Allen, "Hydroelectric Power in Gahan," *Water Power and Dam Construction*, February 1981, p. 48.

15. Stanley Johnson, "A Second Look at Volta Lake," *The Ecologist*, vol. 1, no. 17, 1971, p. 13.

16. E.L. Quartey and L. Allen, op. cit. 1981, p. 48.

17. A. Rapoport, "The Ecology of Housing," *The Ecologist*, vol. 3, no. 1, 1973, p. 11.

18. Ian Archer, "Nabdam Compounds, Northern Ghana," in Paul Oliver, ed. *Shelter in Africa*, Barrie and Jenkins, London, 1971, p. 57.

19. Ibid., p. 52.

20. Ibid., p. 57.

21. E. Durkheim and M. Mauss, *Primitive Classification*, University of Chicago Press, 1963.

22. Ibid., p. 57.

23. J.C. Crocker, "Reciprocity and Hierarchy among the Eastern Bororo," *Man* (NS) vol. 4, no. 1, p. 46.

24. Ibid., p. 46.

25. R. Jaulin, "Ethnocide—The theory and practice of cultural murder," *The Ecologist*, vol. 1, no. 18, December, 1971, p. 15.

26. A. Rapoport, "Culture and Environment," *The Ecologist Quarterly*, Winter 1978, p. 273.

27. Anon., *The Upper Mazaruni Hydro-electric Project—An Approach to the Resettlement of Amerindian and other communities resident in the areas to be inundated*, Seminar on Hydropower and Development, Georgetown, Guyana, October 1976, p. 16.

28. R. Goodland, *Sobradinho Hydro-Electric Project—Environmental Impact Reconnaissance*, prepared for Inter-American Development Bank and The International Bank for Reconstruction and Development. The Carey Arboretum of the New York Botanical Gardens, 1973.

29. R. Goodland, *Environmental Assessment of the Tucuruí Hydroproject*, Electronorte, Brasilia, Brazil, 1978, p. 42. For details of the Tucuruí Scheme, see E. Monosowski in Vol. II, *Case Studies*.

30. Ibid., p. 41.

31. William Ackermann, "Summary and Recommendations," in William Ackermann et al., eds. *Man-made Lakes: Their Problems and Environmental Effects*, American Geophysical Union, Washington, D.C., 1973, p. 28.

32. David Price, *The World Bank and Native Peoples: A Consultant's View*, Testimony presented at hearings on the environmental politics of multilateral development banks, held by the U.S. House of Representatives, Subcommittee on International Development Institutions and Finance, Committee on Banking, Finance and Urban Affairs, Washington D.C., June 29, 1983, pp 2–4.

33. Bruce M. Rich, *Statement on Behalf of the Sierra Club, World Wildlife Fund (U.S.), Friends of the Earth, Izaak Walton League of America, Natural Resources Defence Council, National Audubon Society*, Ibid., June 28, 1983, p. 8.

34. Ibid., pp. 10–11.

35. Ibid., p. 13.

36. K. P. Wimaladharma, *The Signposts of the Mahaweli Human Settlements; An Appraisal of Social Change in Early Settlement Under the Mahaweli Project*, Land Settlement Department, Colombo, 1979, p. 5.

37. National Congress of American Indians, *Tribal Populations and International Banking Practices: A Fundamental Conflict over Development Goals*, Washington, D.C., 1983, p. 8.

38. Godfrey Leinhardt, *Divinity and Experience, The Religion of the Dinka*, Oxford University Press, London, 1961.

39. Stanley Johnson, op. cit. 1971, p. 13.

CHAPTER 4. CLOSING THE DAM: LOSS OF LAND AND
WILDLIFE UPSTREAM, LOSS OF SILT AND FERTILITY
DOWNSTREAM

1. L. Alexis, "The Damnation of Paradise," *The Ecologist*, vol. 14, no. 5/6, December 1984, pp. 206–216.

2. Dr. Satish Chandran Nair, personal communication to Nicholas Hildyard, 1982.

3. Philip Round, *Conservation News* (Thailand), November 1982.

4. Tippetts-Abbett-McCarthy-Stratton (TAMS), *Environmental Assessment: Accelerated Mahaweli Development Program*, vol. 1 (main report), 1980, p. 12.

5. Ibid., p. 20.

6. Ibid., p. 14.

7. Ziauddin Sardar, "Dam threatens Malaysia's national park," *New Scientist*, May 6, 1982, p. 339.

8. J. E. Bardach and B. Dussart, "Effects of Man-Made Lakes on Ecosystems," in W. C. Ackermann et al., eds. *Man-Made Lakes: Their Problems and Environmental Effects*, American Geophysical Union, Washington, D.C., 1973, p. 813.

9. Bruce Johns, "Vast Refuge for African Game May Drown in Quest for Power," *New Zealand Herald*, Jan. 21, 1981, Section 1.

10. Ibid.

11. J. Bardach and B. Dussart, op. cit. 1973, p. 814. See also E. K. Balon, "Kariba: The Dubious Benefits," *Ambio*, vol. 7, no. 2, p. 147.

12. Paul and Anne Ehrlich, *Extinction*, Victor Gollancz, London, 1982.

13. Victor Kovda, quoted by Gilbert F. White in E. Barton Worthington, ed. *Arid Land Irrigation in Developing Countries: Environmental Problems and Effects*, Pergamon, Oxford, 1977, p. 21.

14. John Waterbury, *The Hydropolitics of the Nile Valley*, Syracuse University Press, 1979, p. 131.

15. Gilbert F. White, *Environmental Effects of Arid Land Irrigation in Developing Countries*, MAB Technical Notes no. 8, UNESCO, Paris, 1978, p. 38.

16. Jimoh Omo Fadaka, *Superdams, The Dreams that Failed*.

17. Mohammed Kassas, "Impact of River Control Schemes on the Shoreline of the Nile Delta," in T. Farvar and J. Milton, eds., *The Careless Technology*, Tom Stacey, London, 1973, p. 181.

18. Waterbury, op. cit. 1979, p. 135.

CHAPTER 5. WATER LOSSES: DO THEY EXCEED GAINS?

1. W. B. Langbein, "Water Yields and Reservoir Storage in the United States," *U.S. Geological Survey Circ. 409*, 1959. Quoted by William Ackermann in William Ackermann et al., eds. *Man-Made Lakes: Their Problems and Environmental Effects*, American Geophysical Union, Washington, D.C., 1973, p. 12.

2. Mohammed Kassas, "Environmental Aspects of Water Resource Development," in Asit K. Biswas et al., eds. *Water Management for Arid Lands in Developing Countries*, Pergamon, Oxford, 1980, p. 69.

3. Milós Holy, "The Efficiency of Irrigation Systems: An Overview," in E. Barton Worthington, ed. *Arid Land Irrigation in Developing Countries: Environmental Problems and Effects*, Pergamon, Oxford, 1977, p. 347.

4. K. L. Rao, *India's Water Wealth*, Orient Longman, New Delhi. Quoted by Malin Falkenmirth, "Water and Land: Interdependent but Manipulated Resources," in Carl Widstrand, ed. *Water Conflicts and Research Priorities*, Pergamon, Oxford, 1980, p. 54.

5. Mohammed Kassas, op. cit. 1980, p. 69.

6. W. T. Penfound and T. T. Earle, "The Biology of Water Hyacinth," *Ecological Monographs*, vol. 18, pp. 447–72. Quoted by Mohammed Kassas, op. cit. 1980, p. 69.

7. Gilbert F. White, ed. *Environmental Effects of Arid Land Irrigation in Developing Countries*, MAB Technical Notes No. 8, UNESCO, Paris, 1978, p. 40.

8. Asit K. Biswas, "Environmental Implications of Water Development for Developing Countries," in Carl Widstrand, ed. *The Social and Ecological Effects of Water Development in Developing Countries*, Pergamon, Oxford, 1978, p. 292.

9. Agricultural Research Council Staff Summary Report, *Regional Workshop on Aquatic Weed Management and Utilization in the Nile Valley*, Khartoum, 1975. Quoted by John Waterbury, *The Hydropolitics of the Nile Valley*, Syracuse University Press, 1979, p. 237.

10. Asit K. Biswas, "Water: A Perspective on Global Politics," *Water Resources Journal*, December, 1980. Quoted by Warren Linney and Susan Harrison, *Large Dams and the Developing World: Social and Environmental Costs and Benefits—A Look at Africa*, Environment Liaison Centre, Nairobi, Kenya, 1981, p. 43.

11. Milós Holy, op. cit. 1977, p. 347.

12. Ibid., p. 347.

13. M. M. El Gabaly in Asit K. Biswas et al., eds., op. cit. 1980, p. 62.

14. Gilbert L. Corey and W. Clyma, "Improving Farm Water Management in Pakistan," *Water Management Technical Report*, no. 37, Colo-

rado State University, 1975. Quoted by Carl Widstrand, ed. op. cit. 1980, p. 88.

15. Bruce Stokes, "Bread and Water: Growing Tomorrow's Food," Worldwatch Institute, unpublished manuscript, *circa* 1980, Section 3, p. 8. Other studies have not found the rate to be so high, but even the Department of the Interior acknowledges that 10 to 15 percent of irrigation water is wasted.

16. M. N. Langley and D. C. N. Robb, "Irrigation Water Use Efficiency," Paper presented at the Fourth Technical Conference on Irrigation, Drainage and Flood Control, Phoenix, Arizona, March 27–29, 1969. Quoted by Carl Widstrand, op. cit. 1980, p. 88.

17. Carl Widstrand, op. cit. 1980, pp. 88–89. Figures cited are from Max K. Lowdermilk, D. M. Freeman, A. C. Early, *Social and Organizational Factors for Farm Irrigation Improvement: A Case Study*, Colorado State University, 1977.

18. Milós Holy, op. cit. 1977, p. 348.

19. Ibid., p. 347.

CHAPTER 6. THE EFFECTS OF PERENNIAL IRRIGATION ON PEST POPULATIONS

1. S. T. Ghabbour, "Effect of Irrigation on Soil Fauna," in E. Barton Worthington, ed., *Arid Land Irrigation in Developing Countries: Environmental Problems and Effects*, Pergamon, Oxford, 1977, p. 329.

2. B. P. Uvarov, "Problems of Insect Ecology in Developing Countries," *Journal of Applied Ecology*, 1 (1964), pp. 159–68. Quoted by E. Rivnay in T. Farvar and J. Milton, eds. *The Careless Technology*, Tom Stacey, London, 1973, p. 352.

3. S. T. Ghabbour, op. cit. 1977, p. 330.

4. E. Rivnay, "How to provide a nice wet place where insects you don't want thrive," *Natural History*, 1969.

5. A. Mahir Ali, "Impact of Changing Irrigation on Agricultural Pests on Wildlife in Egypt," in E. Barton Worthington, ed., op. cit. 1977, p. 331.

6. E. Rivnay, "On Irrigation-induced Changes in Insect Populations in Israel," in T. Farvar and J. Milton, eds. op. cit. 1973, p. 350.

7. Ibid., p. 357.

8. Ibid., p. 359.

9. Ibid., p. 354.

10. Ibid., p. 355.

11. Ibid., p. 352.

12. Ibid., pp. 354–55.

13. Ibid., p. 354.

14. Ibid., p. 354.

15. Ibid., p. 350.

CHAPTER 7. DAMS AND DISEASE

1. Anil Agarwal, *Water and Sanitation for All?* Earthscan Briefing Document No. 22, London, 10 November 1980, p. 25.

2. J. L. Cloudsley-Thompson, *Insects and History*, Weidenfeld and Nicolson, London, 1977, p. 83.

3. Sir J. Emmerson Tennent, *Ceylon* (two vols.), London, 1860.

4. George J. Armelagos and Alan McArdle, "The Role of Culture in the Control of Infectious Diseases," *The Ecologist*, vol. 6, no. 5, 1976, p. 179.

5. J. L. Cloudsley-Thompson, op. cit. 1977, p. 84.

6. M. A. Farid, "Irrigation and Malaria in Arid Lands," in E. Barton Worthington, ed. *Arid Land Irrigation in Developing Countries: Environmental Problems and Effects*, Pergamon, Oxford, 1977, p. 416.

7. M. N. Hall, J. A. Chandler, R. B. Highton, "A Comparison of Mosquito Populations in Irrigated and Non-irrigated Areas of the Kano Plains, Nyanza Province, Kenya," in E. Barton Worthington, ed., op. cit. 1977, p. 314.

8. M. A. Farid, op. cit. 1977, p. 417.

9. M. N. Hall, J. A. Chandler, and R. B. Highton, op. cit. 1977, p. 337.

10. M. Larivière, "Santé publique et projets d'irrigation: rôle de l'assainissement et de l'hygiène du milieu," in E. Barton Worthington, ed. op. cit. 1977, p. 396.

11. Robert Goodland, *Environmental Assessment of the Tucuruí Hydroelectric Project*, Electronorte, Brazilia, 1978.

12. M. A. Farid, op. cit. 1977, p. 416.

13. Georganne Chapin and Robert Wasserstrom, "Pesticide Use and Malaria Resurgence in Central America and India," *The Ecologist*, vol. 13, no. 4, 1983, p. 117.

14. Ibid.

15. Frank Graham Jr., *Since Silent Spring*, Hamish Hamilton, London, 1977.

16. Paul and Anne Ehrlich, *Extinction*, Victor Gollancz, London, 1982, pp. 78–79.

17. Mudiyanse Tenakoon, quoted by Edward Goldsmith, "Traditional Agriculture in Sri Lanka," *The Ecologist*, vol. 12, no. 5, 1982, p. 213.

18. Anil Agarwal, op. cit. 1980, p. 25.

19. Letitia E. Obeng, "Schistosomiasis—The Environmental Approach," in E. Barton Worthington, ed. op. cit. 1977, p. 403.

20. Letitia E. Obeng, "Starvation or Bilharzia? A Rural Development Dilemma," in Carl Widstrand, ed. *The Social and Ecological Effects of Water Development in Developing Countries*, Pergamon, Oxford, 1978, p. 343.

21. Ibid., p. 346.

22. Ibid., p. 347.

23. Ibid., p. 346.

24. Gilbert F. White, "The Main Effects and Problems of Irrigation," in E. Barton Worthington, ed. op. cit. 1977, p. 48.

25. Asit K. Biswas, "Environmental Implications of Water Development for Developing Countries," in Carl Widstrand, ed. op. cit. 1978, p. 290.

26. A. W. A. Brown and J. O. Deom, "Health Aspects of Man-Made Lakes," in William Ackermann et al., eds. *Man-Made Lakes: Their Problems and Environmental Effects*, American Geophysical Union, Washington, D.C. 1973, p. 757.

27. John Waterbury, *Hydropolitics of the Nile Valley*, Syracuse University Press, 1979, p. 146.

28. J. N. Lanoix, "Relation between irrigation engineering and Bilharziasis," *Bulletin of the World Health Organization* 18, (1011–35), 1958. Quoted by Letitia Obeng, op. cit. 1978, p. 345.

29. Asit K. Biswas, op. cit. 1978, p. 291.

30. Nigel Pollard, "The Gezira Scheme: A Study in Failure," *The Ecologist*, vol. 11, no. 1, Jan–Feb 1981, p. 24.

31. M. A. Amin, "Schistosomiasis in the Gezira," *Aquatic Weed Management*, University of Gezira, Wad Medani, 1979. Quoted by Nigel Pollard, op. cit. 1981, p. 24.

32. E. Barton Worthington, personal communication to Nicholas Hildyard, 1979.

33. Robert Goodland, personal communication to Nicholas Hildyard, 1979.

34. Robert Goodland, *Rio Parana Hydro-Electric Project: Ecological Impact Reconnaissance*, International Engineering-Electroconsult, The Carey Arboretum of the New York Botanical Gardens (Environmental Protection Program), 1972, p. 43.

35. Letitia Obeng, op. cit. 1978, p. 344.

36. Jane Stein, "Water for the Wealthy," *Environment*, May 1977, p. 9.

37. John Madeley, "The Onchocerciasis Control Program," *Mazingira*, vol. 4, no. 3/4, p. 55.

38. John M. Hunter, "Strategies for the Control of River Blind-

ness," in Melinda S. Meade, ed. *Conceptual and Methodological Issues in Medical Geography.* Studies in Geography no. 15, University of North Carolina at Chapel Hill, 1980, p. 39.

39. John M. Hunter, "Progress and Concerns in the World Health Organization Onchocerciasis Control Program in West Africa," *Social Science and Medicine,* vol. 150, p. 267.

40. Ibid., p. 271.

41. Thayer Scudder, "Ecological Bottlenecks and the Development of the Kariba Lake Basin," in T. Farvar and J. Milton, eds. *The Careless Technology,* Tom Stacey, London, 1973, p. 206.

42. Warren Linney and Susan Harrison, *Large Dams and the Developing World: Social and Environmental Costs and Benefits—A Look at Africa,* Environment Liaison Centre, Nairobi, 1981, p. 28.

43. Gilbert F. White, quoted by Jane Stein, 'Water for the Wealthy,' *Environment,* May 1977, p. 7.

44. Ibid.

45. John M. Hunter, "Past Explosion and Future Threat: Exacerbation of Red Water Diseases (*Schistosomiasis haematobium*) in the Upper Region of Ghana," *International Journal for Physical, Biological, and Human Geosciences and their Application in Environmental Planning and Ecology,* vol. 5, no. 4, 1981, p. 312.

46. Ibid., p. 118.

47. Alexis Coumboros, "Santé et Irrigation," in E. Barton Worthington, ed. op. cit. 1977, p. 3–2.

48. Mutamad A. Amin, "Problems and Effects of Schistosomiasis in Irrigation Schemes in the Sudan," in E. Barton Worthington, ed., op. cit. 1977, p. 410.

49. W. H. Wright, "Schistosomiasis a World Problem," *Bulletin of New York Academy of Medicine,* vol. 44, no. 3, March 1968, pp. 301–13. Quoted by Letitia Obeng, op. cit. 1978, p. 347.

50. M. A. Farooq, "A Possible Approach to the Evolution of the Economic Burdens Imposed on a Community by Schistosomiasis," *Annals of Tropical Medicine and Parasitology,* vol. 57, 1963, pp. 323–31. Quoted by Letitia Obeng, op. cit. 1978, p. 347.

51. John Waterbury, op. cit. 1979, p. 147.

CHAPTER 8. THE EFFECTS OF LARGE-SCALE WATER
PROJECTS ON FISHERIES

1. William Ackermann et al., eds. *Man-Made Lakes: Their Problems and Environmental Effects,* American Geophysical Union, Washington, D.C., 1973, p. 33.

2. D. Tolmazin, "Black Sea, Dead Sea?" *New Scientist*, December 6, 1979, p. 766.

3. Bruce Stokes, "Bread and Water: Growing Tomorrow's Food," unpublished manuscript, *circa* 1980, sec. 3, p. 7.

4. For a detailed discussion of this subject, see Carl J. George, "The Role of the Aswan High Dam in Changing the Fisheries of the Southeastern Mediterranean," in M. T. Farvar and J. Milton, eds. *The Careless Technology*, Tom Stacey, London, 1973, pp. 159–79.

5. D. Tolmazin, op. cit. 1979, p. 769.

6. Peter Freeman, *Environmental Considerations in the Management of International Rivers*, Threshold International Center for Environmental Renewal, Washington D.C., 1978, p. 16. For a recent discussion of the trade in those chemicals that have been banned in the industrialized world, see David Weir and Mark Shapiro, *The Circle of Poison: Pesticides and Poisons in a Hungry World*, Institute for Food and Development Policy, San Francisco, 1981.

7. Mohammed Kassas, "Environmental Aspects of Water Resources Development," in Asit K. Biswas, et al., eds. *Water Management for Arid Lands in Developing Countries*, Pergamon, Oxford, 1980, p. 74.

8. John M. Hunter, "Progress and Concerns in the World Health Organization Onchocerciasis Control Program in West Africa," *Social Science and Medicine*, vol. 150, Pergamon, Oxford, p. 271.

9. Jacques Daget, "La production des poissons de consommation dans les écosystèmes irrigués," in E. Barton Worthington, ed., *Arid Land Irrigation in Developing Countries: Environmental Problems and Effects*, Pergamon, Oxford, 1977, p. 300.

10. MAB Technical Notes no. 8, UNESCO, Paris, 1978, p. 39.

11. See *The State of India's Environment 1982, A Citizen's Report*, Centre for Science and Environment, New Delhi, 1982, pp. 17–25.

12. "Troth-Tiranti Killer Cocktails," *New Internationalist*, July, 1983, p. 5.

13. Carl George, op. cit. 1973, pp. 159–60.

14. V. R. Pantalu, quoted by Peter Freeman, op. cit. 1978, p. 17.

15. Peter Freeman, op. cit. 1978, p. 17.

16. FAO, *Agriculture: Toward 2000*, FAO, Rome, 1983.

17. Eugene Balon, "Kariba; The Dubious Benefits," *Ambio*, vol. 7, no. 2, p. 47.

CHAPTER 9. DAM FAILURES AND EARTHQUAKES

1. David Henry, "Designing for Development: What is Appropriate Technology for Rural Water and Sanitation," in Carl Widstrand, ed.,

The Social and Ecological Effects of Water Development in Developing Coun-tries, Pergamon, Oxford, 1978, p. 365.

2. Philip Williams, "Dam Design: Is the technology faulty?" *New Scientist*, February 2, 1978.

3. Ferdinand Budweg, USCOLD newsletter, November 1982. Quoted by Philip Williams, "Damming the World," *Not Man Apart*, October, 1983, p. 11.

4. J. P. Rothé, personal communication to Edward Goldsmith, 1983.

5. "Landslide Threat to Lima's Power Dam," *WorldWater*, vol. 5, no. 6, June 1982, pp. 7–8.

6. "India's worst dam disaster," *Water Power and Dam Construction*, November, 1979. Quoted by Philip Williams, op. cit. 1983, p. 11.

7. Carl Widstrand, "Conflicts over Water," in Carl Widstrand, ed. *Water Conflicts and Research Priorities*, Pergamon, Oxford, 1980, p. 147.

8. E. G. Giglioli, "The National Organization of Irrigation (Kenya)," in R. Chambers and J. Morris, eds. *Mwea, an Irrigated Rice Settlement Scheme in Kenya*, Weltforum Verlag, Munich, 1973. Quoted by Carl Widstrand, op. cit. 1980, p. 131.

9. Carl Widstrand, op. cit. 1980, p. 132.

10. Ibid., pp. 147–48.

11. "Salvador Rebels Aim for Hydro Dams," *USA Today*, April 12, 1983.

12. Philip Williams, op. cit. 1983, p. 11.

13. Carl Widstrand, op. cit. 1980, p. 138.

14. Philip Williams, op. cit. 1983, p. 11.

15. Philip Williams, *Damming the World*, Philip Williams and Associates, Pier 33 North, The Embarcadero, San Francisco, 1983, p. 13.

16. David W. Simpson, "Seismicity Changes Associated with Reservoir Loading," *Engineering Geology*, vol. 10, 1976, 123–150, p. 123.

17. Ibid., p. 123.

18. Ibid., p. 124.

19. J. P. Rothé, "Man-Made Earthquakes," *Tectonophysics*, 1970, pp. 215–38.

20. J. P. Rothé, "Fill a Lake, Start an Earthquake," *New Scientist*, vol. 39, no. 605, July 11, 1968, p. 78.

21. J. P. Rothé, "Summary: Geophysics Report," in William C. Ackermann et al., eds., *Man-Made Lakes, Their Problems and Environmental Effects*, American Geophysical Union, Washington, D.C., 1973, pp. 441–42.

22. P. M. Mane, "Earth Tremors in Koyna Project Area," *Ninth Congress on Large Dams*, Istanbul, op. cit. 1973, pp. 445–47. Quoted by J. P. Rothé, op. cit. 1973, pp. 446–47.

23. J. P. Rothé, op. cit. 1973, p. 446.

24. UNESCO Working Group on Seismic Phenomena Associated with Large Reservoirs, *Report of First Meeting*, UNESCO, December 14–16, 1970, SC/CONF. 200 4, Paris, 6 March 1971, p. 3.

25. UNESCO Working Group on Seismic Phenomena Associated with Large Reservoirs, *Report of Second Meeting*, UNESCO, December 14–17, 1971, SC-71/CONF. 42/3, p. 4.

26. J. P. Rothé, "Note sur les seismes de Vouglons," unpublished paper, June–July, 1971.

27. J. P. Rothé, op. cit. 1973, p. 445.

28. T. R. Toppozoda and P. W. Morrison, "Earthquakes and Lake Levels at Oroville, Butte Co., California," *Earthquake Notes*, January–March, 1981, vol. 52, no. 1, p. 27.

29. Ibid., p. 28.

30. T. R. Topozoda, J. H. Bennett, and C. H. Kramer, "Earthquakes and Water Levels at Mono Lake, Mono County, California," *Earthquake Notes*, Jan.–March, 1981, vol. 52, no. 1, p. 28.

31. Jean Coulomb, "Sismologies—Un nouvel exemple de sismicité provoqué remarques sur une note de Jean Delannay, Rene Guirand, et Christian Weber", Note du 2 November 1981 de J. P. Rothé, CR Acad. Sc. Paris. t 293 C 7, December 1981, Serie II, p. 953.

32. R. M. Kebeasy, M. Maamour, and E. M. Ibrahim, "Aswan Lake Induced Earthquakes," *Bulletin of the International Institute of Seismology and Earthquake Engineering*, vol. 19, 1981, pp. 155–60.

33. J. P. Rothé, op. cit. 1973, p. 450.

34. David W. Simpson, op. cit. 1976, p. 147.

35. Ibid., p. 130.

36. J. P. Rothé, op. cit. 1973, p. 452.

37. David W. Simpson, op. cit. 1976, p. 141.

38. R. D. Adams, "Incident at the Aswan Dam," *Nature*, vol. 301, January 6, 1983, p. 14.

39. David W. Simpson, op. cit. 1976, p. 146.

40. J. P. Rothé, op. cit. 1978, p. 78.

41. V. D. Saklani, "Tehri Dam Project that Spells Disaster," Tehri Bandh Virodhi Sangharsh Samiti, Tehri Garhwal (undated), p. viii.

CHAPTER 10. THE MYTH OF FLOOD CONTROL

1. Carl Widstrand, "Manageability and Unmanageability of Water," in Carl Widstrand, ed. *Water Conflicts and Research Priorities*, Pergamon, Oxford, 1980, p. 93.

2. Peter Freeman, *Environmental Considerations in the Management of International Rivers: A Review*, (Working Draft), Threshold, Interna-

tional Center for Environmental Renewal, Washington, D.C., March, 1978.

3. Li Jinchang, "Lessons Learned from Heavy Floods," *Mazingira*, vol. 6, no. 2, 1982, p. 58.

4. Department of Irrigation, *Report of the National Commission on Floods*, vol. 1, New Delhi, 1980. Cited by Centre for Science and the Environment, *The State of India's Environment 1982*, New Delhi, 1982, p. 62.

5. Maurice Arnold, "Floods as Man-Made Disasters," *The Ecologist*, vol. 6, no. 5, June 1976, p. 172.

6. Stanley A. Changnon, Jr., "Flood Mitigation: Policy Failure? A Research Agenda to Address the Issue." Paper presented to the AAAS Annual Meeting, May 26–31, 1983, p. 1.

7. B. B. Vohra, "Managing Land and Water Resources," *The Indian Express*, Madras, September 13, 1978. Quoted by Carl Widstrand, op. cit. 1980, p. 94.

8. Maurice Arnold, op. cit. 1976, p. 171. See also: Stanley A. Changnon, Jr., op. cit. 1983, p. 1.

9. Maurice Arnold, op. cit. 1976, p. 172.

10. Ibid., p. 171.

11. Arthur E. Morgan, 1971, *Dams and Other Disasters*, Porter Sargent, Boston, Mass., p. 422. Quoted by Arnold, op. cit. 1976, p. 170.

12. Charles B. Belt, Jr., "The 1973 Flood and the Effects of Man on Stages of the Mississippi, near St. Louis," paper presented at the annual conference of the Geological Society of America, St. Louis, Missouri, 1973. Quoted by Maurice Arnold, op. cit. 1976, p. 170.

13. Maurice Arnold, op. cit. 1976, p. 169.

14. Alan Grainger, "The State of the World's Tropical Forests," *The Ecologist*, vol. 10, no. 1, p. 45.

15. "Savage Waters that Will Not Be Tamed," *The Economist*, September 9, 1978, p. 59.

16. Li Jinchang, op. cit. 1982, p. 58.

17. Ibid., pp. 58–59.

18. Maurice Arnold, op. cit. 1976, p. 169.

19. D. R. Sikka, "Integrated Hydrologic and Societal Interactions of Floods and Droughts in India," in E. F. Schulz et al., eds. *Floods and Droughts: Proceedings of the Second International Symposium in Hydrology*, Water Resources Publications, Fort Collins, Colorado, pp. 237–45. Quoted by Maurice Arnold, op. cit. 1976, p. 171.

20. *The Economist*, op. cit. 1978, p. 59.

21. *The Statesman*, New Delhi, August 19, 1978. Quoted by Carl Widstrand, op. cit. 1980, p. 94.

22. Carl Widstrand, op. cit. 1980, p. 95.

23. *The Indian Express*, 1978. Quoted by Carl Widstrand, op. cit. 1980, p. 95.

24. Carl Widstrand, op. cit. 1980, p. 94.

25. A. L. Mukherjee, *The Sunday Statesman*, Calcutta, September 10, 1978. Quoted by Carl Widstrand, op. cit. 1980, p. 94.

26. William Scobie, *The Observer*, July 10, 1983, p. 10.

27. Maurice Arnold, op. cit. 1976, p. 172.

28. Ibid., p. 171.

29. B. B. Vohra, *A Policy for Land and Water*, Sardar Patel Memorial Lecture 1980, Government of India (Department of Environment), New Delhi, 1980, p. 12.

30. Maurice Arnold, op. cit. 1976, p. 172.

CHAPTER 11. SALTING THE EARTH: THE PROBLEM OF SALINIZATION

1. Arthur F. Pillsbury, "The Salinity of Rivers," *Scientific American*, vol. 245, no. 1, July, 1981, p. 32.

2. V. A. Kovda, "Arid Land Irrigation and Soil Fertility: Problems of Salinity, Alkalinity, Compaction," in E. Barton Worthington, ed. *Arid Land Irrigation in Developing Countries: Environmental Problems and Effects*, Pergamon, Oxford, 1977, p. 216.

3. Ibid., p. 216.

4. Ibid., p. 216.

5. Ibid., p. 218.

6. Bruce Stokes, "Bread and Water: Growing Tomorrow's Food," unpublished manuscript written for Worldwatch Institute, Washington, D.C., undated (*circa* 1980), Section 4, p. 4.

7. V. A. Kovda, op. cit. 1977, p. 221.

8. Gilbert F. White, "The Main Effects and Problems of Irrigation," in E. Barton Worthington, ed. op. cit. 1977, p. 30.

9. Arthur F. Pillsbury, op. cit. 1981, p. 35.

10. John Waterbury, *The Hydropolitics of the Nile Valley*, Syracuse Univ. Press, 1979, p. 143.

11. V. A. Kovda, "Loss of Productive Land due to Salinization," *Ambio*, vol. 12, no. 2, 1983, pp. 92–93.

12. Gilbert F. White, op. cit. 1977, p. 30.

13. V. A. Kovda, op. cit. 1983, p. 92.

14. M. M. El Gabaly, "Problems and Effects of Irrigation in the Near East Region," in E. Barton Worthington, ed. op. cit. 1977, p. 247.

15. Ibid., p. 246.

16. Ibid.

17. Ibid.

18. Guo Huancheng and Xu Zhikang, "Land Use and Crop Allocation in the Proposed Water Transfer Regions," in Asit K. Biswas, et al., eds. *Long Distance Water Transfer: A Chinese Case Study and International Experience*, Tycooly International, Dublin, 1983, p. 121.

19. Xu Yuexian and Hong Jilian, "Impact of Water Transfer on the Natural Environment," in Asit K. Biswas et al., eds. op. cit. 1983, p. 167.

20. John Waterbury, op. cit. 1979, p. 133.

21. M. M. El Gabaly, op. cit. 1977, p. 246.

22. Erik Eckholm, "Salting the Earth," *Environment*, vol. 17, no. 7, p. 10.

23. M. M. El Gabaly, op. cit. 1977, p. 248.

24. Ibid., p. 245.

25. Bruce Stokes, op. cit. (undated, *circa.* 1980), Section 4, p. 2.

26. M. M. El Gabaly, op. cit. 1977, p. 242.

27. Quoted by Bruce Stokes, op. cit. (undated *circa.* 1980), Section 4, p. 2.

28. Quoted by Bruce Stokes, op. cit. (undated *circa.* 1980), Section 4, p. 3.

29. Gilbert F. White, op. cit. 1977, p. 30.

30. V. A. Kovda, op. cit. 1977, p. 219.

31. Ibid.

32. Aloys Michel, "The Impact of Modern Irrigation Technology in the Indus and Helmand Basins of Southwest Asia," in T. Farvar and J. Milton, eds. *The Careless Technology*, Tom Stacey, London, 1973, p. 273.

33. Taghi Farvar in "Discussion" following E. Rivnay's paper in M. T. Farvar and J. P. Milton, op. cit. 1973, p. 365.

34. Aloys Michel, in M. T. Farvar and J. P. Milton, eds. op. cit. 1973, p. 265.

35. Eric Eckholm, *Losing Control*, Norton, New York, 1976. Quoted by Bruce Stokes, op. cit. (undated *circa.* 1980), Section 4, p. 4.

36. M. C. Chaturvedi, *Second India Studies: Water*, Macmillan, New Delhi, 1976. Quoted by Carl Widstrand in Carl Widstrand, ed. *Water Conflicts and Research Priorities*, Pergamon, Oxford, 1980, p. 98.

37. S. Pels and M. E. Stannard, "Environmental Changes due to Irrigation Development in Semi-Arid Parts of New South Wales, Australia," in E. Barton Worthington, ed. op. cit. 1977, p. 181.

38. Bruce Stokes, op. cit. (undated *circa.* 1980), Section 4, p. 5.

39. John Waterbury, op. cit. 1979, p. 134.

40. Carl Widstrand, "Conflicts over Water," in Carl Widstrand, ed. *Water Conflicts and Research Priorities*, Pergamon, Oxford, 1980, p. 131.

41. Quoted by Carl Widstrand, op. cit. 1980, p. 131.

42. A. Azim Abulata, "The Conversion of Basin Irrigation to Peren-

nial Systems in Egypt," in E. Barton Worthington, ed., op. cit. 1977, p. 102.

43. John Waterbury, op. cit. 1977, p. 153.

44. I. P. Gerasimov, "Basic Problems of the Transformation of Nature in Central Asia," from *Problemy Osvoyeniya pustyn*, no. 5 (1967), pp. 3–17. In *Soviet Geography*, vol. 9, no. 6, (June 1968), pp. 444–58.

45. Aloys Michel, op. cit. 1973, p. 273.

46. V. A. Kovda, op. cit. 1977, p. 219.

47. David Sheridan, "The Desert Blooms at a Price," *Environment*, vol. 23, no. 3, April 1981, p. 18.

48. Elizabeth Whitcombe, *Agrarian Conditions in Northern India; The United Provinces under British Rule 1860–1900* (vol. 1), University of California Press, 1972.

49. Quoted by Elizabeth Whitcombe, op. cit. 1972, p. 78.

50. J. A. Voelcker, *Report on the Improvement of Indian Agriculture*, London, 1893. Quoted by Elizabeth Whitcombe, op. cit. 1972, p. 79.

51. Ibid.

52. Chief Commissioner, Punjab, to Government of India (Public Works Department) to Government-General, August 4th 1858, in *Selections from the Records of Governments*, no. 42, p. 1. Quoted by Elizabeth Whitcombe, op. cit. 1972, p. 285.

53. H. B. Medlicott, "Note on the Reh Efflorescence of North-West India, and on the Rivers and Canals," in *Selections from the Records of the Government*, no. 42, pp. 34–39. Cited in Elizabeth Whitcombe, op. cit. 1972, pp. 285–86.

54. Dr. Thomas Anderson, Note of May 29, 1863, in *Selections from the Records of the Government*, no. 42, pp. 71–73. Quoted in Elizabeth Whitcombe, op. cit. 1972, pp. 286–87.

55. Elizabeth Whitcombe, op. cit. 1972, p. 287.

56. NWP, "Irrigation Proceedings," July, 1869, Proceedings nos. 135–37. Quoted by Elizabeth Whitcombe, op. cit. 1972, p. 288.

57. NWP and Oudh, "Revenue Proceedings," June, 1879, Index no. 115, Proceedings no. 53. See Elizabeth Whitcombe, op. cit. 1972, p. 289.

58. Denzil Ibbetson, NWP and Oudh, "Revenue Proceedings," June, 1879, Index no. 116, Proceedings no. 54. Quoted by Elizabeth Whitcombe, op. cit. 1972, p. 289.

59. Arthur Pillsbury, op. cit. 1981, p. 37.

60. Ibid., p. 37.

61. Ibid., p. 38.

62. Richard H. French and William W. Woessner, "Erosion and Salinity Problems in Arid Regions," in V. Dean Adams and Vincent A.

Lamarra," eds. *Aquatic Resources Management of the Colorado River Eco-system*, Ann Arbor Science, Ann Arbor, Mich., 1983, p. 425.

63. Arthur Pillsbury, op. cit. 1981, p. 43.

64. Aloys Michel, op. cit. 1973, p. 269.

65. Peter Beaumont, "The Euphrates River—An International Problem of Water Resources Development," *Environmental Conservation*, vol. 5, Spring 1978, p. 43.

66. Michael Butler, "Perception of Increasing Salinity Associated with the Irrigation of the Murray Valley in South Australia," in R. L. Heathcote, ed. *Perception of Desertification*, United Nations University, Tokyo, 1980, p. 102.

67. Ibid., p. 117.

CHAPTER 12. MANAGEMENT AND MAINTENANCE

1. Anthony Bottrall, "The Management and Operation of Irrigation Schemes in Less Developed Countries," in Carl Widstrand, ed. *The Social and Ecological Effects of Water Development in Developing Countries*, Pergamon, Oxford, 1978, p. 309.

2. Bruce Stokes, "Bread and Water: Growing Tomorrow's Food," Unpublished manuscript, Worldwatch Institute, Washington D.C., undated (*circa.* 1980), Section 7, p. 5.

3. Quoted by Asit K. Biswas, in A. K. Biswas et al., eds. *Long Distance Water Transfer: A Chinese Case Study and the International Experiences*, Tycooly International, Dublin, 1983, p. xiv.

4. James E. Nickum, "Institutions and China's Long Distance Water Transfer Proposal," in Asit K. Biswas et al., eds. op cit. 1983, p. 186.

5. Li Changfang and Zhang Yichang, "A magnificent project which has changed water damage into water benefit," *Guangming Ribao*, October 28, 1980, p. 2. Quoted by James E. Nickum, op. cit. 1983, p. 186.

6. James E. Nickum, op. cit. 1983, p. 186.

7. Ibid., p. 187.

8. Robert Chambers, "Man and Water: The Organization and Operation of Irrigation," in B. H. Farmer, ed. *The Green Revolution*, Westview Press, Boulder, Colorado, pp. 340–67. Quoted by James E. Nickum, op. cit. 1983, p. 187.

9. A. Bottrall, op. cit. 1978, pp. 317–18. See papers read by M. F. Ali and R. Zabala, at the O.D.I. Workshop on Choices in Irrigation Management, Canterbury, September 1976.

10. A. Bottrall, op. cit. 1978, p. 317.

11. Robert Chambers, "Water Management and Paddy Production in the Dryland Zone of Sri Lanka," *Occasional Paper*, no. 8, Agrarian

Research and Training Institute, Colombo, January 1975. Quoted by A. Bottrall, op. cit. 1978, p. 317.

12. Carl Widstrand, "Conflicts over Water," in Carl Widstrand, ed. *Water Conflicts and Research Priorities*, Pergamon, Oxford, 1980, p. 142.

13. Tony Barnett, *The Gezira Scheme: An Illusion of Development*, Frank Cass, London, 1977. Quoted by Carl Widstrand, op. cit. 1980., p. 137.

14. Carl Widstrand, op. cit. 1980, p. 137.

15. Bruce Stokes, op. cit. undated (*circa.* 1980), sec. 7, p. 5.

16. A. Bottrall, op. cit. 1978, p. 312.

17. Carl Widstrand, op. cit. 1980, p. 143.

18. Ashfag H. Mirza, *A Study of Village Organizational Factors Affecting Water Systems*, OECD Development Centre, Paris, 1975. Quoted by Carl Widstrand, op. cit. 1980, p. 143.

19. Carl Widstrand, "Manageability and Unmanageability of Water," in Carl Widstrand, ed. op. cit. 1980, p. 96.

20. R. R. Matango and D. Mayerle, "Maji Na Maendeleo Vijijini— The Experience with rural self-help water scheme in Lushoto District," in Tschannerl, ed. *Water Supply*, BRALUP Research Paper 20, University of Dar es Salaam, 1971. Quoted by Carl Widstrand, op. cit. 1980, p. 96.

21. J. D. Heijnen and D. Conyers, "Impact Studies of Rural Water Supply," in Tschannerl, ed. *Water Supply*, University of Dar es Salaam, 1971. Quoted by Carl Widstrand, op. cit. 1980, p. 96.

22. N. A. De Ridder, *Optimum Use of Water Resources*, International Institute for Land Reclamation and Improvement 21, 1977. Quoted by Carl Widstrand, op. cit. 1980, p. 97.

23. D. F. Salisbury, "Cleansing Earth's Waters," *Water International* 3:1, International Water Resources Association, 1978. Quoted by Widstrand, op. cit. 1980, p. 97.

24. D. Henry, "Designing for Development: What is Appropriate Technology for Rural Water and Sanitation?" *Water Supply and Management* 2:4, Pergamon, Oxford, 1978. Quoted by Carl Widstrand, op. cit. 1980, p. 97.

25. Report from SIDA, Stockholm, 1977. Quoted by Carl Widstrand, op. cit. 1980, pp. 139–40.

26. George Kay, 'Changing Patterns of Settlement and Land Use in the Eastern Province of Northern Rhodesia,' *Occasional Papers in Geography*, no. 2, 1965. Quoted by Carl Widstrand, op. cit. 1980, p. 136.

27. Carl Widstrand, op. cit. 1980, p. 136.

28. Ibid., p. 135.

29. Tony Barnett, *The Gezira Scheme: An Illusion of Development*, Frank Cass, London. Quoted by Carl Widstrand, op. cit. 1980, p. 136.

30. John Gretton, *The Big Dam Strikes Again*, Earthscan Feature, Earthscan, London, 1980, p. 3.

31. Anthony Bottrall, op. cit. 1978, p. 322.

32. Anthony Bottrall, op. cit. 1978, p. 327, See: E. W. Coward, *Irrigation Institutions and Organizations: An International Bibliography*, Cornell University, 1976.

33. E. W. Coward, op. cit. 1976. Quoted by A. Bottrall, op. cit. 1978, p. 323.

34. Gekee Y. Wickham, "The Sociology of Irrigation: Insights from a Philippine Study," *Teaching Forum* 31, The Agricultural Council, New York, 1973. Quoted by Carl Widstrand, op. cit. 1980, p. 85.

35. Asit K. Biswas et al., eds. op. cit. 1983. See in particular the chapter by Bruce Stone, pp. 193–214.

36. Carl Widstrand, op. cit. 1980, p. 87.

37. Ian Carruthers, "Contentious Issues in Planning Irrigation Schemes," in Carl Widstrand, ed. op. cit. 1978, p. 300.

38. René Millon, 'Variations in Social Responses to the Practice of Irrigation Agriculture,' in Richard B. Woodbury, ed., *Civilizations in Desert Lands*, Anthropological Papers no. 62, University of Utah, December 1962, p. 85.

39. Wolf Roder, *The Sabi Valley Irrigation Projects*, University of Chicago, Department of Geography, Research Series 99, 1965. Quoted by Robert C. Hunt and Eva Hunt, "Canal Irrigation and Local Social Organization," *Current Anthropology*, vol. 17, no. 3, September 1976, p. 403.

CHAPTER 13. LOSS OF LAND AND FOOD TO PLANTATIONS

1. S. George, *How the Other Half Dies*, Penguin, London, 1977, p. 39.

2. F. Moore Lappé and J. Collins, *Food First: The Myth of Scarcity*, Souvenir Press, London, 1977, p. 41.

3. B. Dinham and C. Hines, *Agribusiness in Africa*, Earth Resources Research Publications, 1983, p. 187.

4. Ibid., Table A.1, p. 187. See also: S. George, op. cit. 1977, p. 39.

5. B. Dinham and C. Hines, op. cit. 1983, p. 125.

6. F. Moore Lappé and J. Collins, op. cit. 1977, p. 23.

7. Ibid., p. 217.

8. Ibid. See also: S. George, op. cit. 1977, pp. 176–77.

9. B. Dinham and C. Hines, op. cit. 1983, p. 31.

10. Ibid., p. 104.

11. Quoted by F. Mounier, "The Senegal River Scheme: Development for Whom?" in E. Goldsmith and N. Hildyard, eds. *The Social and*

Ecological Effects of Large Dams, Volume 2: *Case Studies*, Wadebridge Ecological Centre, Worthyvale Manor, Camelford, Cornwall, U.K., 1984.

12. F. Mounier, op. cit. 1984.

13. R. Franke and B. Chasin, *Seeds of Famine*, Allanheld, Osmun and Co., 1980, p. 192. Quoted by B. Dinham and C. Hines, op. cit. 1983, p. 150.

14. F. Moore Lappé and J. Collins, op. cit. 1977, p. 199.

15. Ibid., p. 201.

16. "The Sahel: Today's Disaster Area . . . Tomorrow's Glorious Garden," *To the Point International*, October 5, 1974. Quoted by F. Moore Lappé and J. Collins, op. cit. 1977, p. 80.

17. B. Dinham and C. Hines, op. cit. 1983, p. 32.

18. F. Moore Lappé and J. Collins, op. cit. 1977, p. 200.

19. Ibid., p. 40.

20. R. Franke and B. Chasin, "Peasants, Peanuts, Profits, and Pastoralists," *The Ecologist*, vol. 11, no. 4, July/August 1981, p. 161.

21. Ibid., p. 165.

22. Ibid., p. 166.

23. Ibid., p. 164.

24. Ibid., p. 166.

25. F. Moore Lappé and J. Collins, op. cit. 1977, p. 41.

26. R. Franke and B. Chasin, op. cit. 1981, p. 162.

27. G. Borgstrom, *The Hungry Planet*, Collier Books, New York, 1967. Quoted by Andrew P. Vayda, "Plants, Animals, and Man," Keynote address to the 28th Annual Meeting of the Soil Conservation Society of America, Iowa, September, 1973, p. 7.

28. F. Moore Lappé and J. Collins, op. cit. 1977, p. 77.

29. S. George, op. cit. 1977, p. 93.

30. Quoted by S. George, op. cit. 1977, p. 93.

31. S. George, op. cit. 1977, p. 174.

32. Ibid., p. 18.

33. Bruce Stokes, "Bread and Water: Growing Tomorrow's Food," unpublished paper written for the Worldwatch Institute, Washington, D.C., undated (*circa.* 1980), Section 1, p. 2.

CHAPTER 14. THE LOSS OF LAND AND WATER TO INDUSTRY AND URBANIZATION

1. Carrying Capacity, "Report on the Carrying Capacity of the USA," Washington, D.C. unpublished, undated, chap. 6, p. 26.

2. Ibid.

3. David Pimentel, quoted by Peter Freeman, "Environmental Considerations in the Management of International Rivers: A Review,"

unpublished manuscript, International Center for Environmental Renewal, Threshold, Washington, D.C., March 1978, p. 14.

4. Michael Brewer and Robert Boxley, "The Potential Supply of Cropland," paper presented at RFF Symposium on the Adequacy of Agricultural Land, Washington, D.C. Quoted by Neil Sampson, in "Land for Energy or Land for Food?" *The Ecologist*, vol. 12, no. 2, 1982, p. 69.

5. Neil Sampson, "Land for Energy or Land for Food?" *The Ecologist*, vol. 12, no. 2, 1982, p. 69. Less pessimistic projections have been made, but have assumed action to preserve croplands at local, state and national levels. Unfortunately, there is no sign so far of such action being taken.

6. Ibid., p. 67.

7. Alice Coleman, "Is Planning Really Necessary?" *The Geographical Journal*, Vol. 142, part 3, November 1976. Paraphrased by Edward Goldsmith, 'Planning for Starvation,' *The Ecologist*, Vol. 7, No. 2, March 1977, p. 42.

8. Edward Goldsmith, op. cit. 1977, p. 42.

9. Alice Coleman, op. cit. 1976. Paraphrased by Edward Goldsmith, op. cit. 1977, p. 42.

10. Alice Coleman, op. cit. 1976. Paraphrased by Edward Goldsmith, op. cit. 1977, p. 44.

11. Asit K. Biswas, "Loss of Productive Land," *Ecologist Quarterly*, Autumn 1978, p. 210.

12. Ibid., pp. 210–11.

13. John M. Bradley, "Nile Studies Find High Dam Did More Good than Harm," *World Environment Report*, February 28, 1983, p. 1.

14. Mohammed Kassas. The same point is made by Susan Walton though her figures are different. She writes, "In addition to the acreage converted to year-round cultivation, about 950,000 acres of desert land have been reclaimed for agriculture. But since this gain is partially cancelled out by the loss of 600,000 acres to urban expansion—and by additional acreage lost to shoreline erosion along the Mediterranean—the net gain of agricultural land is slight. (see S. Walton, "Egypt: After the Aswan Dam," *Environment*, vol. 23, no. 4, May 1981, p. 32.)

15. John Waterbury, *The Hydropolitics of the Nile Valley*, Syracuse University Press, 1979, p. 138.

16. Ibid., p. 139.

17. Ibid., p. 140.

18. Not too much importance should be attached to these figures, as water policy in the United States will have to be seriously reconsidered in the coming years.

19. Carrying Capacity, op. cit. (undated), p. 28.

20. Ibid., p. 30.

21. Asit K. Biswas, "Water: A Perspective on Global Issues and Politics," in Asit K. Biswas et al., eds. *Water Management for Arid Lands in Developing Countries*, Pergamon, Oxford, 1978, p. 18.

22. Bruce Stokes, "Bread and Water: Growing Tomorrow's Food," unpublished paper prepared for the Worldwatch Institute, Washington, D.C., undated (*circa* 1980), section 3, p. 7.

23. John Waterbury, op. cit. 1979, p. 150.

24. Ibid., p. 223.

25. Ibid., p. 224.

26. Ibid., pp. 226–27.

27. Ibid., p. 225.

28. Ibid., p. 215.

29. Ibid., p. 216.

30. Ibid., p. 216.

31. Ibid., p. 220.

32. Ibid., p. 226.

33. Ibid., p. 231.

34. Malin Falkenmark, "Water and Land: Interdependent but Manipulated Resources," in Carl Widstrand, ed., *Water Conflicts and Research Priorities*, Pergamon, Oxford, 1980, p. 54.

35. Ibid., p. 54.

CHAPTER 15. DAMS, POLLUTION, AND THE REDUCTION OF FOOD SUPPLIES

1. Rob Pardy, *Purari: Overpowering Papua New Guinea?*, International Development Action for Purari Action Group, Fitzroy, Victoria, Australia, 1978, p. 22.

2. *The Oriental Economist*, quoted by Rob Pardy et al., op. cit. 1978, p. 24.

3. Rob Pardy et al., op. cit. 1978, p. 62.

4. Ibid., p. 27.

5. Ibid., p. 29.

6. Ibid., p. 24.

7. Ibid., p. 178.

8. Ibid., pp. 183–84.

9. Ibid., p. 189.

10. Ibid., p. 181.

11. Ibid., p. 179.

12. Carrying Capacity, *Report on the Carrying Capacity of the USA*, Washington, D.C., unpublished, undated, Chapter 6, p. 22.

13. Ibid., chapter 6, pp. 22–23.

14. *Ogemaw County Herald*, September 4, 1975.

15. *Environment* (Spectrum Section), vol. 24, no. 2, March 1982, p. 24.

16. Here one might also note the growing concern regarding the effects of acid rain on crop yields—a subject we cannot examine in this chapter.

17. "Mixtures of Pollutants Can Cause Greater Reductions in Crop Yields than Ozone Alone," *Environmental Science and Technology*, vol. 16, no. 2, 1982, p. 88A.

18. *Chemicals and Industry*, January 21, 1978.

19. *Environment*, p. 24.

20. Carrying Capacity, op. cit. (undated), chapter 6, p. 21.

21. Centre for Science and Environment, *The State of India's Environment 1982*, New Delhi, 1982, p. 73.

22. *The Polluted Seas*, Earthscan Press Briefing Document no. 7, Earthscan, London, 1977.

23. Peter Freeman, "Environmental Considerations in the Management of International Rivers: A Review," unpublished manuscript, International Center for Environmental Renewal, Threshold, Washington, D.C., March, 1978, p. 33.

24. Centre for Science and Environment, op. cit. 1982, p. 17.

25. Ibid., p. 25.

26. Ibid., pp. 20–21.

27. Ibid., p. 17.

28. Alexander A. Jothy, "The Fate of Fisheries and Aquaculture in the Wake of a Deteriorating Aquatic Environment in Malaysia," in Consumers' Association of Penang, *Development and the Environmental Crisis, A Malaysian Case*, 1982, p. 54.

29. Ibid., p. 59.

30. Peter Freeman, op. cit. 1978, p. 34.

CHAPTER 16. SEDIMENTATION, THE WAY OF ALL DAMS

1. Louis M. Glymph, "Summary: Sedimentation of Reservoirs," in William C. Ackermann et al., eds. *Man-Made Lakes, Their Problems and Environmental Effects*, American Geophysical Union, Washington, D.C., 1973, p. 343.

2. F. E. Dendy, W. A. Champin, and R. B. Wilson, "Reservoir Sedimentation Surveys in the United States," in William C. Ackermann et. al., eds. op. cit. 1973, p. 353.

3. Centre for Science and Environment, *The State of India's Environment—1982*, New Delhi, 1982, pp. 62–63. See also Bharat Dogra, "Big Dams in the Indian Subcontinent: Small Gains at High Costs," in

E. Goldsmith and N. Hildyard, eds. *The Social and Ecological Effects of Large Dams, Volume 2: Case Studies*, Wadebridge Ecological Centre, Worthyvale Manor, Camelford, Cornwall, U.K., 1984.

4. Earthscan, *The Improbable Treaty: The Cartagena Convention and the Caribbean Environment*, Press Briefing Documentation no. 34(a), 1983, p. 60.

5. *USCOLD Newsletter*, no. 69, November 1982, p. 15. Quoted by Philip Williams, "Damming the World," *Not Man Apart*, October 1983, p. 11.

6. Warren Linney and Susan Harrison, *Large Dams and the Developing World: Social and Environmental Costs and Benefits—A Look at Africa*, Environmental Liaison Centre, Nairobi, 1981, pp. 19–20.

CHAPTER 17. ARE THESE PROBLEMS INEVITABLE?

1. Barbara J. Bramble, "Statement on behalf of the National Wildlife Federation Before the Subcommittee on International Development Institutions and Finance of the House Committee on Banking, Finance, and Urban Affairs," Washington, D.C., 1983, p. 20.

2. Brent Blackwelder, "Testimony on behalf of the Environment Policy Institute Before the Subcommittee on International Development Institutions and Finance of the House Committee on Banking, Finance, and Urban Affairs, concerning the Multilateral Development Banks and Large-Scale Water-Development Projects," Washington, D.C., June 27, 1983, p. 12.

3. Bruce M. Rich, "Statement on behalf of Sierra Club, World Wildlife Fund, US Friends of the Earth, Izaak Walton League of America, Natural Resources Defense Council, Inc. National Audubon Society Before the Subcommittee on International Development Institutions and Finance of the House Committee on Banking, Finance, and Urban Affairs," Washington, D.C., June 28, 1983, p. 25.

4. Philip B. Williams, *Planning Problems in International Water Development*, Philip Williams and Associates, Pier 33N, The Embarcadero, San Francisco, 1983, p. 4.

5. Ibid.

6. Ibid.

7. Bruce M. Rich, op. cit. 1983, p. 28.

8. Brent Blackwelder, op. cit. 1983, p. 12.

9. Gilbert F. White, "The Main Effects and Problems of Irrigation," in E. Barton Worthington, ed. *Arid Land Irrigation in Developing Countries: Environmental Problems and Effects*, Pergamon, Oxford, 1977, p. 48.

10. Barbara Bramble, op. cit. 1983, p. 21.

11. Bruce M. Rich, op. cit. 1983, p. 29.

12. Brent Blackwelder, op. cit. 1983, p. 12.
13. Ibid.
14. Ibid.
15. Bruce M. Rich, op. cit. 1983, p. 25.
16. Aloys Michel, "The Impact of Modern Irrigation Technology in the Indus and Helmand Basins of Southwest Asia," in T. Farvar and J. Milton, *The Careless Technology*, Tom Stacey, London, 1973, p. 273.
17. Victor Kovda, "Arid Land Irrigation and Soil Fertility," in E. Barton Worthington, ed., op. cit. 1977, p. 219.
18. Philip Williams, op. cit. 1983, p. 4.
19. Brent Blackwelder, op. cit. 1983, p. 12.
20. Bruce M. Rich, op. cit. 1983, p. 28.
21. Brent Blackwelder, op. cit. 1983, p. 4.
22. Ibid.
23. Bruce M. Rich, op. cit. 1983, p. 28.

CHAPTER 18. SOCIAL AND ENVIRONMENTAL IMPACT STUDIES

1. Walter Taylor, "James Bay: Continental Crisis," *Survival* (North American edition), no. 12, March 1973, p. 4.
2. Ibid., p. 1.
3. Quoted by Walter Taylor, op. cit. 1973, p. 2.
4. Quoted by Walter Taylor, op. cit. 1973, p. 5.
5. W. Linney and S. Harrison, *Large Dams and the Developing World: Social and Environmental Costs and Benefits—A Look at Africa*, Environment Liaison Center, P.O. Box 72461, Nairobi, Kenya, 1981, p. 17.
6. R. N. Allen, "The Anchicaya Hydroelectric Project in Colombia: Design and Sedimentation Problems," in T. Farvar and J. Milton, eds. *The Careless Technology*, Tom Stacey, London, 1973, p. 325.
7. Ibid., p. 327.
8. Thomas I. Perry, "The Skagit Valley Controversy: A Case History in Environmental Politics," *Alternatives*, Spring 1975, p. 9.
9. Ibid., p. 12.
10. Aloys Michel, "The Impact of Modern Irrigation Technology in the Indus and Helmand Basins of Southwest Asia," in T. Farvar and J. Milton, op. cit., *The Careless Technology*, Tom Stacey, London, 1973, p. 265.
11. Rosaline Bertolino, *Water Supply: Constraints and Opportunities*, Sierra Club, San Francisco, 1977, p. 7.
12. Earthscan, *The Jonglei Canal*, Press Briefing Document no. 8, p. 3.
13. Quoted by the Environment Liaison Centre, *The Jonglei Canal*,

Environmental and Social Aspects, Abstract of a Report by Oscar Mann for ELC, Nairobi, August 1977, p. 2.

14. Environment Liaison Centre, op. cit. 1977. See in particular pp. 2, 13, 14, 21, 22, 28, 33, 34.

15. Brian Johnson, *The Return of the Big Dam*, Earthscan, London, 1979, p. 3.

16. Anon., "Selingue Dam Project, Mali," Commonwealth Secretariat, undated, p. 43.

17. Brian Johnson, op. cit. 1979, p. 3.

18. Quoted by Rob Pardy et al. *Purari: Overpowering PNG?* International Development Action for Purari Action Group, Victoria, Australia, 1978, p. 104.

19. Quoted by Rob Pardy et al., op. cit. 1978, p. 148.

20. Rob Pardy et al., op. cit. 1978, p. 162.

21. K. Ubell, "Iraq's Water Resources," *Nature and Resources*, vol. 3, no. 2, June 1971, p. 9.

22. Charles Greer, "The Texas Water System: Implications for Environmental Assessment in Planning for Interbasin Water Transfers," in A. K. Biswas et al., eds., *Long-Distance Water Transfer: A Chinese Case Study and International Experiences*, Tycooly International, Dublin, 1983, p. 84.

CHAPTER 19. THE POLITICS OF DAMMING

1. E. Barton Worthington, "The Nile Catchment—Technological Change and Aquatic Biology," in T. Farvar and J. Milton, eds. *The Careless Technology*, Tom Stacey, London, 1973. In the same paper, Worthington remarks: "Every project in Nile control has had to be undertaken with a strictly limited background of knowledge. As a scientist who has participated in development, I have sometimes found it positively frightening to make decisions which will affect the lives of millions of people when the basic facts were unknown. It felt a bit like writing the conclusions of a scientific paper before settling down to do the research." p. 204.

2. Aloys Michel, "The Impact of Modern Irrigation Technology in the Indus and Helmand Basins of Southwest Asia," in T. Farvar and J. Milton, eds., op. cit. 1973, p. 265.

3. Ibid., p. 273.

4. John Waterbury, *The Hydropolitics of the Nile Valley*, Syracuse University Press, 1979, p. 4.

5. Ibid., p. 243.

6. Ibid., p. 247.

7. Ali Fathy, *The High Dam and Its Impact*, General Book, Cairo, 1976, pp. 50–51. Quoted by John Waterbury, op. cit., 1979, p. 116.

8. Quoted by John Waterbury, op. cit. 1979, p. 101.

9. Mackenzie Wallace, *Egypt and the Egyptian Question*, Macmillan, London, 1883, pp. 15, 250. Quoted by John Waterbury, op. cit. 1979, p. 35.

10. John Waterbury, op. cit. 1979, p. 39.

11. Ibid., pp. 40–41.

12. Such fears were not new. Indeed, they date back to an unsuccessful attempt by the French in 1898 to establish a military presence at the head of the Nile. Since then, the British had shown themselves fully aware of the power they held by controlling the major upstream states. Thus, in response to the murder of Sir Lee Stack, commander of the Anglo-Egyptian armies, in 1924, Lord Allenby had announced that the size of the Sudan's Gezira cotton scheme would immediately be increased from 300,000 feddans to "an unlimited figure as need may arise." Although Allenby assured the pasha of Egypt that Britain had "no intention of trespassing upon the natural and historic rights of Egypt in the waters of the Nile," the threat had been clear enough: if Egypt did not control its nationalists, then Britain would interfere with its water supplies.

13. J. Waterbury, op. cit. 1979, p. 63.

14. Ibid., p. 78. Sadat was responding to news that Cuban troops were present in Ethiopia. How much more threatened Nasser must have felt when his fledgling regime first confronted Britain in the 1950s.

15. Ibid., p. 99.

16. Ibid., p. 108.

17. Ibid., p. 116.

18. Gamal Abdel Nasser, *Speech at first closure of the Nile at the High Dam site*, May 14, 1964. Quoted by J. Waterbury, op. cit. 1979, p. 98.

19. J. Waterbury, op. cit. 1979, p. 117.

20. Ibid., p. 122.

21. Ibid., p. 125.

22. William Willcocks, *The Nile in 1904*, London, 1904. Quoted by John Waterbury, op. cit. 1979, p. 39.

23. J. Waterbury, op. cit. 1979, p. 130 (footnote).

24. Ibid., p. 129.

25. Ibid., p. 247.

26. Quoted in Rob Pardy et al., *Purari: Overpowering PNG?* International Development Action for Purari Action Group, p. 136.

27. See: Gordon Bennet et al. *The Damned: The Plight of the Akawaio Indians of Guyana*, Survival International Document VI, London, 1978.

28. Quoted in Earthscan, *The Jonglei Canal*, Press Briefing Document no. 8, London, p. 28.

29. W. Linney and S. Harrison, *Large Dams and the Developing World: Social and Environmental Costs and Benefits—A Look at Africa*, Environment Liaison Centre, P.O. Box 72461, Nairobi, 1981, p. 31.

30. Quoted by F. Powledge, *Water: The Nature, Uses and Future of Our Most Precious and Abused Resource*, Farrar, Straus, and Giroux, New York, 1982, p. 288.

31. George Laycock, *The Diligent Destroyers*, Audubon/Ballantine, New York, 1970, p. 30.

32. Quoted in F. Powledge, op. cit. 1982, p. 286.

33. David Sheridan, "The Underwatered West: Overdrawn at the Well," *Environment*, vol. 23, no. 2, March 1981, p. 9.

34. Ibid., p. 31.

35. George Laycock, op. cit. 1970, p. 8.

36. F. Powledge, op. cit. 1982, p. 309.

37. Peter Thompson, *Power in Tasmania*, Australian Conservation Foundation, 1981.

38. Quoted in Peter Thompson, op. cit. 1981.

CHAPTER 20. FUDGING THE BOOKS

1. For a full discussion of this problem, see N. Hildyard, *Cover-Up*, New English Library, London, 1983.

2. Quoted in T. Palmer, *Stanislaus: The Struggle for a River*, University of California Press, Berkeley, 1982, p. 102.

3. Comptroller General of the United States, *Improvements Needed in Making Benefit-Cost Analyses for Federal Water Resource Projects*, U.S. General Accounting Office, no. B-16794, Washington, D.C., September 1974.

4. J. McCaull, "Dams of Pork," *Environment*, vol. 17, no. 1, Jan/Feb, 1975, p. 11.

5. Ibid., pp. 13–14.

6. Ibid., p. 13.

7. Ibid., p. 14.

8. Ibid., p. 15.

9. Quoted by Onno Kremers, 'Prairie Madness: the Garrison Diversion,' *Alternatives*, Winter 1975, p. 29.

10. Onno Kremers, op. cit. Winter 1975, p. 29.

11. Ibid., p. 29.

12. George Laycock, *The Diligent Destroyers*, Audubon/Ballantine, New York, 1970, p. 31.

13. R. Jeffery Smith, "The Waterway that Cannot Be Stopped," *Science*, vol. 213, August 14, 1981, p. 741.

14. Ibid., p. 742.

15. Representative David Bowen, quoted by R. Jeffery Smith, op. cit. 1981, p. 741.

16. George Laycock, op. cit. 1970, p. 22.

17. Vijay Paranjpye, "Dams, Are We Damned?" in L. T. Sharma et al., eds. *Major Dams: A Second Look*, Environmental Cell, Gandhi Peace Foundation, New Delhi, 1981, p. 23.

18. Ibid., p. 33.

19. George Laycock, op. cit. 1970, pp. 132–33.

20. Water Resources Council, "Proposed Principles and Standards for Planning Water and Related Land Resources," *Federal Register*, vol. 36, no. 245, Part 2, 1971, p. 24167.

21. B. T. Parry and R. B. Norgaard, "Wasting a River," *Environment*, Jan/Feb, 1975, vol. 17, no. 1, p. 26.

22. F. Powledge, *Water: The Nature, Uses and Future of Our Most Precious and Abused Resource*, Farrar, Straus, and Giroux, New York, 1982, p. 291.

23. W. Linney and S. Harrison, *Large Dams and the Developing World: Social and Environmental Costs and Benefits—A Look at Africa*, Environment Liaison Centre, Nairobi, Kenya, 1981, p. 34.

24. Committee for the Defense of James Bay, *The Case Against the James Bay Project*, 1974.

25. F. Powledge, op. cit. 1982, p. 301.

26. W. Linney and S. Harrison, op. cit. 1981, p. 33.

27. T. Palmer, op. cit. 1982, p. 70.

28. Quoted by F. Powledge, op. cit. 1982, p. 293.

29. General Accounting Office, *Congressional Guidance Needed on Federal Cost Share of Water Resource Projects When Project Benefits Are Not Widespread*, Report to the Congress of the United States, CED-81-12, Washington, D.C., November 1980.

30. Ibid., p. 46.

31. Ibid., p. 79.

32. Philip Williams, 'Damming the World,' *Not Man Apart*, October 1983, p. 11.

33. B. T. Parry and R. B. Norgaard, op. cit. 1975, p. 26.

34. Rob Pardy et al., *Purari: Overpowering PNG?* International Development Action for Purari Action Group, Victoria, Australia, 1978, p. 63.

35. Quoted by F. Powledge, op. cit. 1982, p. 292.

36. Ibid., p. 292.

37. Ibid., p. 291.

38. Ibid., p. 286.

39. Ibid., p. 302.

40. B. T. Parry and R. B. Norgaard, op. cit. 1975, pp. 19–20.

41. F. Powledge, op. cit. 1982, p. 293.

42. Ibid., p. 294.

43. Quoted by Rob Pardy et al., op. cit. 1978, p. 152.

44. General Accounting Office, op. cit. 1980, p. 44.

45. Quoted by F. Powledge, op. cit. 1982, p. 321.

46. Personal communication from Dr. Robert Mann, 1983.

47. Rob Pardy, et al., op. cit. 1978, p. 178.

48. Arthur Pillsbury, "The Salinity of Rivers," *Scientific American*, July 1981, p. 38.

49. Ibid., p. 43.

CHAPTER 21. THE QANATS OF IRAN

1. Gunther Garbrecht, "Ancient Water Works—Lessons from History," *Impact of Science on Society*, no. 1, p. 10, UNESCO, 1983.

2. Anil Agarwal, *"Water and Sanitation for All?"* Earthscan Press Briefing Document, no. 22, Earthscan, London, 1980, p. 53.

3. H. E. Wulff, "The Qanats of Iran," *Scientific American*, vol. 218, no. 4, April 1968, p. 94.

4. Ibid., p. 105.

5. H. Pazwash, "Iran's Modes of Modernization: Greening the Desert, Deserting the Greenery?" *Civil Engineering*, March 1983, p. 50.

6. Ibid., p. 50.

7. Gunter Garbrecht, op. cit. 1983, p. 10.

8. H. E. Wulff, op. cit. 1968, p. 100.

9. Ibid., p. 100.

10. H. Pazwash, op. cit. 1983, p. 50.

11. Ibid., p. 50.

12. Ibid., p. 49.

13. Ibid., p. 51.

CHAPTER 22. TWO TRADITIONAL IRRIGATION SYSTEMS IN TANZANIA

1. Robert F. Gray, *The Sonjo of Tanganyika: An Anthropological Study on an Irrigation-Based Society*, Oxford University Press, London, 1963, p. 52.

2. Ibid., p. 52.

3. Ibid., p. 52.

4. Ibid., pp. 47–55.

5. Ibid., p. 54.

6. Ibid., p. 56.

7. Ibid., p. 59.

8. Ibid., p. 60.

9. Ibid., p. 61.

10. Fidelis T. Masao, "The Irrigation System in Uchagga: An Ethno-Historical Approach," *Tanzania Notes and Records*, no. 75, 1974.

11. Ibid., p. 2.

12. Ibid., p. 4.

13. Ibid., p. 4.

14. Charles Dundas, *Kilimanjaro and Its Peoples*, London, 1924, p. 262. Quoted by F. T. Masao, op. cit. 1974, p. 6.

15. F. T. Masao, op. cit. 1974, p. 7.

16. E. Huxley, *The Sorcerer's Apprentice*, London, 1956, p. 67. Quoted by F. T. Masao, op. cit. 1974, p. 8.

Chapter 23. Traditional Irrigation in the Dry Zone of Sri Lanka

1. Sir James Emmerson Tennent, *Ceylon*, (two volumes), London, 1860. Quoted by R. L. Brohier, *Ancient Irrigation Works in Ceylon*. chapter 1, introductory sketch, p. 4.

2. Edmund A. Leach, "Hydraulic Society in Ceylon," *Past and Present*, no. 15 April 1959, p. 21.

3. Ibid., p. 23.

4. Ibid., p. 9.

5. Ibid., p. 8.

6. Upalli Senanayake, quoted by Edward Goldsmith in "Traditional Agriculture in Sri Lanka," *The Ecologist*, vol. 12, no. 5, 1982, p. 215.

7. Edmund A. Leach, op. cit. 1959, p. 24.

8. Sir James Emmerson Tennent, op. cit. 1860, p. 264.

9. Ibid., p. 267.

10. Ibid., p. 268.

11. Upalli Senanayake, quoted by Edward Goldsmith, op. cit. 1982, p. 215.

12. R. L. Brohier, op. cit. chapter 1, p. 2.

13. Mudytanse Tenakoon, quoted by Edward Goldsmith, op. cit. 1982, pp. 214–15.

14. B. Gunersekera, personal communication to Edward Goldsmith, 1982.

15. Edmund A. Leach, op. cit. 1959, p. 24.

16. B. Gunersekera, personal communication to Edward Goldsmith, 1982.

17. Mudiyanse Tenakoon, quoted by Edward Goldsmith, op. cit.

1982, p. 209. According to C. Dreiberg (Superintendent of School Gardens), quoted by C. Wright in *Glimpses of Ceylon*, 1874, three to four hundred varieties of rice were once cultivated.

18. R. L. Brohier, 'The Interrelation of Groups of Ancient Reservoirs and Channels in Ceylon,' *Journal R.A.S.* (Ceylon), vol. 34, no. 90, 1937, p. 65.

19. Ibid., pp. 65–66.

20. Ibid., pp. 66–67.

21. Edmund A. Leach, *Pul Eliya: A Village in Ceylon*, Cambridge University Press, Cambridge, 1961, p. 157. Quoted by René Millon, "Variations in Social Responses to the Practice of Irrigation Agriculture," in Richard B. Woodbury, ed. *Civilizations in Desert Lands*, Anthropological Paper no. 62, University of Utah, December 1962, p. 64.

22. Edmund A. Leach, op. cit. 1961.

23. Ibid.

24. Ibid.

25. Ibid.

26. A comment made by a British official at a Select Committee set up by the British Parliament in 1849. Quoted by Mudiyanse Tenakoon in Edward Goldsmith, op. cit. 1982, p. 216.

CHAPTER 24. TRADITIONAL IRRIGATION IN MESOPOTAMIA

1. Gunther Garbrecht, "Ancient Water Works—Lessons from History," *Impact of Science on Society*, no. 1, UNESCO, Paris, 1983, p. 8.

2. McGuire Gibson, "Violation of Fallow: An Engineered Disaster in Mesopotamian Civilization," in Theodore E. Downing and McGuire Gibson, eds. *Irrigation's Impact on Society*, Anthropological Papers of the University of Arizona, no. 25, University of Arizona Press, Tucson, Arizona, 1974, p. 10.

3. J. C. Russell, in Thorkild Jacobsen, *Salinity and Irrigation: Agriculture in Antiquity*, Diyala Basin Archaelogical Project, Report on Essential Results 1957–58 (mimeographed), p. 67. Quoted by McGuire Gibson, op. cit. 1974, p. 11.

4. Robert A. Fernea, *Shaykh and Effendi: Changing Patterns of Authority among the El Shabana of Southern Iraq*, Harvard University Press, Cambridge, Mass., 1970, p. 13. Quoted by McGuire Gibson, op. cit. 1974, p. 11.

5. Robert A. Fernea, "Irrigation and Social Organization among the El Shabana, a Group of Tribal Cultivators in Southern Iraq," Ph.D. dissertation, University of Chicago, 1959, p. 71.

6. Robert A. Fernea, op. cit. 1970, p. 12. Quoted by McGuire Gibson, op. cit. 1974, p. 12.

7. Robert A. Fernea, op. cit. 1970, pp. 120 and 129 ff. Quoted by McGuire Gibson, op. cit. 1974, p. 12.

8. Robert A. Fernea, op. cit. 1970, p. 54. Quoted by McGuire Gibson, op. cit. 1974, p. 11.

9. McGuire Gibson, op. cit. 1974, p. 11.

10. Ibid., p. 12.

11. Robert M. Adams, "Historic Patterns of Mesopotamian Irrigation Agriculture," in Theodore Downing and McGuire Gibson, eds. op. cit. 1974, p. 3.

12. Robert M. Adams, "A Synopsis of the Historical Demography and Ecology of the Diyala River Basin, Central Iraq," in Richard B. Woodbury, ed. *Civilizations in Desert Lands*, Anthropological Paper no. 62, University of Utah, December 1962, p. 18.

13. T. Jacobsen and Robert M. Adams, "Salt and Silt in Ancient Mesopotamian Agriculture," *Science*, vol. 128, no. 3334, November 21, 1958, p. 1252.

14. Stanley D. Walters, *Water for Larsa. An Old Babylonian Archive Dealing with Irrigation*. New Haven, Yale University Press, 1970, p. 160.

15. T. Jacobsen and R. M. Adams, op. cit. 1958, p. 1252.

16. J. Maleska, *Irrigation Conditions and Problems in Iraq*, 5th Irrigation Practice Seminar, New Delhi, 1964. Quoted by Gunther Garbrecht, op. cit. 1983, p. 9.

17. T. Jacobsen and R. M. Adams, op. cit. 1958, p. 1252.

18. Stanley D. Walters, op. cit. 1970, p. 16.

19. Robert M. Adams, op. cit. 1962, p. 21.

20. Ibid., p. 23.

21. T. Jacobsen and R. M. Adams, op. cit. 1958, p. 1256.

22. Ibid., p. 1257.

23. Robert M. Adams, op. cit. 1962, p. 23.

24. Robert M. Adams, op. cit. 1974, p. 4.

25. T. Jacobsen and R. M. Adams, op. cit. 1958, p. 1257.

26. Robert M. Adams, op. cit. 1962, p. 24.

27. Robert M. Adams, op. cit. 1974, p. 5.

28. McGuire Gibson, op. cit. 1974, p. 13.

29. Ester Boserup, *The Conditions of Agricultural Growth*, Chicago, Aldine, 1965. Quoted by McGuire Gibson, op. cit. 1974, pp. 12–13.

30. McGuire Gibson, op. cit. 1974, p. 12.

31. Ibid., p. 14.

32. Ibid., p. 15.

33. Ibid., p. 13.

34. H. W. Cadoux, "Recent Changes in the Course of the Lower Euphrates," *The Geophysical Journal*, vol. 28, pp. 266–76.

35. Ibid., p. 15.

36. Robert A. Fernea, op. cit. 1959, pp. 108–10. Quoted by René Millon, "Variations in Social Responses to the Practice of Irrigation Agriculture Civilization in Desert Lands," in Richard B. Woodbury, ed. op. cit. 1962, p. 71.

37. Thorkild Jacobsen, *Salinity and Irrigation: Agriculture in Antiqui-ty*, Diyala Basin Archeological Project, Report on Essential Results 1957–58, (mimeographed), p. 85. Quoted by McGuire Gibson, op. cit. 1974, p. 7.

38. McGuire Gibson, op. cit. 1974, p. 7.

39. Robert A. Fernea, op. cit. 1970, p. 47. Quoted by McGuire Gibson, op. cit. 1974, p. 12.

40. Robert A. Fernea, op. cit. 1970, p. 153. Quoted by McGuire Gibson, op. cit. 1974, p. 17.

41. Robert M. Adams, op. cit. 1974, p. 5.

CHAPTER 25. THE LESSONS OF TRADITIONAL IRRIGATION AGRICULTURE: LEARNING TO LIVE WITH NATURE

1. Jimoh Omo Fadaka, *Superdams: The Dream that Failed*, 1978, p. 8.

2. Robert A. Fernea, *Shaykh and Effendi: Changing Patterns of Author-ity among the El Shabana of Southern Iraq*, Harvard University Press, Cambridge, Mass., 1970. Quoted by McGuire Gibson, "Violation of Fallow and Engineering Disaster in Mesopotamian Civilization," in Theodore F. Downing and McGuire Gibson, eds., *Irrigation's Impact on Society*, University of Arizona Press, Tucson, 1974, p. 17.

3. Desmond D. Anthony, *The Ecologist in a Technology Age*, Paper pre-sented at the Seminar on Hydropower and Environment, Georgetown, Guyana, October 4–8, 1976, p. 2.

4. Robert Goodland, *Environmental Assessment of the Tucuruí Hydro-project*, Electronorte, Brasilia, Brazil, 1978, p. 135.

5. William A. Ackermann, "Summary and Recommendations," in William A. Ackermann et al., *Man-Made Lakes: Their Problems and En-vironmental Effects*, American Geophysical Union, Washington, D.C., 1973, p. 6.

6. John M. Hunter, "Strategies for the Control of River Blindness, Conceptual and Methodological Issues," *Medical Studies in Geography*, no. 15, 1980, p. 2.

7. Brian Johnson, *The Return of the Big Dam*, Earthscan, London, 1979, p. 2.

8. Jim Lovelock, personal communication to Edward Goldsmith.

9. E. Washburn Hopkins, *India Old and New*, Charles Scribner, London, 1901, p. 231.

10. Thomas Glick, *Irrigation and Society in Medieval Valencia*, Cam-

bridge, Mass., Harvard University Press, 1970. Quoted by Robert C. Hunt and Eva Hunt, "Canal Irrigation and Local Social Organisation," *Current Anthropology*, vol. 17, no. 3, September 1976, p. 392.

11. Robert C. Hunt and Eva Hunt, "Canal Irrigation and Local Social Organisation," *Current Anthropology*, vol. 17, no. 3, September 1976, p. 392.

12. J. W. Powell, *Report on the Lands of the Arid Region of the United States*, U.S. Government Printing Office, Washington, D.C., 1879, p. 3. Quoted by David Sheridan, "The Underwatered West," *Environment*, vol. 23, no. 2, March 1981, p. 7.

13. Henry Nash Smith, *Virgin Land: The American West as a Symbol and Myth*, Harvard University Press, Cambridge, Mass., 1950, p. 200. Quoted by David Sheridan, op. cit. 1981, p. 7.

14. David Sheridan, op. cit. 1981, p. 7.

15. Wallace Stegner, *Beyond the Hundredth Meridian*, Houghton Mifflin Co., Boston, 1954, pp. 328–38. Quoted by David Sheridan, op. cit. 1981, p. 7.

16. H. E. Thomas, "Water and the Southwest—What Is the Future?" U.S. Geological Service, circular no. 469, 1964: 14. Quoted by D. Sheridan, op. cit. 1981, p. 9.

17. Robert Goodland, "Environmental Optimization in Hydro-Development of Tropical Forest Regions," in R. S. Pardy, ed. *Man-made Lakes and Human Health*, University of Suriname, 1977, p. 12.

18. Quoted by Donald Worster, *Nature's Economy*, Sierra Club Books, San Francisco, 1977, p. 231.

Index